Spire Study System
capture. cross-train. conquer.

ATI TEAS 7 Study Guide

Prep Book with Review Questions for the Test of Essential Academic Skills, Version 7

STUDY SYSTEM + TEST PREP GUIDE + PRACTICE TEST QUESTIONS

Thank you for purchasing the *ATI TEAS 7 Study Guide* from Spire Study System!

Your opinion matters!

As a dedicated educational publisher, we depend on you, our customer, to provide feedback (email: MyBookFeedback@outlook.com). We want to know what we did well and what areas we could further improve.

Likewise, your comments can help other shoppers make informed decisions about whether our system is right for them. If you are happy with your purchase, please take a few minutes to leave a review on Amazon!

Thank you for trusting Spire Study System for your test prep needs. We are always here for you.

-- Your friends at Spire Study System

Contents

INTRODUCTION

ABOUT SPIRE STUDY SYSTEM

Spire was founded by individuals who wanted to drastically improve the quality of educational materials. Our goal was to create a change in thinking in the test prep industry, just like modern technology and innovative companies have done for smartphones and computers.

To facilitate that shift, we assembled a team of seasoned educators, creative professionals, and young entrepreneurs. The result was a specially formulated study system that outperforms traditional study guides in every way.

See, just about every study guide company supplies you with a daunting volume of information with no real instructions on how to dig through it. After you purchase the product, you're on your own.

But Spire is with you every step of the way.

With a 30-day system based on scientific study principles designed to increase retention, you'll know what, when, and how to study. This approach translates into less study time, a better understanding of the material, and a more prepared you on test day.

No more cramming.
No more wasted studying time.
No more guessing at answers and hoping for good luck.

You don't need luck. You've got Spire.

About Our Approach

Since there have been schools, there have been tests, and there have been superstitions and myths about the best way to study for tests. Maybe you have heard—or currently believe—some of these ancient yarns: "Study somewhere quiet where you won't be easily distracted." "Focus on one subject at a time." "The longer you study, the better your score will be."

These yarns sound like good advice—in fact, they are so ingrained in us that they sound intuitively correct. The problem is that they are dead wrong.

In the last half-century, researchers and psychologists have upended a lot of conventional wisdom about the way humans learn and how we can get the most out of studying. Their discoveries have suggested several ways that students can study smarter, not harder.

However, these research findings have been slow to make their way into the school systems, if at all, and the findings are virtually nowhere to be found in most study guides on the market. That means that too many people out there are working too hard for too little gain.

It is time to change that—and that's why we invented the Spire Study System. First, we assembled an experienced team of editors, educators, writers, test designers, and graphic artists. Then, we built a system around findings from decades of scientific research. Lastly, we refined and designed the system for intuitive use and maximum simplicity. The result is what you hold in your hands: not a study guide, but a study system that makes preparation for any test simpler, easier, and more effective.

The Spire Study System operates on the following principles.

Study Multiple Subjects in the Same Session
Since you must answer questions about multiple topics in the same TEAS session, why study one subject at a time? By interleaving multiple subjects in the same session, you will strengthen your powers of discrimination—which are crucial to passing a multiple-choice test! That is why this book is organized into a system of study modules, each containing multiple short chapters spanning a variety of subjects.

Change Your Environment Often
The more often you change your studying conditions, the better off you will be on test day. That means studying in different locations, at different times of day, and even while listening to different kinds of music. The Spire Study System makes this approach easy by providing a schedule and framework for changing your environment often enough to achieve maximum gains from your studies.

Don't Study for Too Long
More studying does not necessarily equal to a better score. There is a point of diminishing returns that, once crossed, could make studying counterproductive. Come the big day of the test, you are going to want to be an expert at retrieving and re-engaging the material you've memorized. The Spire Study System trains those skills by breaking up study sessions and spacing them out over a longer overall period.

Give Yourself Breaks
Most of us were repeatedly told, throughout our childhood, to "pay attention" to lectures that were much longer than our attention spans. Well, trying to pay attention is usually as effective as trying to relax or trying to fall asleep. In other words, trying to pay attention is not at all effective. That is why the Spire Study System incorporates regular breaks timed to the average person's studying speed, to help recharge the innate capacity for focus and jumpstart subconscious synthesis processes.

Start Studying a Month Before the Test
In the time-management nightmare known as modern life, how are you supposed to carve out entire nights to devote to studying? The answer: You can't, until it's too late. At that point, the most primal and effective of motivators—fear—sends you into a cramming frenzy the week before the test. The Spire Study System breaks up studying into short, maximally effective sessions. Rather than trying to find hours upon extra hours to study huge reams of material, you revisit small chunks of the subject matter many times, enabling more reinforcement in less overall study time.

Use Self-Testing as a Memorization Method

Once you have thoroughly studied the material, self-testing is your strongest tool for reinforcement. That is why this book has you complete three practice tests. Taking practice tests, making flash cards to test yourself, and getting someone else to quiz you are all stronger methods to build retention when compared to an equal amount of time spent studying.

There is so much more—but we invented the Spire Study System so that you wouldn't have to become an expert in advanced learning theories. You just need to stick to the following 30-day schedule, and follow the directions in the book. Easy peasy.

CALENDAR

Day 1	Day 2	Day 5	Day 6	Day 8
Pre-Test	Study Module 1	Review Module 1	Study Module 2	Review Module 2

Day 9	Day 11	Day 12	Day 13	Day 15
Study Module 3	Review Module 3	Study Module 4	Review Module 4	Practice Test 1

Day 16	Day 19	Day 20	Day 22	Day 23
Targeted Self-Study	Review Module 1 Self-Test	Review Module 2 Self-Test	Review Module 3 Self-Test	Review Module 4 Self-Test

Day 26	Day 27	Day 28	Day 29	Day 30
Targeted Self-Study	Targeted Self-Study	Review Modules 1-4 Practice Test 2	No Studying Allowed - Celebrate	Take the Test!

TARGETED SELF-STUDY
study your notes and focus on your weakest areas

SELF-TEST
flashcards or a friend

CELEBRATE
reward yourself with a day off, filled with your favorite activities and foods!

ABOUT THE TEAS 7

Congratulations! You have decided to enter the world of nursing. You are in for a long journey ahead, but you've chosen an excellent profession. Your study partners at Spire wish you the best of luck in your new career.

The first order of business is to pass the Test of Essential Academic Skills, more commonly known as the TEAS 7. The ATI TEAS 7 is an admissions exam many nursing schools use to assess potential students and their future success. Nursing students who take the TEAS 7 must be prepared to complete reading, math, science, and English language test sections.

Scoring

To pass the ATI TEAS, you need to know how well you must perform. Some nursing programs require that you score a certain percentage in each exam category, while others evaluate your overall score and compare it with your qualifications and credentials.

Although different nursing schools will require different minimum scores, here are some general guidelines on what you need to score to pass the TEAS 7:

- Reading: 80%
- Mathematics: 75%
- Science: 75%
- English Language: 80%

Minimum scores are dependent on the nursing programs you apply to, so be sure to contact the appropriate admissions offices for specific scoring requirements.

Exam Breakdown

Now that you know the score you need to get, let's talk about the actual test questions. The TEAS evaluates your aptitude in the subtest categories presented in the table below. On test day, you will answer 170 questions total, but only the below 150 questions spread across the four subtest sections are scored. The remaining 20 questions are used for internal purposes only.

Subtest Sections	Number of Questions	Time Allotted (minutes)
Reading	39	64
Mathematics	34	54
Science	44	63
English Language	33	28
Total	**150 questions**	**209 minutes**

FAQs

Question: When I try to make plans, life always throws me a curveball. What should I do if I can't stick perfectly to the schedule?

Answer: Dwight Eisenhower once said, "Plans are useless, but planning is indispensable." If you miss a session or must cut one short because, you know, life happens, then the first order of business is to forgive yourself. What you have (or haven't) done is irrelevant. What matters is what you are doing. Get back to your test prep book, and stick to the schedule as best as you can.

Question: I fear change and want to keep my bad habits. Can I still use this book?

Answer: Of course, you can. This book contains most of the information you need to pass your test, regardless of whether you follow the Spire Study System or want to study on your terms.

Question: Should I do anything specific when I take my breaks?

Answer: Yes! Don't study. Don't think about the material. Don't talk about the material. Do some light activity like taking a walk or dancing in the living room (well, that's what we do—don't judge us). The least productive activities are those designed to distract, so avoid playing video games or anything involving your smartphone, if possible. However, if answering texts or checking the comments on your latest Instagram post are going to free your attention for more studying, then do what you got to do.

Question: AAAAAAAGGGGGGHHHHH! I don't have 30 days! I just got this book, and the test is tomorrow!

Answer: Hey. Take a deep breath. We hate to break this news to you, but you're in for a long, anxious night of that time-tested torture technique: cramming. The good news is that even if you don't gain the distinct studying advantages of long-term spacing and luxurious breaks, you'll still benefit from the interleaved content and the self-testing included in the practice tests at the back of the book. Now quit reading this FAQ, and turn to Practice Test 1, ASAP!

Question: What are some other bad study habits I can break?

Answer: We got you. Here's a handy list: Don't rewrite your notes, don't work from any test outline, and don't restudy subject material from the same module twice in one session.

Question: Should I take notes?

Answer: Yes. Keep them brief and focused on the main points of the subject matter, and be sure to review them during Targeted Self-Study on days 16, 26, and 27.

That's it! You've got a command of the basics, and you understand how the Spire Study System works: just follow the calendar and the directions in the book. Now, your first task is to head to the next section, where you'll find information about the Pre-Test. That's right: Before you read any of the modules, you take the Pre-Test. That may sound counterintuitive, but the science is clear: Testing the material before you start studying yields drastically better results.

Don't even peek at the content first—just get ready to take the Pre-Test. Good Luck!

PRE-TEST

As you read in the FAQs, with the Spire Study System, you take the Pre-Test before you look at any other material in this book.

Here's a little secret: The Pre-Test is simply Practice Test 1. That's right: The same exact test is used for both. But there's a reason for that! Because the Spire Study System will allow you to better retain and recall the information in this book, you can compare your Pre-Test and Practice Test 1 scores to see how much you've learned since you started.

After you complete the first practice test, you'll want to look at the answer key. That way you can establish a baseline for your current knowledge.

Then, after you work through the Spire Study System—according to the 30-day schedule—you'll take Practice Test 1...again.

Later—again, according to the 30-day schedule—you'll take Practice Test 2. Because you will have never seen these questions before, the second practice test will be a bit more challenging than the first.

But don't stress! If you follow the Spire Study System, you'll do great. In fact, you'll be surprised at just how well you do.

But let's not get ahead of ourselves. Once you're ready to experience the magic of the Spire Study System, turn to the back of the book to begin the first test, Practice Test 1 (AKA the Pre-Test).

MODULE 1

VOCABULARY

The most organic way to expand your vocabulary is simply by reading everything you can get your hands on. That means not only blogs, articles, and social media, but also physical books, posted signs, and even the labels on your shampoo bottle. Start looking for opportunities to read a little bit more every day, from now until the day of the test.

Of course, you *do* have that test coming up, so you don't have much time to go au naturel. But don't worry—we've got your back. Here is your first and most crucial vocabulary hack: identifying root words.

What Is the What?

Many words are, in and of themselves, little stories that have a beginning, middle, and end. These parts are the prefix, the root word, and the suffix, respectively.

Not all words have all three parts, however. Sometimes a word has only a prefix and root, sometimes only a root and suffix, and sometimes multiple roots. But importantly, a word is never made up only of prefixes and suffixes. At least one root word is always present because it serves as the main idea of the word. You can't have a complete, grammatically correct sentence without a subject, and you can't have a complete word without a main idea, or root word.

For example, here's a word that's close to your heart lately: *reviewing*. It means viewing something again. Here are its parts:

> Prefix = re
> Root = view
> Suffix = ing

Re is a prefix that basically means *again*. *View* means *see* or *look*. *Ing* is a suffix that tells you the root word is happening. So if you're reviewing, you're viewing something again. Thus, the root word, or main idea, is view.

Let's get concrete: If you approached a friend and just said "again," you'd likely get a funny look and a response something like "What again?"

Similarly, if you just said "doing," your friend would likely say something like "doing what?"

If you just said "look," your friend would look where you're looking to determine what you're seeing. Your friend may not know what to look for, but the idea behind your words is clear.

On the test, almost every vocabulary word will be some combination of prefixes, roots, and suffixes. If you run into a word you don't know, first ask yourself this question: "What is the what?"

Here's another example: *unemployment.* The following list shows the parts of the term:

Prefix = un
Root = employ
Suffix = ment

You can't just say "un" or "ment" and expect to be understood, but when you add the main idea, *employ*, the word makes sense. Unemployment means the *state of not having a job.*

Where Things Get Messy

Of course, we speak the English language, a marvelous, madcap collage of many other languages, but one that relies on mostly Latin, German, and Greek. That means many root words are not English words. On top of that, no hard-and-fast rules exist for how prefixes and suffixes will change root words, so each root may look a little different depending on which prefixes and suffixes are used.

However, you can usually get the gist by first breaking off the parts that you know are prefixes and suffixes and then asking yourself what the remaining part reminds you of.

To break things down, you need to have a grasp of the most common prefixes, suffixes, and root words you'll encounter on the test (these are outlined in the following subsections).

Common Opposite Prefixes

The following table shows some common *opposite* prefixes you'll encounter frequently on the test:

Prefix	Variations	Meaning	Examples
Anti-	Ant-	against or opposite	anti-inflammatory, antagonist
De-		opposite	decontaminate, deconstruct
Dis-		not or opposite	disagree, dis (slang for insult)
In-	Im-, Il-, Ir-	not	incapable, impossible, illegitimate, irreplaceable
Non-		not	noncompliant, nonsense
Un-		not	unfair, unjust

Other Common Prefixes

The following table presents a quick list of some other common prefixes:

Prefix	Variations	Meaning	Examples
En-	Em-	cause	enlighten, empower
Fore-		before	foresee, foretell
In-		inside of	inland, income
Inter-		between	interrupt, interaction
Mid-		in the middle of	midair, midlife
Mis-		wrong	mistake, misdiagnose
Pre-		before	pregame, prefix
Re-		again	review, recompress
Semi-		half or partial	semitruck, semiannual
Sub-		under	subconscious, subpar
Super-		above	superimpose, superstar
Trans-		across	translate, transform

Suffixes

The following table presents some common suffixes you'll encounter on the test:

Suffix	Variations	Meaning	Examples
-able	-ible	can be accomplished	capable, possible
-al	-ial	has traits of	additional, beneficial
-en		made of	molten, wooden
-er		more than	luckier, richer
-er	-or	agent that does	mover, actor
-est		most	largest, happiest
-ic		has traits of	acidic, dynamic
-ing		continues to do	reviewing, happening
-ion	-tion, -ation, -ition	process of	occasion, motion, rotation, condition
-ity		the state of	ability, simplicity
-ly		has traits of	friendly, kindly
-ment		process/state of	enlightenment, establishment
-ness		state of	happiness, easiness
-ous	-eous, -ious	has traits of	porous, gaseous, conscious
-y		has traits of	artsy, classy

Common Root Words

If you can't identify a word because it seems like it's in another language, that's most likely because the word *is* in another language. This isn't always true, of course, but a good general rule is that longer, more academic English words tend to have their roots in Latin and Greek, while shorter English words tend to have their roots in German. For example, *amorous* and *loving* are synonyms, but one has its roots in the Latin *amor* and the other in the German *lieb*, respectively.

Latin/Greek

Because vocabulary words on the test tend to be of the longer, more academic variety, you'll get the most benefit from studying some common Latin and Greek roots:

Root	Variations	Meaning	Examples
Aster	Astro	star	astronomy, disaster
Aqua		water	aquatic, aquarium
Aud		hear	auditorium, audience
Bene		good	benevolent, benign
Bio		life	biology, autobiography
Cent		hundred	century, cent (money)
Chrono		time	chronological, synchronize
Circum	Circa	around	circumspect, circumnavigate
Contra	Counter	against or conflict	contraband, encounter
Dict		speak or say	dictate, dictation
Duc	Duct, duce	lead or leader	produce, conduct
Fac		make or do	manufacture, facsimile (fax)
Fract	Frag	break	fraction, defragment
Gen		birth or create	genetics, generate
Graph		write	telegraph, calligraphy
Ject		throw	inject, projection
Jur	Jus	law	juror, justice
Log	Logue	concept or thought	logo, dialogue
Mal		bad	maladaptive, malevolent
Man		hand	manuscript, manual
Mater		mother	maternal, material
Mis	Mit	send	mission, submit
Pater	Pat	father	paternal, patriot
Path		feel	sympathy, empathetic
Phile	Philo	love	philosophy, anglophile
Phon		sound	telephone, phonetic
Photo		light	photograph, photosynthesis
Port		carry	transport, portable
Psych	Psycho	soul or spirit	psychiatrist, psyche
Qui	Quit	quiet or rest	acquittal, tranquility
Rupt		break	rupture, interrupt
Scope		see, inspect	telescope, microscopic
Scrib	Script	write	describe, transcription
Sens	Sent	feel	sensory, consent
Spect		look	spectate, circumspect
Struct		build	construct, obstruction
Techno	Tech	art or science	technical, technology
Tele		far	teleport, television
Therm		heat	thermometer, thermal
Vac		empty	vacation, evacuate
Vis	Vid	see	visual, video
Voc		speak or call	vocal, vocation

CRITICAL READING

Many of the reading comprehension questions you will encounter on the TEAS 7 are structured around finding the main idea of a paragraph. In the last section on root words, you learned all about finding the main idea of a word—notice a theme developing here?

In this section, you will need to find the main idea of a paragraph. Luckily, doing so is simple once you know what to look for.

Before looking at an example and practice questions, though, we're first going to re-define a few terms in the following subsections that you might think you already know, so don't rush through this part.

Paragraph

A paragraph is a tool for organizing information. In simple terms, a paragraph is a container for sentences in the same way that a sentence is a container for words. Okay, maybe you knew that already, but you'd be surprised how many professional writers get their minds blown when they realize that almost all books are structured in the same way.

Books are made of chapters, which are made of sections, which are made of paragraphs, which are made of sentences, which are made of words. That structure creates a simple hierarchy, and smack in the center is the humble paragraph. For the purposes of the TEAS 7, you need to be able to comb through the provided paragraphs to identify two kinds of sentences: topic and detail.

Topic Sentence
A well-written paragraph—which all the paragraphs on the test will certainly be—contains just one topic. That topic is framed into the topic sentence, which is the backbone of the paragraph. The topic sentence tells you what the paragraph is about. All other sentences in the paragraph exist solely to support the topic sentence, which is often the first or last sentence in the paragraph. However, "often" does not mean always. To get it right no matter where the topic sentence lands in the paragraph, use the following foolproof method by first asking yourself who or what the paragraph is about and then finding the sentence that answers that question.

Detail Sentence
Detail sentences exist to support the topic sentence. They do so with all kinds of additional information, such as descriptions, arguments, and nuances. An author includes detail sentences to explain the reason for writing about the topic. In other words, the detail sentences contain the author's point, which you'll need to find the main idea. To easily spot the author's point, ask yourself the following question: "Why is the author writing about this topic?" Then pay close attention to the detail sentences to pry out the author's motivations.

Got it? Good. Now, let's do some easy math: The topic + the author's point = the main idea. And in English, that math translates to the following: What + why = main idea.

In the Real World

All right, you've got the abstract concepts nailed down. Now, let's get concrete. Imagine a scenario where a friend is explaining the movie *Toy Story* to you. Also imagine that your friend has already picked her jaw up off the floor because, seriously, how have you not seen *Toy Story*? You should fix that.

She tells you what the movie is about: "There are these toys that get lost, and they have a bunch of adventures trying to get back to their owner." Then she tells you why you should see the movie: "It's cute and funny, and it's a classic."

Those two sentences reveal the topic (what the movie is about) and your friend's point (why she's telling you about it). And now you have the main idea: Your friend thinks you should see the movie *Toy Story* because it's a cute, funny classic about toys having adventures.

Identifying the topic and author's point in written text works in the same way.

Illustrating the Main Idea

The following paragraph resembles one you might encounter on the test, followed by the types of questions that you will need to answer:

> *Example (from* The Art of Conversation *by Catherine Blyth):*
>
> "Silence is meaningful. You may imagine that silence says nothing. In fact, in any spoken communication, it plays a repertoire of roles. Just as, mathematically speaking, Earth should be called Sea, since most of the planet is covered in it, so conversation might be renamed silence, as it comprises 40 to 50 percent of an average utterance, excluding pauses for others to talk and the enveloping silence of those paying attention (or not, as the case may be)."

This example is relatively easy, but let's break it down:

1. Who/What is the paragraph about?
   Answer: Silence.

2. Why is the author writing about this topic?
   Answer: Silence is often overlooked, but it's an important part of conversation.

3. What is the main idea?
   Answer: Silence is an important part of conversation. Or put another way, "Silence is meaningful"—it's the first sentence!

Okay, you've seen the technique in action, so now it's your turn. In the example passages in the next subsections, you'll need to read the paragraphs and determine the topic sentence, the author's main point, and the main idea.

To find the main idea of any piece of writing, remember the following: The topic + the author's point = the main idea (or what + why = main idea).

Now it is practice time! Let's see what you have learned about finding the main idea and focal points of a passage. First, read the following passages. While doing so, search for the topic and main idea in each passage, and try to determine the focus of each. Then answer the questions presented after each passage.

Good luck!

Passage 1

Regardless of the reasons and motivations, if you choose to homeschool your child, many factors must be considered. One of the most hotly debated factors is that of providing a means of socialization for students. The fear some people have is that students taught at home rather than in a traditional school setting do not get the social interaction with peers that regular students do. But there are many ways children can socialize and interact with others their age:

Group field trips: Groups and certain organizations help host group fields trips. Homeschooled students can also get together and attend field trips together with other homeschooled students or friends and peers who are in public or private schools. These trips can also serve as credit for the homeschooled students' class work—for example, historical monuments can count as history credit, and a report written about what was seen can count as an English assignment. The homeschooled students also get the benefit of having time with their friends and peers.

Community service: There is always an opportunity to get involved in the community, and community service activities offer the perfect opportunities to interact with others. Students can get together to work on a project or can work on their own and/or alongside others volunteering at the same location. Such activities help get your child interacting with others and can help instill valuable life lessons at the same time.

Scouts, clubs, and programs: Many organizations offer the opportunity for students to work, learn, and grow alongside each other. Boy Scouts and Girl Scouts offer a chance for students to interact with their peers while developing life skills. The 4-H Program also offers a unique opportunity for homeschooled students to get life experiences and interaction; some 4-H clubs are set up especially for homeschooled students.

Co-op groups: These groups exist to help families organize group events with fellow homeschooled students. Group projects and study sessions are just some of the options available. Group study sessions can also be prepared to practice for things such as SAT testing. Finally, homeschool families can take advantage of co-op groups to help set up study sessions and events for students.

These options are just a handful of simple ways homeschool families can answer society's question about how students can be socially active and interact with same-aged students. Following those simple tips and trying any others that may be out there is a great way to meet your homeschooled children's socialization needs while providing the peace, protection, and education you want your children to receive.

1. Which sentence best states the main idea of this passage?
   A. Homeschooled children lack any good socialization and peer interaction
   B. There are many ways children can socialize and interact with others their age
   C. Children who are homeschooled lack major social skills
   D. None of the above

Answer: B
Rationale: Throughout the piece, the author talks about how homeschooled children can still find ways to socialize and interact with peers.

2. Which of the following was not discussed in the passage as a way homeschooled students can interact with their peers?
   A. Join a club or social group
   B. Volunteer in the local community
   C. Go on field trips
   D. All the above

Answer: D
Rationale: All three of the listed methods of socialization were talked about in detail within the passage. Every method had several examples and explanations given regarding why they were effective means for having homeschooled students socialize with their peer groups.

Passage 2

The world around us is filled with the weird and the unusual. When we think of "freaks of nature" (i.e., the weird), we usually envision images of massive rabbits, six-legged cows, and two-headed dogs.

However, the unusual species and freaks of nature also spill over into the plant world. Unusual plants offer a unique look at plant biology gone haywire. From plants of excessive size to those with an unusual smell, freaky plants are real and can be found today—if you know where to look.

Although more than 90% of plant types have leaves, used for photosynthesis, some plant species and varieties do not. The most common of these are members of the mushroom family that are parasitic in nature. They feed off the decaying material of plants or suck nutrients from healthy living plants. One such parasitic plant truly earns the title of unusual: the Rafflesia arnoldii. This plant bears a bloom that can grow more than three feet in diameter. The flower smells like rotting flesh and has a hole in the center big and deep enough to hold up to six quarts of water. Topping off the list of unusual traits, this plant has no stems, roots, or leaves—making it a true freak of nature.

Flowers can range in size from a fraction of the size of the plant to more than 80% of the plant itself. Serving as the reproductive part of the plant, flowers are responsible for producing seeds to further the next batch of plants to be grown according to that plant's individual biology. One of the plants that shows a wide range in plant size is the group of plants known as Amorphophallus. Closely related to the peace lily, these plants have a similar flower. The plant group is found in the subtropics, and more than 200 species and varieties have been identified. One of these species, Amorphophallus titanium, has a bloom several times larger than the plant itself; on some plants, the blooms get so large that they can exceed the height and width of a grown adult. What plant biology is capable of is truly amazing.

Many species of trees and flowering plants are quite old. The methuselah trees of the desert and the great redwood giants of the forests are just two well-known examples of ancient species still living. But perhaps the most ancient of all is a plant that was believed to have been long extinct. Until 1944, the Wollemia nobilis plant was known only by fossil remains. Then living plants of this type were discovered in remote tropical areas. The plant's unique bark is a deep chocolate color and looks like it is composed of many tiny bubbles. This plant is not tiny either as some specimens have reached record heights of over 120 feet. It is believed that only about 100 of these plants remain in the wild.

Plant biology is an interesting branch of science, and a great deal can be learned about nature and the world around us by studying plants. When the unusual plant species that populate the world are considered, this field of study gets even more interesting. Every corner of the world holds surprises. Who knows, there may still be colossal giants hidden away in remote rainforests and miniscule plants hiding in the crevasse of a mountain side just waiting to be discovered.

1. Which point do the details in this passage support?
   A. Plants have many different features
   B. All plants basically have the same biologic makeup
   C. Plants must share similar characteristics to be considered plants
   D. None of the above

Answer: A
Rationale: All the details in this passage talk about how plants differ from each other yet are all considered to be plants—some have whole leaves, while others do not; some are big, while others are little. In sum, plants can look vastly different from each other and still belong to the plant family.

2. What did the author want the reader to take away from reading this passage?
   A. That plants are amazing and very diverse in how they look
   B. Not all plants look like the flowers and trees we are familiar with
   C. Some plants are very old, and some are still waiting to be discovered
   D. All the above

Answer: D
Rationale: All these points are correct because they are all mentioned within the passage and discussed and described in detail.

How did you do? If you still need some help figuring out the main idea and topic in passages like those you just worked through, keep practicing!

ARITHMETIC BASICS

Many math exams will assess your memory of basic math definitions, vocabulary, and formulas that have become so distant that the questions on this type of exam may feel unfair. You likely do not refer to quotients and integers in your day-to-day life, so testing your recall of high school math class vocabulary and concepts doesn't exactly feel like a valid way to gauge your mathematical reasoning abilities.

In this section, you should ideally begin with the following refresher list so that you can quickly master basic math terminology.

Integer. Any whole number, i.e., any number that doesn't include a non-zero fraction or decimal. Negative whole numbers, positive whole numbers, and 0 are all integers. 3.1415 is not an integer. $1/2$ is not an integer. But −47, −12, 0, 15, and 1,415,000 are all integers.

Positive and negative numbers. A positive number is any number greater than zero. A negative number is any number less than zero. Zero is neither positive nor negative. Adding a negative number is the same as subtracting the positive value of that number. Subtracting a negative number is the same as adding a positive number.

Even and odd numbers. An even number is any number that can be evenly divided by 2, with no remainder left over. −4, 2, 6, 24, and 114 are all even numbers. An odd number has a remainder of 1 when divided by 2. −19, 1, 3, 5, 17, and 451 are all odd numbers. Another way to think about even/odd is that even numbers are all integers that are multiples of two, and odd numbers are any integers that are *not* multiples of two.

Factors and multiples. The factors of a number (or a polynomial) are all the numbers that can be multiplied together to get the first number. For example, the following pairs of numbers can be multiplied to get 16: 1 * 16, 2 * 8, and 4 * 4. Therefore, the factors of 16 are 1, 2, 4, 8, and 16. Note that a polynomial is an expression that can have constants, variables, and exponents that can be combined using addition, subtraction, multiplication, and division.

Prime number. An integer that only has two factors: 1 and itself. Remember two things about prime numbers: (1) among all infinite integers in existence, only one prime number is even, number 2, and (2) you can handle almost any prime number question on the test by memorizing all the primes between 0 and 100. This memorization is not required, but you will save time and mental anguish if you take the time to memorize the following primes:

2, 3, 5, 7, 11, 13, 17, 19, 23, 29, 31, 37, 41, 43, 47, 53, 59, 61, 67, 71, 73, 79, 83, 87, 89

Prime factorization. The prime factors are the prime numbers you must multiply to get a number. Take the number 24 as an example. First, you should find the factors of 24, which are 1, 2, 3, 4, 6, 8, and 12. Then, you must pull out all the numbers that are not prime (i.e., 1, 4, 6, 8, and 12). What's left? 2 and 3, which are the prime factors of 24. That's a simple example, but the concept remains the same no matter how large the number. When in doubt, start working from the number 2 (the smallest prime), which will be a factor of any number that ends with an even number. Be on the lookout for sneaky questions. If the exam asks you for the prime factors of the number 31, for instance, recall that 31 is a prime number, but 1 is not! Therefore, the only possible prime factor of 31 is itself (i.e., 31). The same mechanisms are true for all prime numbers.

Sum. The number you get when you add one number to another number.

Difference. The number you get when you subtract one number from another number.

Product. The number you get when you multiply one number by another number.

Quotient. The number you get when you divide one number by another number.

Expressions

An expression is made up of terms that are numbers, variables, and operators that are added together. If that explanation sounds complicated, think of it this way: expressions are simply made up of the basic symbols used to create everything from first-grade addition problems to formulas and equations used in calculus. The individual terms of the expression are added to each other as individual parts of the expression. Remember that expressions can stand for single numbers and use basic operators such as $*$ and $\div$.

While a single expression does not suggest a comparison (or equivalency), an equation does and can be represented by a simple expression equal to a number. For example, $3 + 2 = 1 + 4$ is an equation because it uses the equal sign. Thus, think of $3 + 2$ and $1 + 4$ as building blocks—they are the expressions that, when joined together by an equal sign, make up an equation. Another way to think of an expression is that it is a math metaphor used to represent another number.

Order of Operations

An operation is what a symbol does. The operation of a + sign, for instance, is to add. That's easy enough, but what happens if you run into something like the following problem?

$$44 - (3^2 + 6) = ?$$

To solve this problem, you must simplify it, but if you do it in the wrong order, you will get the wrong answer. This concept—using the order of operations—is incredibly important. Here's the order you must remember.

1. Parentheses
2. Exponents
3. Multiplication and division (from left to right)
4. Addition and subtraction (from left to right)

You must do the operations in that order, starting first with anything in parentheses and finishing with addition/subtraction last, to get the correct answer. Let's revisit the prior equation:

$$44 - (3^2 * 2 + 6) = ?$$

Start by first focusing on the expression in parentheses. Inside the parentheses is an exponent, so do that first so that you can then do the operation within the parentheses:

$$3^2 = 3 * 3 = 9$$

The expression then becomes the following:

$$(9 * 2 + 6)$$

To complete the operation within the parentheses, do the multiplication operation first:

$$9 * 2 = 18$$
$$(18 + 6) = 24$$

You don't need the parentheses anymore because no operations are left to complete inside the parentheses. Now the problem looks like the following equation:

$$44 - 24 = ?$$
$$20 = ?$$

You can use the phrase **P**lease **E**xcuse **M**y **D**ear **A**unt **S**ally as a useful mnemonic. The words in the phrase have the same first letters as parentheses, exponents, multiplication, division, addition, and subtraction.

The most common mistake involving the order of operations is the following: doing division and multiplication after subtraction and addition, which results in the wrong answer. You must do multiplication and division first as you encounter them from left to right, and then addition and subtraction. Also remember to evaluate what's inside parentheses first.

Here's another example of this concept:

$$(4^2 + 5^3 - 120) * 3 = ?$$

You start with the exponents:

$$4^2 = 4 * 4 = 16$$

$$5^3 = 5 * 5 * 5 = 125$$

The original equation then becomes the following, which can be solved as follows:

$$(16 + 125 - 120) * 3 = ?$$
$$21 * 3 = ?$$
$$63 = ?$$

If you didn't understand this example, go back and review the order of operations again.

Occasionally, you may encounter an equation that uses brackets. In such cases, evaluate what's in the parentheses first and then what's in the brackets.

Equations

Equations relate expressions to one another with an equal sign. In algebra, equations can get complicated, but in arithmetic, equations often center around finding the equivalent of a single expression. See the following example:

$$3 + 2 = 5$$

While saying $3 + 2$ expresses 5 may seem simple because both have a clear and simple relationship, they are equal. Other kinds of equations (i.e., relationships) include symbols such as > (greater than) and < (less than), which can join two expressions. Such equations are often called *inequalities* due to not being equal. The greater than or less than relationship is thus a sign of inequality.

Remember that equations can be rearranged by doing the same operations to each side of the equivalency. Here's an example of subtracting 6 from both sides of the equation:

$$34 - 23 = 6 + ?$$
$$34 - 23 - 6 = 6 + ? - 6$$

The two instances of the number 6 subtracted on both sides of the equation cancel each other out. Therefore, the equality of the relationship remains unaffected, as the following shows:

$$11 - 6 = ?$$
$$5 = ?$$

Greatest Common Factor

Sometimes the term *greatest common factor* is called the *greatest common divisor*, but the concept remains the same regardless of the specific words used. The concept refers to the largest factor that two (or more) numbers share.

To use this concept, you should first work out all the factors for each number, and then find the largest factor the numbers have in common. For example, to find the greatest common factor of 18 and 30, the factors could be listed as follows:

- **Factors of 18:** 1, 2, 3, 6, 9, and 18
- **Factors of 30:** 1, 2, 3, 5, 6, 10, 15, and 30

The highest number in both sets (i.e., the highest number common to both sets) is 6, so that's the greatest common factor.

Least Common Multiple

Sometimes the term *least common multiple* is called the *lower common multiple*, the *smallest common multiple*, or the *lowest common denominator* (the latter when used in a fraction). But in any case, the concept remains the same—without knowing this term, you can't compare, add, or subtract fractions, all of which are important steps in mathematics.

The least common multiple is the smallest number that can be divided by two (or more) given numbers. To get this number, first write out the multiples for each number, and then find the smallest multiple that the numbers share.

For example, to find the least common multiple of 3 and 7, the multiples could be listed as follows:

- **Multiples of 3:** 3, 6, 9, 12, 15, 18, 21, 24, 27...
- **Multiples of 7:** 7, 14, 21, 28, 35, 42, 49, 56...

The lowest common number in both sets is 21, which is the least common multiple. Notice that other multiples are present, but you are looking only for the lowest, or least of the common multiples.

Exponents and Roots

Exponents

An exponent is an algebraic operation that tells you to multiply a number by itself.

For example, 4^2 is the same as $4 * 4$, and 4^3 is the same as $4 * 4 * 4$. The exponent tells you how many times to multiply the number by itself.

Exponents have a few special properties (you can think of them as shortcuts or even helpful tricks if desired):

1. If two numbers with exponents share the same base number, you can multiply them by adding the exponents:

$$2^5 * 2^3 = 2^8$$

2. If two numbers with exponents share the same base number, you can divide them by subtracting the exponents:

$$2^5 \div 2^3 = 2^2$$

3. A number with an exponent raised to a negative power is the same as 1 over or the reciprocal of that number with an exponent raised to the positive power:

$$5^{-2} = 1/5^2$$

$$1/5^2 = 1/25 \text{ or } 1 \div 25 = 0.04$$

4. A number raised to a fraction power is the same as a root, or radical:

$$9^{1/2} = 3 \text{ (the square root indicated by the 2 in 1/2)}$$

Remember that the root of a number x is another number, which when multiplied by itself a given number of times equals x. For example, the second root of 9 is 3 because $3 * 3 = 9$. The second root is usually called the *square root*. The third root is usually called the *cube root*. Because $2 * 2 * 2 = 8$, 2 is the cube root of 8. Two special exponent properties are further explained in the following two examples.

5. 1 raised to any power is 1:

$$1^2 = 1$$
$$1^{-4} = 1$$
$$1^{912} = 1$$

6. Any number raised to the power of 0 equals 1—sounds crazy, but it's true! Here's an example:

$$253^0 = 1$$

If you can remember these six properties, you'll be able to simplify almost any problem with exponents.

Roots and Radicals

Roots and radicals are sometimes held up as cliché symbols for difficult math problems, but in the real world, roots and radicals are easy to understand and use to solve equations.

A radical is an expression that has a square root, cube root, etc.; the symbol is a $\sqrt{}$. The number under that radical sign is called a *radicand*. Meanwhile, a square is an expression (not an equation!) in which a number is multiplied by itself. A given number is often raised to the power of 2. Here's an example: 4^2 is a square; $4 * 4$ is the same square, expressed differently.

The square root of a number is a second number that, when multiplied by itself, equals the first number. Therefore, finding the square root is the same as squaring a number, but in the opposite direction. For example, to find the square root of 25, you need to figure out what number, when squared, equals 25. With enough experience, you will automatically know many common square roots. For example, 5 is commonly known as the square root of 25. Square and square root are operations often used to undo or cancel out each other in problem-solving situations.

A mental image that works like a numerical mnemonic and helps some people is envisioning the given number and the square root (in the prior case, 25 and 5) as a tree and its much smaller roots in the ground, respectively.

The previous example uses the number 25, which is an example of a perfect square. Only some numbers are perfect squares—those equal to the product of two integers. The following table shows the first 10 perfect squares.

Factors	Perfect Square
1 * 1	1
2 * 2	4
3 * 3	9
4 * 4	16
5 * 5	25
6 * 6	36
7 * 7	49
8 * 8	64
9 * 9	81
10 * 10	100

Remember that, if you find that the square root of any radicand is a whole number (not a fraction or a decimal), the given number is a perfect square.

To deal with radicals that are not perfect, rewrite them as radical factors and then simplify until you get one factor that's a perfect square. This process is sometimes called *extracting* or *taking out the square root*. As an example, that process would be used for the following number:

$$\sqrt{18}$$

First, notice that 18 has within it the perfect square 9:

$$18 = 9 * 2 = 3^2 * 2$$

Therefore, $\sqrt{18}$ is not in its simplest form. Now, you need to extract the square root of 9:

$$\sqrt{18} = \sqrt{9} * 2 = 3\sqrt{2}$$

Now the radicand no longer has any perfect square factors.

$\sqrt{2}$ is an irrational number that is equal to approximately 1.414. Therefore, the approximate answer is the following:

$$\sqrt{18} = 3 * 1.414 = approximately\ 4.242$$

Note that the answer can only be an approximate one since $\sqrt{2}$ is an irrational number, which is any real number that cannot be expressed as a ratio of integers. Irrational numbers cannot be represented as terminating or repeating decimals.

Factorials

If you have ever seen a number followed by an exclamation point, don't worry—you're not being yelled at! That formation is called a *factorial*. Simply put, a factorial is the product of a number and all the positive integers below it, stopping at 1. For example, if you see 5!, its value is determined as shown in the following equation:

$$5! = 5 * 4 * 3 * 2 * 1 = 120$$

Factorials are typically used in relation to the fundamental principle of counting or for the combinations or permutations of sets.

ALGEBRA CONCEPTS

Algebra is not only a branch of mathematics with symbols (referred to as *variables*) and numbers, but also a system of rules for the manipulation of both. Solving higher-order word problems is a valuable application of the algebra properties described in this chapter.

Expressions

Algebra uses variables, numbers, and operations as basic components in algebraic expressions. Variables are typically represented by letters and may have any number of values in a problem. Usually, the variable is the unknown quantity in a problem. All letters can and often are used, but the letters x, y, and z appear most often in algebra textbooks. In a testing situation, letters other than x, y, and z are often used to mislead test takers.

Algebraic expressions are variables and numbers with operations such as addition, subtraction, multiplication, and division. The following examples are all algebraic expressions:

Type of Expression	Example Expressions		
Letters	x	y	a
Product of a variable and number	$7u$	$q/2$	$3.9p$
Sum of a variable and number	$s + 5$	$u + v$	$2.3 + r$
Difference of a variable and number	$z - 3.5$	$k - n$	$t - 1.3$
Quotient of a variable and number	$m/6$	$(z/2)$	$3.9/p$
Variable or number with an exponent	c^2	$b^{0.5}$	$\sqrt{3}$

Finally, the sum, difference, product, or quotient of the expressions are also expressions.

Equations

Equations are defined as algebraic expressions set equal to a number, variable, or another expression. The simplest identifier of an equation is the equal sign (=). When an equation is written to express a condition or represent a problem-solving situation, the solution is normally completed by manipulating the equation correctly so that a variable or unknown quantity is on one side of the equal sign and the numerical answer(s) is on the other side. Let's review some problem-solving methods in the following examples.

If a simple equation is written in word form, the first step toward solving the equation is to write the equation that represents that written question. The simple problem of determining the ages of individuals is a common example:

Example Problem: Jane is 8 years older than Nancy. In 5 years, Jane will be 27 years old. What is her current age?

Solution: The variable J will represent Jane's age, and the expression $J + 5$ will represent Jane's age in 5 years. In this example, the expression is equal to a number, in this case 27. The following equation shows the equation to be solved:

$$J + 5 = 27$$

In the words of the problem, the correct expression is set equal to a number. The basic principle for solving the problem is to perform algebraic operations until the J is alone on one side of the equation and the numerical answer is on the other side. This type of solution involves the opposite of the addition (+5) in the previous equation, so 5 is subtracted from both sides:

$$\begin{aligned} J + 5 &= 27 \\ -5 \quad &-5 \\ \hline J + 0 &= 22 \end{aligned}$$

Therefore, the answer says that variable J, Jane's age, is currently 22 years.

If the simple equation involved multiplication, the steps would involve an opposite operation, in this case division:

$$7J = 84$$

$$\frac{7J}{7} = \frac{84}{7}$$

$$J = 12$$

These examples are typical of "one-step solutions" since a single operation is needed to solve the problem.

Of course, more involved, complex problems have multi-step solutions. But the rules remain the same:

1. Opposite operations are performed to solve an equation.
2. The same operations must be performed on both sides of the equation.
3. The solution is complete when a variable is on one side and the answer is on the other side.

Let's try another example.

Example Problem: Jane is 8 years older than Nancy. In 5 years, Jane will be twice as old as Nancy. What is Jane's current age?

Solution: The first step to solving this type of problem is to identify the variable. In this solution, we will select the variable J to represent Jane's age and N to represent Nancy's age.

The two equations from the word description, become the following equations:

$$J - 8 = N$$

and

$$J + 5 = 2(N + 5)$$

Dividing both sides of the second equation by 2 means obtains the following:

$$(J + 5)/2 = N + 5$$

Adding 5 to the first equation ($J - 8 = N$) so that both equations equal $N + 5$ results in the following:

$$J - 8 + 5 = N + 5$$

In this method, two expressions contain J, and both equal $N + 5$. Therefore, the expressions must be equal. The following equation can thus be formed:

$$J - 3 = (J + 5)/2$$

Multiply both sides by 2 (same operation on both sides) to obtain the following:

$$2J - 6 = J + 5$$

Now subtract J and add 6 to both sides to obtain the answer, as shown in the following solution:

$$
\begin{array}{rcl}
2J - 6 &=& J + 5 \\
-J + 6 & & -J + 6 \\
\hline
J &=& 11
\end{array}
$$

Through this solution, the problem is completed, and the following statements are clarified:

1. Currently, Jane is 11 years old, while Nancy is 3 years old.
2. In 5 years, Jane will be 16 years old, and Nancy will be 8 years old.

We could answer the question "What is Jane's current age?" and identify all the other ages in the problem because of an algebra principle that requires two equations for two unknowns. The problem has two variables (J and N) and two relationships between them (currently and 5 years from now). If we can formulate two equations with the two unknowns, then algebra principles allow for finding the solution for a complex problem.

Quadratic Equations

Quadratic equations are algebraic equations where the largest variable exponent is equal to two. This type of equation is often referred to as a *second-degree equation*. If there are multiple terms, the equation can also be referred to as a *second-degree polynomial*, where *polynomial* indicates that the equation has multiple terms. Quadratic equations are valuable in higher-order problem-solving situations, with particularly important applications in physics. See the following examples of quadratic equations:

$$7x^2 = 0$$

$$\frac{1}{2} * (9.8) * t^2 - 27$$

$$ax^2 + bx + c = 0 \text{ where } a, b, \text{ and } c \text{ are real numbers}$$

Note that all quadratic equations can be written in the form of the last example because coefficients can be zero, and algebra operations can be performed so that the 0 is on the right side of the equation. This last statement is the standard form and is important. **Every** quadratic equation in this form can be solved with the quadratic formula.

The quadratic formula is presented below with a qualifying statement. In a timed testing environment, the use of the following formula is typically used when factoring is not feasible due to it being time-consuming. Below is the quadratic formula for equations in the standard form:

$$x = \frac{-b \pm \sqrt{b^2 - 4ac}}{2a}$$

In the context of the exam, the quadratic formula will normally be used when the following situations are true:

$$b^2 - 4ac = 0, \text{ or}$$

$$b^2 - 4ac = \text{a perfect square}$$

Since the use of technology is not allowed in timed testing environments, any more intricate application of the quadratic formula would be too time consuming to be useful. Note that the operations before the square root sign are both correct. The plus and minus signs indicate that every quadratic equation has two possible answers. That does not mean, however, that both answers will be valid for the multiple-choice word problem in quadratic form. This concept is easily explained with a simple statement: Since two negative numbers and two positive numbers multiplied together give a positive answer, any quadratic equation may have two possible correct answers. When answering multiple-choice questions about quadratic equations, that statement should be considered.

FOIL—Polynomial Multiplication

Polynomial multiplication is routinely taught with a method described as FOIL, which stands for first, outside, inside, and last. In a binomial multiplication problem, the form will usually look like the following expression, with $A, B, C,$ and D all being whole number coefficients:

$$(Ax + B) * (Cx + D)$$

- The "first" means that Ax and Cx are multiplied together to equal ACx^2.
- The "outside" means that Ax and D are multiplied together to equal ADx.
- The "inside" means that B and Cx are multiplied together to equal BCx.
- The "last" means that B and D are multiplied together to equal BD.

The polynomial answer becomes the following expression:

$$ACx^2 + (AD + BC)x + BD$$

In testing conditions, this method can be cumbersome, confusing, and unreliable because mistakes are too common.

A simplified alternative is the box method, which is simpler than FOIL for multiple reasons:

- A box provides the organization for the multiplication.
- The box also provides organization for the addition of like terms.
- This method is expandable for use with longer polynomial multiplication.

To use the box method for polynomial multiplication, use the following five steps:

5. Create a box that has a row and column for each term in the multiplication problem.
6. Perform the multiplication for each pair of terms.
7. Place the answers in the cells of the box.
8. Add the like terms that are aligned diagonally.
9. Write the polynomial.

The following diagram explains the outcome with the previously noted example:

$$(Ax + B) * (Cx + D) \text{ becomes the following:}$$

	Ax	B
Cx	ACx^2	BCx
D	ADx	BD

The diagonal boxes in the upper right and lower left are always the "like terms," leaving no questions regarding which terms must be added together. This aspect is always true if you have correctly ordered the binomials with the "x term" of the binomials on the left and on top, respectively.

The outcome is the same as the FOIL answer previously noted:

$$ACx^2 + (AD + BC)x + BD$$

Notice also that the box method has the additional benefit of completely separating the addition and multiplication operations.

In a multiple-choice problem with polynomial multiplication, using the box method offers a significant benefit to consider—saving time.

Example: $(x + 6)(4x + 8) = $ _____ (choose the correct answer from the following answer choices):

        A. $4x^2 + 32x + 48$
        B. $4x^2 + 32x + 32$
        C. $4x^2 + 32x + 14$
        D. $4x^2 + 14x + 48$

Using the box method, the lower right box entry means that the last term in the answer must be $6 * 8$, or 48. Therefore, both answer choices B and C can be eliminated since the last term is not 48 in either answer option.

The upper right and lower left box entries are added, so the middle term must be $24x + 8x = 32x$. Therefore, answer D can be eliminated because the middle term is not $14x$ in that answer option.

The correct answer must be A, a choice that can be made logically by looking at the box entries. Eliminating choices is expedited with the box method because the box entries can be easily compared to coefficients in the answer choices.

Substitute Variables

Many mathematics applications require using equations and then substituting variables. This terminology means that the algebra equation will typically have a single variable, with all other parameters defined as whole, decimal, or fractional numbers. When solving a problem, the value of the specific variable will then be uniquely defined (in some cases, multiple values may be supplied for comparison), and the variables are then used to determine a problem solution. For example, let's use an equation for a car traveling 40 kilometers per hour, assuming the distance traveled equals 40 km/h multiplied by time in hours.

Without the words, the equation in strictly algebraic terms would be as follows:
$$D = 40t \ (t \ in \ hours)$$

To find the distance traveled, you would solve the equation by substituting the value of time appropriate for the problem. If the problem stated that the time traveled was 2.5 hours, then the problem would be solved with the following equation:

$$D = 40 * 2.5$$

After multiplying, the answer for the distance traveled is 100 kilometers.

In some equations, you may be asked to evaluate an equation that involves a second-degree variable. For example, a word description might read as follows:

Distance traveled is equal to one-half 9.8 m/sec² multiplied by the time squared.

Again, without words, the question equation would be as follows in strictly algebraic terms:

$$D = \frac{1}{2} * 9.8 * t^2$$

Evaluating this equation for a time of 2 seconds results in the following:

$$D = \frac{1}{2} * 9.8 * 2^2$$
$$D = \frac{1}{2} * 9.8 * 4$$
$$D = 2 * 9.8$$
$$D = 19.6 \; meters$$

The distance unit for the answer is determined by the unit of measure given in the word problem.

Kilometers per hour multiplied by hours will provide distances in hours. Meters per second multiplied by seconds will provide distances in meters. The units of time and distance within the problem must be consistent. If variables are consistent, substituting variables will be simple.

Inequalities: Greater Than and Less Than

In mathematics, inequalities provide a powerful way to express relationships between quantities that may not be equal. An inequality is a statement that compares two expressions or values and asserts their relative size. There are several types of inequalities, including less than (<), greater than (>), less than or equal to (≤), greater than or equal to (≥), and not equal to (≠).

Inequalities are essential in various fields, such as algebra, calculus, and real-world applications like economics and physics. They allow us to describe ranges of values, express constraints, and model relationships where exact equality is not applicable.

Solving inequalities involves determining the set of values that satisfy the given conditions, which often requires applying mathematical principles (e.g., addition principle, multiplication principle, logical reasoning). Understanding inequalities is fundamental for solving problems, making decisions, and analyzing situations in diverse mathematical and practical contexts.

Addition Principle: If you add the same value to both sides of an inequality, the inequality remains unchanged.

Example: If $a > b$, then $a + c > b + c$.

Subtraction Principle: If you subtract the same value from both sides of an inequality, the inequality remains unchanged.

Example: If $a > b$, then $a - c > b - c$.

Multiplication Principle: If you multiply both sides of an inequality by a positive number, the inequality remains unchanged. If you multiply both sides by a negative number, the inequality sign flips direction.

Example 1: If $a > b$ and $c > 0$, then $ac > bc$.
Example 2: If $a > b$ and $c < 0$, then $ac < bc$.

Division Principle: If you divide both sides of an inequality by a positive number, the inequality remains unchanged. If you divide both sides by a negative number, the inequality sign flips direction.

Example 1: If $a > b$ and $c > 0$, then $a/c > b/c$.
Example 2: If $a > b$ and $c < 0$, then $a/c < b/c$.

To solve an inequality, you will want to apply the above principles and isolate the variable to one side of the inequality sign.

Example: Solve $2x + 3 > 7$.
Step 1: Subtract 3 from both sides: $2x > 7 - 3$.
Step 2: Simplify: $2x > 4$.
Step 3: Divide both sides by 2: $x > 4/2$.
Step 4: Simplify: $x > 2$.

Again, remember that it is crucial to flip the inequality sign when you multiply or divide both sides of the sign with a negative number. Here's an example:

$$-3x > 9$$

To solve this inequality, we need to divide both sides by -3. However, since we are dividing by a negative number, we need to remember to flip the inequality sign. Dividing both sides of the inequality by -3 and flip the sign, we get:

$$x < -3$$

In this example, we started with the inequality -3x > 9. Since we divided both sides by -3 (a negative number), we flipped the inequality sign from ">" to "<".

MODULE 2

LIFE AND PHYSICAL SCIENCE

The questions contained in the science sections of the TEAS are designed to evaluate the level of knowledge of the chemical basis of life, cellular biology, human anatomy, and human physiology. These topic areas include all the content of a full year of introductory high school-level biology and general chemistry.

Additionally, the TEAS will likely include questions that test other topics that might not be covered by such courses and that might only be available in higher-level courses such as organic chemistry, biochemistry, cell physiology, human physiology, anatomy, embryology, and genetics.

It is impractical to try to provide a complete science review in a single manual to include the entire range of material covered in multiple years of science coursework at the high school or college level. No study manual can cover everything in the TEAS.

The information provided in this manual is, to the best of our knowledge, likely to be of high yield—meaning the material is highly likely to be on the actual TEAS science questions.

Additionally, the material is presented as a logical progression of topics—as a storyline that makes sense and is interesting. We also believe that most of the lower-yield science information you'll encountered on TEAS science questions will likely be found in this section of the manual.

When deemed necessary, we may also introduce concepts that are unlikely to be directly tested on the TEAS but that greatly clarify and simplify the explanation of high-yield information. This material eliminates the need for memorizing a ton of high-yield facts when preparing for the TEAS.

This approach allows us to introduce advanced science topics in an efficient, easily understood manner while providing a deeper level of understanding of complicated topics. Although we cannot guarantee this manual will prepare you for every possible TEAS science question, we are confident that it will prepare you to succeed at the highest levels of the TEAS science section.

Properties of Matter

The physical properties of matter are those that can be observed or measured, such as color, elasticity, mass, volume, and temperature.

Mass measures the amount of a substance in an object. **Weight** is the amount of gravitational pull of Earth on an object. **Volume** is the amount of space an object occupies. **Density** is the amount of mass per unit volume.

Mass

Nearly everything in the universe relevant to the TEAS can be defined as matter or as energy. Matter is everything that has mass. Nearly all matter on Earth is composed of atoms, and atoms are composed of three basic subatomic particles: the proton, the neutron, and the electron. Each of these subatomic particles has a fundamental physical property known as mass.

For macroscopic objects such as a rock, a glass of water, or a balloon full of helium gas, the SI unit of mass is the kilogram (kg). In the laboratory, it is more common to work with smaller units of mass than kilograms; the most common of these mass units are grams and milligrams. Grams (g) are 1/1000th of a kilogram, and milligrams (mg) are 1/1000th of a gram.

On the atomic scale, masses are incredibly small. The mass of a proton is 1.6726×10^{-27} kg while the mass of the neutron is slightly more than that of a proton, however, the mass of an electron is 1,827 times lighter than that of a proton.

For atomic scales, masses are expressed in atomic mass units (AMUs) which are significantly smaller than the kilogram as a unit. The mass of a proton in AMUs is approximately 1.007 AMU. The mass of an electron is so small that it can be approximated to zero for most cases (likely to be encountered on the TEAS).

Density

All matter has a volume in addition to mass. For any given sample of matter, volume is the amount of space that the sample occupies. The density of a sample matter is calculated by dividing its mass by its volume or simply mass per unit volume (m/V).

$$Density = \frac{mass}{volume}$$

$$D = \frac{m}{V}$$

The density of liquid water at a temperature of 40 °C is equal to 1 gram per cubic centimeter (1 g/cm3).

Weight

The physical quantities of weight and mass are often misunderstood. Mass is an intrinsic property of matter that is determined by the type and number of atoms that comprise a given sample of matter. Weight is a force that acts on matter in a gravitational field.

Basic Atomic Structure

The Atom

The atom is the smallest unit of matter that can retain the physical and chemical properties of a specific substance. Atoms are composed of three subatomic particles: electrons (which are fundamental, i.e., not composed of smaller subatomic particles), protons, and neutrons. The latter two are composed of quarks. Quarks are fundamental subatomic particles.

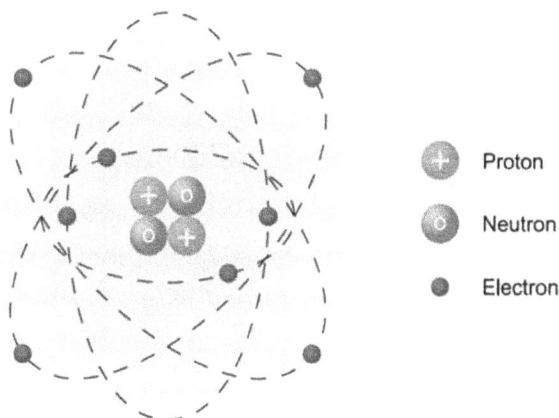

Atomic and Molecular Weights

The terms atomic and molecular weights are often used in science and should be equivalent to atomic mass and molecular mass. The term "atomic weight" refers to the average mass of an atom of an element.

The unit for atomic weight is grams and for atomic mass is AMU (atomic weight = grams, atomic mass = AMU).

For example, an atom with an atomic mass of 10 AMU has an atomic weight of 10 grams.

As mentioned earlier, an atom's atomic mass is approximately equal to the sum of the masses of its protons and neutrons.

The Atomic Nucleus

The central region of an atom—the nucleus—is composed of protons and neutrons. The only exception is one isotope of the element hydrogen, hydrogen 1, which is made up of a nucleus with a single proton and no neutrons.

Protons and neutrons are more generally classified as "nucleons." Nucleons are held together by a strong nuclear force.

Atomic Mass

The mass of a proton is exactly equal to one atomic mass unit (1 AMU). The mass of a neutron is slightly higher than that of a proton. For the TEAS, the mass of the neutron is also considered 1 AMU.

The mass of an electron is several thousand times less than 1 AMU, and for the TEAS, the mass of the electron is so small that it will be irrelevant in comparison to the proton and neutron masses.

The mass of a single atom is therefore almost entirely due to the sum of the masses of the nucleons (protons and neutrons) in the atom's nucleus.

For example, an atom whose nucleus contains six protons and seven neutrons has an atomic mass of $6\ AMU + 7\ AMU = 13\ AMU$.

Electrons and Atomic Charge

The nucleus is surrounded by electrons with an electric charge of -1, whereas protons have an electric charge of +1, and neutrons have a zero charge.

Particles with opposite electric charges are attracted to one another by electromagnetic forces while those with the same electric charge repel each other. This force attracts electrons to an atom's positively charged nucleus. When an atom contains the same number of electrons and protons, the positive charge of protons in the nucleus and the negative charge of electrons surrounding the nucleus cancel each other out, resulting in a neutral atom or an atom with a net electric charge of zero.

Elements

An element refers to an atom with the same number of protons in the nucleus. For instance, the element carbon refers to all atoms that have exactly six protons in their atomic nuclei.

Most carbon atoms have six neutrons in their nuclei; therefore, most carbon atoms have an atomic mass of approximately 12 AMU (6 protons + 6 neutrons). The actual average value depends on the percentage of the naturally occurring heavier carbon atoms. This average elemental atom mass is defined as the element's atomic mass, also frequently described as the element's atomic weight.

In the laboratory, the term "atomic weight" is equivalent to the element's atomic mass in grams. This is an important definition to understand because it is the scientific basis for designing most chemical experiments. This is because the atomic masses of all elements have been determined experimentally.

The absolute values of these elemental masses are less important than the fact that we also know what the elemental masses are relative to each other. For instance, the atomic mass (average mass) of a carbon atom is approximately 12 AMU (21.01), and the atomic mass of an oxygen atom is approximately 16 AMU.

Ions

Atoms can have fewer or more electrons than protons. When the number of electrons exceeds the number of protons, the atom has a net negative charge. When the number of protons exceeds the number of electrons, the atom has a net positive charge. The net charge is equal to the sum of the positive charges caused by protons and the negative charges caused by electrons. For instance, if an atom has eight electrons and six protons, then the net charge of the atom is $(-8) + (6) = -2$.

Atoms (and molecules) with net charges are called ions. Negative ions are called anions, and positive ions are called cations.

Larger particles such as molecules and even macroscopic objects can also have a net charge due to an unbalanced number of electrons and protons within the particle or object.

Importantly, nearly all the macroscopic mechanical forces such as mechanical friction, air resistance, and the pressures exerted by fluids and gases are due to the repulsive electromagnetic force at the atomic level between the electrons of different atoms.

Isotopes

The simplest atom is the hydrogen atom, which contains only one proton but may also contain one or two neutrons in its atomic nucleus. There are three types of hydrogen nuclei: one with a single proton only, one with a proton and a neutron, and one with a proton and two neutrons. Each of the three types of hydrogen nuclei has one proton in its nucleus but has a different number of neutrons. Elemental atoms with different numbers of neutrons in their nucleus are called isotopes of the element. Therefore, there are three isotopes of the element hydrogen.

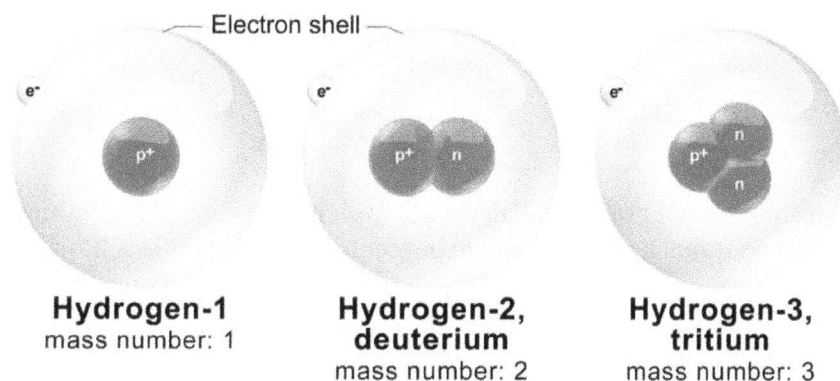

Other elements have varying numbers of isotopes. Atoms with nuclei that contain different numbers of protons are different elements, and the atoms of every individual element have a unique set of physical and chemical properties. Isotopes of an element have virtually identical chemical properties but can have different physical properties due to the difference in mass among the isotopes.

Atomic Weight

The atomic weight of an element is defined as the average atomic mass of its atoms. Since most elements have at least two isotopes, the average mass of the elemental atoms depends on the masses of the isotopes and the fractional percentage (relative abundance) of the isotopes that occur in nature.

Hypothetically, imagine that hydrogen's three isotopes occur naturally in percentages of 50% H-1 (one proton or 1 AMU), 20% H-2 (1 proton and 1 neutron or 2 AMU), and 30% H-3 (one proton and 2 neutrons or 3 AMU). The average atomic weight of hydrogen atoms in general would be as follows:

$$(0.5)(1\ AMU) + (0.2)(2\ AMU) + (0.3)(3\ AMU) = 0.5\ AMU + 0.4\ AMU + 0.9\ AMU$$
$$= 1.8\ AMU$$

If these were the actual percentages of hydrogen's three isotopes, then the average mass of hydrogen atoms would be 1.8 AMU, and the atomic mass of the element hydrogen would be 1.8. Nearly all the hydrogen occurring in nature (99.99%) is the isotope H-1.

Therefore, the tiny fractions of heavier isotopes are too small to change the mass except at several digits to the right of the decimal point. Therefore, the atomic mass of the element hydrogen is very nearly equal to that of the hydrogen-1 isotope, which is 1.008.

For the lighter elements, the most common isotope by far is the isotope that has equal numbers of protons and neutrons. Most atomic weights are thus close to twice the element's atomic number, though this is not always true—as the element chlorine illustrates.

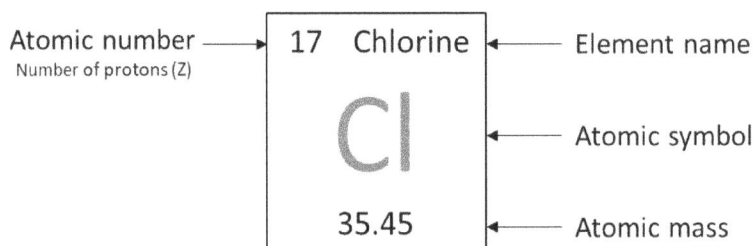

Chlorine has an atomic number of 17 and an atomic weight of 35.45. Those values indicate that the element chlorine contains a relatively large percentage of the heavier chlorine isotopes.

The Periodic Table

The periodic table arranges elements in a modified grid-like chart, with each element occupying a unique position in the table that correlates with the element's atomic number.

Reminder: The atomic number of an element is equal to the number of protons found in its nucleus.

The first element, hydrogen, occupies the upper left corner of the table.

Elements with increasing atomic numbers are added to the next available position to the right on the same row until the row is complete.

The element after that will occupy the first position to the left on the next row.

PERIODIC TABLE OF THE ELEMENTS

Groups and Periods

The rows of the periodic table are called periods, while the columns are called groups. There are 7 periods and 18 groups in the periodic table. Groups are numbered from left to right (from 1 to 18).

The first period of the periodic table only has a Group 1 position (hydrogen) and a Group 18 position (helium) seen separated by a wide gap on the periodic table.

The second and third periods have eight positions for Groups 1, 2, 13, 14, 15, 16,17, and 18. The fourth through seventh periods have the complete 18 groups.

The gaps in the periods reflect differences in the properties of the elements that emerge as electrons arrange themselves in various configurations. This topic will be discussed later.

Atomic Energy States

All atoms strive to attain their lowest possible energy states. The most favorable energy state of an atom is the neutral state. The nuclei of atoms have a positive charge equal to the number of protons they contain. All protons have a charge of +1. An electron has a charge of -1 (the exact opposite charge of a proton).

When an atom contains an equal number of protons and electrons, the proton and electron charges cancel each other out, leading to a net charge of zero. This type of atom is called a neutral atom.

Neutral atoms can further lower their overall energy state if they achieve a certain arrangement of electrons.

Electron Shells (N levels)

Electrons that are electromagnetically bound to an atom arrange themselves in concentric electron shells around the nucleus.

The innermost electron shell is the "n = 1" electron shell, which contains the lowest energy level positions available to electrons. It is the first shell to be filled by electrons.

The n level can be any positive integer n = 1,2,3... The larger the integer value for n, the higher the energy of the n electron shell.

Electron Subshells (Orbitals)

The regions within an electron shell that electrons occupy are called subshells or electron orbitals. The n = 1 shell has only one type of subshell called an "s" orbital.

Since this s orbital is located on the n = 1 shell, it is designated as the "1s" orbital. Individual subshell orbitals can accommodate no more than two electrons. Since only a single s orbital exists at any given n-shell level, only two electrons can be accommodated at the n = 1 level.

An atom achieves a significant lowering of its energy state when filling the n = 1 shell. Atoms of the element helium have two protons and therefore will achieve charge neutrality by acquiring two electrons. Additionally, these two electrons will fill the 1s orbital. This also simultaneously completes the n = 1 electron shell. There is no additional electron configuration that will further lower the energy state of helium atoms. Helium is therefore chemically inert, meaning it will never participate in any chemical reactions with other elements.

Period 2 Elements and p Orbitals

For elements with atomic numbers higher than 2 (meaning the nuclei contain more than two protons), additional electrons must be acquired for the atoms to achieve charge neutrality. Additional electrons will occupy higher energy positions within orbitals beginning at the n = 2 electron shell.

At the n = 2 level, there are two types of orbitals: the s orbital and a new type of orbital, the "p" orbital. For the n = 2 shell level and at all subsequently higher shell levels (n = 3, 4 ...) there is a single s orbital and three p orbitals. The p orbital is at a higher energy level compared to the s orbital.

Since the maximal electron capacity of any single orbital is always two electrons, the n = 2 shell can accommodate a total of eight electrons: two in the single s orbital and two electrons in each of the three p orbitals. These orbitals at the n = 2 level are designated as the 2s orbital and the 2px, 2py, and 2pz orbitals.

Elements in the second period (row) of the periodic table have electrons that occupy positions within the orbitals of the n = 2 electron shell. There are eight elements in the second period of the table, beginning with lithium on the left in *Group 1* column directly beneath hydrogen. The elements to the right of lithium sequentially have one additional electron in their n = 2 level orbitals.

At the final position on the right (the 8th position of the period) is the element neon (atomic number 10). Notice that neon has a full n = 2 electron shell and is in the *Group 13* column directly below helium.

Electron Configuration Notation
The electron configuration (positions) of an atom can be specified by listing the electron shells and orbitals that contain them.

Electron positions are specified beginning with the lowest energy orbital on the left and then going to progressively higher energy orbitals.

- For hydrogen, this would be indicated by the following notation: $1s^1$.
- For helium (atomic number 2), this would be indicated by: $1s^2$.
- For neon (atomic number 10), this would be indicated by: $1s^2 2s^2 2p^6$.

Since at any given n electron shell level, the s orbitals are lower energy than the *p* orbitals, the *s* orbitals fill before electrons begin to occupy positions in the *p* orbitals.

NOTE: The electron energy level notation indicates the lowest possible electron energy state of an atom. This is called the ground state of electrons. Electrons can acquire energy by absorbing photons and consequently jump to higher energy level orbitals. This is called an "excited energy state."

If an electron absorbs enough energy, it can escape from the parent atom entirely. The energy required for this is equal to the parent atom's elemental ionization energy.

Valence Electrons
We can begin to explain and even predict the chemical and physical properties of elements.

The innermost electrons in an element are very tightly bound to their atomic nuclei and under normal circumstances never participate in chemical reactions.

On the other hand, electrons in the outermost electron shell are the ones that participate in chemical reactions and are called valence electrons.

Elements in the same group have the same number of valence electrons and thus have similar chemical properties.

The Octet Rule
The energy of an atom is significantly lowered when the n = 1 electron shell is completed with two electrons in the 1s orbital. From the n = 2 energy level, an additional significant reduction of energy occurs when the 2s orbital and the three 2p orbitals of a shell are filled by electrons. This is the explanation of the octet rule.

The octet rule states that atoms engage in chemical reactions for a fundamental reason, which is to acquire exactly eight electrons in their valence s and p orbitals. Acquiring this eight-electron configuration will significantly reduce their electron energy level.

Atoms that do not have a filled valence octet can fill their octet by acquiring electrons from other atoms, consequently becoming an anion. Alternatively, they may achieve a valence octet by sharing electrons with other atoms through the formation of covalent chemical bonds.

Periodic Properties of the Elements

The term "periodic" in the periodic table refers to the periodically repeated chemical and physical properties of the elemental atoms. This is because elemental atoms with the same number of s and p orbital valence electrons attempt to satisfy the octet rule in the same manner. Atoms of elements in the same column (group) have the same number of s and p valence electrons.

All the elements in Group 18 (the noble gases) except helium have satisfied the octet rule as neutral atoms. Noble gases are chemically inert, and thus participating in chemical reactions with other elemental atoms provides no energetic advantage.

The Trends in the Periodic Table—From Left to Right

Electronegativity

The ability of an elemental atom to draw electrons from other atoms to share in a covalent bond or, in extreme cases, take an electron away from an atom is determined by its electronegativity.

The electronegativity of elemental atoms is mainly influenced by their proximity to achieving a valence octet.

Group 17 elements, or the halogens, are one electron short of completing their valence octets and are therefore the most electronegative element group.

Group 1 elements (the alkali metals) are the further away from completing their valence octet as they need seven electrons to complete their valence octets. They thus have the lowest electronegativity of the elemental groups.

The electronegativity of elements in the periodic table increases from left to right across a period. This trend stops at the last element to the right (Group 18) or the noble gases group, which has no desire for additional electrons and therefore has almost zero electronegativity.

ELECTRONEGATIVITY

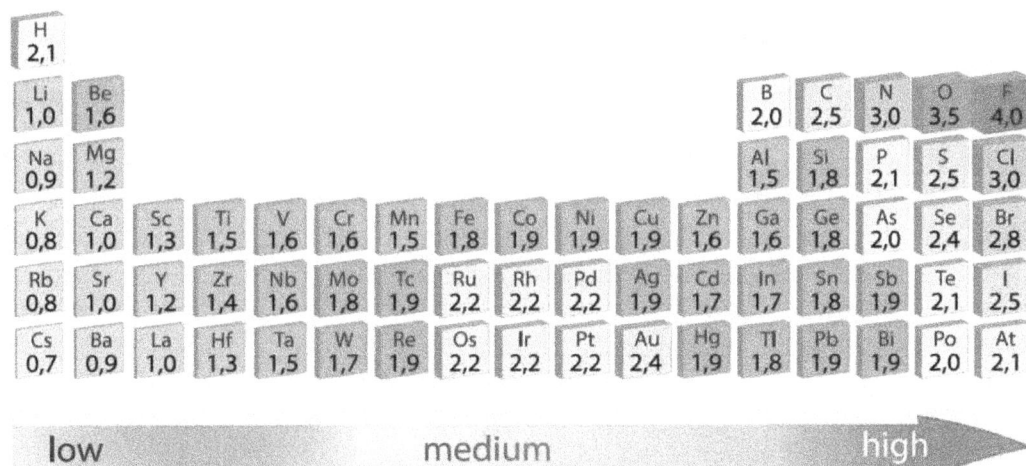

H 2,1																	
Li 1,0	Be 1,6											B 2,0	C 2,5	N 3,0	O 3,5	F 4,0	
Na 0,9	Mg 1,2											Al 1,5	Si 1,8	P 2,1	S 2,5	Cl 3,0	
K 0,8	Ca 1,0	Sc 1,3	Ti 1,5	V 1,6	Cr 1,6	Mn 1,5	Fe 1,8	Co 1,9	Ni 1,9	Cu 1,9	Zn 1,6	Ga 1,6	Ge 1,8	As 2,0	Se 2,4	Br 2,8	
Rb 0,8	Sr 1,0	Y 1,2	Zr 1,4	Nb 1,6	Mo 1,8	Tc 1,9	Ru 2,2	Rh 2,2	Pd 2,2	Ag 1,9	Cd 1,7	In 1,7	Sn 1,8	Sb 1,9	Te 2,1	I 2,5	
Cs 0,7	Ba 0,9	La 1,0	Hf 1,3	Ta 1,5	W 1,7	Re 1,9	Os 2,2	Ir 2,2	Pt 2,2	Au 2,4	Hg 1,9	Tl 1,8	Pb 1,9	Bi 1,9	Po 2,0	At 2,1	

low   medium   high →

Ionization Energies

The ionization energy of an atom is the amount of energy required to overcome an electron's attraction to its nucleus.

The first ionization energy is the least energy to extract the first electron from an atom, which results in a +1 charged atomic ion.

The energy required to remove the second electron is called "second ionization energy," requires a larger amount of energy, and results in a +2 charged atomic ion.

An elemental atom's ionization energies are usually correlated to its electronegativity. Elements with the lowest first ionization energies are Group 1 elements, and those with the highest first ionization energies are Group 18 elements. The exception is noble gases, which have the lowest electronegativities and highest ionization energies of all the periodic groups.

Ionization energies of elements increase with increasing atomic number within a given period except when a new subshell begins (as in the case of boron and beryllium) the first ionization energy decreases. The first ionization energy of boron (atomic number 5) is less than that of beryllium (atomic number 4) since the electron removed in boron is a p electron ($2s^2 2p^1$), while the electron removed in beryllium is a s electron ($2s^2$).

Atomic Radius

The atomic radius measures the size of an atom. It represents half the distance between the nuclei of two identical atoms bonded together, or the distance from the center of the nucleus to the outermost electron orbital.

Generally, the atomic radius decreases as the atomic number increases within each period. This is due to the increasing number of protons in the nucleus, which increases the element's positive nuclear charge as it moves from left to right.

The increasing positive nuclear charge exerts a stronger electromagnetic force on the electrons orbiting the nucleus, causing them, including those in the outermost electron shell, to be physically drawn closer to the nucleus. Since the outermost electron shell determines the outer boundary of an atom, the increasing nuclear charge will decrease the atom's radius.

Additionally, going down within each group, there is a greater distance between the nucleus and the electron's outermost orbital as the number of energy levels (n) increases the atomic radius.

Trends in the Periodic Table—From Top to Bottom

The atomic radius increases from top to bottom within each group due to an increased number of energy levels, resulting in a greater distance between the nucleus and the outermost orbital of electrons. Therefore, electrons in the outermost orbital are less strongly attracted to the nucleus and require less energy to be removed. Accordingly, the ionization energy within each group decreases from top to bottom.

Additionally, electronegativity decreases within each group. As the number of energy levels (n) increases, atoms have a weaker ability to attract electrons.

Physical Properties of Transition Metals:

Malleability and Ductility

The ability of atoms to roll into new positions and retain their metallic bond explains the physical properties of transition metals, such as ductility, malleability, and tensile strength. A metal's ability to be permanently pressed or hammered out of shape without breaking is known as malleability.

A metal's ability to be deformed under tensile stress and stretched into a wire when pulled is known as ductility. Because of these properties, metals are used as construction materials, parts of complex machinery, tools, and weapons.

Electrical and Thermal Conductivity

Transition metals have mobile and loosely bound electrons in their d-orbitals. These act as charge and thermal energy carriers, which results in excellent electrical and thermal conductivity.

Additionally, transition metals have a high boiling and melting point, allowing them to conduct a large amount of current and heat without melting.

Non-Metals

The TEAS expects that you'll understand several chemical and physical properties of non-metals. These should be understood in contrast to transition metals and alkali metals (Group 1). Explaining these is too technical and counterproductive for preparation for the TEAS. Instead, it is best to simply memorize that the most significant non-metal elements are carbon (*C*), nitrogen (*N*), oxygen (*O*), phosphorus (*P*), sulfur (*S*), and all the halides (Group 17 elements).

The properties of non-metals are generally the opposite of transition metals. Non-metals form small molecules with strong covalent bonds but weak intermolecular attractions both in their elemental form and as molecular compounds with other elemental atoms. These compounds in their solid state tend to be brittle or powdery. Non-metals are extremely poor electrical and thermal conductors and, therefore, excellent electrical and thermal insulators.

Non-metals include Group 18 (halogens) together with carbon, nitrogen, oxygen, fluorine, phosphorus, sulfur, chlorine, selenium, bromine, and iodine.

Metalloids

Metalloids are elements that exist along a stepped line between metals and non-metals. They conduct heat and electricity moderately well and have properties that are partially metallic and partially non-metallic. Due to their intermediate electrical conductivity, they are often classified as semiconductors and are used in the electronics industry.

Metalloids include boron, silicon, germanium, arsenic, antimony, tellurium, polonium, and astatine.

The Fifth and Higher Periods of the Periodic Table

At the fifth and higher periods of the periodic table, additional electrons begin to be added to new types of n orbitals. In the fourth period, the f orbital becomes available, and in the fifth period, a g class orbital becomes available. Elements that are adding electrons to these new orbitals are the lanthanide and actinide elements.

Once these f and g orbitals are filled, d orbitals will begin to fill. The chemistry of the lanthanide and actinide orbitals is beyond the scope of the TEAS.

Groups 1 (alkali metals), 2 (alkali earth metals), 17 (halogens), and 18 (noble gases) at all higher periods of the periodic table retain their specific group properties (this is expected knowledge for the TEAS).

Chemical Bonds Between Atoms

Except for Group 18 elements, all elemental atoms will, to varying degrees, engage in chemical reactions with other atoms. Groups 1 through 17 elemental atoms attempt to satisfy the octet rule either by taking one or more electrons away from other atoms (ionization) or by sharing electrons with other atoms through the formation of interatomic bonds.

Ionic Bonds

An ionic bond occurs when one or more electrons are transferred completely from one atom to another and the resulting ions are held together by pure electrostatic forces.

When an atom succeeds in taking one or more electrons from another atom, the atom that takes the electron(s) becomes negatively charged, called an anion, and the atom that loses the electron(s) becomes positively charged, called a cation. Usually, the electron donor and electron acceptor atoms become strongly bonded due to the electromagnetic force between the negative and positive charges of the two atoms. This type of interatomic or molecular bond is called an ionic bond.

Atoms with very high electronegativities can take electrons away from atoms with very low electronegativities. As a result, ionic bonds form between atoms of very high electronegativity and those with very low electronegativity.

The tendency to form ionic bonds is highest for elements located on the left and right sides of the periodic table—Groups 1 and 2 as cations and Groups 16 and 17 as anions—and progressively lowers toward the middle of the table.

The formation of a cation in an ionic bond requires less energy and is thus more likely to progress from top to bottom in the periodic table, while the formation of an anion is less energetically favorable and is therefore less likely to progress from top to bottom.

Hydrogen Bonds

Hydrogen bonding is the attractive force between a hydrogen atom attached to a highly electronegative atom of one molecule and a highly electronegative atom of a different molecule.

Hydrogen has a partial positive charge. The electronegative atom is usually oxygen, nitrogen, or fluorine, which have a partial negative charge. Hydrogen bonds are seen in water molecules (H_2O), chloroform molecules ($CHCl_3$) and ammonia molecules (NH_3).

Covalent (nonpolar) Bonds

Covalent (nonpolar) bonds are stronger than hydrogen bonds. In most cases, the difference in electronegativity between bonding atoms is insufficient for one atom to take an electron away from the other bonding atom, resulting in the two atoms sharing one electron each through a covalent bond.

Atoms can share additional electrons through the formation of additional covalent bonds with other atoms or with the same atom, resulting in double or triple covalent bonds. A purely covalent (nonpolar) bond occurs when electrons are shared equally between two atoms.

The number of covalent bonds that an atom can form depends on the number of electrons it requires to complete its valence octet. For example, oxygen has six valence electrons and is two electrons short of completing its valence octet. Therefore, oxygen shares two more electrons with other atoms, producing two covalent bonds that result in completing its valence octet.

Polar Bonds

A polar covalent bond occurs where electrons are not equally shared and there is a significant difference in electronegativity between the bonding atoms.

Identifying whether a molecule has nonpolar or polar bonds is important because polar molecules (those with high polarity) are hydrophilic (water-loving) and mix well with other polar compounds such as water.

On the other hand, nonpolar molecules are hydrophilic (resistant to water) and mix well with other nonpolar compounds such as oil, benzene, and hydrocarbon.

The ionic character of a bond is the magnitude of the charge required for separation in a polar covalent bond or the difference in electronegativity between two atoms.

If there is a large difference between the electronegativities of two atoms in a polar covalent bond, then it is called a partial ionic character. For example, in the molecule hydrogen fluoride (HF) fluorine is much more electronegative than hydrogen. Thus, a hydrogen fluoride molecule has a partially negative pole near the fluorine atom and a partially positive pole near the hydrogen atom. The covalent bond between hydrogen and fluorine is said to have a partial ionic character.

The ionic character of a bond can be predicted based on the position of atoms in the periodic table. Ionic bonds involve a metal and a non-metal, whereas covalent bonds involve two non-metal atoms. Some compounds can contain both covalent and ionic bonds.

Changes in States of Matter

The Four States (Phases) of Matter
On the human or macroscopic scale, matter molecules can exist in four phases or states: the solid phase, the liquid phase, the gas phase, and the plasma phase. When we are discussing the phases of matter, we are usually describing a macroscopic sample of a substance or a pure sample of a molecule.

A molecule is a particle that consists of more than one atom strongly bound together by electromagnetic forces, either in the form of ionic bonds between oppositely charged atoms or in the form of electrons in covalent bonds between two atoms.

These binding forces are called intramolecular forces, and except for the fourth state of matter—the plasma phase—the intramolecular covalent binding forces are not disrupted or broken during phase changes of the substance.

Ionic crystalline solids are bound by an ionic bond, which is a very strong bond that occurs between positive and negative ions, that must be disrupted to transition from a solid state to a liquid or gaseous state.

Ionic solids are not composed of small molecules; instead, the solids are composed of a three-dimensional lattice of alternating anions and cations.

For the TEAS, any mention of the phases and phase changes of matter almost certainly refers to substances that are covalent molecular compounds and not ionic crystalline solid or liquid compounds.

The phase of a substance is affected by temperature and pressure. Increasing the temperature separates the matter particles while increasing the pressure brings them closer together.

Intermolecular Forces

Intermolecular forces are the attractive electrical forces between molecules and are responsible for the unique properties of the solid and liquid phases of matter. These forces are weaker than the intramolecular forces of covalent bonds but stronger than hydrogen bonds.

Temperature

Although a motionless object has no net kinetic energy, every object has a temperature. Heat, either of atomic or molecular size, is typically the energy that is transformed into kinetic energy.

The temperature of an object—whether solid, liquid, or gas—is proportional to the average kinetic energy of the atoms contained within the object. The higher the temperature of a substance, the greater the average kinetic energy of the individual particles contained in the substance. The addition of heat to a substance usually increases the temperature of the object.

The Temperature Scales - Celsius, Kelvin, and Fahrenheit

The three most used temperature scales are Fahrenheit (expressed as °F), Celsius (°C), and Kelvin (K).

The Fahrenheit (°F) temperature scale defines the freezing point of water as 32 °F and the boiling point of water as 212 °F.

The Celsius (°C) temperature scale defines the freezing point of water as 0 °C and the boiling point of water as 100 °C.

The Kelvin and Celsius scales are both related as units of measurement. One unit increase in the Kelvin scale equals a one-degree increase in the Celsius scale. Their only distinction is that they have different absolute zero and triple points of water. The absolute zero of the Kelvin scale is 0 K, but -273 on the Celsius scale, and the triple point of water on the Kelvin scale is 273.16 degrees and 0.01 on the Celsius scale.

Absolute zero is the theoretically lowest possible temperature of matter and corresponds to a state where the atoms of matter have no kinetic energy at all. In other words, they are completely motionless. The laws of quantum mechanics show that this temperature can never occur in nature—it is physically impossible to cool anything down to a temperature of absolute zero.

Fahrenheit to Celsius conversion formula: $T\ (°C) = [T\ (°F) - 32] \times \dfrac{5}{9}$

Kelvin to Celsius conversion formula: $T\ (°C) = T\ (°K) - 273.15$

Solids

In solids, intermolecular forces are strong enough to prevent individual particles from changing position relative to each other. The particles in a solid have no translational velocity, however, they vibrate at a certain frequency; hence, the kinetic energy of particles is described as vibrational motion. As the particles in the solid acquire more energy, they vibrate faster, and the temperature of the solid increases.

Matter in the solid state maintains a constant three-dimensional configuration (shape) and has a definite volume and definite shape.

Liquids

When heat is continuously added to a solid, the temperature eventually rises until it reaches the melting point. At this point, the vibrational kinetic energy of individual particles will allow them to move or flow freely among the other particles in the solid. The continued addition of heat to a liquid increases the particles' kinetic energy by increasing the vibrational motion of the particles. This transition from the solid phase to the liquid phase is known as melting.

In the liquid phase, the particles still have little net translational motion and remain in contact with one another.

As heat is continuously removed from a liquid, the temperature of the liquid will eventually drop to its freezing point. The liquid-to-solid phase transition begins at this point, which is the inverse of the solid-to-liquid phase transition. Notably, a substance's freezing and boiling point temperatures are the same.

The ability of particles in a liquid to move freely within the liquid explains the physical property of liquids to conform to the interior shape of the vessel that contains them.

Additionally, a liquid has a definite volume but no definite shape and will seek the lowest spaces available within a container to form a continuous horizontally leveled surface while occupying all the container's accessible interior volume that is below this liquid-level surface.

Gases

When heat is continuously added to a liquid, its particles move faster and faster, both vibrationally and translationally. When the particles accumulate enough kinetic energy to overcome their attraction to other particles, they begin to leave the liquid surface and enter the vapor phase, which corresponds to the boiling point of the liquid.

This liquid-to-gas transition is called evaporation. Particles in the gas phase behave as if no intermolecular forces exist between them. The kinetic energy of gas particles is no longer caused by vibrational motion but by translational motion, which is the linear distance traveled by an object per unit of time.

Temperature can be used to calculate the average speed of gas molecules. At 20 °C, the average speed of air molecules is 500 m/s. This translates to about 1,100 miles per hour.
As gas molecules lose heat energy, their gas temperature falls to the condensation point, and they return to the liquid phase. The condensation point occurs at the same temperature as the boiling point of a substance. This gas-to-liquid transition is called condensation.

Gases are highly compressible and change in volume, but liquids and solids are non-compressible.

Plasmas

The plasma phase of matter occurs when matter reaches extremely high temperatures, where the atom's electrons absorb additional energy, and the kinetic energy of individual molecules overcomes the strength of intramolecular bonds. This causes molecules to be ripped apart into individual atoms and electrons to be stripped away from atomic nuclei, resulting in a collection of naked, positively charged atomic nuclei and negatively charged free electrons.

The plasma phase seldom occurs on Earth except when artificially generated by highly specialized and sophisticated technological processes. Elsewhere in the universe, the plasma phase of matter is the most common since it is the phase of matter that exists within stars and interstellar dust. It is unlikely that TEAS questions will involve detailed knowledge regarding the plasma phase of matter.

Sublimation and Deposition

Under certain conditions, substances in the solid phase can transition directly to the gas phase in a process called sublimation. Similarly, substances in the gas phase can transition directly to the solid phase in a process called deposition. The temperature at which this occurs is the substance's sublimation and deposition point.

Carbon dioxide, for example, transitions directly from a solid to a gas at atmospheric pressure with a sublimation and deposition point of $-78.5\ °C$.

Evaporation and Condensation

A liquid can transition into a gas in a process called evaporation. When a liquid is sufficiently heated or the pressure on the liquid is sufficiently reduced, the forces of attraction between molecules are overcome, and the liquid evaporates into a gas.

On the other hand, a gas or vapor can transition into a liquid in a process called condensation. When a gas is sufficiently cooled or, in many cases, when the pressure on the gas is sufficiently increased, the forces of attraction between molecules prevent them from moving apart, and the gas condenses into a liquid.

Specific Heat Capacity

The specific heat capacity of a substance is the amount of heat required to increase the temperature of 1 gram of the substance by 1 degree Celsius (or 1 Kelvin).

This value is determined by several factors, but the actual value must be determined experimentally for each substance. It is calculated as energy per unit mass degree Celsius, either *Joules/kg °C* or *calories/g °C*.

For example, the specific heat capacity of water is 4.18 *Joules/g °C*. This means that 1 gram of water requires 4.18 *Joules* of heat energy to increase its temperature by 1 *°C*. Water has one of the highest specific heat capacities of any substance.

On the other hand, solid iron has a heat capacity of 0.45 *Joules/g* °C. This means that raising the temperature of 1 g of water by 1 °C requires approximately ten times the heat energy required to raise the temperature of 1 g of solid iron by 1 °C.

Let's calculate the amount of energy required to raise the temperature of 20 *g* of liquid water by 15 °C. The calculation is shown below.

$$(4.18 \, J/g°C)(20 \, g)(15 °C) = 1254J$$

Characteristic Properties of Substances

Cellular Homeostasis

<u>Cell Membranes</u>
For biological cells, homeostasis requires a physical barrier called a cell membrane to separate the cell's internal contents from the surrounding external environment. The cell membrane is a selective, semi-permeable double-layered lipid membrane.

It is permeable to water, oxygen, and carbon dioxide molecules but not to other molecules. These other molecules require trans-membrane proteins that act as transporters if they were to enter or leave the cell.

<u>Osmolality</u>
In the context of human cellular biology, all intracellular processes occur in solutions where the solvent is water. The particles dissolved in the intracellular water include oxygen, carbon dioxide, electrolytes, small molecules such as glucose, and a vast number of other chemicals and proteins.

Osmolality is the total concentration of all these dissolved particles in body fluid.

<u>Hypertonic and Hypotonic Solutions</u>
A liquid environment usually exists outside of cells as well. This environment also has an osmolality. Water tends to diffuse between two regions, causing the osmolality of both regions to equalize.

Osmosis is the flow of the solvent from the side with a lower concentration of solute to the side with a higher concentration of solute.

For cellular homeostasis, the internal and external osmolality levels are slightly different. The internal cellular osmolality is artificially maintained at a slightly higher concentration level than the external cellular osmolality. This causes water to be drawn into cells via osmosis, resulting in higher internal fluid pressure. The desired homeostatic state for cells is to be surrounded by a hypotonic solution, which means that the surrounding external solution has a lower osmolality than the cell's internal osmolality.

A hypertonic external solution (when the external environment of the cell has a higher osmolality than the inner solution of the cell) causes water to move out of the cell via osmosis, causing the cell to shrivel and eventually die.

Conversely, a hypotonic solution (when the external environment of the cell has a lower osmolality than the inner solution of the cell) causes water to enter the cell, causing it to swell and eventually rupture its membrane. This phenomenon can be observed microscopically by placing red blood cells in a Petri dish filled with pure water, which is hypotonic.

Semipermeable Membranes
Semipermeable membranes are typically thin sheets of material that separate at least two fluid compartments. They are generally permeable to solvent liquids within the compartments.

Permeable means "able to pass through." The semipermeable membrane is permeable to some but not all molecules within the compartments.

Semipermeable membranes are important in biology because the cell membrane is semipermeable; it is permeable to water (which is the solvent in biological solutions) but impermeable to most other substances that are dissolved in biological solutions.

Diffusion
Diffusion is the passive, non-energy-requiring process by which solvents and solutes move from one local region to another due to their differences in solute concentrations. When there is a concentration gradient between two regions, the solute particles in the higher concentration region will move or flow to the lower concentration region. The greater the concentration difference between the two regions, the greater the driving force for the solute movement.

The distance between the highest and lowest concentration regions is another factor in determining how strong the driving force of diffusion is. The shorter the distance between the high and low-concentration regions, the stronger the driving force of diffusion. The diffusion process will continue until the concentrations in both regions are equal.

If a semipermeable barrier exists between high and low solute concentration regions, where the barrier is permeable to the solvent but not to the solutes, the solvent will diffuse through the semipermeable barrier and eventually equalize the concentration of the solution between high and low regions.

Simple Diffusion
We have discussed the details of diffusion in general. Let's review! All dissolved particles in a solution will, if possible, move by diffusion spontaneously from regions of higher solute concentrations to regions of lower solute concentrations which is referred to as a movement with or down a concentration gradient. This is referred to as "simple diffusion," which does not require energy. In fact, diffusion can be a source of chemical energy that drives chemical reactions.

Within the human body, oxygen will typically diffuse into the cell and carbon dioxide will typically diffuse out of the cell via simple diffusion.

Facilitated Diffusion
Facilitated diffusion is the movement of a solute from a high to a low solute concentration area that does not require energy. It is faster than simple diffusion; however, it requires a carrier to transport molecules.

The glucose transporter GLUT acts as a carrier for glucose transport across the plasma membrane via facilitated diffusion.

Osmotic Pressure
Osmotic pressure is a colligative property that is present in solutions when a semipermeable barrier exists between two solutions with different solute concentrations. It is the required pressure to stop water from diffusing through a barrier by osmosis.

Chemical Reactions
Chemical reactions are reversible and, depending on conditions, can occur in both forward and reverse directions. In a chemical equilibrium, these forward and reverse reactions occur at equal rates, with the concentrations of their products and reactants remaining constant.

General Form of a Chemical Reaction
When writing chemical reactions, the reactants are placed on the left, followed by a rightward pointing arrow, and the products of the reaction to the right.

$$aA + bB \rightarrow cC + dD$$

The small letters a, b, c, and d refer to the relative amounts (number) of particles for each participant A, B, C, and D in the reaction (called the stoichiometric coefficients of the reaction).

The General Types of Chemical Reactions
The general types of chemical reactions include synthesis reactions, decomposition reactions, single replacement reactions, and double replacement reactions. The general formulas for each of these types of reactions are as follows:

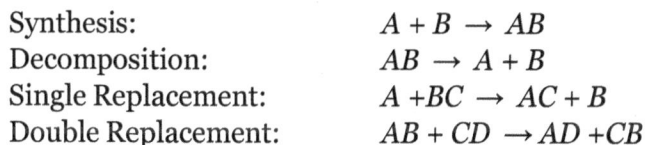

Synthesis:	$A + B \rightarrow AB$
Decomposition:	$AB \rightarrow A + B$
Single Replacement:	$A + BC \rightarrow AC + B$
Double Replacement:	$AB + CD \rightarrow AD + CB$

In terms of what happens during these reactions, the general formulae for these four types of reactions should be self-explanatory.

There are more complex reactions that are much more important to recognize, which are combinations of these four basic reactions that occur simultaneously. Other types of reactions include acid-base reactions, reduction-oxidation reactions, hydrolysis or dehydration reactions, polymerization reactions, and phosphorylation or dephosphorylation reactions.

Stoichiometric Coefficients
In most cases, a chemical reaction involves molecules on the left side, A and B, whose atoms react to rearrange themselves into new types of molecules on the right side, C and D.

The molecules A and B on the left side of the equation are called reactants, and the molecules C and D on the right side of the equation are the products of the reaction. The reactant molecules rearrange into the product molecules by breaking existing chemical bonds and forming new chemical bonds.

The lowercase letters a, b, c, and d are called stoichiometric coefficients. They are integer numbers that indicate the proportional numbers of the molecules A, B, C, and D that participate in the reaction. For instance, this could be stated as follows:

$$2A + 3B \rightarrow C + 4D$$

This indicates a reaction where two molecules of A and three molecules of B react to produce one molecule of C and four molecules of D. Notice that when the stoichiometric coefficient is 1, the number 1 is not written, as is the case for the product molecule C. When reactant or product molecules are not preceded by a coefficient, it is understood that the coefficient is 1.
As discussed earlier, the coefficients may be thought of as numbers of individual molecules. However, they often represent a very large collection of molecules given by moles. The key concept is that the stoichiometric coefficient describes the relative amounts of reactants and products participating in the chemical reaction.

Balancing Reactions
Balancing chemical reactions involves the elements of molecules that constitute the reactants and products of a chemical reaction where neither ratios of the elements that compose molecules nor their stoichiometric ratios are balanced.

To balance a chemical reaction, the total number of each type of atom on the left must equal the total number of each type of atom on the right. When the ratios of elements are unknown for the molecules that participate in chemical reactions, the information provided in the periodic table and the octet or equivalent rule for individual elements can be used to predict what the ratios of elements should be.

Once this information is known, the stoichiometric coefficients can be concluded using common sense or simple algebra. The following example illustrates this balancing process.

Example: Synthesis of liquid water from molecular hydrogen gas and molecular oxygen gas. Perhaps the most basic chemical reaction is the reaction of hydrogen (H_2) and oxygen (O_2) molecules to form a hydrogen-oxygen molecule:

$$H_2(g) + O_2(g) \rightarrow HO(l)$$

This reaction is an unbalanced chemical reaction where hydrogen and oxygen combine to form a molecule consisting of hydrogen and oxygen. The (g) for H_2 and O_2 indicates that both O_2 and H_2 react as gases. The (l) for HO indicates the product HO is a liquid.

On the left, there are two atoms of hydrogen and two atoms of oxygen. On the right, one atom of each of hydrogen and oxygen is contained in the molecule HO on the left. A balanced reaction could be written as follows:

$$H_2(g) + O_2(g) \rightarrow 2HO(l)$$

This is a balanced reaction where there is the same number of hydrogen and oxygen atoms on the left and right sides of the reaction. However, this is incompatible with what we know atoms are attempting to do in chemical reactions, which is to satisfy the octet rule.

Remember that oxygen requires two additional electrons to satisfy the octet rule. Hydrogen is unique in that it does not have an octet rule but has the equivalent. When hydrogen has two electrons, it achieves a substantial reduction in energy by filling the n = 1 electron shell. Oxygen, therefore, wishes to share two electrons by creating two covalent bonds, and hydrogen wishes to share one electron by creating one covalent bond. Thus, we can predict that one oxygen atom will form two covalent bonds, one with each of the two hydrogen atoms. The Lewis dot structure for this is as follows:

$$H : \overset{\cdot\cdot}{\underset{\cdot\cdot}{O}} :$$
$$H$$

The two dots between the hydrogen and oxygen atoms represent the covalent bonds between them. Each atom shares one of its valence electrons in each covalent bond.

This structure demonstrates that both hydrogen and oxygen atoms have all attained the desired electron configuration where each hydrogen atom has two electrons that are shared in a covalent bond with the oxygen atom, and oxygen has eight octet valence electrons. The following is the correct chemical reaction for this reaction:

$$2H_2(g) + O_2(g) \rightarrow H_2O(l)$$

Reduction-Oxidation (Redox) Reactions

A major alternative classification of reactions is the reduction-oxidation, or "redox," class of chemical reactions. Any of the four categories of general chemical reactions—synthesis, dissociation (or decomposition), single replacement, and double replacement—can be redox reactions. The critical element in determining whether a reaction is a redox reaction or not is to determine whether, during the reaction, any atom participating in the reaction has changed its oxidation number.

Combustion Reactions

Combustion reactions are oxidation-reduction reactions in which the reactants are oxygen molecules and molecules containing carbon-hydrogen, and the products are carbon dioxide and water. A typical combustion reaction is one that occurs in an internal combustion engine with the reactant oxygen and the mixture of hydrocarbon molecules in gasoline.

Here is an example of this type of combustion reaction, in which ethane and oxygen are the reactants:

$$2C_2H_6 + 7O_2 \rightarrow 4CO_2 + 6H_2O$$

This is a balanced reaction, but it is more commonly written as follows:

$$C_2H_6 + 3\frac{1}{2}O_2 \rightarrow 2CO_2 + 3H_2O$$

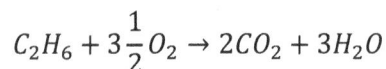

Because all combustion reactions are self-sustaining and highly exothermic, they produce a large amount of heat energy.

Pressure Change Effects on Reactions

Another way to drive reactions in a desired direction is to take advantage of the effects that changes in the partial pressures of chemical participants can have on chemical reactions. In the example of a pure gas-phase reaction $A(g) + B(g) \rightleftharpoons C(g) + 2D(g)$, the forward reaction produces 3 moles of product (1 mole of C and 2 moles of D) from 2 moles of reactant (one mole of A and one mole of B). As a result, the forward reaction generates a greater number of gas molecules from a smaller number of gas molecules.

In a sealed reaction vessel, the forward reaction tends to increase the partial pressures of the reaction participants. If the reaction vessel is a piston, the external force can be exerted by the piston head on the gas in the reaction vessel.

As the partial pressures increase, the reaction moves farther away from equilibrium, and the reverse reaction becomes more favorable since this causes a lowering of the partial pressures within the vessel by converting a larger number of gas molecules into a smaller number of gas molecules through the reverse reaction.

By increasing the volume of the reaction vessel, the forward reaction is favored by the same reasoning. It is important to realize that this effect is due to the increased concentration of the participant gases. Other methods to increase the pressure of the reaction vessel, such as pumping additional non-reactive gas into the vessel, will not have any effect on the reaction.

Temperature Effects on Reactions

For exothermic reactions, increases in temperature drive the reverse reaction, which removes heat from the system. Lowering the temperature increases the forward reaction, which adds heat to the reaction environment.

The opposite is true for endothermic reactions, increasing the temperature of the reaction environment will favor the forward reaction since this removes heat from the reaction environment, and decreasing the temperature will favor the reverse reaction.

Enzymes

Catalysts are substances that increase the rate of chemical reactions without being transformed or consumed by the chemical reaction. Enzymes are complex, three-dimensional protein structures that function as biological catalysts, which lower the activation energy of biological reactions.

Enzymes attract reactants to a specific site known as the "active site," causing changes in the configuration site of the enzyme. This process orients the reactants for a chemical reaction to occur and is known as the "induced fit mechanism."

The activity of an enzyme is defined as the rate at which the reaction catalyzed by the enzyme occurs. The higher the enzyme activity, the greater the rate of an enzyme-catalyzed reaction.

Acids, Bases, and pH Balance

In living organisms, there are critical acid-base reactions that must occur to maintain homeostasis and the carefully regulated narrow range of pH of 7.35 to 7.45 for fluids located within them.

Organic acids are waste products of a living organism's metabolic processes and must be neutralized and excreted from the body. If this does not happen, the organism's internal fluids will become increasingly acidic, eventually reaching fatally low pH levels.

One of the most important organic acids in the body is carbonic acid, which is a weak acid produced from a series of reactions used by biological organisms to neutralize and/or excrete excess acid.

Acids

In solution, acids partially or completely dissociate into hydrogen ions and a conjugate base. Additionally, an acid is a proton (hydrogen ion) donor molecule.

Bases

A base is a substance that dissolves in water, produces OH^- ions, and can accept a proton (hydrogen ion). Acids and bases react together to produce water and salt.

pH

For solutions that contain hydrogen ions (H+), the negative log of the hydrogen ion concentration is defined as the pH of the solution. As mentioned before, in pure liquid water, the hydrogen ion concentration is 1×10^{-7}. Therefore, the pH of pure liquid water is 7, which is the neutral pH.

Solutions with higher concentrations of H+ have pH values lower than 7 and are called acidic solutions, while those with lower concentrations of H+ have pH values higher than 7 and are called basic solutions. The pH of the human body's fluids is tightly regulated to an ideal pH of 7.4.

The pH Scale

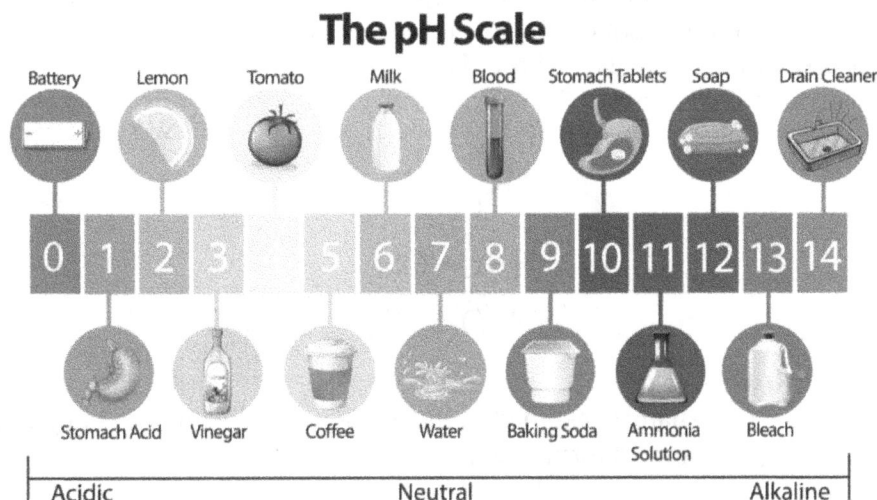

Battery	Lemon	Tomato	Milk	Blood	Stomach Tablets	Soap	Drain Cleaner

0 1 2 3 4 5 6 7 8 9 10 11 12 13 14

Stomach Acid	Vinegar	Coffee	Water	Baking Soda	Ammonia Solution	Bleach

Acidic — Neutral — Alkaline

Basic Macromolecules in a Biological System

Carbohydrate Chemistry in Biology

Carbohydrates play a crucial role in human biology. They provide cells with chemical energy and structural support, play an important role in immune system function and cell-to-cell recognition, and are components of the backbones of our genetic material (DNA and RNA).

Carbohydrates are generally defined as sugar molecules composed of carbon, hydrogen, and oxygen atoms. Carbohydrates are classified according to the number of sugar units (saccharides) they contain: monosaccharides have one sugar unit, disaccharides have two sugar units, oligosaccharides have two to ten sugar units, and polysaccharides have more than ten sugar units.

Glucose

Glucose is a monosaccharide and is the simplest sugar, with a molecular formula of $C_6H_{12}O_6$. It is composed of six carbon units. Carbons 1 is single-bonded to hydrogens and double-bonded to oxygen (also known as an aldehyde or ketone functional group) and Carbons 2-6 are single-bonded to oxygen of hydroxide groups (OH) (also known as an alcohol functional group). The chemical structure of glucose ($C_6H_{12}O_6$) is shown below.

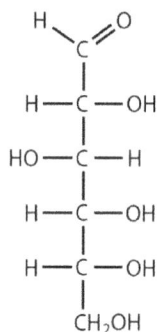

Monosaccharides (Single or Simple Sugars)

Nearly all monosaccharides are classified as "single" or "simple" sugars. They are the chemical subunits or building blocks of more complex carbohydrates.

The name of monosaccharides that are sugars begins with the Latin prefix of the number of carbons in its carbon chain backbone—"tri" for three, "pent" for five, and "hex-" for six—and ends with the suffix "-ose." The sugar "ribose" is a five-carbon sugar, so it is a pentose. Glucose is a six-carbon sugar, so it is a hexose.

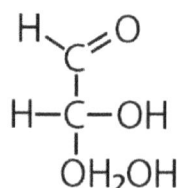

Starch and Cellulose

Dietary carbohydrates are usually consumed in the form of starch contained in grains and vegetables. Starch is a polymerized form of glucose.

Cellulose is a glucose polymer with glycosidic bonds that are incapable of being broken down by human digestion. Cellulose forms most non-digestible fiber in the human diet.

Nucleotides

Nucleotides are the basic components of DNA (deoxyribonucleic acid) and RNA (ribonucleic acid), which contain the genetic information of cells needed for growth and reproduction. DNA protects the cell's genetic information, while RNA translates the information and transports it to protein synthesis sites.

Both DNA and RNA molecules are very large linear-chain polymers composed of nucleotide subunits. Nucleotides have the following structures:

RNA nucleotide: PO_4 – (C5) Ribose (C1) – (N) base

DNA nucleotide: PO_4 – (C5) Deoxyribose (C1) – (N) base

Lipid Chemistry in Biology

Lipids are molecules that have a wide range of functions in the human body:

- Triglycerides stored in adipose tissue serve as energy storage.
- Phospholipids seen in cell membranes serve as a barrier.
- Cholesterol is used in the production of steroid hormones.
- Prostaglandins are used in cell signaling and the inflammatory response.
- The absorption of fat-soluble vitamins A, D, E, and K.

Nearly all types of lipids involved in biological processes are derivatives of either fatty acids or cholesterol.

Triglycerides make up most dietary fat and the fat stored in adipocytes. Dietary triglycerides are hydrolyzed in the small intestine by the enzyme lipase to monoglyceride molecules and fatty acid molecules. After absorption in the small intestine, some fatty acids are recombined with monoglycerides to reform triglycerides, and most of them are stored in fat cells while some remain in the circulation as free triglycerides.

The remainder of fatty acids are packaged along with cholesterol and proteins into circulating complexes called lipoproteins. The most notable lipoproteins are the high-density lipoprotein (HDL) and low-density lipoprotein (LDL) complexes. Fatty acid and cholesterol molecules are transferred from lipoprotein complexes in the bloodstream into cells, where they serve as raw materials for the construction of cell membranes, as a source of energy production, and many other functions.

A high concentration of triglycerides and lipoproteins in the bloodstream is a major risk factor for the development of atherosclerosis and coronary artery disease, which are the primary causes of heart disease and cerebral stroke. These two conditions are by far the most common causes of death in the industrialized world. High levels of triglycerides and LDL increase the risk of these diseases, whereas high levels of HDL reduce the risk of these diseases.

Cholesterol

Cholesterol is a four-ringed lipid-based molecule that is an important component of cell membranes and a precursor molecule for many biochemical processes, including the synthesis of the steroid hormones (cortisol, aldosterone, and progesterone), the sex hormones (testosterone and estrogen), and vitamin D. Most of the cholesterol used in the body is synthesized rather than of dietary origin.

Amino Acids and Proteins

Amino acids are the building blocks of proteins. The general form of an amino acid is a central carbon atom singly bonded to a hydrogen atom and three functional groups: an amine *(-NH$_2$)* group, a carboxylic acid *(-COOH)* group, and a side group designated as an "R" group.

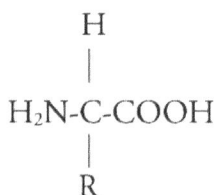

$$
\begin{array}{c}
\text{H} \\
| \\
\text{H}_2\text{N-C-COOH} \\
| \\
\text{R}
\end{array}
$$

Each type of amino acid has a unique functional side group that determines its chemical properties. The R, or side group, of the simplest amino acid—glycine—is a hydrogen atom.

The TEAS most likely doesn't expect you to memorize the R groups for all 20 amino acids; however, it is useful to know that the R groups include hydroxyl groups OH (as in the amino acid serine), hydrocarbon groups CH3 (as in the amino acid alanine), amine groups NH2 (as in the amino acid lysine), and carboxylic acid groups COOH (as in the amino acid glutamic acid, glutamate).

In a typical American diet, most protein is acquired by eating meat, but all amino acid requirements can be met by a carefully selected vegetarian diet. Excess dietary proteins can be converted to fat by the body and used as energy storage. Severe protein deficiency due to inadequate protein intake during early childhood can result in malnutrition known as kwashiorkor.

Protein Structure

Proteins are formed from amino acids linked by peptide bonds. Each protein has a primary, secondary, and tertiary structure. The primary structure is a linear chain of amino acids, the secondary structure is an alpha-helix and beta-pleated sheets, and the tertiary structure is its three-dimensional shape. The 20 different amino acids can be used multiple times in a single polypeptide chain to create a specific primary protein structure.

Structural Proteins

The primary function of proteins is to provide mechanical and structural support within the body, maintaining cell shape and integrity, and offering the elastic properties necessary for tendons and ligaments.

In general, structural proteins exhibit a fibrillar (fiber-like) shape, unlike globular proteins, which typically serve enzymatic or transport functions.

Collagen

The most important extracellular structural protein is collagen, which has many different forms and unique mechanical properties.
Rigid collagen found in bones provides mechanical and structural support.

Elastic collagen is found in tendons (that connect muscles to bone), ligaments (that connect two bones at a joint), the skin, and blood vessels. It allows these structures to stretch and relax.

The collagen found in cartilage has mechanical properties intermediate between rigid and elastic collagen. This property forms a protective layer over the ends of bones and at movable joints, as well as structural support in the nose, ears, skeletal system, and elsewhere in the body.

Overall, collagen comprises approximately 30% of the total protein mass of the human body. It is synthesized by different types of cells, the most important of which are the fibroblasts. These cells are found throughout the body and constantly produce collagen, particularly in inflammation, tissue regeneration, and repair processes.

Keratin

Keratin is another major extracellular structural protein in humans. It provides protective and mechanical support to the outer layers of skin and is the primary component of hair and nails in humans. In other animals, it also forms horns and claws.

Heredity Material

Nitrogenous Bases

All cells contain the nucleic acids DNA and RNA. The DNA molecules within a cell contain all the genetic information required to synthesize all the proteins that the cell requires to carry out its metabolic, physiological, and structural functions.

This information is stored as a linear sequence of nitrogenous bases. The nitrogenous bases occur in two forms: purines and pyrimidines. Both forms are small nitrogen-containing molecules that have either one structural ring (the pyrimidines), or a double ring (the purines).

The nitrogenous bases in DNA are the purines adenine (A) and guanine (G), and the pyrimidines thymine (T) and cytosine (C). The nitrogenous bases found in RNA molecules are the same as those found in DNA molecules, with the exception that, in RNA, another pyrimidine called uracil substitutes thymine.

The DNA Double-Helix

The structure of a DNA molecule in a cell is usually the double-stranded form of DNA. This double-stranded structure is a spiraling (helical) ladder consisting of linear backbones of alternating deoxyribose sugars and phosphate groups. One deoxyribose phosphate polymer backbone forms the left side rail of the DNA ladder, and the other one forms the right-side rail of the DNA ladder.

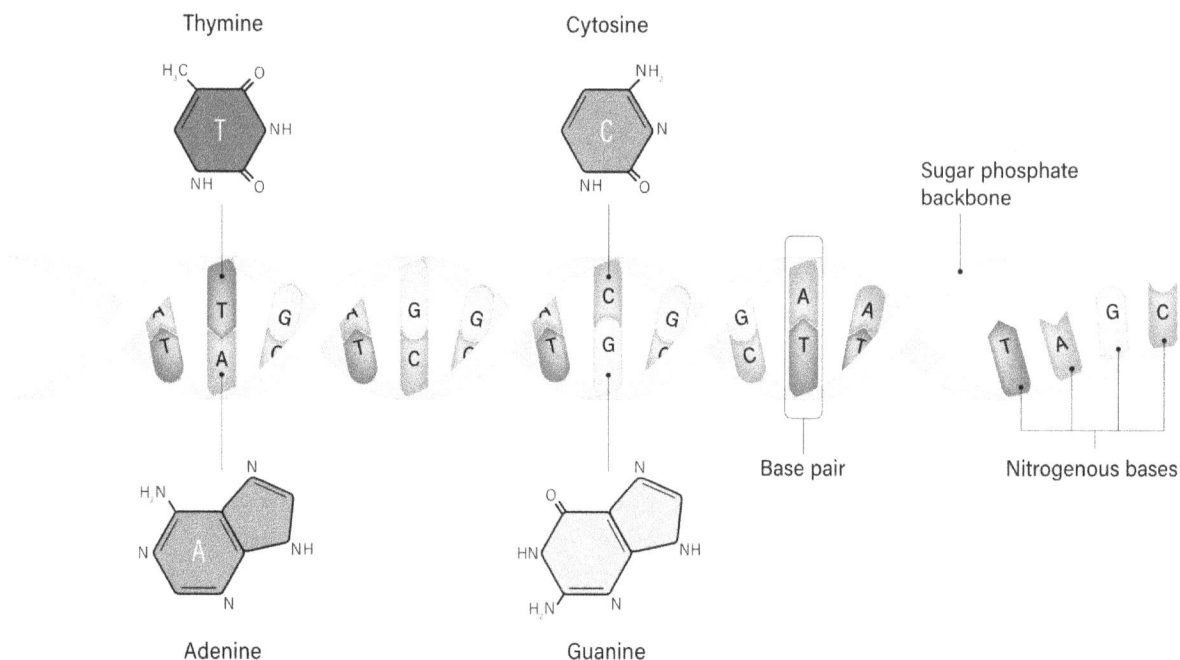

Complementary Base Pairing in Double-Stranded DNA

Each deoxyribose sugar mentioned above is also bonded to a single nitrogenous base. In double-stranded DNA, each of these bases is hydrogen bonded to its complementary base, which is similarly bonded to a deoxyribose sugar on the opposing sugar-phosphate backbone of the DNA molecule. These hydrogen-bonded nitrogenous base pairs form the rungs of the double-stranded DNA ladder.

The term *complementary* in complementary base-pair bonding refers to the fact that each nitrogenous base will pair (bond) with one and only one specific complementary base; for example, adenine (A) will only pair bond with thymine (T), and guanine (G) will only pair bond with cytosine (C). There are two hydrogen bonds formed between the base-pairing adenine and thymine in double-stranded DNA and three hydrogen bonds formed between the base-pairing guanine and cytosine.

Nucleotides

Nucleotide is the term used for a nucleic acid molecular subunit consisting of either a ribose or a deoxyribose sugar bonded to a phosphate group and a nitrogenous base.

Any DNA molecule can be assembled entirely from deoxyribose-containing nucleotides, and any RNA molecule can be assembled entirely from ribose-containing nucleotides.

Chromosomes

In eukaryotic cells, DNA is usually in an extended linear form that allows cells to access the nitrogenous base sequences for DNA replication and transcription into messenger RNA molecules.

During cell division, these DNA strands are highly condensed into structures called chromosomes. The formation of chromosomes during the cell division cycle involves a series of coiling and supercoiling actions of the DNA molecule. This process involves the physical wrapping of the DNA molecule around specialized spherical proteins called histone proteins, or histones.

Chromatids
Each chromosome can exist in two forms: a single condensed strand of DNA or a two condensed identical strands of DNA.

These two condensed DNA strands are called chromatids individually, and together they are called sister chromatids. The sister chromatid form occurs only after the replication of an entire DNA strand is completed.

Homologous Chromosomes
Human somatic cells have 46 chromosomes, which occur as 23 pairs of chromosomes or homologous chromosomes (22 pairs of autosomes and 1 pair of sex chromosomes). The sex chromosome pair in males is not an actual pair since it consists of one "X" chromosome and one "Y" chromosome. The sex chromosomes in females are a pair of chromosomes made up of two "X" chromosomes.

Protein Synthesis
When a cell begins the process of constructing a protein, it must first expose and disrupt the hydrogen bonds between the nitrogenous base sequences of the gene that codes for the desired protein. This separates the left and right halves of the DNA ladder as if it were being unzipped down the middle of the nitrogenous base-pair rungs.

Transcription of DNA into mRNA—The 3' to 5' Direction
After the separation of the DNA ladder, a protein complex called RNA polymerase then inserts itself into the cleft created by the disruption of the hydrogen bonds between complementary base pairs.

RNA polymerase then begins to assemble a single-strand RNA molecule that is complementary to the DNA strand that contains the base sequence code for the protein that will be constructed. The transcription of the DNA strand begins at the 3' end of the DNA molecule and continues in the 5' direction.

The Sense and Antisense Strands of DNA
When hydrogen bonds between the complementary base pairs are disrupted, it produces two strands, namely the sense and antisense strands. The antisense DNA strand will serve as the template and will be transcribed by RNA polymerase into a sense messenger RNA that matches the sense DNA strand.

The mRNA base sequence is identical to the sense strand DNA sequence, with the exception that the nitrogenous base uracil in the mRNA base sequence replaces the nitrogenous base thymine in the sense strand of the DNA molecule.

Since the base sequence of the DNA sense strand is the complementary sequence of the DNA antisense strand, the sense strand does not code for functional proteins, and it is not read by RNA polymerase.

Genes

The base sequence in the sense strand that codes for a single-chain protein is called a gene. One gene always codes for one and only one polypeptide chain. All polypeptide chains are single-chain proteins, while some complex proteins are composed of more than one type of polypeptide chain.

Codons

The individual amino acids that will form a protein's chain are coded for by three-base sequences called codons. Since four different bases can occur at any point in the DNA base sequence, there are statistically 64 possible combinations of the three-base sequences (codons).

Only 20 amino acids are used to assemble proteins, so more than one codon may be used for a given amino acid. But no individual codon codes for more than one specific amino acid.

Transcription of DNA

As RNA polymerase assembles an RNA molecule, a new nitrogenous base, uracil (U), is used in place of the base thymine. Uracil is the RNA base that is complementary to adenine. The process of constructing an RNA molecule that contains a complementary base sequence to a DNA gene sequence is defined as *transcription*.

Anticodons and Ribosomes

Once a complete RNA transcript of a gene has been completed, the transcript, known as a messenger RNA (mRNA) molecule, leaves the nucleus and enters the cell cytoplasm. Eventually, the mRNA molecule encounters a ribosome, which attaches itself to the mRNA transcript. The ribosome then reads the RNA as three-base complements of the DNA codons. These three-base RNA sequences are called anticodons.

Translation of mRNA

When the ribosome reads an anticodon, it inserts the amino acid that corresponds to the anticodon onto a growing polypeptide chain. When the entire mRNA molecule has been processed by the ribosome, it results in a newly synthesized single-chain protein.

This polypeptide chain is the protein coded for by the gene that was transcribed at the beginning of this process. The reading of mRNA by ribosomes and the construction of the corresponding protein is called translation.

Transfer RNA

During the assembly of a protein chain in a ribosome, individual amino acids are transported to the ribosome by transfer RNA (tRNA) molecules. These molecules are short RNA segments with a three-leaf-clover configuration, with one end of the stem of the clover that binds to an amino acid. There are 20 different types of tRNA molecules, and each binds to one and only one type of amino acid.

DNA Replication

During DNA replication, the unzipping of double-stranded DNA is accompanied by the construction of new complementary DNA for each of its original strands. The synthesis of these two new complementary strands continues for the entire length of the DNA molecule, resulting in two exact copies of the original DNA molecule. Each of the new DNA molecules contains either the right or left strand of the original DNA molecule as well as a completely new synthesized complementary strand. This type of DNA replication is called semi-conservative replication.

DNA Polymerase

During DNA replication, DNA polymerase is the enzyme complex that inserts itself into gaps created by the disruption of complementary base-pair hydrogen bonds. These DNA replication molecules synthesize complementary DNA strands to both the original sense and antisense strands simultaneously.

Genetic Variability

Remember that homologous chromosome pairs do not necessarily have identical genes but instead have variants of each gene (known as alleles). Therefore, the two daughter cells resulting from the first cell division by meiosis have one-half of the total number of chromosomes—23 instead of 46—and these cellular sets of genes are not identical sequences of DNA.

The individual chromosomes from homologous chromosome pairs that are now in different cells, almost certainly have a wide variety of different alleles for a wide variety of individual genes.

Additionally, during the pair separation process in the anaphase of meiosis 1, small segments from chromatids on different chromosomes of the homologous pairs can be exchanged, resulting in hybrid chromatids.
This process is called crossing over, and it increases the genetic variability of the chromosomes.

Meiosis 2

The next phase of cell division follows immediately without any further replication of DNA and is called the meiosis 2 phase of meiotic cell division.

The events of meiosis 2 cell division are identical to the events of mitosis cell division. In each of the two daughter cells created by meiosis 1 cell division, the 23 individual chromosomes align at the metaphase plate of each daughter cell, and the individual sister chromatids of each chromosome are pulled apart and separated into the second-generation daughter cells.

This process, beginning with the original diploid progenitor cell, results in the production of four haploid cells.

Each haploid cell contains one chromosome in the form of a sister chromatid from each of the 23 pairs of chromosomes contained in the progenitor cell. In the human male, meiosis results in the production of sperm cells, while in the female, meiosis results in the production of ova.

Molecular Genetics

In an individual member of a species, the total amount of genetic information contained in the genes of a diploid cell represents the individual's genome. The specific types of genes within the genome are the individual's genotype, and the way an individual's genotype is expressed in physical form is the individual's phenotype.

Calculating Gene Frequencies

For species where there are multiple alleles for a given gene, individual members of the species may have different combinations of these alleles in their genomes.

When there are two alleles for a given gene—for instance, if we annotate them to be alleles "A" and "a" for a specific gene—individuals may possess one of three possible combinations of the two alleles within their genotype. These are "AA," "aa," and "Aa."

The combinations AA and aa are the two possible homozygous genotypes, while the combination Aa is the heterozygous genotype. This type of mating is often described as an "Aa x Aa" cross. When a mating Aa male and Aa female pair of a species create a zygote (an Aa x Aa cross), the probability (or predicted frequencies) of the alleles in the zygote can be calculated using a Punnett square.

The following Punnett square is a representation of an Aa x Aa cross between two heterozygous (Aa) parents:

	A	a
A	AA	Aa
a	Aa	aa

The Punnett square shows the possible combinations of zygotes resulting from a mother and father where both are heterozygous for the gene with alleles A and a. Since each parent can contribute only one allele to any zygote, the alleles for one parent are separated into an "A" column and an "a" column. The other parent's alleles are represented by an "A" row and an "a" row. The four squares show the combination of alleles that results from combining a parental row with a corresponding parental column.

Notice that, for two heterozygous individuals, there is one AA square, one aa square, and two Aa squares. This indicates that the parents have a 1 in a 4 (or 25%) chance of producing a zygote with AA alleles, a 1 in 4 (or 25%) chance of producing a zygote with aa alleles, and a 2 in 4 (or 50%) chance of producing a zygote with Aa alleles. Since zygotes can develop into children, for humans, these are the probabilities of heterozygous parents having children with the AA, Aa, and aa genotypes.

The expected gene frequencies resulting from mating between parents with other genotypes can be calculated in the same fashion using the Punnett square technique. The gene frequencies for the gene with two alleles A and a in the offspring of one heterozygous (Aa) parent and one homozygous (AA) parent (an AA x Aa cross) are shown in the following Punnett square:

	A	A
A	AA	AA
a	Aa	Aa

The Punnett square is a representation of an AA x Aa cross between one heterozygous parent (Aa) and one homozygous parent (AA).

There is only one possible gamete for the homozygous parent (AA) for the gene: the allele A. The homozygous parent gametes are represented as A and A at the top margin of the 2×2 Punnett square in horizontal orientation. The heterozygous parent (Aa) can produce two different gametes for the gene: either the allele A or the allele a. The heterozygous parent gametes are represented in the vertical left margin orientation as A and a.

We see that there are two possible zygotes from this heterozygous/homozygous cross: AA and Aa. Of the four possible crosses (represented by the allele pair in each of the four individual squares), two are AA and two are Aa. The gene frequencies for both AA and Aa are 2/4, or 50%. Notice that there is a zero percent chance of a homozygous aa offspring.

There is another possible cross for the homozygous/heterozygous state. This would be a cross between a parent homozygous for the "a" allele of the gene (aa) and a parent heterozygous for the gene (Aa). This would be an Aa x aa cross, depicted in the following Punnett square:

	A	a
a	Aa	aa
a	Aa	aa

Notice that the gene frequencies are the same as for an AA x Aa cross except that it is the aa homozygous state that is 50% (instead of the AA homozygous state) and that there is no chance of an AA homozygous state (instead of an aa homozygous state).The heterozygous state (Aa) has the same 50% probability as the AA x Aa cross.

There are three other possible crosses for a single gene with two alleles (A and a). Two are homozygous crosses of aa x aa and AA x AA. It should be obvious that each has only one possible zygote outcome. For the aa x aa cross, there is only an "a" allele, and so all offspring must be homozygous for the "a" allele (aa). Similarly, the offspring of an AA x AA cross can only have one combination of alleles AA.

The final possible combination for a cross of a single gene with two alleles (a and a) is the cross between a homozygous AA parent and a homozygous aa parent. The cross between two homozygous parents is represented in the following Punnett square where one parent is homozygous for the allele A (AA) and the other for the allele a (aa).

	A	A
a	Aa	Aa
a	Aa	Aa

From this cross, only one combination of zygotes is possible: heterozygous combination (Aa).

Dominant and Recessive Alleles

Often, the phenotypic appearance or the physical trait that results from a gene depends on whether the alleles for the gene are dominant or recessive. The classic example is eye color, where the brown allele is "B" and the blue allele is "b."

Brown (B) is the dominant allele, and blue (b) is the recessive allele. Homozygous brown-eyed individuals (who are BB) and heterozygous brown-eyed individuals (who are Bb) always have brown eyes. Only homozygous blue (bb) individuals have blue eyes. Notice that the offspring of parents who are heterozygous for eye color (Bb) will have the same expected genotype frequencies shown in the prior Punnett square example, but the blue-eyed phenotype is only the bb genotype. Therefore, heterozygous, brown-eyed parents will have a 1 in 4 (25%) chance of having a blue-eyed child.

Notice that two blue-eyed parents will never have brown-eyed children since both parents possess only the blue-eye color allele. Finally, notice that in any couple where at least one parent is homozygous brown (BB), there is no possibility of an offspring who will be homozygous blue (bb), and therefore these parents have no chance of having a blue-eyed child.

Dihybrid Crosses

A classic topic in Mendelian genetics is the calculation of the types of different gene combinations that can occur in the offspring of parents with two genes, each with two alleles that assort independently. This type of cross is called a dihybrid cross.

If we represent the two alleles for these two genes as A and a for the alleles of the first gene and B and b for the alleles of the second gene, then we can construct a Punnett square to calculate the possible gene combinations and frequencies for the offspring of any two parents with any possible combination of the alleles for the two genes (A, a, B, and b). We have partially completed the construction of a Punnett square to calculate these gene combinations and frequencies for a dihybrid cross where both parents are heterozygous for both genes. This would be a diploid state of AaBb for each parent. As the following Punnett square illustrates, each parent can generate gametes with four possible combinations of the alleles for the two genes.

These possible combinations are AB, Ab, aB, and ab. Each of the four combinations in the following Punnett square is listed at the top margin for one parent and is listed at the left margin for the other parent. Notice that the possible zygote for any square is the combination of the horizontal and vertical gametes that correspond to the row and column of the square below.

	AB	Ab	aB	ab
AB	AABB			
Ab		AAbb		
aB			aaBB	
ab				aabb

There are 16 squares for a dihybrid cross, but the actual number of different combinations of alleles that are possible for the parental offspring depends on the alleles of the genes possessed by each parent. For instance, in our example of a dihybrid cross where both parents are heterozygous for both genes, several of the 16 possible combinations are equivalent. For example, an AaBb combination is identical to an aAbB combination. Both combinations have exactly one of each allele (A, a, B, and b); it makes no difference which parent contributed which allele.

	AB	Ab	aB	ab
AB				AaBb
Ab			AaBb	
aB		AaBb		
ab	AaBb			

The above Punnett square shows that four squares have the equivalent allele combination of AaBb. The frequency for this combination is therefore 4/16 (or 25%.). At this point, we have partially completed the Punnett square:

	AB	Ab	aB	ab
AB	AABB			AaBb
Ab		AAbb	AaBb	
aB		AaBb	aaBB	
ab	AaBb			aabb

If we continue the process of assigning allele combinations for the remaining empty squares, the result would be as follows:

	AB	Ab	aB	ab
AB	AABB	AABb	AaBB	AaBb
Ab	AABb	AAbb	AaBb	Aabb
aB	AaBB	AaBb	aaBB	aaBb
ab	AaBb	Aabb	aaBb	aabb

We have listed capital alleles (A, B) before lowercase alleles (a and b) in the squares to make it easier to identify equivalent combinations. It is still difficult to recognize all the possible combinations by looking at the squares.

The TEAS will unlikely ask a question with this degree of difficulty required to exactly determine the frequencies of all the allele combinations for this type of dihybrid cross. However, you should be able to construct a Punnett square for any dihybrid cross and identify frequencies for simpler examples of a dihybrid cross.

SCIENTIFIC REASONING

Basic Scientific Measurements Using Laboratory Tools

Accurate measurement, recording, and charting data are essential when performing scientific investigations and authoring reports.

SI Units

The International System of Units, also known as the metric system, supports measurement in meters, kilograms, seconds, amperes (electric current), Kelvin, candelas (luminous intensity), and moles (amount of substance).

The metric system uses a base unit of 10 and prefixes to increase or decrease the base unit's size.

Mass is the amount of material an object consumes by gaining weight in a gravitational field and is measured in kilograms (kg).

Length measures the distance from end to end of an object, which is measured in meters (m).

The duration of time is measured in increments of 1 second (s or sec).

The volume of a three-dimensional object is the product of its length, height, and width. All measurements are recorded as length measurements, with the meter as a base.

The volume of a container measuring 10 cm x 10 cm x 10 cm = 1,000 cm³. A liter (L) more accurately describes the volume of a container.

SI UNIT MEASUREMENTS				
Prefix	**Symbol**	**Base 10**	**Decimal**	**English Word**
Milli-	m	10-3	0.001	one-thousandth
Centi-	c	10-2	0.01	one-hundredth
Deci-	d	10-1	0.1	one-tenth
Base		100	1	one
Deca-	da	101	10	ten
Hecto-	h	102	100	hundred
Kilo-	k	103	1000	thousand

Scale Unit

When measuring, it is essential to use the most appropriate scaled unit. Use kilograms when measuring a large volume rather than centigrams. When measuring something small, such as a chocolate chip, it is more appropriate to use millimeters instead of meters. It is more logical to state one chocolate chip measures 0.004 mm rather than a million chocolate chips measure 4 meters.

Tool Selection

The triple beam balance and the electronic balance are tools that measure the mass of an object. The electronic (or digital) balance is more commonly used due to ease of use and is faster and easier for weighing smaller amounts.

However, balance beam scales are the most precise measuring device for determining an object's mass.

Glassware

Numerous types of glassware are available to measure the volume of liquids:

- A volumetric flask provides the most accurate measurement when measuring large volumes.
- A volumetric pipette provides efficiency when measuring small volumes.
- Graduated cylinders provide less accurate measurement data.

The volume of solids is calculated by multiplying the length, width, and height of the object using rulers, meter sticks, or measuring wheels.

Scientific Explanation Using Logic and Evidence

It is essential to draw logical scientific explanations by analyzing the scientific process with logic and evidence and drawing conclusions from data. Additionally, analyzing scientific arguments for evidence will help identify scientific information and content and construct meaningful scientific conclusions.

Empirical Evidence

Empirical evidence is the evidence obtained through conducting experiments. When reviewing or reproducing data, scientists will benefit from appropriately collecting relevant data and understanding how to draw logical conclusions based on the data.

Conclusions

Many scientists base their conclusions on evidence that supports the scientific explanation's cause-and-effect relationship. Understanding the conclusion requires utilizing and analyzing the strengths of the evidence used to support an argument.

Strong conclusions are demonstrated by replicable and convincing data. The process of analyzing data must be predicated on the following: the absence of bias (intentional or unintentional), a controlled setting with only one variable change allowed at a time, accurate data collection, impeccable record keeping, and the ability to reproduce the results.

Relationships Among Events, Objects, and Processes

Relationships and processes are ever-changing, so it is essential to differentiate between the magnitude of events, objects, and processes.

Every measurement necessitates the use of a specific unit, which determines the scale.

Determining a causal relationship may be challenging, but it is necessary to determine the cause-and-effect relationship from the given scientific information. It may be necessary to determine the sequence of events leading to a result as this may serve as additional information relevant to the scientific investigation.

The Design of a Scientific Investigation

A scientist finds answers and solutions to questions and problems using a scientific method. This method consists of drawing observations, formulating hypotheses, planning and performing experiments, analyzing data, accepting or rejecting a hypothesis, and formulating a theory.

When presented with a question or problem, scientists make observations to then formulate and determine if a cause-and-effect relationship exists between the two variables. When the scientist wants to learn more about an observation, he or she will formulate a hypothesis, which is a temporary explanation or relationship of that observation. The context of the hypotheses establishes the strength of the investigation, and the hypothesis may be accepted or rejected.

Scientists will plan and carry out experiments related to their observations to prove their hypothesis. The collection of experimental data during the investigation leads to the development of theories. To do this, scientists must implement strategies to control variables.

The independent variable is the one manipulated by the scientists and is measured as the possible cause of the hypothesis. The dependent variable is the observed condition that responds to the manipulation of the independent variable, creating a causal relationship between the independent and dependent variables. A controlled investigation manages and maintains all other variables.

Scientists collect and analyze data to determine whether their hypothesis should be accepted or rejected. The results and conclusions, supported by evidence, will be published in journals.

VOCABULARY

For items 1–5, try to identify the root and then write an English translation or synonym for the root. We did the first one for you as an example.

#	Word	Root	Translation/Synonym
Ex	Description	Script	Something written
1	Irresponsible		
2	Entombment		
3	Professorial		
4	Unconscionable		
5	Gainfully		

For items 6–10, try to identify the prefix and then write an English translation or synonym for the prefix. We did the first one for you as an example.

#	Word	Prefix	Translation/Synonym
Ex	Prepare	Pre	Before
6	Proceed		
7	Misapprehend		
8	Antibiotic		
9	Hyperactive		
10	Cacophony		

For items 11–15, try to identify the suffix and then write an English translation or synonym for the suffix. We did the first one for you as an example.

#	Word	Suffix	Translation/Synonym
Ex	Lovable	Able	Can be accomplished
11	Tedious		
12	Absolution		
13	Cathartic		
14	Merriment		
15	Inspector		

Now let's test your current vocabulary. For the following questions, select the best answer:

1. The word <u>achromatic</u> most closely means _____:
   A. Full of color
   B. Fragrant
   C. Without color
   D. Vivid

2. The word <u>cursory</u> most closely means _____:
   A. Meticulous; careful
   B. Undetailed; rapid
   C. Thorough
   D. Expletive

3. The word <u>hearsay</u> most closely means _____:
   A. Blasphemy
   B. Unverified secondhand information
   C. Evidence that can be confirmed
   D. Testimony

4. The word <u>magnanimous</u> most closely means _____:
   A. Suspicious
   B. Uncontested
   C. Forgiving; not petty
   D. Stingy; cheap

5. The word <u>terrestrial</u> most closely means _____:
   A. Of the earth
   B. Cosmic
   C. Otherworldly/unearthly
   D. Supernatural

Let's see how you did based on the answer key:

1. **Answer:** C. Without color
2. **Answer:** B. Undetailed; rapid
3. **Answer:** B. Unverified secondhand information
4. **Answer:** C. Forgiving; not petty
5. **Answer:** A. Of the earth

CRITICAL READING

Detail Questions

Reading passages and identifying important details are also an important part of the critical reading process. Detail questions ask the reader to recall specific information about the main idea. These details are often found in the examples given in the passage and can contain anecdotes, data, or descriptions, among other details.

For example, if you are reading a passage about certain types of dogs, you may be asked to remember details about breeds, sizes, and coat colors and patterns. As you read the following passages, take note of numbers, figures, and the details given about the topic. You'll likely need to remember at least some of that information.

Within any passage you read, a wealth of information, facts, pieces of data, and details can be presented. The key to uncovering the main idea and understanding the details presented is to take your time and read everything contained in the passage. For all the examples and figures presented, think about how the details relate to the main idea, how they support the focus, and how those details add to the information and value of the passage.

Read the following news article, and answer the questions that follow the passage.

Passage 1

The Chicago Police are searching for two men under investigation for impersonating cops. The men stopped a person on the city's Northwest Side. In a bit of an ironic twist, the two fake cops pulled over an actual Chicago cop.

Officials say that the officer, who is in his 40s, was finishing his shift and on his way home when he was pulled over. It was in Chicago's Avondale neighborhood just after midnight when a white SUV pulled up behind the officer and flashed its lights. The officer saw the signaling, said the SUV looked like a police-issued undercover vehicle, and pulled over. According to reports, one of the two men exited the unmarked car wearing normal civilian clothes. The man approached the cop, who was still wearing his bulletproof vest, and said he was with the Chicago Police.

The officer said that the civilian clothes and lack of standard police-issued items alerted him that something was wrong, and he challenged the fake officer on that statement. The man ran back to the unmarked car, sped off, and disappeared into the dark streets. The Chicago Police describe the suspects as two Hispanic men in their early to mid-20s who are both around 6 feet tall and 150 pounds. Anyone with tips about the two men should call the Chicago Police Department.

1. What is the passage mostly about?
   A. Problems with the Chicago Police Department
   B. A news report about people pretending to be police officers
   C. A crime crackdown by Chicago Police
   D. None of the above

Answer: B

Rationale: One sentence in the passage specifically states that the report is about two men who were pretending to be Chicago Police officers.

2. According to the passage, what details were given about the incident?
   A. Civilian clothes and lack of standard police-issued items made the cop suspicious
   B. The event occurred in Chicago's Avondale neighborhood just after midnight
   C. The two men who posed as Chicago Police officers were of Hispanic decent
   D. The police officer was in his 40s, and the two fake cops were in their 20s
   E. All the above

Answer: E
Rationale: All the listed details were mentioned throughout the news report.

3. All the following details are stated about the real officer in this story except:
   A. His age
   B. His duty status at the time
   C. How long he's been with the Chicago Police
   D. All the above

Answer: C
Rationale The article doesn't mention how long the real officer has been serving with the Chicago Police Department.

Remember:
A wealth of information and many facts, pieces of data, and details can be presented within any passage you read. The key to uncovering the main idea and understanding all the details presented is to take your time and carefully read everything in the passage. Take the time to consider every example and every figure presented. Then, see how each detail relates to the main idea, supports the focus, and adds to the information and value of the passage you are reading.

Reading passages and picking out these important details are a big part of being an effective reader. Practice makes perfect. The more you read, analyze, and practice, the better you will get, and the more you will be able to pull from any article, blog, story, or report you read!

Understanding Question Stems
In addition to careful reading of the passages (including by marking up the text for topic and concluding sentences, transitional words, and key terms), you must also be able to identify what is being asked of you in each question. Recognizing the task in each question can be easily accomplished if you are familiar with question stems, or the common wording that will be associated with each type of question on the test. Keep reading for an explanation of each question type, sample question stems based on the question type, and suggested strategies.

Main Idea
Questions asking you to identify the main idea expect that you will be able to determine the overall point of the passage (often called the thesis), NOT secondary details or supporting points. Attempting to put the main idea into your own words after reading, WITHOUT looking at the text again, is a very helpful strategy for answering this type of question. If you can sum up

the author's main point in your own words, then you will find it easier to find the right "match" among the answer choices provided. Notably, the main idea can often be found in the opening or concluding paragraphs, two common places where authors introduce topics and personal perspectives on the topics, or summarize the main points.

Here are some common stems used when this type of question is asked:

- The main idea for this paragraph...
- The central point of the passage...
- A possible title for the passage...
- The author's primary point...

Supporting Details

Supporting details are those that back up the main ideas presented in the passage. These details can include examples, clarifying explanations, or elaborations of basic ideas presented earlier in the reading. Supporting details are directly stated in the passage, so you must rely on your careful reading to guide you to the correct answer. Answers may not be stated in the original language of the passage, but the basic ideas will be the same.

Here are some common stems used when this type of question is asked:

- The passage states...
- The author says...
- According to what you read...

Inference

Inferences are those ideas that can be gleaned from the suggestions implied in other statements made by the author. Inferences are never explicitly stated, but we understand that they are true from "reading between the lines." The answers to inference questions, therefore, are assumptions and cannot be found from direct statements in the text. You will have to rely on your ability to logically deduce conclusions from your careful reading. More than one answer may sound correct, but only one is correct. Ensure that, whatever your answer, you can find statements in the text to support that idea. If you cannot, then that choice is likely not the right answer.

Here are some common stems used when this type of question is asked:

- The passage implies...
- The author suggests...
- The reader could logically conclude that...
- The reader would be correct in assuming that...

Tone/Attitude

Some questions will ask you about the author's tone or attitude. A good place to start with this type of question is to consider whether the passage is positive, negative, or neutral. Does the author seem angry? Maybe sad? Or torn between two points of view? The language that an author uses can be very telling regarding the tone and attitude. Is the author critical? Praiseworthy? Disappointed? Even if you find some finer details of the passage difficult to understand, the tone and attitude are often easy to identify. Look for adjectives and statements that reveal the author's opinion, rather than facts, and this approach will help you recognize the tone or attitude.

Here are some common stems used when this type of question is asked:

- The tone of the passage is...
- The attitude of the author is...
- The writer's overall feeling...

Style

Style refers to a writer's "way with words." Most seasoned writers have a well-developed and easily recognizable style. Often, however, the topic of a written work can dictate style. If the topic is serious, the language will likely be more formal. Works for academic settings might be heavy with the jargon of that discipline. Personal reflections can be rife with imagery, while instructional manuals will use simple and straightforward language. Whatever the case, identifying style is not difficult; simply pay attention to the words used (simple or fancy?), the sentence structure (simple or compound-complex?), and the overall structure of the piece (stream of consciousness or 5-paragraph essay?). You must answer these questions to determine the style of the passage.

Here are some common stems used when this type of question is asked:

- The overall writing style used in the passage...
- The author's style is...
- The organizational style of the passage is...

Pattern of Organization

Pattern-of-organization questions want you to consider how the writing of a piece was developed. What features did the writer utilize to make the main point? Were personal anecdotes included? What about data or statistics? Quotes from authorities on the topic? These angles are all modes of organizing a passage that help the writer support claims and provide a logical focus for the work.

Here are some common stems used when this type of question is asked:

- The author proves a point through...
- In the passage, the author uses...
- Throughout the passage, the author seems to rely on...

Purpose and Attitude

Questions asking about purpose and attitude require you to consider why the author took the time to write. The author's motivations are directly behind the purpose of the piece. What question did the author wish to answer? What cause did the author want to show support for? What action did the author wish to persuade you to take? Identifying these reasons for writing will reveal the purpose and attitude of the passage.

Here are some common stems used when this type of question is asked:

- The purpose of the passage is...
- The author's intent for writing the passage is...
- The attitude the author displays is...

Fact/Opinion

Some questions on the test will ask you whether a statement is a fact or an opinion. Without being able to fact check, how will you decide? A rule of thumb would be that opinions reflect only the thoughts, feelings, or ideas of the writer, whereas facts are verifiable as true or false, regardless of one's feelings. If a writer cites a statistic about the environmental effects of oil drilling on migratory mammals in the Pacific Northwest, then that information is verifiable and can be considered factual. If, however, the writer claims that oil drilling in the U.S. Pacific Northwest is bad and should be stopped, then that detail is the author's opinion. The author may at some point provide examples of why the claim is true, but that viewpoint is based on that author's thoughts and feelings about oil drilling, and can thus only be considered opinion.

Here are some common stems used when this type of question is asked:

- Which statement is a fact rather than an opinion?
- This statement is meant to be...
- An example fact is when the author says...
- An example of opinion is when the author states that...

ARITHMETIC REASONING

Decimals and Fractions

Operations with Decimals

The sign conventions for positive and negative decimal arithmetic operations are the same as those for whole number operations outlined in Module 1. But some special details need to be recalled when performing arithmetic operations with decimal values to ensure the correct answers are obtained.

When adding and subtracting decimal values, ensure the decimal points are aligned vertically. This method is the simplest way to ensure a reliable result. For example, adding 0.522 and 0.035 should be performed as follows:

$$\begin{array}{r} 0.522 \\ + \ 0.035 \\ \hline 0.557 \end{array}$$

Subtraction operations should be similarly aligned:

$$\begin{array}{r} 0.522 \\ - \ 0.035 \\ \hline 0.487 \end{array}$$

Importantly, multiplication requires a different convention to be followed. When multiplying decimals, the operations are NOT necessarily aligned the same way as addition and subtraction. For example, multiplying 0.7 and 2.15 is performed as follows:

$$\begin{array}{r} 2.15 \\ \times \ 0.07 \\ \hline 1.505 \end{array}$$

When you're multiplying decimal values, the decimal point placement in the answer is determined by counting the total number of digits to the right of the decimal point in the multiplied numbers. This detail is often overlooked in testing choices where the same numbers may appear in several multiple-choice answers, but with different decimal point placements.

The division of decimal values is simplified by first visualizing the equivalent fractions. The mathematics terminology is that $\frac{dividend}{divisor} = quotient$, as shown in the following example:

7.35/1.05 is the same as 73.5/10.5, which is the same operation as 735/105.

The last fraction in the example means that, to solve 7.35/1.05, you can divide 735 by 105 to find the correct whole number answer. This method just requires that, when dividing by a decimal number, the divisor must be corrected to be a whole number, which can be achieved by moving the decimal points in **both the dividend and divisor** the same number of decimal places. If the dividend still contains a decimal point, the place is maintained in the long division operation, and the correct quotient is still achieved. The quotient remains in the form of a decimal number.

Operations with Fractions

The sign conventions for positive and negative fractional arithmetic operations are the same as those for whole number operations outlined in Module 1. However, some special details should be recalled when performing arithmetic operations with fractional values to ensure the correct answers are obtained.

Remember that fractions are made up of a numerator and a denominator. The top number of the fraction (the numerator) conveys how many of the fractional parts are being represented. The bottom number (the denominator) conveys how many equal parts the whole is divided into. For this reason, fractions with different denominators cannot be added together because different denominators are as different as apples and oranges. Therefore, when adding or subtracting fractions with different denominators, a common denominator must be found. In this case, simple geometric models will be used to explain the common denominator principle. This principle is usually illustrated with circles divided into "pie slices." A simpler and more effective example involves the use of squares or rectangles divided into fractional parts.

Representing fraction parts, $1/3$ and $1/4$ can be demonstrated with the following square diagrams. The whole square equals the number 1, and the fractional parts are the slices of the square:

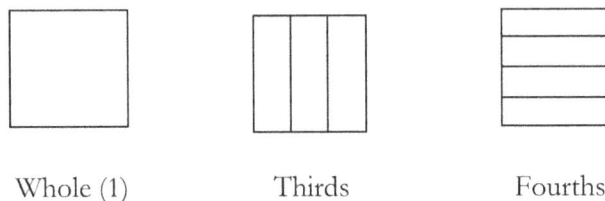

Whole (1)   Thirds   Fourths

If you superimpose the four horizontal slices over the three vertical slices, the result is 12 separate parts of the whole, as shown in the following depiction:

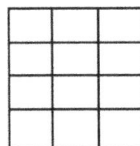

In the last diagram, any column representing a third has four of the 12 small rectangles from the diagram, or $4/12$ as the equivalent fraction.

Similarly, any row of the last diagram, representing a fourth, has three of the 12 small rectangles from the diagram, or $3/12$ as the equivalent fraction. With this modification of the two fractions, both are now in the form of a common denominator, and the addition of the two fractions can be completed:

$$\frac{1}{3} + \frac{1}{4} = \frac{4}{12} + \frac{3}{12} = \frac{7}{12}$$

Notice that this result is exactly analogous to the prior simple diagram. Common denominator fractions need not be simplified with this type of diagram, but the example is valuable to help explain the principle. The common denominator is required whenever adding or subtracting fractions with different denominators. If the denominators are the same, then the addition or subtraction of numerators is all that is required to solve the problem. If more assistance is needed on how to find common denominators, the Arithmetic Basics chapter in Module 1 provides information on finding the least common multiple or the lowest common denominator required for addition and subtraction. Remember that the individual fractions will retain the same value only if the numerator and denominator are multiplied by the same value.

The multiplication of fractions is a simple operation because fractions are multiplied as follows:

$$\frac{7}{8} * \frac{3}{4} = \frac{7 * 3}{8 * 4} = \frac{21}{32}$$

The final fraction is in its simplest form because there are no common factors. If common factors exist in the numerator and denominator of a fraction, then that fraction must be simplified.

The division of fractions should never be attempted in the form of a ratio. The method is confusing, elaborate, and unreliable in a testing situation. Instead, **every** fraction division problem is a simple operation because the division operation can be rewritten as a multiplication operation. To begin, consider the previously stated equation:

$$\frac{dividend}{divisor} = quotient$$

This equation can be rewritten as a multiplication operation as follows:

$$dividend \times \frac{1}{divisor} = quotient$$

The multiplication operation yields the same outcome as division. The quantity $(^1/_{divisor})$ is called a *reciprocal*, and for a fraction, you simply need to flip the fraction upside down, as demonstrated in the following equation:

$$\frac{5}{8} \div \frac{1}{4} = \frac{5}{8} * \frac{4}{1} = \frac{20}{8} = 2.5 \ (in \ simplified \ form)$$

Fraction to Decimal Conversions

Every fraction represents a division problem. For any fraction, the decimal value is represented by the numerator (top value) divided by the denominator (bottom value). Certain combinations, such as $^1/_3$, will result in repeating decimals that will always be rounded in a multiple-choice testing situation.

The fraction $1/2$ has a decimal value of 0.5, which is the value of 1 divided by 2. The values of improper fractions (larger numerator than denominator)—such as $3/2$, $5/2$, or $7/2$—are determined by either dividing as previously stated or, more easily, by multiplying the numerator by 0.5 (the decimal value of the unit fraction, or 1 divided by the denominator). Therefore, the improper fraction of $7/2$ is 7 * 0.5, or 3.5. Often, the determination of the unit fraction followed by the decimal multiplication is simpler in a testing situation.

For example, the fraction $3/5$ has a decimal value of 0.6, which is the value of 3 divided by 5. Alternately, the value of the unit fraction of $1/5$ is 0.2, and that unit fraction multiplied by 3 is 0.6. If you know the unit fractions for common fraction values, the answer selection process may be simplified.

When a fraction such as $5/7$ is evaluated, the quotient of 5 divided by 7 results in a lengthy decimal value of 0.71428.... That extended value will never appear as a multiple-choice test answer selection. Typically, that value will be rounded to either 0.71 or 0.714. Remember that testing instructions say to choose the **best answer**. Your best choice is sometimes a rounded number.

Decimal to Fraction Conversions

All decimals are also fractions and can be written in that form. The fractions that result all have powers of 10 in the denominator and usually need to be simplified to be compared to multiple-choice answers in a testing situation.

For example, simple decimal values, such as 0.25, can be written as the fraction $25/100$. This fraction must be simplified to be correct. $25/100$ can be rewritten as a product:

$$\frac{(25 * 1)}{(25 * 4)}$$

or

$$\frac{25}{25} * \frac{1}{4}$$

The fraction can be expressed correctly as $1/4$ since the fraction $25/25$ is simplified to 1. Recognizing the common factors in the numerator and denominator is essential for making these conversions.

For testing purposes, decimal conversions will often be based on common fraction values. For example, $1/16$, if divided with long division, is 0.0625. Any integer multiple of this value results in a fraction with 16 in the denominator.

The value 0.0625 is first rewritten as the fraction:

$$\frac{625}{10,000}$$

Simplifying with factors of 5 in the numerator and denominator gives the following fraction:

$$\frac{125}{2,000}$$

Simplifying with factors of 25 in the numerator and denominator gives the following fraction:

$$\frac{5}{80}$$

Simplifying with factors of 5 in the numerator and denominator one more time gives the simplified fraction:

$$\frac{1}{16}$$

While either of these methods may require extra time to complete, the answer choices can usually be logically reduced to two of the four examples. Testing the answer choices is simply a matter of multiplying the decimal value by the denominator to determine whether the numerator is correct.

Another solution method, logical deduction, can be used as a simple, reliable, and time-saving approach for finding the fractional value of 0.4375.

For example, the following is a list of possible multiple-choice answers:

A. $^{3}/_{16}$
B. $^{5}/_{16}$
C. $^{7}/_{16}$
D. $^{9}/_{16}$

Logically, any fraction greater than $^{1}/_{2}$ is immediately eliminated since the following is true:

$$0.4375 < 0.5$$

Therefore, first eliminate answer D, which illustrates how incorrect answer choices can be eliminated with this type of logical deduction.

Second, notice the following regarding answer choice A:

$$\frac{3}{16} < \frac{1}{4}$$

And in decimal form, the expression would be as follows:

$$\frac{3}{16} < 0.25$$

Choice A can thus logically be eliminated since the comparison is with 0.4375. Third, notice the following in the answer choices:

$$\frac{5}{16} > \frac{1}{4}$$

And in decimal form, the expression would be as follows:

$$\frac{5}{16} > 0.25$$

Since $5/16$ is just slightly more than $1/4$, choice B can be eliminated since our comparison is with 0.4375. Finally, C is chosen as the best and most logical answer choice given the following:

$$\frac{7}{16} < \frac{1}{2}$$
$$\text{and}$$
$$0.4375 < 0.5$$

Percentages

You're likely most familiar with percentages as a concept from real-world applications, so these math problems are some of the less scary math problems that appear on tests. However, test writers take that confidence into account and can use it against you, so be careful on problems with percentages. Let's look at an example.

Example: A sweater went on sale and now costs $25.20. If the original price was $42.00, what is the percent discount?

    A. 16.8%
    B. 20.0%
    C. 25.0%
    D. 40.0%
    E. 60.0%

Take a minute to work out the problem yourself. If you get the wrong answer, it will be helpful for you to see where you went wrong—several of the answer choices are distinct traps that often appear on test questions like this example question.

Solution: With percentages, you can always set up a fraction. First, you want to know what percent the sale price is of the original price. The reference point, or original price, will go on the bottom of the fraction. The numerator will be the sale price. The ratio of $25.2/42$ is equal to $6/10$. The sale price, $25.20, is 0.6, or 60% of the original price. A percentage is just the decimal times 100.

This correct answer for sale price amount would therefore be answer choice E. However, the question did NOT ask what percent the new price is of the original price. Read carefully: the question asks for the percent *discount.* This language is commonly used for questions with prices. Here's what it means, in math terms:

$$Percentage\ discount = 100\% - percentage\ of\ sale\ price$$

The percentage discount represents the amount less than 100% that the sale price is of the original price. We can use this equation to solve the question, which yields the following:

$$(42 - 25.2)/42 = 0.40$$

Remember, a percent is a decimal multiplied by 100%. You can thus convert the decimal on the right side to a percentage by multiplying by 100%:

$$100\% * 0.40 = 40\%$$

The sale price is 40% *less than* the original price, which is answer choice D. Another mathematical reasoning approach would be to take the original fraction subtracted from 1:

$$1 - 25.2 \div 42 = 0.4$$

From here, just recognize that if the sale price *is* 60% of the original price, then it is 40% *less than* the original price.

You can also solve for the discounted amount and then find that amount as a percent of the original amount to solve for the percentage of the discount:

$$42 - 25.2 = 16.80$$

$$16.80/42 = 0.4$$

Those three approaches show how you can solve one problem in multiple ways by using the same concept of percentage and recognizing that a percent *discount* requires subtraction from the original price.

Here's another percentage problem, this time with a different trick:

Example Problem: 168 is 120% of what number?

Solution: First, convert 120% to a decimal. Remember, converting a percentage to a decimal is done by dividing by 100%:

$$120/100 = 1.2$$

The problem states that 168 is this percent *of* some other number. To set up the equation, then, 168 goes in the numerator position of the percent fraction equation. Here is the resulting equation:

$$168/x = 1.2$$

Here, x signifies the unknown number in the problem. Writing the percent equation is indispensable to solving this type of problem. Multiply both sides by x, and then divide both sides by 1.2 to isolate the variable:

$$168(x)/x = 1.2(x)$$
$$168 = 1.2x$$
$$168/1.2 = 1.2x/1.2$$
$$140 = x$$

Therefore, 168 is 120% of 140. You can verify this answer by plugging the numbers back into the original equation:

$$168/140 = 1.2$$

This problem is tricky because the percentage is greater than 100%, or greater than 1.0, so it violates our intuition that the bigger number should go on the bottom of the fraction. Percentages are usually less than 100. However, when percentages are larger than 100, the numerator is bigger than the denominator. The inverse of the original question could be the following: 168 is what percent of 140?

Many people, after reading this question, would automatically set up the following fraction equation:

$$140/168 = 0.83$$

On the test, 83% would be a likely answer choice, but would also be the wrong answer. The question is asking for 168/140. Read these questions carefully, and don't automatically place the larger number in the denominator.

Let's look at one more example that combines these concepts and then do a couple practice problems:

Example Problem: An ingredient in a recipe is decreased by 20%. By what percentage does the new amount need to be increased to obtain the original amount of the ingredient?

Solution: Here's a pro's tip for working with percentages: When a problem is given only in percentages with no given numbers, you can substitute in any value to work with as your original amount. Since you are solving for a percentage, you'll get the same answer no matter what numbers are used because percentages are ratios. The easiest number to work with in problems like this is 100, so use that as the original recipe amount. 100 what? Cups of flour? Chicken tenders? Chocolate chips? Doesn't matter. Here's how your equation should look:

$$x/100 = 0.20$$

Solve for x, which gives the amount the ingredient has been decreased by:

$$x = 100 * 0.20$$

Remember that 20% is a decimal, so $0.20 * 100 = 20$. The ingredient has been decreased by 20 units. What is the new amount?

$$100 - 20 = 80$$

What was the original question asking? *By what percent does the new amount need to be increased to obtain the original amount of the ingredient?* Let's parse this mathematical language. We've found the new amount of the ingredient, 80 units. The original amount, we decided, was 100 units.

The next step in answering the question is to find the *amount* that we would need to add to get back to the original amount. This part is easy:

$$80 + x = 100$$
$$x = 20$$

It's the same amount that we subtracted from the original amount, 20. But the question asks what percentage of 80 is required to add 20?

Set up the percentage equation. 80 times what percent ($x/100$) will give that extra 20 units?
$$80 * x/100 = 20$$

Solve as normal by dividing both sides by 80 and then multiplying both sides by 100:

$$x/100 = 0.25$$
$$x = 25$$

The new amount must be increased by 25% to equal the original amount.

MATHEMATICS KNOWLEDGE

Rates

Rate-related questions are some of the most common questions on standardized math exams. A *rate* is anything that relates two types of measurement: distance and time, dollars and workers, mass and volume, *x* per *y*, and so on. Exchange rates convey how much of one currency you can get for a certain amount of another currency. Speedometers tell you how many kilometers you travel per unit of time. Growth rates tell you how much the population has grown over time. In sum, rates are everywhere in the world, and they are everywhere on standardized math tests. To express a rate mathematically, think of the following:

All rates express one measurement *in terms of* another.

For example, *km per hour* gives a measurement of distance (kilometers) for one unit of time (an hour). *Per* is a term that means divide. How "per" divides is defined in the following statement: If a car is traveling 40 kilometers per hour, it travels 40 kilometers for every one hour of time that passes.

All rates work this way. If you can get €0.81 (euros) for one American dollar (i.e., per every American dollar), the exchange rate is depicted mathematically as follows:

$$\frac{€0.81\ (euros)}{1\ dollar} = 0.81\ euros\ per\ dollar$$

A rate is written as a fraction. A rate *equation* gives you a value of one of the measurements if you know the rate and the value of the other measurement.

If a car can travel 40 km/h, the following equation can be used:

$$Distance = 40km/hour * hours$$

This recipe for the equation always works for a rate problem:

Examine the mph example: When you multiply 40 km/h times the number of hours, the hours units cancel out, leaving you with the number of kilometers. This process works for any type of rate. The thing being measured on the *top* (numerator) of the rate measurement is equal to the rate times the unit being measured on the *bottom* of the rate measurement.
To solve a rate problem, follow these steps:

1. **Read the question carefully to determine what the question is asking you to solve.** Is it an amount of time? A distance? Something else? Ensure you understand this aspect before doing anything else. It can be helpful to name the variables at this point.

2. **Write equations to express all the information given in the problem.** This step is just like what was demonstrated for percentage problems, averaging problems, etc. The ability to express information in an equation is one of the main mathematical

reasoning abilities that you can demonstrate to succeed on tests like these. Remember the equation from above distance:

$$Distance = Rate * Time$$

3. **Solve!**

   First, here's a simple example problem: A train is traveling west at 75 km/h. How long will it take for the train to travel 60 kilometers?

   Step 1: Identify what the question is asking for: in this instance, you need to determine *how long*, or the time it takes to travel 60 kilometers.

   Step 2: Write the equation to solve: $60 = 75 * time$

   Step 3: Solve! You know that the rate is 75 kilometers per hour and that 60 kilometers were traveled. To solve for time, just plug those values into the equation, and then isolate the *x hours* by dividing both sides by 75 km/h:

   $$60 \ km/75 \ km \ per \ hour = 0.8 \ hours$$
   $$0.8 \ hours * 60 \ minutes \ per \ hour = 48 \ minutes$$

Rate problems can also require a system of equations. That just means you need to write two equations to relate two unknown variables, instead of one equation to solve for one unknown variable like in the problem we just solved. The algebra is not any more difficult for these types of problems. They just require the extra step of writing another equation.

Example Problem: Jessica assembles one model airplane per hour. James assembles one model airplane per 45 minutes. If they work for the same amount of time and assemble 12 planes all together, how many planes did James assemble?

Solution:

   Step 1: Identify what the question is asking you to solve: the number of planes that James assembled.

   Step 2: Write equations:

   $$x = Jessica's \ rate * T$$
   $$x = \frac{1 \ airplane}{hr} * T$$
   $$y = James' \ rate * T$$
   $$y = \frac{\frac{1}{0.75} airplanes}{hr} * T$$
   $$x + y = 12 \ airplanes$$

You convert "45 minutes" to 0.75 hours, since $\frac{45}{60} = 0.75$. If you'd rather not do that, you could leave the rate in minutes, but then change Jessica's rate to 60 minutes instead of one hour. The important thing is to use the same units for time across the whole equation.

Step 3: Solve! Notice that the "T hours" term is the same in both rate equations. The problem stated that Jessica and James worked for the same amount of time. To solve for the number of planes James assembled, you first need to find T hours. The *number of planes Jessica assembled* and the *number of planes James assembled* can be added together since the sum is 12. The following new equation results from adding those together:

$$12 \; airplanes = x + y$$
$$12 \; airplanes = \left(\frac{1 \; airplane}{hr} * T\right) + \left(\frac{\frac{1}{0.75}airplanes}{hr} * T\right)$$

The algebra here is a little bit hairy, but you can handle it! To solve for time, isolate T step by step. First, multiply every term in the equation by "1 hour."

Now, the unit "hour" cancels out in both terms on the right side of the equation. Remember, when you multiply *and* divide a term by something, it cancels out:

$$12 \; planes \times (1 \; hour) = \cancel{(1 \; hour)} * \frac{1 \; plane}{\cancel{1 \; hour}} * T \; hours + \cancel{(1 \; hour)} * \frac{1 \; plane}{0.75 \; \cancel{hours}} * T \; hours$$

Now, after adjusting that equation, you're left with the following:

$$12 \; plane \; hours = 1 \; plane * T \; hours + 1/0.75 * T \; hours$$

Now, you need to isolate "T hours." Gather the "T hours" terms on the right side of the equation. Right now, they are separated into an addition expression. If you add them together, they will be collected into one term. Since 1/0.75 is equal to 4/3, change that term first:

$$12 \; plane \; hours = 1 \; plane * T \; hours + 4/3 \; plane * T \; hours$$

Now add through the following equation:

$$12 \; plane \; hours = (1 \; plane \; + \; 4/3 \; plane) \times T \; hours$$

$$12 \; plane \; hours = (1 \; and \; 4/3 \; plane) \times T \; hours$$

When you add together 1 and $^4/_3$, the effect is the same as saying that $1x + 2x = 3x$. We just collected the like terms.

Now, divide both sides by 1 plane to isolate the T hours term. Since mixed fractions are difficult to work with, change the mixed fraction into an improper one:

$$12 \text{ } plane \text{ } hours = (7/3 \text{ } plane) * T \text{ } hours$$

The planes unit cancels out on the right side, leaving you with the following equation:

$$12 \text{ } hours/(7/3) = T \text{ } hours$$

One arithmetic trick is that dividing by a fraction is the same as multiplying by the inverse of the fraction. If you are comfortable dividing by fractions on your calculator, you can do the rest of the problem that way, or else you can flip the fraction over and simplify the arithmetic:

$$12 * 3/7 = T \text{ } hours$$
$$36/7 = T \text{ } hours$$
$$5\frac{1}{7} = T \text{ } hours$$

The answer is $x = 5\frac{1}{7}$ hours, or approximately 5.14 hours.

Phew! That problem was a long one! But it included rates, a system of equations, unit conversions (changing minutes into fractions of an hour), and algebra with complex fractions. That type of question is one of the most difficult types of rate problems you would ever see on a standardized math exam. If you could follow along with the solution, then you're well-prepared for taking the test.

Remember, on exams like this, most points come from the easier problems. The harder problems (which on most exams tend to be at the end of a section) are always worth giving a shot, but they are not necessary to earn a good score. Problems like the prior examples are great for practice because they include a lot of different concepts, though. But don't be discouraged if you don't always get the tougher problems correct on the first try. They are preparing you to do well on a wide range of different problem types!

MODULE 3

VOCABULARY

Let's face it. Vocabulary just isn't that interesting. So let's change it up! Below is a crossword puzzle to help you learn some new words and expand your vocabulary.

The word list that follows the puzzle contains all the words to solve the list of clues. As you solve each clue, enter the relevant word into the crossword puzzle and cross it off your word list.

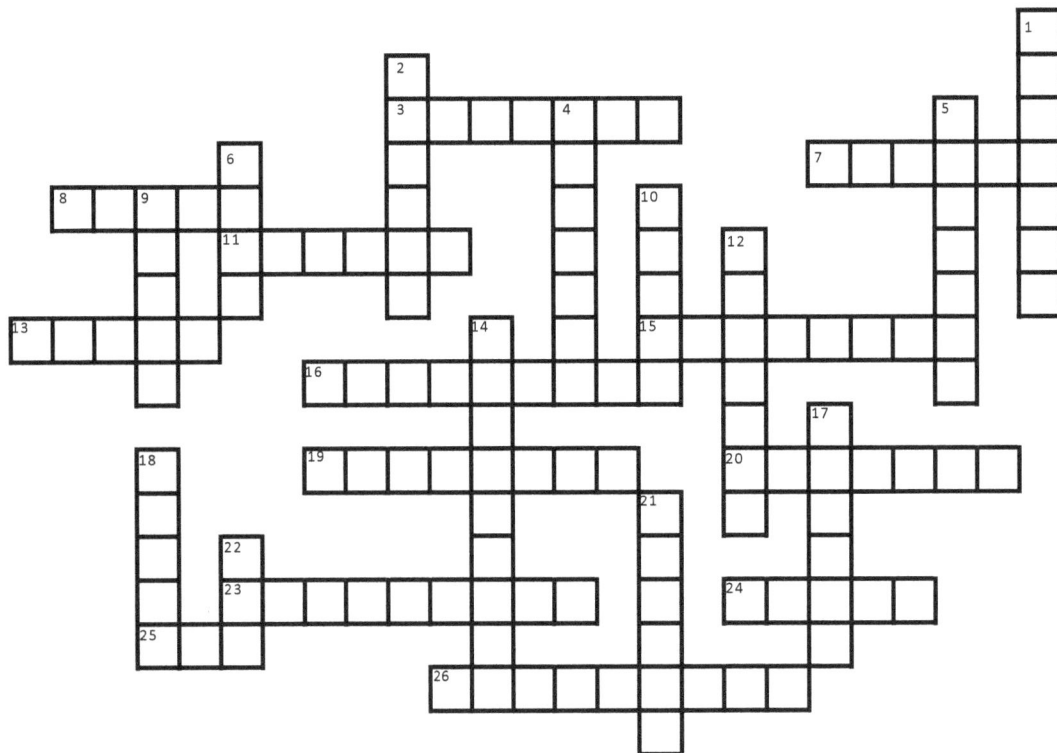

Word List

abhorrent	frail	parity
abscond	glut	perpetual
ambiguous	haughty	ravage
amity	hoist	slander
bar	immerse	surmount
carcass	jargon	transpose
chide	lofty	unison
debonair	malign	vague
err	obscure	

Clues

Across

3. to escape quickly

7. destroy or ruin

8. weak

11. together or at once

13. of considerable height

15. to overcome something

16. disgusting or hateful

19. stylish and charming

20. speaking falsely about someone

23. having more than one explanation

24. unclear or uncertain

25. to make a mistake

26. a state of being without change

Down

1. cover completely

2. specialized words

4. relatively unknown

5. arrogant

6. too much of something

9. friendly relations between two people

10. raise with a mechanical device

12. the remains of a dead animal

14. to change an arrangement

17. speak badly about

18. to scold

21. the equivalent of something

22. forbid or prevent

Hopefully, that wasn't too difficult! Ready to see how you did? Head to the following page to check your answers against the solution.

Solution

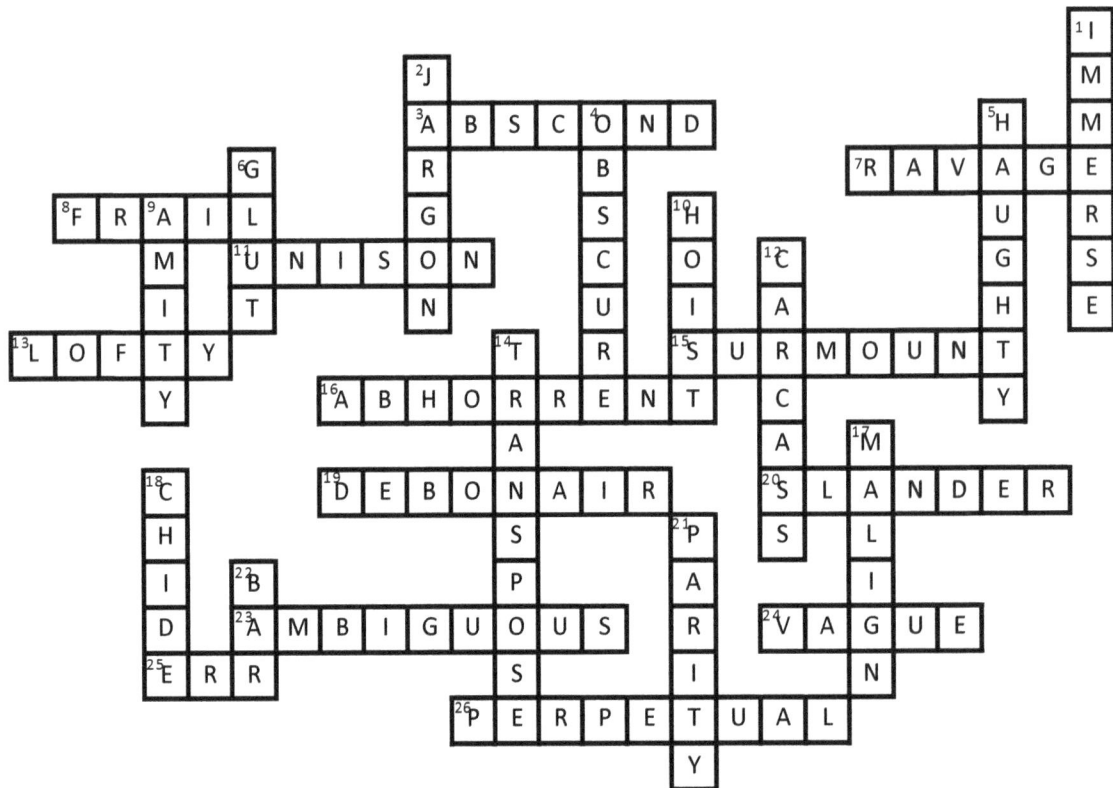

Across

3. to escape quickly [ABSCOND]

7. destroy or ruin [RAVAGE]

8. weak [FRAIL]

11. together or at once [UNISON]

13. of considerable height [LOFTY]

15. to overcome something [SURMOUNT]

16. disgusting or hateful [ABHORRENT]

19. stylish and charming [DEBONAIR]

20. speaking falsely about someone [SLANDER]

23. having more than one explanation [AMBIGUOUS]

24. unclear or uncertain [VAGUE]

25. to make a mistake [ERR]

26. a state of being without change [PERPETUAL]

Down

1. cover completely [IMMERSE]

2. specialized words [JARGON]

4. relatively unknown [OBSCURE]

5. arrogant [HAUGHTY]

6. too much of something [GLUT]

9. friendly relations between two people [AMITY]

10. raise with a mechanical device [HOIST]

12. the remains of a dead animal [CARCASS]

14. to change an arrangement [TRANSPOSE]

17. speak badly about [MALIGN]

18. to scold [CHIDE]

21. the equivalent of something [PARITY]

22. forbid or prevent [BAR]

Words in Context

When reading through a chapter in a book or a passage on a test, you will sometimes encounter a word you've never seen before. You may not know what it means, but don't worry! You can still figure out a basic definition of the word, even if you don't have a dictionary on hand (or if you don't want to get off the sofa and get one).

In every sentence, any given word is surrounded by clauses, phrases, and other words. When you find a word that you don't recognize, you can learn more about it by studying the context surrounding the word. The surrounding words, phrases, and clauses are called *context clues*. Using these clues, you can determine the definition for almost every unfamiliar word you encounter. This skill will become especially helpful when you start reading higher-level texts with fancy words or training manuals with lots of jargon.

Types of Context Clues

While reading, you can use several types of context clues to help you discover the meaning of unknown words. Some important and common types of context clues are outlined in the following subsections. For each, try to use the specific context clue to determine the meaning of the bolded word.

Root Word & Affix

This type of context clue uses your existing knowledge of common root words and affixes.

> *Example:* Scientists who dig up dinosaur bones are experts in **paleontology**.

Here, the root word and affix are "paleo" (meaning old, ancient) and "-ology" (meaning the academic study or practice of a certain field), respectively. Thus, if you know that dinosaurs are very old/ancient and know what the affix means, then you can use the context clue to deduce what "paleontology" roughly means. Here is the exact definition of paleontology: The scientific study of life of the geologic past that involves the analysis of plant and animal fossils. A paleontologist studies the bone fossils of the dinosaurs, among other flora and fauna fossils.

Compare/Contrast

This type of context clue signals a similarity or difference by using words or phrases that denote a comparison or contrast. Words that imply similarity (or comparison) include *like, also, just as, too*, etc. Words that imply difference (or contrast) include *whereas, opposed to, unlike, versus,* etc.

> *Example:* A comet, like an **asteroid**, is made from leftover matter in the universe.

This context clue compares an "asteroid" with a comet to imply a similarity to the given definition of a comet.

Logic

This context clue requires you to infer the definition of the unknown word by using the relationships within the sentence.

Example: Builders routinely use **fasteners** that will help hold structures and buildings in place.

This context clue describes the job that "fasteners" do (i.e., help hold structures and buildings in place).

Definition

This type of context clue includes a basic definition of the unknown word.

Example: New biological species can be formed through a process called **speciation**.

This context clue explicitly defines "speciation" (i.e., the process through which new biological species can be formed).

Example or Illustration

This context clue uses an example or illustration of the unknown word.

Example: Animals classified in the phylum porifera live in a **marine** habitat like the Atlantic and Pacific Oceans.

This context clue uses the Atlantic and Pacific Oceans as examples of "marine" habitats.

Homographs

Now that you've had a refresher on context clues, let's talk about homographs. A *homograph* is a word that is spelled exactly like another word, but has a different meaning. For example, *bass* can mean *a low, deep sound* OR *a type of fish*. Here's a more complex homograph: *Minute* can mean *a unit of time* OR *something exceedingly small.*

Although questions with homographs aren't necessarily difficult, you'll need to pay extra attention to the context clues. If you're rushing or don't read the entire sentence, you can accidentally mark an incorrect answer by mistaking the homograph for the wrong meaning. Just take your time, and use context clues. By doing both, you'll most likely have no problem recognizing the correct meaning.

Here's something to consider when you take the exam. Within the question, replace the vocabulary term with your selected answer choice. Read the sentence, and check whether it makes sense with the selected answer swapped in for the vocabulary term. This approach won't guarantee a correct answer, but it will at least help you weed out some incorrect ones.

Another point to keep in mind, sometimes no answer choice will fit perfectly into the sentence. Don't panic! You probably did not misread the context clues or identify an incorrect meaning. Many times, questions will ask you to select the *best* word from the given answer choices, even though that correct answer choice may not be the best *possible* answer overall. These types of questions are looking for you to choose the *most* correct answer choice. While tricky to tackle, such questions will appear on the exam. Just remember the tips given here, and you'll do just fine.

CRITICAL READING

Eliminating Wrong Answers

Authors often write with an intended purpose in mind, and they will support their main ideas with examples, facts, data, and stories that help ensure clarity in the overall meaning of the written text. You may be asked a question regarding one of these details or examples or regarding the overall theme or main idea of the passage. These types of questions require you to carefully read the passage for meaning and to look at all the supporting details used. However, you must also learn how to identify incorrect answer choices and eliminate them right away. This step will help you narrow down the answer choices that are likely to be correct. Here's how you do it:

Strategies for Answering Specific Detail Questions

- Identify the key words in the question to help you find details and examples that will help answer the question.
- As you read the passage, make mental notes about how words are used and any repeated phrases. Also look for the overall meaning of each paragraph and passage.
- Some questions will pull words or phrases from the passage and use them in the question. In this case, look through the passage and find those words or phrases and ensure they're being used the same way in both the passage and the question. The wording in many questions will change the meaning of the wording, which can make the question wrong or confuse the reader.

Some questions will ask you to determine whether a particular statement about the passage or its topic is true or false. In this case, look over the paragraphs, and find the overall theme or idea of the passage. Compare your theme or idea to the statement in the question.

Now it's your turn to try out the strategies to see how you do. Read the following passages, and answer the questions that follow, ensuring you eliminate the wrong answers while looking for the right one. There will be three passages for you to read and several questions about each passage. Each question will have one right answer and at least three wrong answers, the latter of which you will need to eliminate as you read.

Good luck!

Passage 1

Online game play has become standard for many video games. This format allows kids the opportunity to play their favorite games with other like-minded fans, but also brings new risks and dangers. By being proactive and staying active with their children, however, parents can ensure their kids remain safe and have fun when playing video games online.

Parents need to stay current on several things: video game ratings, content clues, and kids' use and involvement. In that regard, the ratings on video games can help parents know what is and is not acceptable content for their kids.

Parents also need to keep an eye on the content of the games once game play starts—namely by peeking in now and then to ensure nothing surprising lurks within a game that parents originally thought was fine. Parents must also monitor how often kids are playing the games, the time spent playing, and how much time is spent thinking about the game. Balance is critical to ensure video game use remains fun and safe.

Parents should ultimately keep open lines of communication with their kids. They need to know that they can come to their parents with questions, concerns, or problems. In addition, kids need to feel safe talking to their parents and not be fearful that parents will get angry. When your child comes to you with a problem, do not brush it off—give the problem the attention it deserves, and ensure your kids know you are glad they are coming to you.

1. What can parents do to ensure their children remain safe and have fun when they play video games online?
   A. Be proactive with decisions
   B. Be active and involved with kids
   C. Be willing to let kids do what they want
   D. a and b
   E. b and c

Answer: D
Rationale: Both A and B are correct since they were mentioned in the opening paragraph of the passage.

2. What must parents do to keep their kids safe when they play video games online?
   A. Stay current on trends and news
   B. Monitor kid's game activities
   C. Communicate with kids often
   D. All the above
   E. None of the above

Answer: D
Rationale: All these things are mentioned in the passage when it discusses the things people can do to keep their kids safe when they play games online.

Remember that reading all the paragraphs is a great way to get the overall idea of the passage. In addition, remember that every paragraph of a passage should be discussing a different example or point that connects back to the main idea of the passage, which helps further demonstrate the main idea.

Passage 2
Kids of all ages have long loved drawing, and many kids will draw on anything and everything they can get their hands on. Accordingly, kids will draw on paper, the floor, their clothes, themselves, and of course, the walls! Many parents thus turn to the tried-and-true chalkboards for children's playroom or play area.

However, chalk can be messy and difficult to clean up, and some kids just don't like the light powdery look of their chalk artwork. If facing this situation, consider dry-erase paint as the most practical solution to your dilemma. Years ago, when dry erase was something found only in schools or office buildings, it was hard to come by if you wanted that option at home.

Dry erase easels and boards were cumbersome, bulky, heavy, and expensive. However, now you can get specially formulated dry erase paint to use on your walls to turn them into massive dry erase boards! Dry erase paint has low-odor, low-chemical content and is suitable for a range of surfaces, such as wood, brick, concrete, and many others.

Why stifle kids' creativity when you can unleash it and let them create, design, and explore the wonders of their own imaginations? Many companies carry dry erase paint, so you can transform your child's bedroom or playroom into the best place in the world. Whether you want to give your kids a section of the wall, one entire wall, or all the wall space they can reach, the addition of dry erase paint can help make it easy for you to give them ample space to be creative.

Imagine the smile on your child's face upon seeing a daily message written on the wall upon waking up or coming home from school. You can also send gentle reminders about chores and homework, or use the dry erase space for a fun approach to nightly homework sessions. Be creative, and you will never run out of uses for dry erase paint.

1. What are some reasons mentioned in the passage for why dry erase walls are a good choice for a kid's room?
    A. Easy to clean and helps kids be creative
    B. Safe and fewer chemicals
    C. Can be used for everyday needs
    D. All the above

Answer: D
Rationale: All the answers are correct and are mentioned in the passage. All the details are not mentioned in one paragraph, but they are mentioned throughout the passage. All the details also tie back to the idea of dry erase paint being a good option for a kid's bedroom.

2. Only a few companies carry dry erase paint to be used on walls, which makes it hard to find and use for kids' room designs.
    A. True
    B. False

Answer: B
Rationale: The passage mentions getting dry erase paint from companies and that many companies carry it. Thus, the paint is easy to find and easy to use, making it a good choice for kid's rooms.

Passage 3
We hear a lot of talk about recycling today. We recycle glass, plastic, newspaper, and more, and there are countless ways to reuse everyday items to keep them out of landfills for a little longer. An equally important, but less discussed method of recycling is scrap metal recycling. You may be wondering why it's such a big deal and what good metal recycling does—well, let's look what it means and its effects.

As one of its biggest impacts, this form of recycling conserves raw resources and has eliminated the carbon footprint for many metal production facilities. The Institute of Scrap Recycling Industries (ISRI) states that, in 2010, more than $64 billion was added to the U.S. economy from the recycling, reuse, and production of new products from recycled metals. All this metal scrap would otherwise end up in landfills or in the environment, meaning that much more raw material would have to be mined, refined, and produced from scratch to make new tools, machines, and products. Scrap metal recycling is therefore a very important aspect of conservation and pollution reduction.

In addition to the economic impact from the profits of reusing scrap metal, the act of metal recycling also generates jobs. The ISRI estimated that, in 2008, over 85,000 jobs were supported and made possible in some way thanks to scrap metal recycling. It also helps in trades and exports; more than an estimated $28 billion and roughly 44 million metric tons of metal were shipped and sold overseas.

Scrap metal recycling comes in many forms. Sometimes a junk yard or scrap yard buys scrap metal and then sells it to manufacturers who can melt it down, refine it, and use it to make new products and materials. Or the neighborhood scrap collector could visit yard sales and stop by your trash pile to pick up that old dishwasher or microwave you threw out.

Community-sponsored recycling programs also exist. In such programs, cans are collected and turned in for cash. Other types of programs include electronics recycling and business incentives for recycling scrap metal left over from production or building projects.

The benefits and importance of scrap metal recycling are clear. Whether recycling some materials left over after a home renovation project, tin cans your kids collected, or the last remaining pieces to that old junk car you scraped, recycling scrap metal can do a world of good and have a lasting impact on the environment, economy, and your local community. So do your part, and be on the lookout for scrap metal to add to your recycling piles.

1. The ISRI is a company that oversees scrap metal and recycling practices.
   A. True
   B. False

Answer: A
Rationale: ISRI stands for the Institute of Scrap Recycling Industries, and the passage states that they offer reports about money earned from scrap metal recycling and mentions the job market associated with scrap metal recycling.

2. Recycling scrap metal helps the environment by keeping that junk out of landfills.
   A. True
   B. False

Answer: A
Rationale: The passage talks about recycling and how it's a vital aspect of conservation and pollution reduction.

Good job! Remember to carefully read every passage you are given, and don't be afraid to go back and read something again or re-scan the passage for key words and phrases that show up in the questions.

Inferences and How to Make and Use Them

Inference is a mental process through which we reach a conclusion based on a given set of facts and numbers, and on our ability to reason. The ability to use inference is needed when information is implied, but not directly stated. For example, people's motives and intentions are often not overtly stated, we need to deduce what they are based on people's actions and words, and on our knowledge and experiences.

In fact, we use inference in daily life all the time. When we see a person wearing a lot clothes, we will conclude he might be feeling cold. When we see a stranger on the street, by paying attention to his grooming, mannerism, and clothes, we very quickly draw conclusions about his background and intentions. When we have a conversation with someone, we infer a wealth of information from the body language and facial expressions. Thus, we all have inborn capabilities of inferencing.

In all these examples, we make observations and draw conclusions with varying degrees of confidence, and we fill in information that is not directly and literally presented to us.

In the context of exam preparation, inference is usually a process that we find clues in the text, consider multiple pieces of information, connect the dots, and combine these with our knowledge and experiences to figure out the unspoken.

ARITHMETIC REASONING

Sets

Working with Sets
All standardized math exams will touch on the basic statistical descriptions of sets of numbers: mean (the same as an average, for a set), median, mode and range. These are terms to know. Let's look at an example set and examine what each of these terms means:

Set of numbers: 42, 18, 21, 26, 22, 21

Mean
The mean of a set of numbers is the average value of the set. The following formula is used to find the mean:

$$\frac{Sum\ of\ the\ numbers\ in\ the\ set}{Quantity\ of\ numbers\ in\ the\ set} = mean$$

Then, that formula is used to find the mean of the example set:

$$\frac{42 + 18 + 21 + 26 + 22 + 21}{6} = \frac{150}{6} = 25$$

As that equation shows, you add together all the numbers that appear in the set and then divide by the quantity of numbers in the set. The mean, or average, value in the set is 25. Notice that the mean is not necessarily a number that appears in the set, although it can be.

Median
The median of a set is the number that appears in the middle **when the set is ordered from least to greatest.** Therefore, the first step in finding the median is to put the numbers in the correct order, if they are not already. You should always do this physically, on your scratch paper, to ensure you don't leave any numbers out of the reordering. For the example set previously given, the reordered set would look like the following set:

18, 21, 21, 22, 26, 42

Ensure you've included all the numbers in order, even if there are duplicates. When working with a set with a lot of numbers, you might find it helpful to cross them off in the original set as you order them on your scratch paper. This process helps ensure you don't leave any numbers out.

If there is an odd quantity of numbers in the set, the median will be the middle number. For example, if a set has nine numbers, the median will be the fifth number of the ordered set.

However, the example set has six numbers. Since no single number is in the exact middle, you want to average the two middle numbers (i.e., the third and fourth numbers) to find the median, as shown in the following equation:

$$\frac{21 + 22}{2} = 21.5$$

The median of this set is 21.5.

Mode

The mode of a set of numbers is the number that appears most often. Speakers of French will find this easy to remember since *mode* is the French word for style. The number that appears the most is "in style" for the set.

The example set has one number that appears more than once: 21. Therefore, 21 is the mode. Sometimes, any repeated numbers are easier to see after the set is ordered, when duplicate numbers appear next to one another.

If a set has two numbers that equally appear most often, such as two 21s and two 22s, then both 21 *and* 22 are the mode. You don't average them together as that is done for the median. Therefore, the mode is the only descriptor of a set that must always be a number in the set. Since there are two modes, the set would be described as "bimodal."

If all the values in the set appear the same number of times in a number set, there is no mode.

Range

The range of a set of numbers is the distance between the highest and lowest values. Once you've reordered a set, these values are easy to identify. Simply subtract the two values to obtain the range:

Highest value − Lowest value = Range

For the example set, the range would be calculated as follows:

$$42 - 18 = 24$$

The range of the set is 24.

Sets can include negative numbers, decimals, fractions, duplicates, etc. In addition, sets can appear in table form. Let's look at another example set to see what kinds of tricky questions you may encounter on the test.

Example Problem: Based on the following table, what is the average rainfall for the months spanning September, October, November, and December?

Month	Rainfall (cm)
August	0.8
September	1.3
October	2.1
November	1.3
December	3.7

Solution: Notice the first trick in this question: you are asked for the average of only four months, not all five listed in the table. This trick introduces two potential sources of error—you could add all five months' rainfall and/or divide the total rainfall of all months by five when calculating the average. To find the average of *only* the four months stated in the question, use the following solution:

$$\frac{1.3 + 2.1 + 1.3 + 3.7}{4} = 2.1 \; cm$$

The following example is another question for the same data table, but the problem uses a different approach to averaging.

Example Problem: The average monthly rainfall from July through December was 1.7 cm. What was the rainfall, in centimeters, in July?

Solution: This question gives you the average and asks you to find the missing rainfall value. This approach is a common way to make a mean/average problem a little tricky for the average (mean) test-taker. Don't fret, though! You can solve these types of questions by applying the basic equation for finding the mean:

$$\frac{Sum \; of \; the \; numbers \; in \; the \; set}{Quantity \; of \; numbers \; in \; the \; set} = mean$$

Next, fill in all the known values:

$$\frac{July + 0.8 + 1.3 + 2.1 + 1.3 + 3.7}{6} = 1.7$$

Then solve the equation algebraically:

$$July + 0.8 + 1.3 + 2.1 + 1.3 + 3.7 = 1.7 * 6$$
$$July = (1.7 * 6) - 0.8 - 1.3 - 2.1 - 1.3 - 3.7$$
$$July = 1 \; inch$$

The following example problem is yet another question for you to solve based on the previous table.

Example Problem: What is the difference between the mode and the median of the rainfalls for August through December?

Solution: To solve this problem, simply find the mode and median values. Remember, the first step is to order the set: 0.8, 1.3, 1.3, 2.1, 3.7

The mode is 1.3 because that is the only number that appears more than once. The median is 1.3 because, of the five numbers in the set, 1.3 is the third (middle) number.

Therefore, the difference between the mode and the median is $1.3 - 1.3 = 0$.

Mathematics Knowledge

Probability and Ratios

Probability
Every probability is determined using the following ratio:

$$Probability = \frac{Total\ number\ of\ desired\ events}{Total\ number\ of\ possible\ outcomes}$$

The simplest example of this type of ratio is found when tossing a coin. Since only two total outcomes (heads, tails) are possible, the probability of either outcome is always $1/2$ for that coin.

Similarly, if you tossed that same coin 14 times, you would expect it to land 7 times with the head showing and 7 times with the tail showing. Because these events are random, however, flipping the coin 14 times will not always provide an equal number of outcomes in a group of trials. The number of heads in a trial of 14 is thus considered the "expected value" of 7. Similarly, 7 would be the "expected value" for tails.

A common misconception is that there "has to be" a certain outcome based on the number of outcomes that have already occurred. In the repeated trial of an event, each outcome is its own trial and is not influenced by the previous trial or trials.

The other common type of probability problem is with dice, where each of the six faces of a cube has its own number from 1 to 6. Each number has the probability of 1/6 for a single die roll. A table of outcomes formulated for two dice, thrown together, shows that the details are slightly different. In the following table, individual numbers are shown across the top and vertically on the side. The entries in table cells represent the total of both dice, Cube A and Cube B.

	1	2	3	4	5	6
1	2	3	4	5	6	7
2	3	4	5	6	7	8
3	4	5	6	7	8	9
4	5	6	7	8	9	10
5	6	7	8	9	10	11
6	7	8	9	10	11	12

Cube "A" (top), Cube "B" (side)

A look at the table shows that there are 36 potential outcomes (6 * 6) when the two dice are thrown together. The individual probabilities are shown in the following table.

Individual Probabilities			
$P(1) =$	0		(never appears)
$P(2) =$	$1/36$	does not simplify	(appears once)
$P(3) =$	$2/36$	simplifies to $1/18$	(appears twice)
$P(4) =$	$3/36$	simplifies to $1/12$	(appears three times)
$P(5) =$	$4/36$	simplifies to $1/9$	(appears four times)
$P(6) =$	$5/36$	does not simplify	(appears five times)
$P(7) =$	$6/36$	simplifies to $1/6$	(appears six times)
$P(8) =$	$5/36$	does not simplify	(appears five times)
$P(9) =$	$4/36$	simplifies to $1/9$	(appears four times)
$P(10) =$	$3/36$	simplifies to $1/12$	(appears three times)
$P(11) =$	$2/36$	simplifies to $1/18$	(appears twice)
$P(12) =$	$1/36$	does not simplify	(appears once)
$P(13) =$	0		(never occurs)

The symmetry of the table makes it easier to visualize the probability ratios for the individual outcomes. Based on the definition of probability, any number larger than 13 will never appear in the table, so the probability of rolling 13 must be zero. The probability of any impossible outcome must always be zero. By the same reasoning, any event that must happen will have a probability of one. Therefore, the probability of rolling a number from 2 to 12 is one.

If you are finding the probability of two events happening, the individual probabilities are added. For example, the probability of rolling a 10 or 11 is the same as the probability of rolling an 8. The number appears in the table the same number of times as the combined total for appearances of 10 or 11.

The formulation of ratios for probabilities is simplest when using fractions. Often, the expression of a probability answer will be in a percent or a decimal. A coin from the first example would have the following probabilities $P(heads) = 50\%$, or 0.5.

Formulating probabilities from a word problem can always be structured around the ratio defined at the beginning of this section. However, the words can mislead or misdirect problem-solving efforts.

For example, a problem that describes a class distribution may often be stated as the number of boys and the number of girls. The probability of selecting a boy in a random sample is defined as the number of boys divided by the TOTAL number of boys AND girls. This dynamic is simple to see in theory, but problems can be worded to mislead you into selecting the incorrect answer or drawing the wrong conclusion when calculating an answer.

Another way that probability problems can be misleading is when multiple choices are used when simplified ratios are required. For example, if a class is made up of 6 girls and 10 boys, the probability of randomly selecting a girl from the classroom is $6/16$ or $3/8$. The misleading multiple choices that may be listed would often include 60% ($6/10$) or 50% (since there are two outcomes—boys and girls). Reading a probability problem carefully is therefore extremely important in both formulating the probability ratio and ensuring the correct ratio is selected in the correct form. If the probability ratio for the example is formulated as $^6/_{16}$, the simplified form of $^3/_8$ is the only correct answer.

Ratios and Proportions

Ratios and fractions are synonymous when discussing numerical values. The ratios or fractions always imply division of the numerator by the denominator. In this section, the discussion is directed toward how words appear in ratio problems and how those words should be interpreted.

A commonly used ratio is contained in the term *kilometers per hour*, usually abbreviated by km/h. When interpreted numerically, the term kilometers per hour is the ratio of the total number of kilometers traveled divided by the number of hours traveled. The key word in this commonly used term is *per*, which means for each hour of travel a specific number of kilometers will be traveled. Per has the same implication when the term is *gallons per hour* (how fast a tub is filled or a lawn is watered) or *tons per year* (how much ore is mined in one year).

Another way that ratios can appear is when a phrase defines a ratio as one value to another. A commonly used comparison is the ratio of *men to women* or *boys to girls*. When such terminology is used, the first term is in the numerator, and the second term is in the denominator by convention.

An inherent problem exists, however, when this terminology is used in the way illustrated by the following example problem.

Example Problem: In a classroom setting, the ratio of girls to boys is 3 to 4 (or 3:4 in strictly mathematical terms). How many boys are there in the classroom if the total number of students is 28?

Solution: This word problem can be easily solved in two ways. If the ratio of ($^{girls}/_{boys}$) is $^3/_4$, the actual numbers could be $^3/_4$, $^6/_8$, $^9/_{12}$, $^{12}/_{16}$, and so forth. These fractions are all equivalent fractions since they all simplify to the value of $^3/_4$. The equivalent fractions are easily determined as the ratios of multiples of the numerator and denominator of the original fraction. Only one fraction exists where the numerator and denominator add to 28, the ratio $^{12}/_{16}$. Therefore, the solution is the classroom has 16 boys and 12 girls.

Notice that the words specify which group (boys or girls) is the numerator and denominator in the original problem and in the solution. When choosing multiple-choice answers, ensure you choose the correct based upon the wording in the original problem. Most often, the correct ratio and its reciprocal are in the answer choices. For example, if the sample problem appeared on the exam, the multiple-choice answers would most likely include 16 boys and 12 girls AND 12 boys and 16 girls. But 16 boys and 12 girls would be the correct answer choice.

MODULE 4

GENERAL HUMAN ANATOMY

Cell Biology

The cell is the fundamental living unit of all organisms. Tissues are a group of cells with the same function. Tissues are grouped into organs, which carry out a single task. A group of organs that work together to perform coordinated functions are called organ systems.

When many cells are organized to create a multicellular organism, the individual cells are usually specialized to serve specific functions within the organism. The broadest category of these functions is summarized below.

Basic Cell Parts

Organelles
The lowest hierarchical level is the organelles within a cell. Each organelle has a specific function that combines to complete the larger function of the individual cell.

ANIMAL CELL

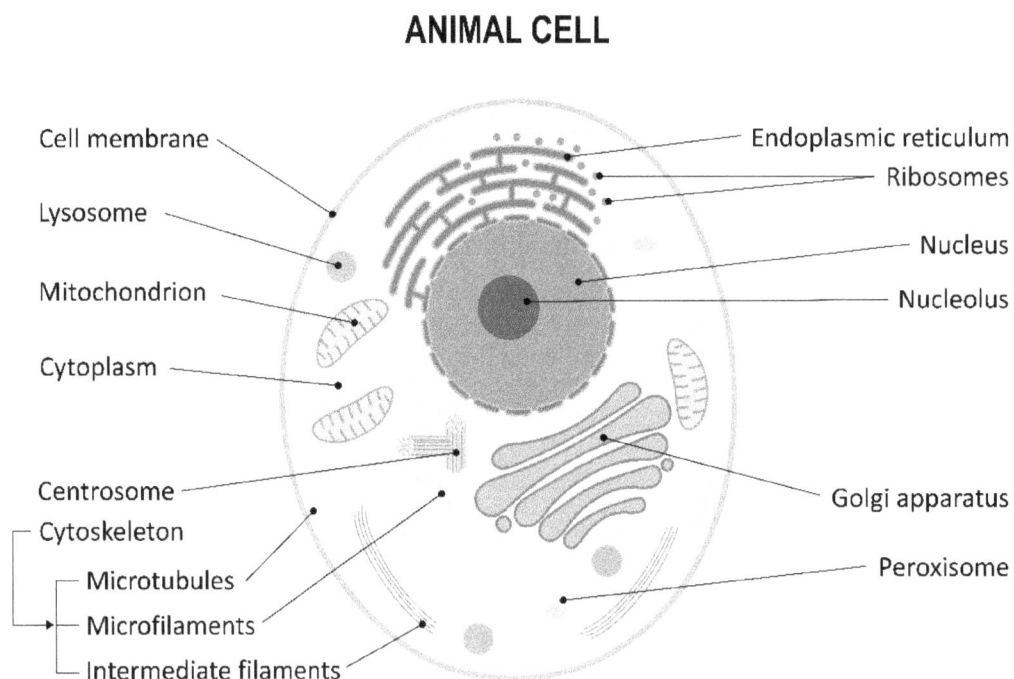

CellMembrane
All cells have a cell membrane that separates the internal contents of the cell from the cell's external environment. This membrane is a bilayer of long, linear phospholipid molecules and hydrocarbon chains that are attached as chain pairs to a phosphate group at one end of the molecule.

The phosphate "heads" of molecules face outward in the outer layer of the membrane bilayer and inward in the inner layer thus forming the exterior and interior surfaces of the cell membrane.

The hydrocarbon chains or "tails" of the molecule align and face inward toward the center of the bilayer.

Cytoskeleton
All human cells contain a cytoskeleton, which is a structural system that provides mechanical support and numerous other intracellular functions.

Cytoplasm
All cells contain cytoplasm. The cytoplasm consists of all the material enclosed within a cell membrane except the material enclosed within the membrane of the cell nucleus (the nuclear membrane). The contents of the nucleus are called the nucleoplasm.

The cytoplasm contains all the cell organelles and the cytosol, which is the gel-like aqueous (watery) solution that fills the interior of the cell. The cytosol consists primarily of water but also contains countless other dissolved chemicals and proteins.

Flagella and Cilia
Flagella and cilia are extensions or attachments of cell membranes. Flagella are long whip-like energetically driven structures that can generate the locomotion of a cell. Cilia are hair-like extensions of the cell membrane. The primary function of cilia is locomotion with independent movement ability of either the cell itself or fluids on the cell surface.

The Nucleus
Nearly all human cells contain a nucleus (mature red blood cells are a notable exception). The nucleus is a membrane-bound structure that contains the DNA of a cell and the nucleolus. The nucleolus is a structure where ribosomes are constructed. There are membrane pores in the nuclear membrane that allow various small molecules to enter—primarily building blocks of DNA and RNA molecules. Nuclear pores also allow messenger RNA (mRNA) molecules and ribosomes to exit from the nucleus into the cell cytoplasm.

Mitochondria
Mitochondria and chloroplasts are complex organelles that possess both inner and outer encapsulating membranes. Mitochondria contain enzymes that extract chemical energy from nutrients (usually glucose molecules) and convert the energy into potential energy stored in high-energy molecules such as ATP or NADH.

Nucleic Acids, Enzymes, and Other Proteins
All cells contain nucleic acids (DNA and RNA molecules). These are the genetic information molecules of the cell. All cells have proteins that can replicate their DNA.

All cells have enzymes that can convert an energy source (such as sunlight or chemicals obtained from the outside environment) into high-energy molecules that can drive other chemical reactions within a cell.

Ribosomes

All cells contain ribosomes. Ribosomes are small spherical complexes of proteins and RNA that can read messenger RNA transcripts and assemble the proteins coded for in the mRNA. The ribosomes assemble these proteins from individual amino acids that are dissolved in the cell cytosol.

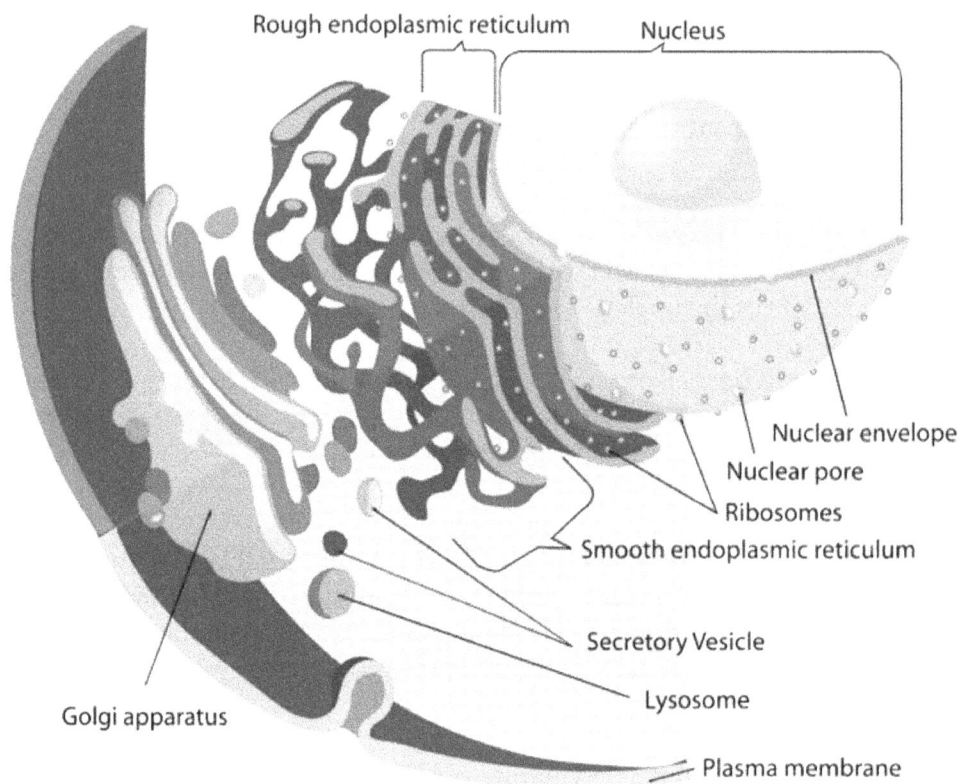

Endoplasmic Reticulum

The rough and smooth endoplasmic reticulum (ER) are a convoluted network of membrane passageways that are connected to the cell nucleus and then continue extensively into the cell cytoplasm.

Smooth ER is involved in the synthesis of lipid compounds and the transport and packaging of various compounds produced by the cell. Smooth ER functions in close coordination with the Golgi apparatus.

Rough ER (RER) is so called because ribosomes are distributed on its membranes, giving a granular or rough appearance to its membranes. Cells that produce large amounts of proteins for transport outside of the cell contain prominent amounts of RER.

The Golgi Apparatus (the Golgi)

The Golgi is a highly folded series of membrane compartments that resembles a stack of pancakes. This apparatus functions with the smooth ER to process, package, and transport a wide variety of products synthesized within the cell.

Most often, these products are packaged into secretory vesicles that are subsequently carried to the cell membrane and then secreted out of the cell into the external environment. In some types of cells, these vesicles remain inside the cell and are involved in the intracellular digestion of phagocytized substances.

Centrosomes

Centrosomes are structures in eukaryotic cells that assemble and organize microtubule structures. These are required for a wide variety of purposes within the cell.

For example, they are central elements in the construction of flagella in human sperm cells and the construction of the spindle apparatus during the mitosis and meiosis stages of cell division.

Anatomical Positions

We've covered the anatomy of words themselves and how to dissect and decipher the prefixes, roots, and suffixes. Now, we'll dive into the anatomy of the human body, how the terminology is used, and what it specifically means in a medical setting.

The anatomy of the human body and the discrete structures within it are described in part by their spatial orientations and relationships. Accordingly, the terms used to describe the relative positions of anatomical structures to one another are also used to describe specific regions of individual anatomical structures. In the definitions of these terms, some overlap exists, and occasionally, they may be used interchangeably. Most of the terms are best understood as pairs of opposing directions or relative locations. Below, we've broken down some of the most common pairs.

Dorsal vs. Ventral: "Dorsal" means toward the back of the body, and "ventral" means toward the front of the body. At the outer body surface, the back of the head, neck, torso, upper and lower legs and arms, the back of the hands and the upper surface and the top (vs. the soles) of the feet are the dorsal exterior surfaces. The most significant dorsal region landmarks are the midline of the spine and the shoulder blades, or left and right scapulae.

The exterior ventral surfaces are the front of the neck, chest, abdomen, pelvis, upper and lower arms and upper and lower legs, and the soles of the feet. Prominent ventral surfaces landmarks include the trachea (or windpipe) in the midline ventral neck, the sternum (or breastbone), the clavicles (or collarbones), the breasts in the ventral thorax (chest), the umbilicus (belly button) in the midline of the ventral abdomen, and the external genitalia in the ventral pelvis. The ventral surfaces of the arms are the surfaces that face upward when the arms are extended straight out with the palms facing upward.

Important dorsal/ventral regions are the dorsal and ventral regions of the spine and spinal cord, and the dorsum of the hands and feet (vs. the palms of the hands and the soles of the feet).

Anterior vs. Posterior: These terms are largely analogous to the terms dorsal and ventral, but are usually the terms preferentially used to describe relative positions. Commonly, one structure is defined as being "anterior to" or "posterior to" another structure rather than saying "dorsal to" or "ventral to." For instance, the esophagus is correctly described as being located "dorsal to" the heart, but the esophagus is usually described as located "posterior to" the heart, and conversely, the heart is located "anterior to" the esophagus.

Notable anatomical regions identified with these terms include the anterior and posterior pituitary (sub regions of the pituitary gland) and the coronary arteries (arteries that supply oxygenated blood to the muscle tissue of the heart); the left anterior descending coronary artery is one example.

Lateral vs. Medial: "Lateral" means to the side or the side(s) of. "Medial" means toward the center or closer to the midline. Lateral and medial are often used in combination with other positional terms to produce a more precisely defined location (e.g., dorsolateral, ventromedial, anterolateral, etc.). The ventromedial hypothalamus is a notable region described in this manner.

One anatomical structure is commonly said to be located lateral or medial to another anatomical structure. Externally, the major lateral regions are the lateral chest regions, the lateral abdominal regions, and the lateral thigh and knee regions. The prominent medial regions of the external surfaces of the body are the medial thigh and medial knee regions.

Inferior vs. Superior: "Superior" means above, over, or toward the top of the head. "Inferior" means below, underneath, or toward the feet. These terms can be combined with other positional terms to identify more precise and discrete anatomical regions, such as the anterior superior ischial spine region of the pelvis.

Rostral vs. Caudal: This pair of descriptive terms is somewhat analogous to the terms superior and inferior. "Rostral" means toward the head or cranium, and "Caudal" means toward the pelvis or the base of the spine. These terms are rarely used comparatively. Instead, the terms are most often used in reference to the regions between the head and pelvis, and are not used to describe the appendages (arms and legs).

Superficial vs. Deep: "Superficial" means shallow, or toward the surface of, or closer to the skin. "Deep" means closer to the center of or farther from the surface of. Superficial body structures include skin, hair, facial structures (e.g., eyes, nose, and mouth), nipples of the breast, the umbilicus, and external genitalia.

The deepest structures in the appendages of the body (arms and legs) include the medullary cavities of the long bones. The deepest regions of the skull are the ventricles at the center of the brain. With respect to the external body surfaces, the heart, digestive organs, kidneys, urinary bladder, and female reproductive organs are deep structures.
When describing relative positions of two or more anatomical structures or locations, the superficial structure or location is closer to the external surface of the body compared to the deep structure or location. For example, the esophagus is posterior to the trachea, but describing the esophagus as being "deep to the trachea" is equally correct.

Proximal vs. Distal: "Proximal" means close or nearer to, and "distal" means distant, farther away from, or toward the end of. The reference point used to define proximal or distal varies depending on what is being described. In the broadest sense, proximal is closer to the center mass of the body within the deep chest or abdomen, while distal is nearer to the tips of the toes or fingers, or the top of the head.

Usually, the reference point is more specific. The aorta, the main artery of the body, for instance, begins at the heart and passes from the chest into the abdomen with a first major branch at the femoral arteries. In this case, the reference point is the heart; the abdominal aorta is proximal to the femoral arteries and distal to the thoracic aorta with respect to proximity to the heart. In the kidneys, small filtering units have structures called renal tubules. The tubule is divided into proximal and distal renal tubule segments. In this case, the reference point is Bowman's capsule, a central region of these small filtering units of the kidney.

Prone vs. Supine: This term pair defines two general positions of the entire human body. The "supine" position occurs when lying flat on one's back, arms and legs are extended (straight, not bent at a joint such as the knee or elbow). The palms of the hands are facing upward, and the heels of the feet are in contact with the ground.

The "prone" position is the reverse of the supine position, occurring when one is lying flat and face down, with the palms of the hands and the tops of the feet in contact with the ground. In the supine position all the ventral anatomical surfaces of the body are facing upward. For the prone position, the reverse is true: all the dorsal surfaces of the body are facing upward (except for the upper arms, where the lateral surfaces face upward).

Cross Sections of the Body

The anatomy of the body can be visually displayed as cross sections, either of the entire body or of body structures (e.g., heart or brain). These sections are defined in relation to a human body being in an upright standing position. Three primary types of cross-sectional views exist: the transverse, the sagittal, and the coronal cross-sectional views. In the following image, all three planes are depicted.

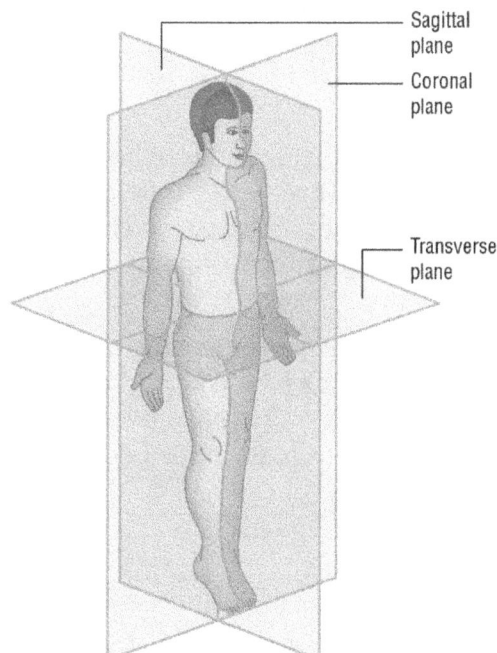

Transverse sections are the views represented as if the body has been sliced cleanly in two on the horizontal plane. A mid-sagittal view will divide the upper body (head, arms, chest, and upper abdomen) and the lower body (lower abdomen, pelvis, and legs) at about the waistline of a typical individual. Cross-sections of the body may occur at any higher or lower horizontal height, moving either toward the top of the head or toward the soles of the feet.

Sagittal sections divide the body into a left and a right side. The mid-sagittal section will divide the body into equal right and left sides, as if a knife had cut cleanly through the body beginning at the top of the head and then proceeded downward through the midline axis of the body. The left section will include the left side of the face, neck, chest, abdomen, and pelvis, and the left leg. The reverse is true for the right section of the body.

Coronal sections are identical to sagittal sections except that the dissection plane is rotated by 90 degrees. This rotation results in a transection of the body that results in a front, ventral, or anterior section and a back, dorsal, or posterior section. A mid-coronal section divides the body into front and back sections at the midline of the body.

Any sagittal section of the body may be obtained by moving the dissection plane parallel and lateral to the mid-sagittal section. Any coronal section of the body may be obtained by moving the dissection plane parallel and lateral to the mid-coronal section.

Anatomical Direction and Motion

Nearly all voluntary movements of the human body occur through muscle contractions that result in motions of bones at joints designed for body movement (notable exceptions are facial expression movements and the motion of the diaphragm during breathing).

Generally, these motions refer to movement of the arms and legs (the appendages), but considerable numbers and types of movements occur along the skull-spine and spine-pelvis axis. The appendages are capable of complex motions, particularly at the shoulder, wrist, and ankle regions.

Flexion vs. Extension: At a joint, the adjacent ends of bones can move in ways that cause the joint angle between the bones to increase (open) or decrease (close) in a simple hinge-like fashion, usually within a maximum range of 180 degrees. The simple, hinge-like joint motion notably occurs at the elbow and knee joints, but most joints can produce this motion.

Extension is the increase in the angle of the joint (opening or extending out). Flexion is the opposite or reverse of extension. Flexion at a joint causes the bones at the joint to move in a manner that causes the joint angle to decrease (close or bend inward). In the following image, flexion and extension movements at various parts of the body are depicted.

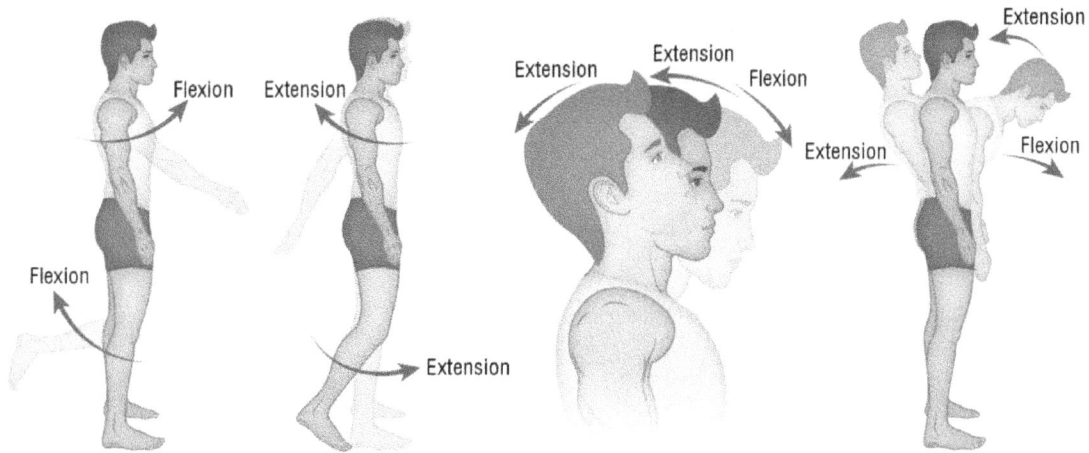

Abduction vs. Adduction: This type of motion is almost always in reference to motion of the upper arms at the shoulder joints and the upper legs at the hip joints. Abduction results in movement of the arms or legs outward, away from the midlines of the body. Adduction, the reverse of the motion of abduction, involves the movement of arms or legs toward the midlines of the body. Below, the image depicts these motions at the shoulder joint.

Medial Rotation vs. Lateral Rotation: "Lateral" means away from the midline, and "medial" means toward the midline. Any rotation toward the midline is a medial rotation, and any rotation away from the midline is a lateral rotation. In the following image, these motions are depicted.

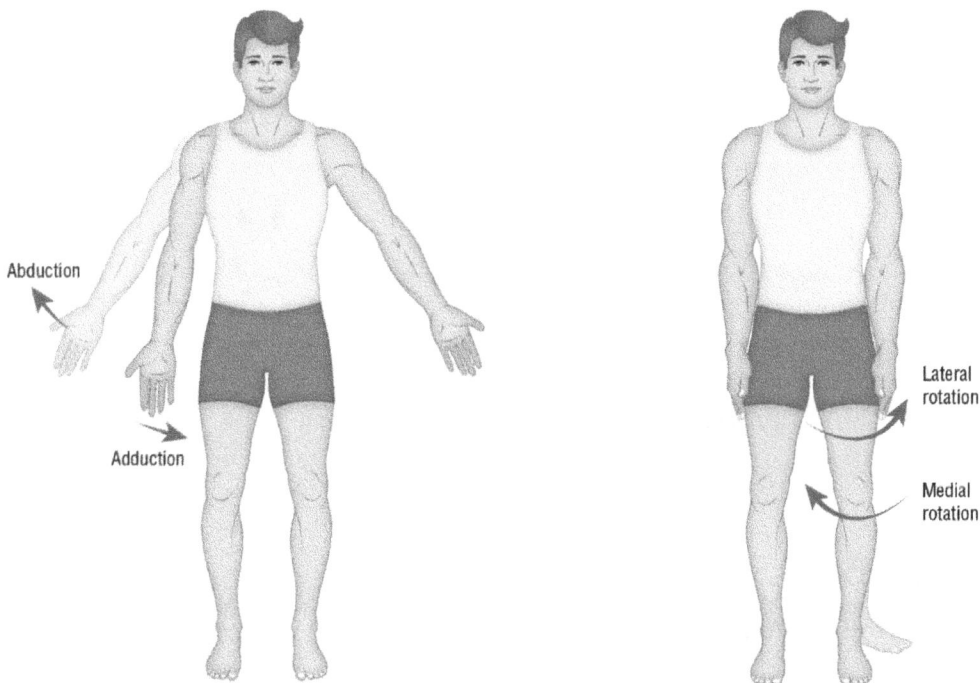

Dorsiflexion vs. Plantar Flexion: These movements involve the entire foot in relation to the ankle. "Dorsiflexion" means flexing the foot upward or superiorly. Conversely, "plantar flexion" means pointing the foot downward or inferiorly. In the following image, these motions are depicted.

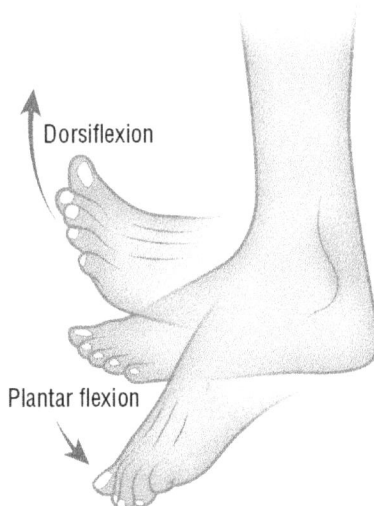

Pronation vs. Supination: In plain English terms, "prone" means being face down, and supine means being face up. When related to the hand, pronation simply means palm down and supination means palm up. Easy enough, right? But the identifying pronation and supination of the ankle can cause confusion with lateral and medial rotations. Pronation of the ankle to foot means a shift "inward" occurs, and supination of the ankle means a shift or angle where the weight is shifted to the outside the ankle. In the following image, the pronation and supination of the ankle on the RIGHT foot are depicted.

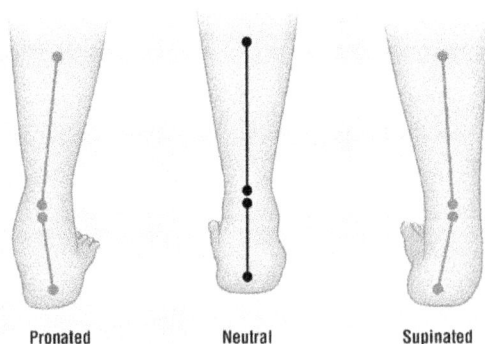

Regions of the Body

(Note: All regions in the lists are in order of superior to inferior.)

Head Regions
The cranial region encompasses the upper part of the head, while the facial region encompasses the lower half of the head, beginning below the ears.

- **Cephalic region:** the entire head region
- **Occipital region:** back of the head
- **Frontal region:** forehead
- **Orbital or ocular region:** eyes
- **Buccal region:** cheeks
- **Auricle or otic region:** ears
- **Nasal region:** nose
- **Oral region:** mouth
- **Mental region:** chin
- **Cervical region:** neck

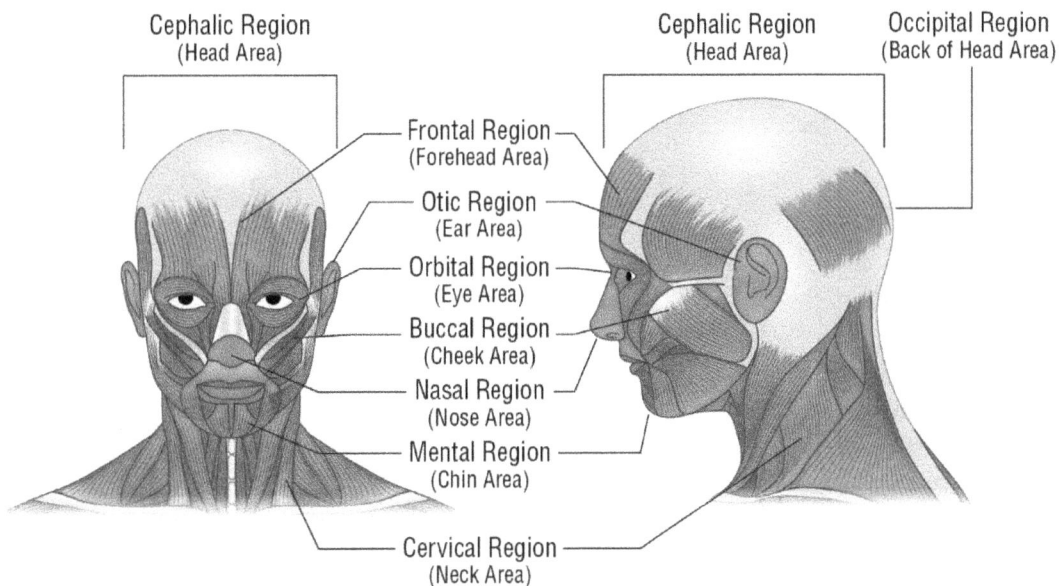

Trunk Regions

- **Thoracic region:** the chest
- **Mammary region:** each breast
- **Sternal region:** the sternum
- **Abdominal region:** the stomach area
- **Umbilicus, or naval region:** the area located at the center of the abdomen.
- **Coxal region:** the belt line
- **Pubic region:** the area above the genitals
- **Cervical region:** the neck
- **Scapular region:** the scapulae and the area around
- **Dorsal region:** the upper back
- **Lumbar region:** the lower back
- **Sacral region:** the end of the spine, directly above the buttocks
- **Acromial region:** the shoulder
- **Brachial region:** the upper arm
- **Olecranal region:** the back of the elbow
- **Antebrachial region:** the back of the arm
- **Manual or manus region:** the back of the hand

Mammary Region
(Breast Area)

Acromial Region
(Shoulder Area)

Vertebral Region
(Spine Area)

Cervical Region
(Neck Area)

Scapular Region
(Shoulder Blade Area)

Axillary Region
(Armpit Area)

Sternal Region
(Breast Bone)

Brachial Region
(Upper Arm Area)

Abdominal Region
(Stomach Area)

Thoracic Region
(Chest Area)

Axillary Region
(Armpit Area)

Umbilicus Region
(Belly Button Area)

Lumbar Region
(Lower Back Area)

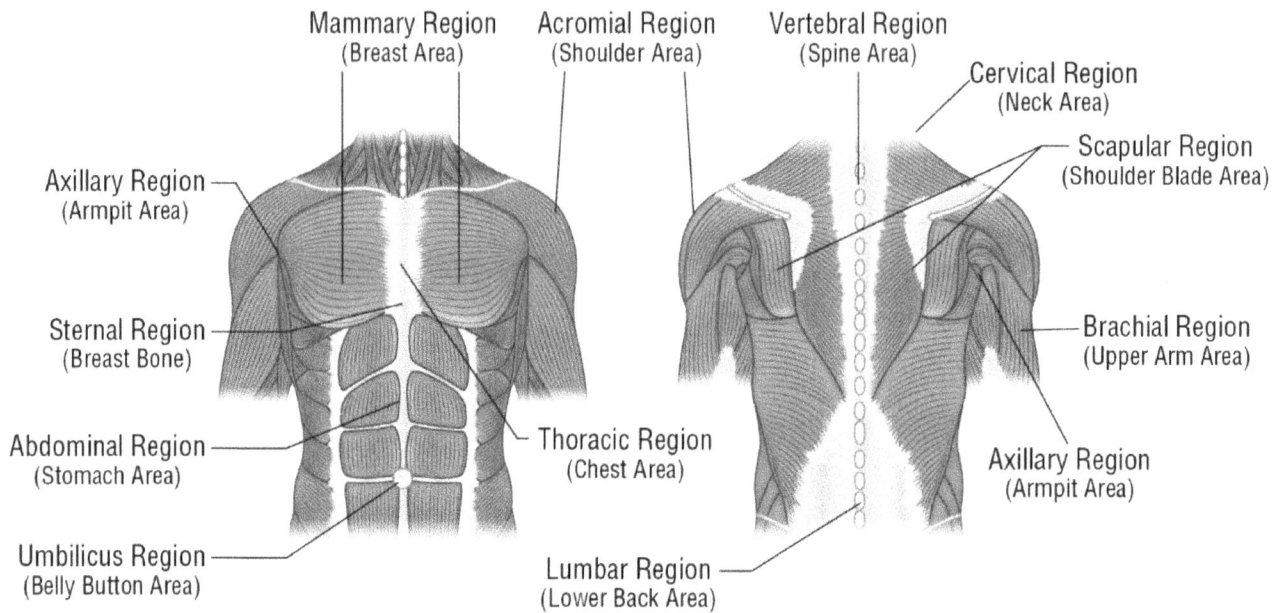

Pelvic and Leg Regions

- **Inguinal or groin region:** between the legs and the genitals
- **Pubic region:** the genitals and surrounding areas
- **Gluteal region:** the buttocks
- **Femoral region:** the thigh
- **Popliteal region:** the back of the knee
- **Sural region:** the back of the lower leg
- **Lumbar region:** the lower back, vertebrae L1 through L5
- **Sacral region:** the portion of spine between lower back and tailbone
- **Coxal region:** the lateral side of hips

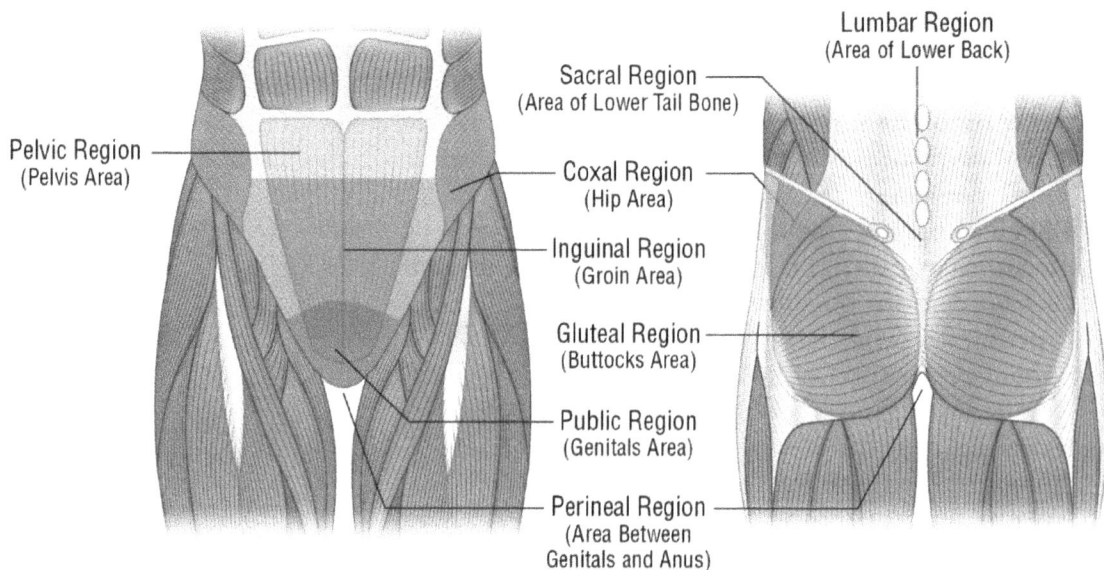

Pelvic Region
(Pelvis Area)

Sacral Region
(Area of Lower Tail Bone)

Lumbar Region
(Area of Lower Back)

Coxal Region
(Hip Area)

Inguinal Region
(Groin Area)

Gluteal Region
(Buttocks Area)

Public Region
(Genitals Area)

Perineal Region
(Area Between
Genitals and Anus)

Upper Limb Regions

- **Axillary region:** the armpit
- **Brachial region:** the upper arm
- **Antecubital region:** the front of the elbow
- **Antebrachial region:** the forearm
- **Acromial region:** the shoulder
- **Scapular region:** the upper thoracic region on the dorsal surface of the rib cage
- **Olecranal region:** the back of the elbow

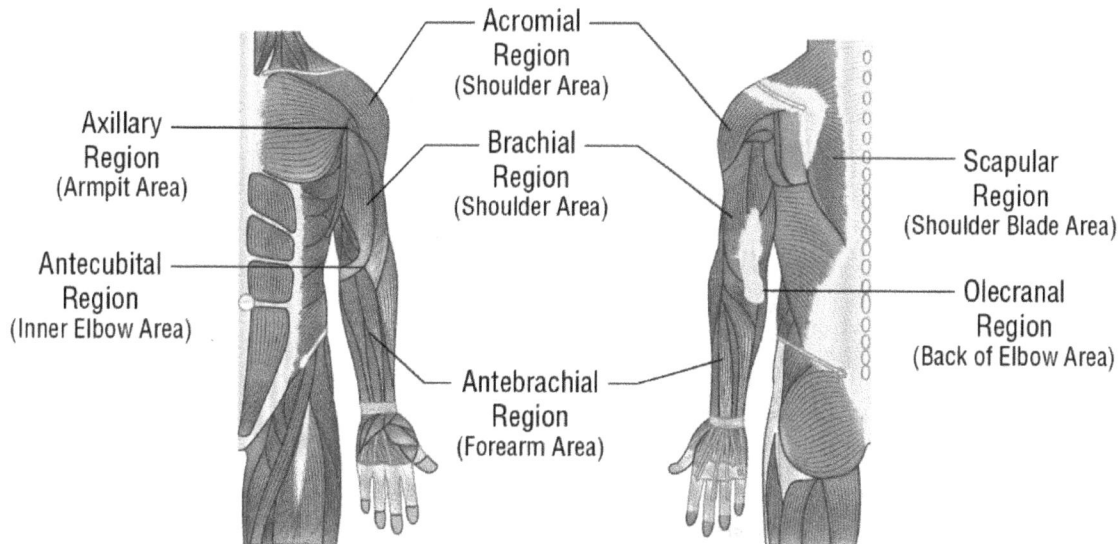

Hand and Wrist Regions

- **Carpal region:** the wrist
- **Palmar region:** the palm
- **Digital/phalangeal region:** the fingers
- **Pollex region:** the thumb
- **Manus region:** the hand area

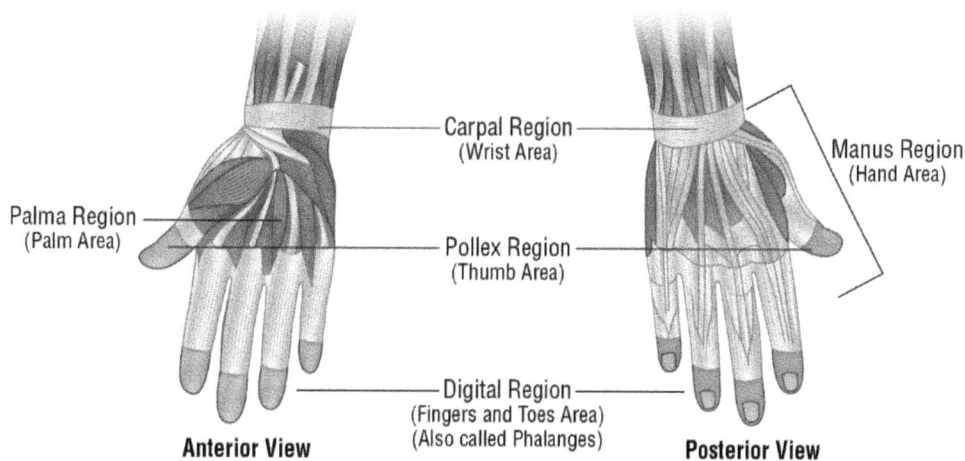

Leg Regions

- **Femoral region:** the thigh
- **Patellar region:** the knee
- **Crural region:** the shin area of the leg
- **Fibular region:** the outside of the lower leg
- **Gluteal region:** the buttocks
- **Popliteal region:** the back of the knee
- **Sural region:** the back of the lower leg

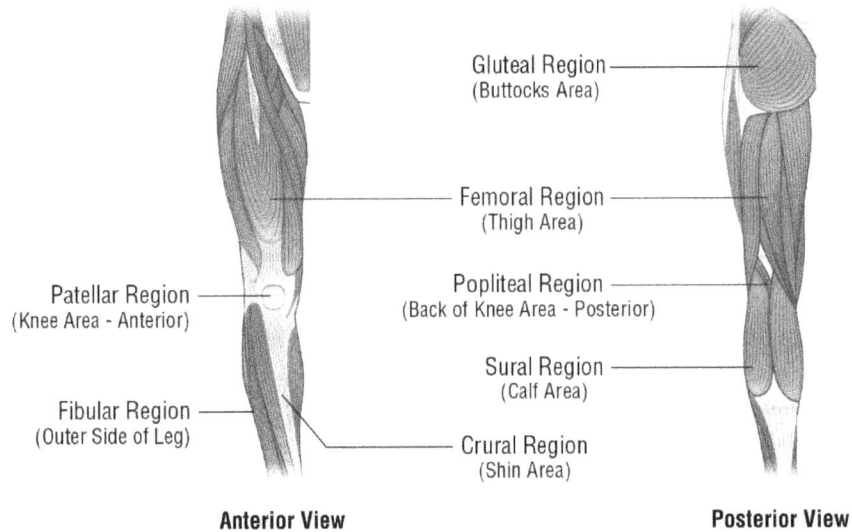

Gluteal Region
(Buttocks Area)

Femoral Region
(Thigh Area)

Patellar Region
(Knee Area - Anterior)

Popliteal Region
(Back of Knee Area - Posterior)

Sural Region
(Calf Area)

Fibular Region
(Outer Side of Leg)

Crural Region
(Shin Area)

Anterior View

Posterior View

Feet and Ankle Regions

- **Tarsal region:** the ankle
- **Pedal region:** the foot
- **Digital/phalangeal region:** the toes
- **Hallux:** the "big" toe
- **Calcaneal region:** the heel
- **Plantar region:** the sole of the foot

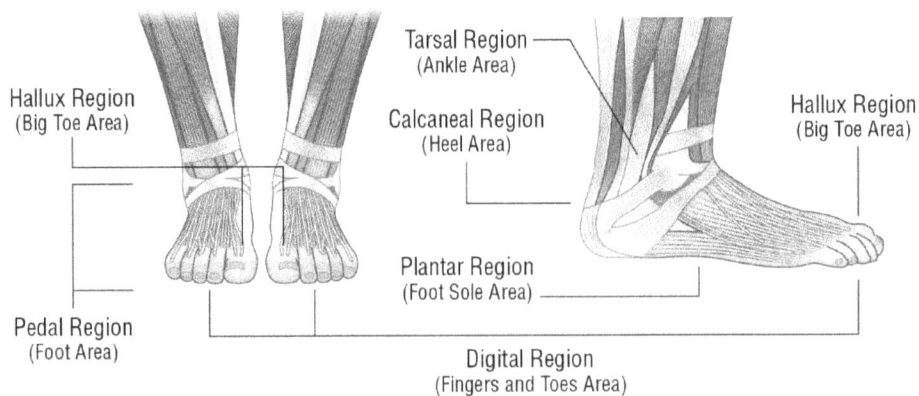

Hallux Region
(Big Toe Area)

Tarsal Region
(Ankle Area)

Calcaneal Region
(Heel Area)

Hallux Region
(Big Toe Area)

Pedal Region
(Foot Area)

Plantar Region
(Foot Sole Area)

Digital Region
(Fingers and Toes Area)

Abdominal Regions

Specific to the abdominal area, sub-regions exist within this area. This important area of the body includes additional details due to the internal organs in and around the abdomen.

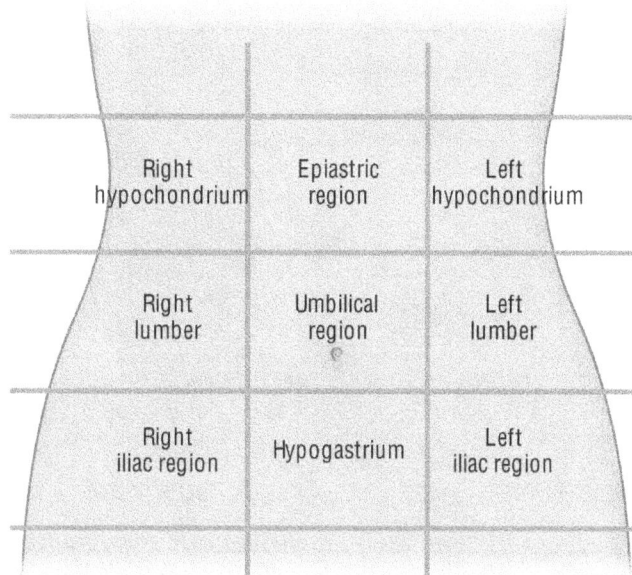

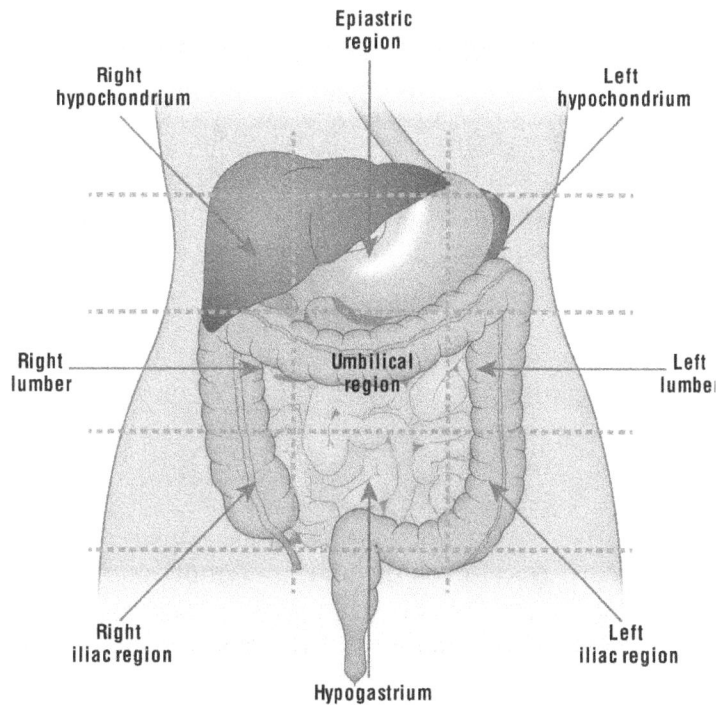

Cavities of the Body

Two major cavities exist in the human body: the **dorsal** and the **ventral** body cavities.

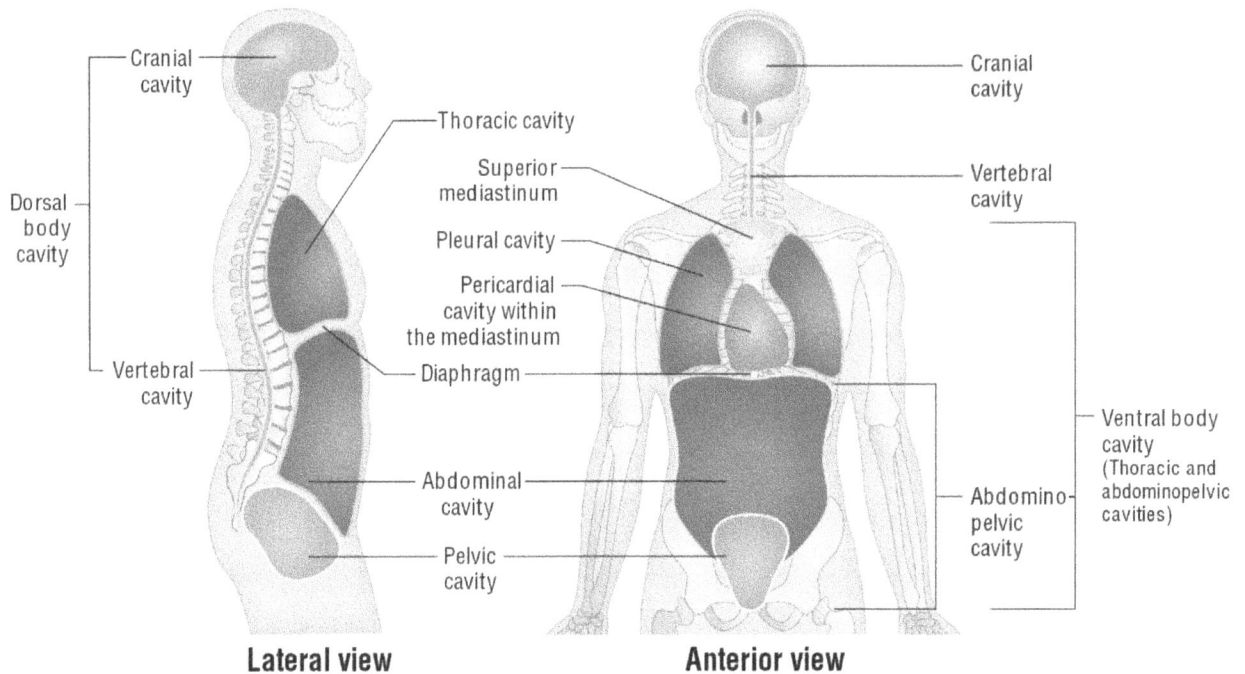

Lateral view   Anterior view

The Dorsal Cavity

The dorsal cavity is a body cavity located on the posterior (back) side of the human body. The ventral cavity is located on the anterior (front) side of the body. These cavities are almost completely sealed off from the external environment by surrounding bone and/or muscle and other connective tissue.

The dorsal cavity is subdivided into two main cavities: the cranial cavity and the vertebral or spinal cavity. The cranial cavity sits within the skull and encloses the brain, while the vertebral cavity sits within the spinal column and encloses the spinal cord. The dorsal cavity is lined with a layer of connective tissue called the meninges, which helps protect the delicate structures inside. It is also filled with cerebrospinal fluid, which acts as a cushion for the brain and spinal cord.

The dorsal cavity plays a crucial role in protecting and supporting the central nervous system, which is responsible for coordinating and controlling many of the body's functions. Any damage or injury to this area can result in serious consequences, including paralysis, loss of sensation, and even death.

The Ventral Cavity

The ventral cavity is a body cavity located on the anterior (front) side of the human body. The ventral cavity is larger and more complex than the dorsal cavity. It is enclosed by the inner walls of the thorax (i.e., thoracic muscles, ribs sternum, and thoracic vertebrae); the inner surfaces of the ventral, lateral, and dorsal abdominal wall muscles; and the inner surface bones and associated muscles of the pelvis.

The ventral cavity is divided into an upper cavity (thoracic cavity) and a lower cavity (abdominopelvic cavity) by a transverse dome-shaped muscle, the diaphragm. The thoracic cavity sits within the chest and contains the heart, lungs, and other structures of the respiratory and cardiovascular systems. The abdominopelvic cavity sits within the abdomen and pelvis and contains the digestive organs, reproductive organs, urinary system, and other structures.

The ventral cavity is lined with a thin layer of connective tissue called the serous membrane, which helps to protect and support the organs inside. This membrane produces a lubricating fluid that allows the organs to move against each other without causing friction or damage.

The ventral cavity plays a crucial role in maintaining the health and well-being of the body by containing and protecting many vital organs and systems. Any damage or injury to this area can have serious consequences, including respiratory failure, heart failure, organ failure, and other life-threatening conditions.

Skeletal System

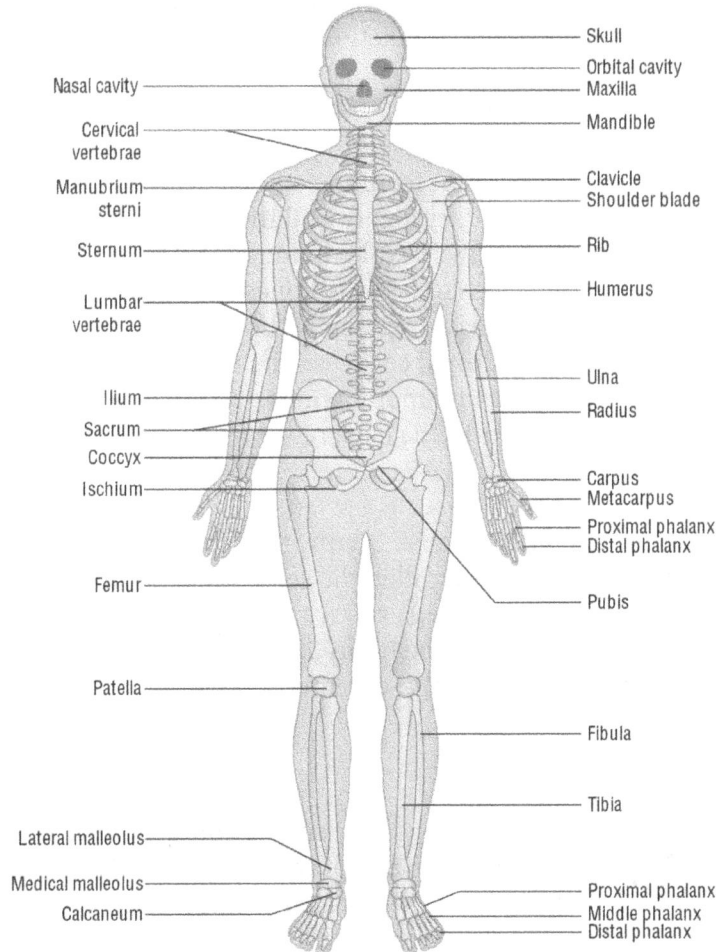

The Axial Skeleton
The axial skeleton consists of the skull bones and the spinal column, ribs, and sternum.

The Spine

In many respects, the spine is the fundamental structure of the human body. The spine consists of individual bones known as vertebrae arranged linearly to form a continuous, flexible, bony column.

The Vertebral Canal

The surfaces and underlying sub-regions of the spine and the individual vertebrae are the dorsal, ventral, lateral, and central regions. The central vertebral-spinal region is hollow and forms the vertebral canal. The vertebral canal contains the spinal cord of the central nervous system. The spinal cord begins as the distal extension of the brainstem and enters the vertebral canal through the foramen magnum, a large opening in the posterior base of the skull.

The spinal cord does not extend for the entire length of the vertebral canal. Instead, the spinal cord terminates distally (or caudally) at the junction level of the first and second lumbar vertebrae. The dorsal and ventral spinal nerve roots that combine to form the 31 sets of spinal nerves of the somatic or voluntary nervous system emerge from the spinal cord at the dorsolateral and ventrolateral intervertebral junctions in the cervical, thoracic, and lumbar spinal regions.

The Skull

The skull consists of tightly fused bones that form the cranial vault and the facial bones. The cranial vault contains the brain and pituitary gland, and the facial bones include the upper jaw bones (i.e., the maxillae) and the lower jaw (i.e., the mandible). The mandible is the only moveable bone of the skull. The inner surfaces of the bones that form the cranial cavity (cranial vault) correspond to the adjacent underlying regions of the cerebral cortex of the brain. The frontal bone overlies the left and right frontal cortices. The midline parietal bones overlie the parietal cortices. The laterally positioned temporal bones overlie the temporal cortices and the posteriorly positioned occipital bones form the back of the skull and overlie the occipital cortices.

The cerebellum and brainstem of the brain also occupy the occipital region of the cranial cavity at the base of the brain. A small depression called the sella turcica is in the media anterior inner surface of the base of the skull. Within the sella turcica, the pituitary gland is partially contained. The 12 pairs of cranial nerves emerge from the brain through various openings in the skull. Together with the 31 pairs of spinal nerves, these cranial nerves and spinal nerves form the somatic nervous system.

The Thoracic Skeleton

The thoracic (chest and upper back) skeleton comprises the thoracic vertebrae, 12 sets of ribs, the sternum (breastbone), and the medial sections of the clavicles (collarbones). The ribs connect to the lateral surfaces of the thoracic vertebrae and then extend laterally to form the dorsal thorax. Next, the ribs first curve anteriorly to form the lateral walls of the thorax and then curve medially, continuing to medially articulate with the sternum. The sternum is in the midline of the anterior (ventral) wall of the thorax. The medial ends of the clavicles articulate to the superolateral angles of the sternum.

The thoracic skeleton creates a cage-like structural framework. When the associated muscles and connective tissues are added to this framework, an interior thoracic cavity is created. This cavity contains the heart, lungs, and several other important anatomical structures. The floor of the thoracic cavity is formed via a single dome-shaped sheet of muscle, the diaphragm.

The Appendicular Skeleton

The upper appendicular (attached) skeleton consists of the bones of the shoulder girdles, arms, wrists, hands, and fingers. The shoulder girdles are formed by the clavicles and the scapulae. The medial ends of the clavicles articulate with the superolateral angles of the sternum. This connection is the only direct bony connection of the upper appendicular skeleton to the axial skeleton. The distal end of the scapula and a lateral extension of the clavicle (the acromion) articulate distally and, along with the proximal end of the humerus, form the bony elements of the rotator cuff, the complex shoulder joint.

The distal end of the long bone of the upper arm (the humerus) forms the elbow joint with the proximal ends of the two lower arm bones, the radius and the ulna. The distal ends of the radius and the ulna articulate with several of the wrist bones (the carpals) to form the complex wrist joint. The carpals articulate with the metacarpal bones of the hand. The distal ends of the metacarpals articulate with the bones of the fingers, the phalanges.

The lower appendicular skeleton consists of the bones of the pelvis (except for the sacrum, which is part of the axial skeleton), and the bones of the legs, ankles, feet, and toes. The left and right portions of the bony pelvis are fused to the axial skeleton medially at the lateral edges of the sacrum. The proximal end or "head" of the femur fits into a semicircular depression of the inferolateral borders in the bones of the pelvis. Along with associated muscles and connective tissues, they form the ball and socket joint of the hip. The distal end of the femur articulates with the proximal ends of the tibia and fibula at the knee joint. The distal ends of the tibia and fibula articulate with several tarsal bones to form the complex ankle joint. Tarsal bones in the ankle region articulate with proximal ends of metatarsal bones in the foot. Distal ends of metatarsal bones articulate with the bones of the toes, the phalanges.

Skeletal Muscles

The skeletal structure of the body is mostly covered by layers of muscles. The anterior surface of the tibiae or shins and the wrists, ankles, cranium, and dorsal surface of the spine the ribs and the sternum and the clavicles have comparatively thin or extremely thin overlying layers of muscles. Major skeletal muscle groups include the following:

- Upper arm muscles, the biceps and triceps
- Deltoid muscles of the shoulders
- Large muscles of the anterior chest, the pectoralis major muscles
- Large lateral muscles of the back, the latissimus dorsi
- Large muscles of the pelvis (hips), the gluteal muscles
- Anterior muscles of the upper leg, the quadriceps
- Large muscles of the posterior upper leg, the hamstrings
- Largest muscles of the lower leg, the gastrocnemius (calf) muscles

Synovial Joints

The adult human body has 206 major bones and many other smaller bones called sesamoid bones. Nearly all the major bones form articulations with adjacent bones (the patellae and the hyoid bone are notable exceptions). The widest range of motion occurs at synovial joints, which consist of a fibrous joint capsule that encloses the ends of two articulating bones. Ligaments between the articulating bone ends surround the exterior of the fibrous capsule and bind together the joint. The ends of the bones within the joint capsule are covered by pads of cartilage called articular cartilage, which provides mechanical protection to the ends of the bone; the pads are also slippery, allowing for ease of movement for bones within the synovial capsule.

Synovial Fluid

The interior surfaces of the synovial capsule are covered with specialized connective tissue that forms a synovial membrane. Fibroblasts within the synovial membrane secrete components of synovial fluid. These contributions to synovial fluid consist of long-chain sugar polymer molecules called hyaluronic acid and another molecule called lubrin. Both hyaluronic acid and lubrin provide lubrication to the joint structures within the synovial capsule. Additional elements of synovial fluid include water and dissolved oxygen and nutrients that diffuse from the capillaries within the synovial capsule.

Fibrous Joints and Sutures

Compared to synovial joints, fibrous joints are much simpler in structure. Fibrous joints consist of varying proportions of cartilage and/or collagen and elastic fibers; such joints allow very limited mobility. Fibrous joints are typically located between the edges of two adjacent bones, forming a seam between the bone borders like the mortar between bricks or masonry stones. Joint movement is limited to hinge-like flexion and extension at the fibrous seam between adjacent bone edges. The sternomanubrial joint and the sacroiliac joints are fibrous joints that have a moderated amount of flexibility. Suture joints, which have very little fibrous content and almost no range of motion, are the strongest joints and are analogous to seam welds between adjacent bone edges. The skull bones (except for the mandible) articulate with suture joints.

Bone Classification by Shape

The bones of the human body can be classified by shape into one of five general categories: long bones, short bones, flat bones, irregular bones, and sesamoid bones.

Long Bones

Long bones have a tubular shape with a long axis several times greater than a cross-sectional diameter. The longest section of long bones is the bone shaft or diaphysis. The ends of long bones are called epiphyses. They are located at either end of the shaft (diaphysis) and have expanded and often complex geometries beautifully designed to allow the types of motion that occur when the long bones articulate with adjacent epiphyses within a synovial joint. The major bones of the upper and lower arms and legs (the humerus, femur, radius, ulna, tibia, and fibula) are long bones. The phalanges (finger and toe bones) and the clavicles (collarbones) are also long bones. Most long bones have medullary cavities and are a major site of erythropoiesis.

Epiphyseal plates

The cartilaginous epiphyseal plates of the upper and lower extremities are a primary site for growth resulting in increased bone length. The adult height of an individual is determined by the amount of growth that occurs at the epiphyseal plates of these long bones and in the vertebrae of the spine. When the cartilage of the epiphyseal plates of long bones and vertebrae become fully mineralized into bone, no further increase in height can occur in an individual. The closure of these epiphyseal plates is a primary indication that an individual has reach adulthood.

Short Bones
Short bones have variable shapes, often cuboidal with dimensions of roughly equivalent length, width, and height.

The Wrist and Ankle Bones
The bones of the wrists and ankles (metacarpals and the metatarsals, respectively) and the middle bones of the hands and feet (the carpals and tarsals, respectively) are short bones. Each hand has eight carpal bones; each foot has seven tarsal bones. These bones are closely packed and have multiple interfaces with adjacent carpals or tarsals. At the ankle and wrist, for example, some tarsal or carpal bones articulate with metacarpals or metatarsals.

Metacarpals and metatarsals also articulate with adjacent long bone epiphyses of the radius and ulna, or the tibia and fibula. In addition, some tarsals and carpals articulate with epiphyses of phalanges in the hands to form the "knuckle" joints.

Due to multiple articulations with adjacent bones, carpals, metacarpals, tarsals, and metatarsals tend to have complex surface geometry and irregular overall three-dimensional shapes. These bones are designed to function as a group of subunits that allow for very complex and subtle rearrangements of the contours of the palms of the hands and soles of the feet. These continuous alterations in the contours of the palms and soles are required particularly when walking on uneven surfaces or when grasping and manipulating objects. While these multi-bone systems allow for remarkable adaptability during walking and running activities and exceptional dexterity of the hands, even seemingly minor injuries to an individual ankle or wrist bone can destabilize the entire wrist or ankle system, leading to severe impairment of function.

Irregular Bones
As a general category, irregular bones have complex three dimensional geometries. The range of irregularity varies greatly, however. By far the most irregular bones are two of the skull bones, the vomer and the sphenoid bones. These bones have complex three-dimensional overall and local structures consisting of bony walls, partitions, shelves, protuberances, compartments, passageways, and openings that accommodate a variety of contents. For example, the sphenoid is particularly designed for a broad range of structural and functional purposes. Many anatomists have opined that the sphenoid is a bone whose structure is so complex that "it defies description." Several other bones of the cranium and the face are irregular bones or have irregular regions. For example, the ethmoid, mastoid, and maxillary bones. The bones of the pelvis (the ilium, ischium pubis, and sacroiliac bones) are also irregular bones.

The bones of the middle ear—the incus, malleus, and stapes (anvil, hammer, and stirrup)—are irregular in the sense of not having a simple shape, but they each have a very specific shape that allows them to function together as a unit. These three middle ear bones form a linked bony mechanical system that transduces sound waves arriving at the tympanum (eardrum) in the outer ear canal to fluid waves within the canals of the inner ear.

The Spinal Vertebrae

The individual vertebrae of the spine are classified as irregular bones but are comparable in structure and in articulations with adjacent vertebrae to the short bones of the ankle and wrists. The "irregularity" of the vertebrae consists of their vertebral foramen, left and right transverse processes, and dorsal midline single spinous processes.

The central canal of a vertebra is a tubular passage that aligns with the vertebral foramen of adjacent vertebrae. In the spine, these central canals form a continuous tube called the spinal canal. The spinal cord is contained within the spinal canal. The dorsal spinous process of a vertebra is a single long projection of the dorsal surface of a vertebra. The tips of spinous processes can, as a group, be seen and felt as the longitudinal arrangement of bumps that define the location of spine underlying the skin in the midline of the dorsal surface of the torso.

These additional features of a vertebrae are very regular and differ slightly but regularly between vertebrae, primarily in the length and thickness of the spinous processes in the cervical, thoracic, and lumbar sections of the spine and in the mass of the main body of the vertebrae, from smallest at the first cervical vertebrae (Cl and C2) to largest at the most caudal lumbar vertebrae (L4 and LS). The vertebrae function as subunits of the overall spine. Although the range of motion between adjacent vertebrae is limited, when coordinated along the length of the spine, these motions can cumulatively produce a remarkable range of bending and twisting spinal movements. As a result, the human body can adopt a vast number of specific postures in three dimensions and coordinate changing postures to create complex, dynamic choreographies of continuous body movements.

Intervertebral Discs

A unique feature of the spinal vertebrae is the intervertebral discs. These are shock-absorbing structures consisting of a tough outer fibrous capsule that encases a gel-like substance called the nucleus pulposus. The discs act as a fibrocartilaginous joint between adjacent vertebrae.

Flat Bones and Sesamoid Bones

Flat bones are thin with a high surface area. They have an outer layer of cortical bone and a thin central layer of trabecular bone. In the cranium, most bones are flat bones. Flat bones have a primary protective function—particularly the protection of the brain—and have little if any role in erythropoiesis.

On the other hand, sesamoid bones are formed with muscle tendons and have a mechanical function related to the amount of leverage that a muscle can generate on an attached bone. Most sesamoid bones are relatively small; a notable exception is the patella, which is located anterior to the synovial joint of the knee.

Bone and Joint Disorders

Many diseases and other pathological conditions of bones and joints are notable for the frequency and/or severity in humans. Joint disorders are so common that one medical specialty—rheumatology—focuses exclusively on the diagnosis and treatment of these conditions.

Disorders of the Synovial Joints

The two most important synovial joint disorders are rheumatoid arthritis and osteoarthritis. Rheumatoid arthritis is an autoimmune disorder that attacks synovial joints, resulting in progressive, painful disfigurement and loss of function in joints throughout the body. Modern treatment involves monoclonal antibodies and other immunological therapies that can prevent the progression of the disease if the condition is diagnosed in its early stages.

Osteoarthritis is a result of the wear-and-tear damage to the articular cartilage in synovial joints. The mechanical forces acting on joints over decades of physical activity eventually wear away the cartilage in synovial joints, resulting in the loss of the protection the cartilage provides to underlying bone. The unprotected articulating bones grind against each other and cause severe pain and eventually loss of function. Most middle-aged to elderly males have some degree of osteoarthritis. The condition is most serious when the knee and hip joints are involved. In the United States, damage due to osteoarthritis is the number one reason for hip and knee replacements.

Infection, Inflammation, and Physical Injury

Synovial fluid is susceptible to accumulations of uric acid crystals, resulting in the excruciatingly painful inflammatory condition known as gout. Bacteria that enter the bloodstream often settle in synovial joints and cause infection or septic arthritis. Many viral and autoimmune diseases also attack synovial joints and cause sterile or aseptic arthritis. The joints are common sites of severe physical injuries, including ligament and tendon tears and ruptures, and joint sprains and dislocations. The deep tendon reflexes are a specialized local neuromuscular reflex that has evolved to limit such injuries.

A particularly significant class of joint disorders are those of the intervertebral discs. Herniated vertebral discs usually occur due to awkward and/or strenuous lifting and twisting activities. Degenerative disc disease (DJD) is a progressive deterioration of the intervertebral discs. Both conditions are very common; in fact, lower back pain associated with these disorders is one of the leading causes people seek medical attention.

Disorders of the Bone

Osteoporosis is the most common serious bone disorder and most commonly occurs in postmenopausal women. The condition is a loss of bone density and disruption of bone structure primarily due to inadequate calcium content. People with osteoporosis are at greatly increased risk of bone fractures, most seriously fractures of the pelvic bones or the femur. Estrogen replacement therapy in postmenopausal women can greatly reduce the incidence of osteoporosis, but this form of treatment must be balanced against the risks of the therapy, including increased risk of cardiovascular disease. Regular physical activity and weight-bearing exercise reduces the risk of osteoporosis.

Although rare in developed countries, rickets is a common bone disorder elsewhere in the world. The disorder is caused by vitamin D deficiency. If left untreated, rickets results in deterioration of bone tissue; bones become increasingly brittle and fracture easily. Osteomalacia (vitamin D-resistant rickets), which causes a disease that resembles rickets, leads to not only bone weakness but also abnormal bone formation. The condition is the result of a defect in vitamin D metabolism.

Paget's disease is characterized by abnormal structural development, including enlargement and thickening of bones that are brittle and easily broken. The condition results from abnormalities of osteoblast and osteoclast functions.

Perthes' disease, which occurs primarily in children, is a disorder of the femoral head of the tibia at the ball-and-socket joint of the hip. The condition is caused by inadequate blood supply to the femoral head and results in pain and an impaired ability to walk or run.

Osteogenesis imperfecta (brittle bone disease) is an autosomal dominant genetic disorder caused by defects in the enzymes involved in collagen production. The result is brittle bones that fracture easily.

Acromegaly is a condition caused by an excess of growth hormone and continued growth hormone production after individuals have completed puberty. Most commonly, the abnormal growth hormone production is due to a benign tumor of the pituitary gland. If left untreated, acromegaly results in progressive enlargement of the facial, hand, and feet bones. This process can continue over the entire life of an individual.

Bone Marrow Disorders

Bone marrow suppression and bone marrow failure occur as a relatively common and often life-threatening condition. The hematopoietic cells of bone marrow are particularly sensitive to a wide variety of drugs, including antibiotics, anti-inflammatories, anti-cancer drugs, and many other commonly used drugs. Bone marrow cells are also easily damaged by environmental toxins, such as cleaning agents, heavy metals, and insecticides and herbicides. In addition, bone marrow is very vulnerable to radiation-induced injuries from medical and dental x-ray imagery and from artificial and naturally occurring radioactive compounds in the environment.

As these conditions worsen and persist, the granulocytes and lymphocyte cell production drop or even cease, resulting in profound impairment of the immune system. Impaired red cell production results in severe anemia, and impaired platelet production results in spontaneous hemorrhages. All these effects can be rapidly fatal if not corrected promptly. Most blood cancers, including leukemias and lymphomas, originate from abnormal cells in the bone marrow.

Muscular System

Most of the body skeletal structure body is covered by layers of muscles. Areas of the body that have comparatively thin or extremely thin overlying layers of muscles include: the anterior surface of the tibiae or shins; the wrists, ankles, cranium, and dorsal surface of the spine; the ribs and the sternum; and the clavicles.

Orbicularis oculi — Sternocleidomastoid

Orbicularis oris — Trapezius

Deltoid

Pectoralis major

Latissimus dorsi — Biceps

Serratus anterior — Brachialis

Brachioradialis

Rectus abdomin — Iliopsoas

External oblique —

Tensor — Sartorius

fasciae latae — Gracilis

Rectus femoris

Vastus lateralis

Vastus medialis

Peroneus longus

Tibialis anterior

Gastrocnemius — Extensor

digitorum longus

Soleus

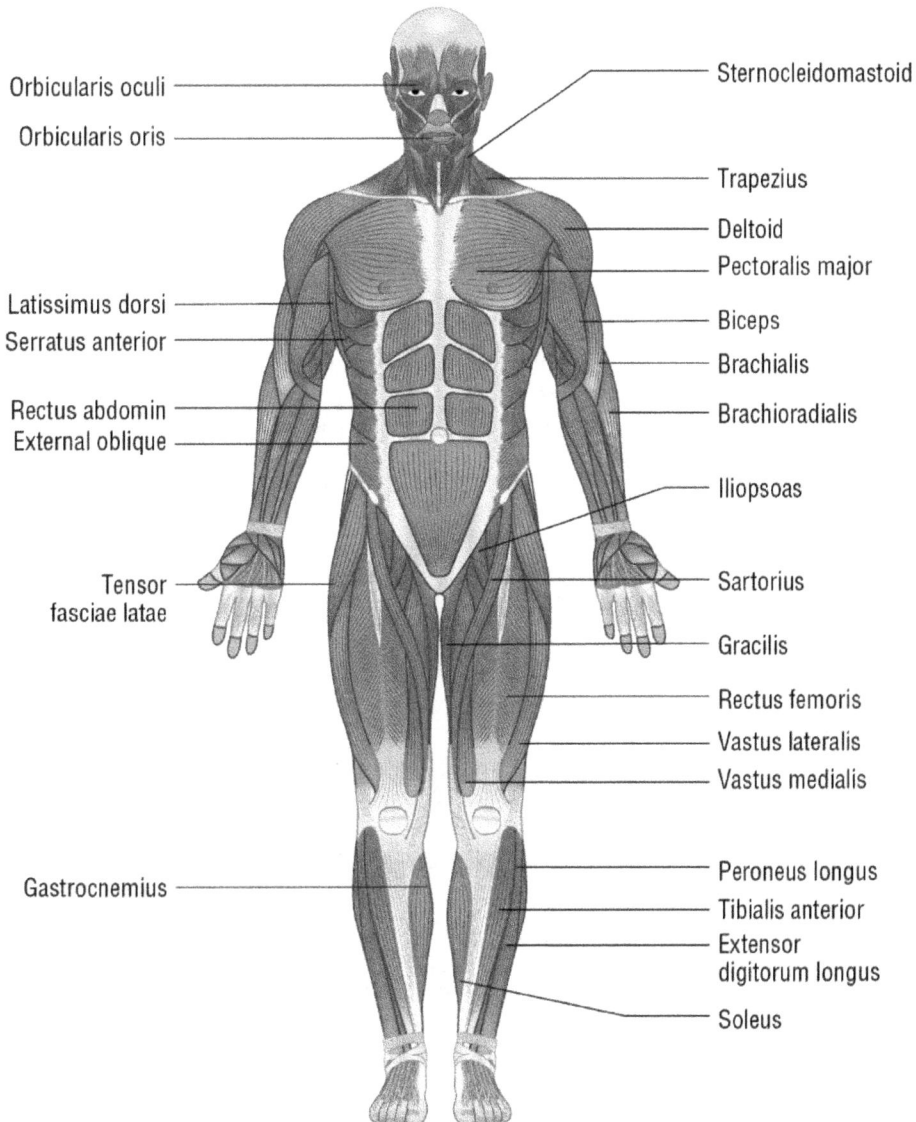

The muscular system is composed of muscle fibers. Muscle fiber's main function is to contract and enable movement (contractility). Almost all movement in the body is caused by muscle contraction. To move the skeletal bones, the muscle fibers contact, create tension, and the tension is transferred to the tendons (which are strong bands of dense connective tissue that connect muscles to bones), and then to the periosteum to pull on the bone for movement of the skeleton. When not contracting, a muscle can relax and revert to its original length (elasticity). Muscle tissue can also stretch or extend (extensibility). Contractility, elasticity, and extensibility make muscle one of the most versatile tissue types of the human body.

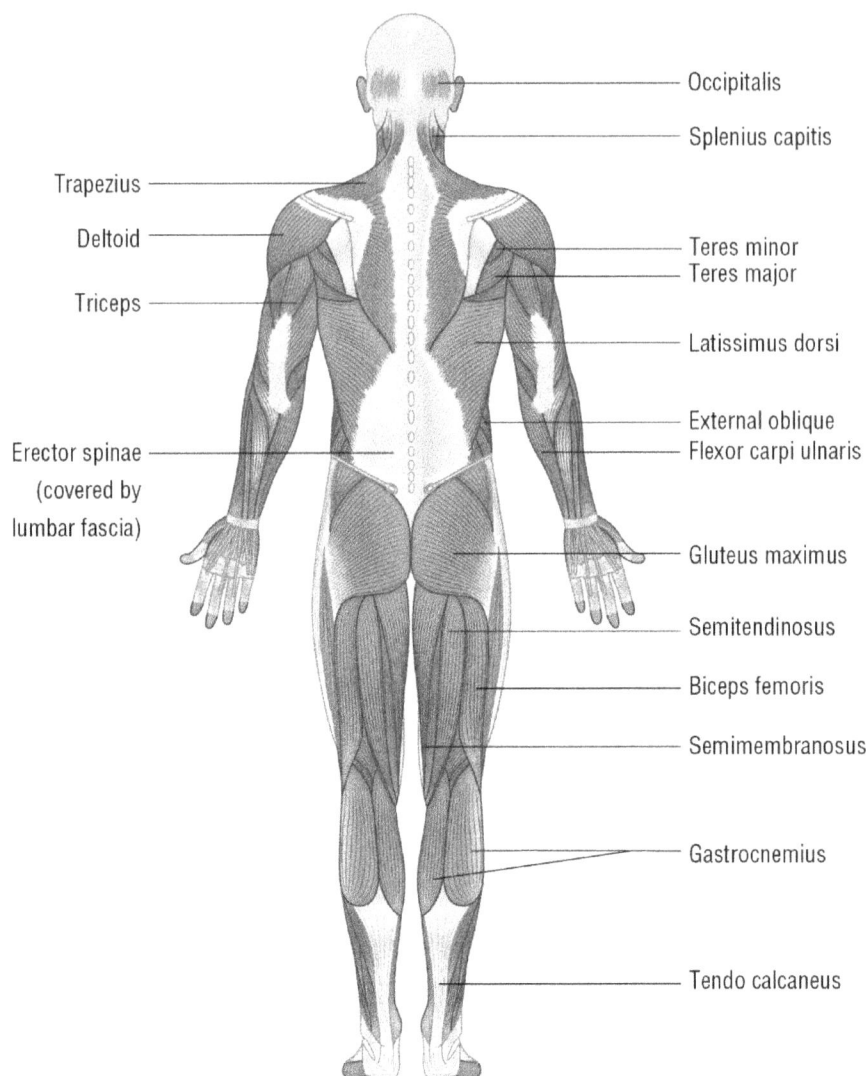

Skeletal muscles do not work by in isolation. Instead, they are attached to the bones of the skeleton in pairs. The integrated action of tendons, joints, bones, and skeletal muscles enables movements such as lifting, walking, and running, or other more subtle movements such as facial expressions. Muscle contraction also helps maintain body posture, joint stability, and is largely responsible for the body's heat production.

Major Muscle Groups
Major skeletal muscle groups include the following groups:
- Upper arm muscles (biceps and triceps)
- Deltoid muscles of the shoulders
- Large muscles of the anterior chest the pectoralis major muscles
- Large lateral muscles of the back, the latissimus dorsi
- Large muscles of the pelvis (hips), the gluteal muscles
- Anterior muscles of the upper leg, the quadriceps
- Large muscles of the posterior upper leg, the hamstrings
- Largest muscle of the lower leg, the gastrocnemius (calf) muscles

Muscle Naming Conventions

A skeletal muscle is oftentimes named after its distinguishing features. Here is a list of such features, followed by examples:

- Anatomical location or relationship to the bone(s) a muscle is attached to temporalis, which is in the temple area and attached to the temporal bone: pectoralis (chest), gluteus (buttock), brachii (arm), lateralis (lateral).
- Position relative to the body midline: medialis (toward the midline), lateralis (toward the outside and away from the midline).
- Shape of the muscle: orbicularis (the Latin root word "orbiculus" means "small disk"), deltoid (triangular), rhomboid (like a rhombus with equal and parallel sides).
- Size of the muscle: gluteus minimus, gluteus maximus, gluteus medius.
- Length of the muscle: brevis (short), longus (long), peroneus brevis, adductor longus.
- Movement produced by the muscle: flexor, extensor, abductor, adductor, levator, flexor pollicis longus, adductor longus, adductor magnus.
- Direction of the muscle fibers and fascicles: external oblique of the abdomen, rectus (straight) abdominis.
- Number of muscles in a group or origins a muscle has: biceps, triceps, quadriceps.

Muscle Types

The three types of muscle are skeletal, smooth, and cardiac.

Skeletal Muscle

Skeletal muscle is attached to bones, and its contraction produces skeletal movements, facial expressions, posture, and other voluntary movements of the body. The peripheral portion of the central nervous system controls the skeletal muscles. Skeletal muscle cells have many nuclei squeezed along the membranes. Skeletal muscle fibers are striated with transverse streaks. The striation can be attributed to 1) the regular alternation of the contractile proteins actin and myosin; and 2) the structural proteins that couple the contractile proteins to connective tissues. Skeletal muscle fibers act independently of neighboring muscle fibers.

Skeletal muscles not only enable body movements, but they also contribute to the maintenance of homeostasis by generating heat. Skeletal muscle is richly supplied by blood vessels for nutrition supply, oxygen delivery, and waste removal. The energy supply required for muscle contraction is produced through breaking down ATP, and heat is generated in this process as a byproduct. Such heat production is very noticeable during physical activity. During low temperature, the body's involuntary shivering produces heat to maintain body temperature.

Skeletal muscle fiber is also supplied by the axon branch of a somatic motor neuron, which controls the contraction and relaxation of muscle fiber. Under the conscious control of the central nervous system, skeletal muscles initiate movement, stop movement, maintain posture and balance. Muscles also maintain skeletal and joint stability and integrity by preventing excess movement of the bones and joints. Muscles located throughout the body, such as the genioglossus muscle, styloglossus muscle, urethral sphincter, and anal sphincter, also help control basic bodily functions such as food intake, urination, and defecation.

<u>Smooth Muscle</u>
Smooth muscle is in the walls of the hollow internal organs such as blood vessels, the gastrointestinal tract, bladder, uterus, reproductive systems, and the airways. Smooth muscle is under control of the autonomic nervous system and its contraction cannot be controlled consciously. The non-striated (smooth) muscle cell is spindle-shaped, with a single central nucleus. Smooth muscle contracts slowly and rhythmically.

<u>Cardiac Muscle</u>
Cardiac muscle forms the contractile walls of the heart. It is under the control of the autonomic nervous system and cannot be controlled consciously. The cells of cardiac muscle, known as cardiomyocytes, are striated, like those of the skeletal muscle fiber. However, unlike skeletal muscle fibers, cardiomyocytes are single cells that typically have a single nucleus that resembles that of the smooth muscle. The contraction of cardiac muscle is strong and rhythmical. A mechanical and electrochemical syncytium allows the cardiac cells to synchronize their contractions and relaxations.

Cardiovascular System

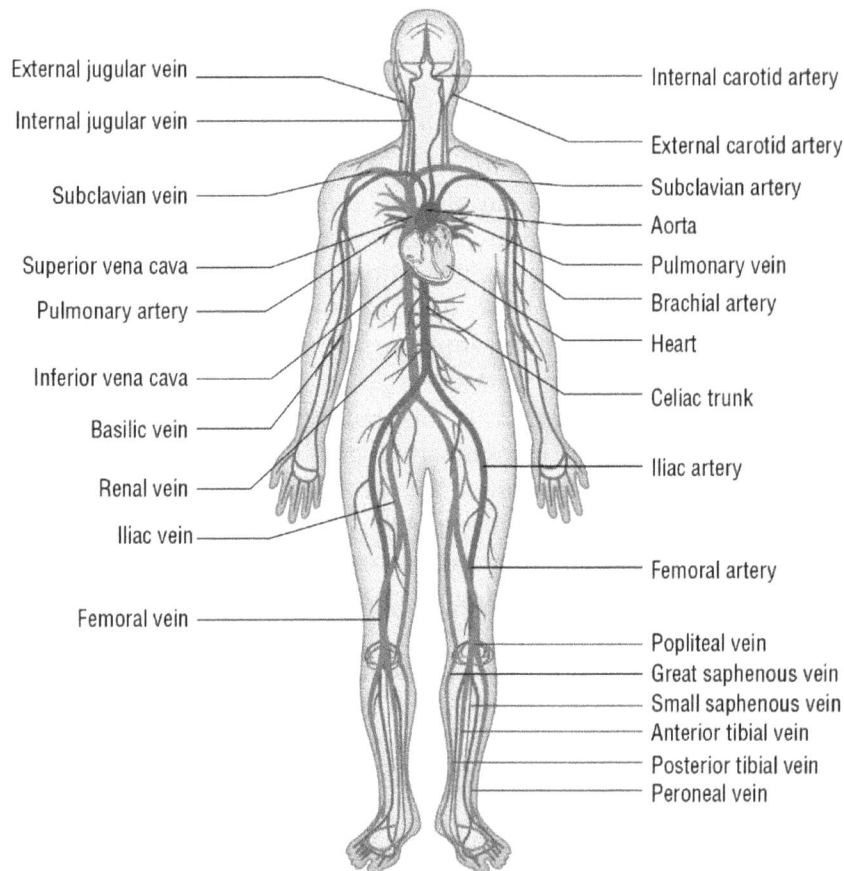

The anatomy of the cardiovascular circulatory system begins with the heart, located at the base of the thoracic cavity directly superior to the diaphragm and centered slightly left of the midline of the sternum. The lower lobes of the left and right lungs are immediately lateral to the lateral walls of the heart.

The heart consists of muscular walls that enclose four chambers: the thin-walled right and left atria, and the thick-walled right and left ventricles. The right and left ventricles share a common medial wall (interventricular septum), as do the right and left atria (interatrial septum). The right atrium is directly superior to the right ventricle, and the left atrium is directly superior to the left ventricle. The atria and ventricles are separated by a common septum (atrioventricular septum), which forms the bases or floors of the atria and the ceilings of the underling ventricles of each atrium.

Cardiovascular Blood Flow

Deoxygenated blood from all other body regions arrives at the heart via veins. The smaller veins eventually pass blood through to either the superior or inferior vena cava, the largest veins of the body. The superior and inferior vena cava both empty into the right atrium. Blood then passes from the right atrium through a three-leaflet valve (the tricuspid valve) into the right ventricle. Subsequently, this blood is pumped out the right ventricle through a two-leaflet valve (the pulmonic valve) into the main pulmonary artery. Blood in the main pulmonary artery continues to either the left or right pulmonary arteries, which then enter either the left or the right lung.

Pulmonary Blood Flow

The pulmonary arteries branch into increasingly smaller and more numerous arteries. The smallest terminal arterial branches are the arterioles. From the arterioles, blood passes into capillaries (one-cell thick walled vessels). Blood passing through these capillaries exchanges oxygen from inspired (inhaled) air in alveolar airspaces. Carbon dioxide diffuses from the blood in the capillaries and into the alveolar airspaces before being expelled from the body via respiratory airways during exhalation (expiration).

The capillary blood, now oxygenated, passes first to venules, then to larger veins, and finally returns to the heart via the main pulmonary veins. The main pulmonary veins (usually four these) empty into the left atrium. Blood from the left atrium passes into the left ventricle through a two-leaflet valve (the mitral valve). The blood is then pumped from the heart via the left ventricle through a two-leaflet valve (the aortic valve) into the aorta.

The aorta is the largest artery in the body. From the aorta, oxygenated blood is delivered via a network of branching arterial trees to all body regions. Oxygen and nutrients are transferred to tissues, and carbon dioxide and other waste products are absorbed in capillary beds, which refers to the interweaving network of capillaries supplying tissues and organs. Capillary blood, now deoxygenated, returns to the heart via networks of veins, as already described.

Portal Vein Systems

An important anatomical concept in the cardiovascular system is that blood pumped away from the heart, either via the left or the right ventricle, always first enters a main artery, then travels to sequentially smaller arteries, travels to the smallest arteries (arterioles), and finally enters capillaries. From the capillaries, this blood travels to the smallest veins (venules), and then to the larger veins. Most of this blood travels to sequentially larger veins and directly back to the heart, but some blood is routed through a second set of capillary beds. Most notably, the latter occurs with venous blood traveling from capillary beds in the intestines to capillary beds in the liver. This type of circulatory anatomy is classified as a "portal system" or "portal circulation."

Cardiovascular (Circulatory) Physiology

The primary functions of the cardiovascular system are to (1) deliver oxygen from the lungs to all the cells of the body along with water, electrolytes, glucose, and other essential substances, and (2) transport waste products to the organs responsible for detoxifying and excreting waste products from the body. Carbon dioxide is delivered to the lungs, and other wastes are delivered either directly or indirectly to the kidneys through the liver. To accomplish these functions, the circulatory vessels must maintain a large, driving blood-pressure differential between the arterial side of the heart (the left heart) and the venous side of the heart (the right heart).

Mechanics of Cardiac Pressure and Blood Flow

The heart is a muscular organ composed primarily of cardiac muscle. The atria of the heart are thin-walled compared to the ventricles of the heart. This difference exists because atria receive low pressure venous blood from the body and do not need to generate high blood pressure to pump blood to the ventricles. Comparatively, ventricles are thick-walled and designed to generate high blood pressures that drive blood through the arterial vessels. The direction of blood flow within the heart is accomplished by the arrangement of one-way valves within the heart and the sequence in which various regions of the heart contract during a cardiac cycle.

Arteries

Arteries are designed to withstand the high pressure generated by the ventricles of the heart. Arteries must also be able to stretch when blood flow volumes increase greatly during ventricular contractions and contract to maintain adequate blood pressures in the intervals between ventricular contractions. This ability requires thick arterial walls with elastic protein fibers and a layer of smooth muscle cells.

Arterioles

As the arterial vasculature progresses from the heart, large arteries split into numerous branches of smaller diameter arteries. The final arterial branches are the arterioles. As the smallest diameter arteries, the arterioles connect to capillaries. The arteriole walls contain smooth muscles that can relax or contract in response to numerous types of stimuli, some local and some in the form of hormonal or electrical to signals from the nervous system. Arteriolar contraction can completely close off blood flow to capillary beds, and arteriolar relaxation increases blood flow to capillary beds. At this level, many body systems regulate blood distribution and organ function based on the needs of the body at any given time.

Capillaries

Capillaries are designed to maximize the diffusion of substances entering and leaving the circulatory system. This maximization is accomplished by minimizing the structures and distances that substances must cross when passing through capillary walls. To facilitate this process, capillaries are only one-cell layer in thickness.

Fluid Compartments of the Body

The body has three major fluid compartments: the intravascular space (space inside blood vessels and the heart; the extracellular space (space outside blood vessels, the heart, and all cells of the body); and the intracellular space (total space within all the cells of the body). Oxygen, nutrients, water, waste products, and all other water-soluble biological substances diffuse between the intravascular space and the extracellular space, and between the extracellular space and the intracellular space. Water diffuses freely between all three spaces; the distribution of water is determined by the osmolality of the fluid compartments. The major osmotic particles in fluid compartments are proteins, which do not diffuse across cell membranes that separate fluid compartments (except by active transport processes).When the arterioles feeding capillaries are open, the blood pressure within capillaries is higher than the fluid pressure in the extracellular compartment; this higher pressure drives water from the capillaries. The proteins in the blood inside capillaries limit the water loss from the intravascular space via osmotic pressure effects. Oxygen, nutrients, and other essential biological substances diffuse down concentration gradients from the capillaries and into the extravascular space. The reverse process occurs for waste products in the extracellular space.

Veins

Excess water is reabsorbed by lymphatic vessels and by the venules, the venous vessels at the other end of capillaries. Venules are the terminal branches of the venous side of the circulatory system. Veins return blood to the heart (except in portal systems). Venules converge on large veins and then to still larger veins, eventually converging into the superior and inferior vena cava. The blood pressure in veins is much lower than on the arterial side; consequently, veins are thin-walled since they are not subject to high arterial pressure. Venous blood flow from the extremities is greatly aided by skeletal muscle contractions and associated limb movements. Veins also have internal one-way valves that allow blood to flow freely toward the heart but prevent blood flow in the opposite direction (backflow).

Nervous System

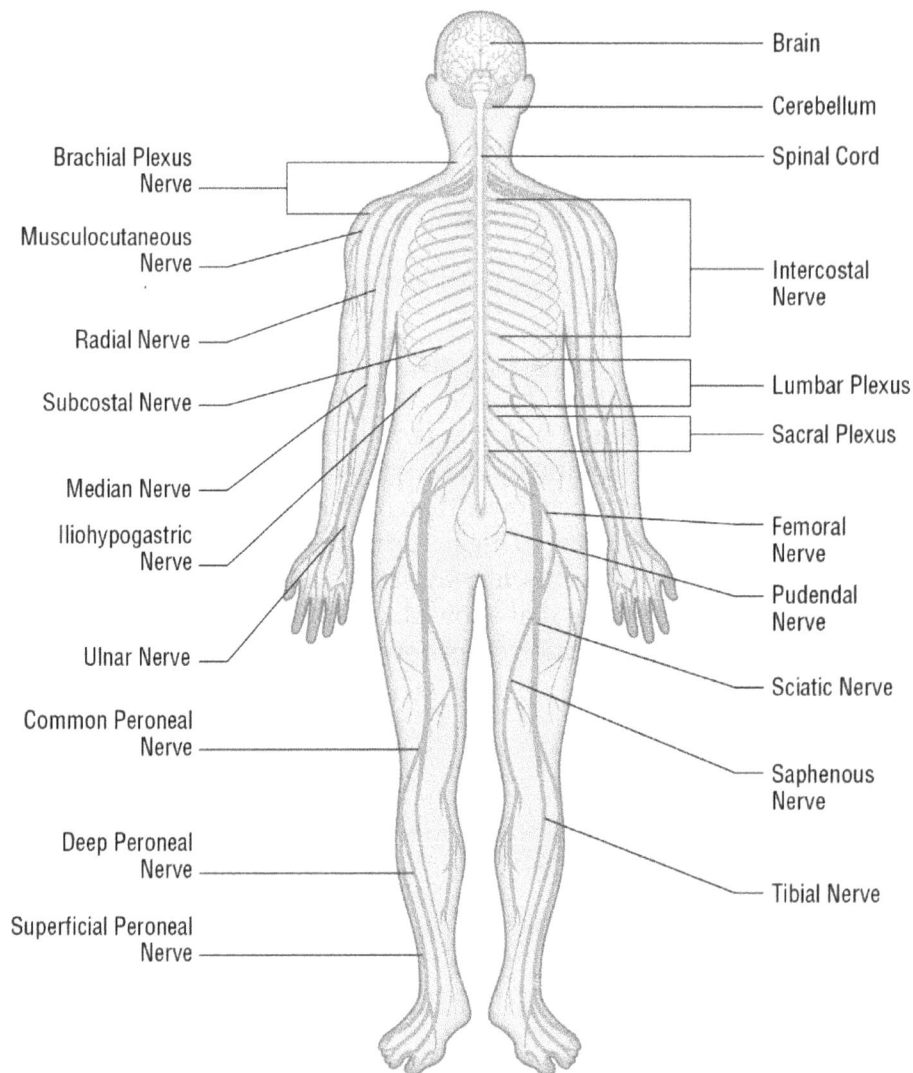

Brain
Cerebellum
Spinal Cord

Brachial Plexus Nerve
Musculocutaneous Nerve
Radial Nerve
Subcostal Nerve
Median Nerve
Iliohypogastric Nerve
Ulnar Nerve
Common Peroneal Nerve
Deep Peroneal Nerve
Superficial Peroneal Nerve

Intercostal Nerve
Lumbar Plexus
Sacral Plexus
Femoral Nerve
Pudendal Nerve
Sciatic Nerve
Saphenous Nerve
Tibial Nerve

NERVOUS SYSTEM

The nervous system can be anatomically divided into the central nervous system and the peripheral nervous systems.

The Central Nervous System

The central nervous system, as previously noted, consists of the brain (in the cranial cavity) and the spinal cord (in the vertebral canal of the spine). Also mentioned was that the outermost or most superficial region of the terminal end of the brain, the cerebral cortex, consists of five regions or lobes. The frontal, parietal temporal, and occipital lobes underlie the cranial bones of the corresponding designations. The cerebral cortex is divided into two hemispheres, right and left, connected by large nerve tracts. The largest of these tracts is the corpus callosum. Each hemisphere consists of the five cerebral cortical lobes; thus, there are right and left frontal, parietal temporal, and occipital lobes.

The regions of the brain between the cerebral cortex and the spinal cord include the midbrain, the cerebellum, and the brainstem. The brainstem is continuous with the spinal cord as the spinal cord enters the brain at the base of the skull. More specific notable brain regions include the medulla oblongata (in the brainstem) and the hypothalamus (in the midbrain at the base of the skull). The pituitary gland is an important endocrine structure adjacent and inferior to the hypothalamus.

The spinal cord is the distal continuation of the brain stem and is contained within the vertebral canal. Beginning at the base of the occipital region of the skull, the spinal cord continues to its terminus at the junction of the first and second lumbar vertebrae. The spinal cord has relatively few neuron cell bodies, instead consistently of mainly nerves that relay information between the brain and neurons of the peripheral nervous system. The 31 pairs of spinal nerves exit the spinal cord at the interspaces between adjoining vertebrae, one pair per intervertebral junction.

The 12 pairs of cranial nerves and 31 pairs of spinal nerves become important elements of the peripheral nervous system once they have exited from the cranial or vertebral cavities.

The Peripheral Nervous System

The peripheral nervous system is the portion of the nervous system that lies outside the brain and spinal cord. It collects information from different areas of the body and delivers that information back to the brain; and it also carries out commands from the brain to various parts of the body. All elements of the nervous system—neurons, nerves (axons of neurons), sensory cells, effector cells (muscle cells and glands), and supporting cells and structures not located either inside the skull or the spinal column—are also elements of the peripheral nervous system.

Importantly, the distinction between the central nervous system and the peripheral nervous system is purely an anatomical one. All the neurological activity in the body is ultimately under the control of the central nervous system, and all the neurons in the peripheral nervous system have nerve pathways that connect to the brain.

Two broad divisions exist in the peripheral nervous system: (1) the voluntary or somatic nervous system and (2) the involuntary or autonomic nervous system.

The Somatic (Voluntary) Nervous System

The somatic nervous system, as previously mentioned, consists of 12 pairs of cranial nerves and 31 pairs of spinal nerves. These nerves carry sensory information from sensory receptor cells located throughout the body to the brain. The nerves also carry instructions, in the form of electrical impulses, from the brain to effector cells located throughout the body. In most cases, the effector cells are skeletal muscle cells or glands (endocrine and exocrine glands). The sensory information provided by the peripheral nervous system is integrated with other conscious thought processes and allow people to make voluntary decisions to complete physical actions. These decisions are translated into actions, starting with the generation and transmission of electrical signals through the somatic nerves to skeletal muscles. Skeletal muscles relax and contract in a way that results in the desired body movements. Often, these highly complex movements occur in the muscles of the vocal cords to produce speech.

Somatic Ganglia

An important anatomical feature of the somatic nervous system is that the spinal peripheral nerves originate from collections of neuron cell bodies in discrete regions of the vertebrae but outside the vertebral canal. Collections of neuron cell bodies not inside the central nervous system are classified as "ganglia." The sensory ganglia are found in the dorsal regions of vertebrae and are called dorsal root ganglia. Neurons in the dorsal ganglia contribute the sensory nerve fibers to spinal nerves. In ventral regions of the vertebrae, ventral root ganglia neurons contribute the nerve fibers that send signals to effector cells. These types of nerves are called motor nerves.

The Autonomic (Involuntary) Nervous System

Most of the neural regulatory activity of the body is not under voluntary control. The central nervous system regulates most body functions through the involuntary or autonomic nervous system. The two divisions of the autonomic nervous system are the sympathetic and the parasympathetic nervous systems. These systems are commonly described as the "fight or flight" nervous system (sympathetic division) and the "rest and digest" nervous system (parasympathetic division). Again, realizing both systems are directly connected to specific regions of the brain is important. The systems are not an independent peripheral nervous system. Rather, they have an extensive peripheral component and a highly complex central component.

One notable general anatomical feature is that the autonomic nerve fibers are usually not organized into separate specific nerves, but often are nerve fibers that follow the course of and may even be adherent to blood vessels or somatic nerves.

The Sympathetic Nervous System

The peripheral component of the sympathetic nervous system begins with the neuron cell bodies in the sympathetic ganglia. Most of these ganglia are in pairs just lateral to the spinal cord and are therefore often referred to as the sympathetic "chain" ganglia. These ganglia send nerve fibers throughout the body, particularly to the organs, glands, and blood vessels of the body.

The Parasympathetic Nervous System

The peripheral component of the parasympathetic nervous system begins with the neuron cell bodies in the parasympathetic ganglia. In contrast to the sympathetic ganglia, the parasympathetic ganglia are usually located close to the organs and local anatomic regions that they innervate (supply nerves to). The Vagus nerve or 10th (X) cranial nerve is particularly important in the parasympathetic nervous system. This nerve carries parasympathetic nerve fibers to most of the major organs of the body, including the heart, the lungs, and much of the digestive system.

Neurophysiology

Nervous tissue consists of two types of cells, neurons and glial cells. Neurons are responsible for the computation and communication functions of the nervous system. They can send electrical and chemical signals to target cells. Glial cells, or glia, play a supporting role for the nervous tissue.

Neurons

At the cellular level, the production, transmission, and processing or integration of information in the form of electrical impulses is carried out by neurons. Neurons are electrically excitable cells (muscle cells are also electrically excitable cells). All cells in the body maintain concentration levels of ions inside the cell (particularly for Na+, K+, Na+, and Cl) that are different than the ion concentrations outside the cell. This difference of ion concentrations causes a voltage difference across the cell membrane.

Electrically excitable cells have specialized membrane pores and ion pumps that can use this voltage difference to generate a voltage spike called an action potential, which travels along the cell membrane.

Axons, Dendrites, and Synapses

The neuron has, in most cases, a very long membrane extension called the axon, which looks like a tail. The nerves of the body comprise these neuron axons. The sciatic nerve, which extends from the spine to the toes, can consist of numerous individual neuron axons, each several feet in length. Action potentials generated by the neuron at the base of the axon travel along the axon to its terminal end.

At the end of the axon, a dendrite (a branch-like extension of another neuron) is usually found. The action potential in the first neuron axon causes the release of neurotransmitters, which are small molecules that diffuse across the gap between the axon and the dendrite of the second neuron. The neurotransmitter molecules bind to receptors on the second neuron's dendritic membrane. This binding can cause the second neuron to generate its own action potential, which again travels down the second neuron's axon.

Through this method, electrical impulses can be transmitted from one neuron to another. The location at which the diffusion of neurotransmitters between two neurons occurs is called a synapse. The human brain has more than an estimated 100 trillion synapses.

The Medulla Oblongata

Among the most ancient regions of the brain, the medulla oblongata is in the brainstem adjacent to the spinal cord. The medulla is responsible for maintaining heart rate, breathing rate, and blood pressure, but plays other key roles in the homeostatic control of all body systems.

The Hypothalamus

A midbrain structure located at the base of the skull, the hypothalamus, is a critical region in homeostatic regulation. The hypothalamus either directly or indirectly detects blood pH and osmolality levels, oxygen levels, and numerous other biochemical and physiological metrics. Most of the drive state sensations—including hunger, thirst, and excessive heat and cold—are generated by the hypothalamus. The hypothalamus is integrated with other brain regions to respond to homeostatic needs via activation of the sympathetic and parasympathetic nervous system, and through the secretion of hypothalamic hormones that directly influence the activity of all other endocrine glands throughout the body.

The Autonomic Nervous System

The autonomic nervous system, consisting of the sympathetic and parasympathetic nervous systems, is activated through complex processing at all levels of the central nervous system. The homeostatic control systems of the central nervous system often exert regulatory control over a wide variety of biochemical and physiological functions through a combination of sympathetic- and parasympathetic- sympathetic-induced physiological and biochemical responses. The sympathetic response can be nearly instantaneous, particularly with the effects on the cardiovascular system.

The Sympathetic Nervous System

Sympathetic nerves release neurotransmitters to cardiac muscle and smooth muscle in the bronchial walls, intestinal tract walls, and blood vessel walls. The neurotransmitters generate a rapid response to environmental circumstances that require aggressive and highly energetic responses (fight-or-flight responses). The sympathetic effects in such circumstances include increased force of heart contractions, increased heart rate, increased blood pressure, redirection of the blood flow from the intestines to the skeletal muscles, suppression of peristalsis, and dilation of the bronchial airways.

The sympathetic system also innervates the adrenal medulla and can cause the release of epinephrine and norepinephrine into the bloodstream, which creates a maximal and persistent overall state of dynamic alertness and physiological readiness to engage in the pursuit of prey, engage in physical combat, or escape from life-threatening situations.

The Parasympathetic Nervous System

The parasympathetic nervous system innervates most of the same glands, cardiac muscle, and smooth muscle cells as the sympathetic system. However, the effects of the parasympathetic system are the opposite of the sympathetic effects in most cases. The parasympathetic system is predominately activated during periods when the body requires rest and regeneration and/or must digest food. Perhaps most importantly, the body requires a continuously adjusting balance between the sympathetic and parasympathetic states. This balancing act is called the autonomic tone of the body and is essential for the continuous optimal performance of all body systems.

Protective Reflexes

A vital class of specialized nervous system functions is the protective reflex class of functions. Notably, other primitive reflexes (e.g., the Babinski reflex, the root reflex, and others) are rather complex. The simple protective reflexes, most notably the deep tendon reflexes, are extremely simple two- or three-neuron circuits completely outside the central nervous system.

These reflexes respond instantaneously to stimuli that represent potentially dangerous forces acting on the body. Examples include the instantaneous withdrawal of a body part from a hot surface. The deep tendon reflexes are usually involved in this type of reflex, but they are also crucial when the limbs and joints are experiencing possibly catastrophic mechanical forces. The deep tendon reflexes have mechanoreceptors that trigger impulses when a dangerous level of mechanical stress is detected. Then, the mechanoreceptor signal travels through one or two neurons and synapses on a skeletal muscle that contracts to counteract the forces threatening injury at a bone or joint region. As a specific example of a deep tendon reflex, the patellar tendon reflex is elicited by tapping the patellar tendon of the knee with a reflex hammer.

Respiratory System

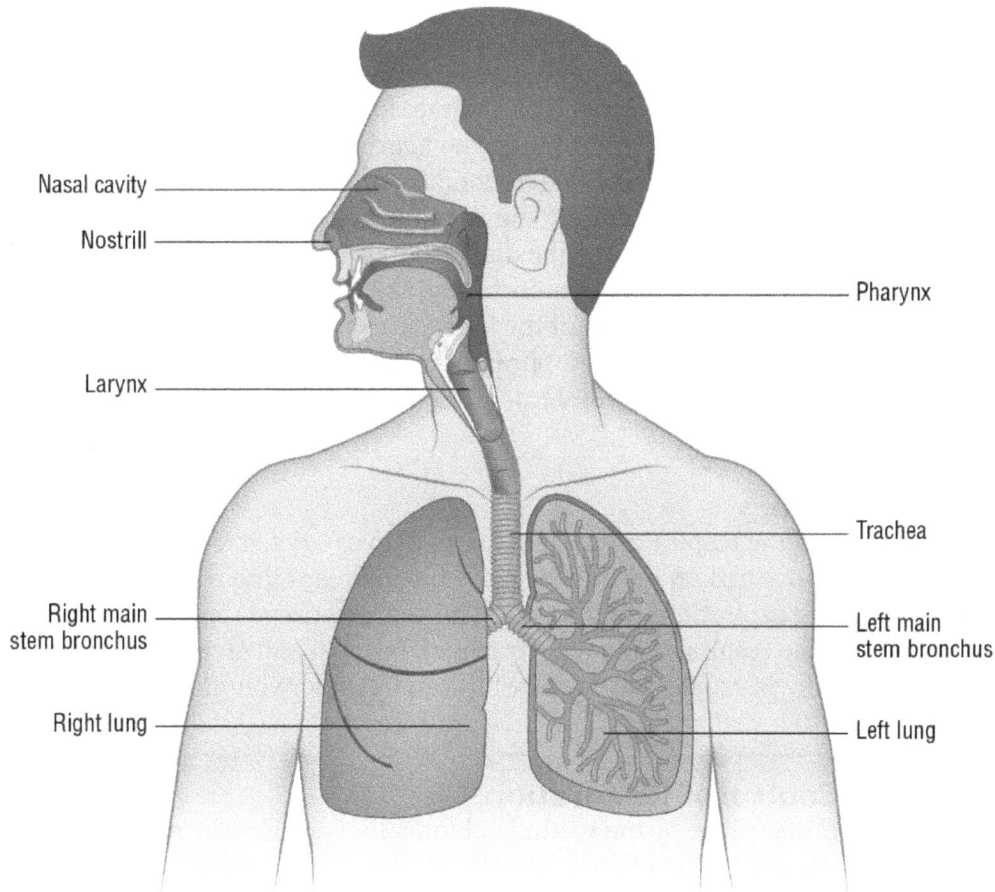

Nasal cavity

Nostrill

Pharynx

Larynx

Trachea

Right main stem bronchus

Left main stem bronchus

Right lung

Left lung

The Respiratory Tract

The initial segment of the respiratory tract is the trachea. The initial segment of the digestive tract is the esophagus. During swallowing, a specialized hinged plate structure (the epiglottis) can drop across the top of the trachea. This process prevents ingested solids and liquids from entering the trachea. The tracheal tube, which consists of rings of cartilage, descends through the anterior region of the neck (the trachea can be felt with one's fingers beneath the surface of the anterior neck). At the midpoint of the neck, a specialized region of the trachea (the larynx) can be seen and is commonly called the Adam's apple. The larynx contains the vocal cords and associated structures involved in the production of speech.

The trachea continues to the base of the neck and then enters the thoracic cavity. At about the mid-sternum level, the trachea bifurcates into a left and right main-stem bronchus. The right and left main-stem bronchi then enter their respective right and left lungs, then break into numerous subsequent and increasingly smaller branches and increasingly more air passages.

These divisions result in a dense tree-like network of airways that infiltrate the entirety of the lung tissues. The thinnest terminal branches of this respiratory airway tree are called bronchioles. At the terminal ends of the bronchioles, grape-like clusters of spherical air sacs called alveoli serve as the site of oxygen and carbon dioxide exchange between the blood contained in capillaries encircling the alveoli and the inspired air in the alveoli.

The Respiratory System
Along with the respiratory tract anatomy already described, the respiratory system comprises the lungs, internal spaces of the thoracic cavity, and the muscular diaphragm that forms the thoracic cavity floor The lungs are composed of separate lobes, two on the left and three on the right. Positioned between the left and right lungs, the heart is directly adjacent to the medial surfaces of the left-lung lower lobe. Individual secondary bronchi branch off the main-stem bronchi and enter the lung lobes. The diaphragm is a dome-shaped muscle that is convex into the thoracic cavity. The superior surface of the diaphragm is adjacent to the inferior surfaces of the left and right lower lobes of the lungs. Importantly, the left and right phrenic nerves pass from the cervical spine through the center of the thoracic cavity and innervate the diaphragm. Damage to these nerves can paralyze the diaphragm, making the act of breathing impossible. The nasal sinuses also play a role in this system. These nasal sinuses are in cavities within the facial and occipital skull bones.

Respiratory Physiology
The primary functions of the respiratory system are to deliver oxygen from the air to the bloodstream and to remove carbon dioxide from the bloodstream into the air in the lungs and then out the body during expiration (exhalation). The primary tissues and structures of the respiratory system are the respiratory airway (trachea), bronchi and alveoli, the lung tissue, and the diaphragm. Breathing is usually involuntary but can be under voluntary control for short periods of time.

Nervous System Control of Respiration
The basal breathing rate is driven by the medulla oblongata. Peripheral sensory receptors in major arteries and veins and within the brain itself monitor oxygen and pH levels and report this information to the hypothalamus and the medulla. Breathing depth and rate is modified as necessary to maintain optimum levels of oxygen and blood PH.

The smooth muscle cells in bronchial airways are also innervated by the sympathetic and parasympathetic nervous system. Sympathetic signals cause relaxation of bronchial smooth muscle, which results in dilation of the bronchial airways. Parasympathetic signals have the opposite effect. In addition, a protective gag reflex functions at the epiglottic region to prevent inhalation of solids or liquids.

Cilia
The epithelial cells lining the bronchial airways secrete mucous, and have numerous densely packed cilia, which have tiny, hair-like structures. The cilia on the bronchial airway membranes are in constant coordinated motion to propel mucus and inhaled particulate matter out of the lungs through the trachea, so the mucus can be more easily coughed up or swallowed.

Breathing Mechanics

When the epiglottis is open, the respiratory airways are continuous with the outside air. The flow of air is determined by the relative air pressures inside of the airway and the outside air. When the diaphragm contracts, the convex surface of the diaphragm within the thoracic cavity flattens; this increases the volume of the thoracic cavity surrounding the lungs, which causes a drop of pressure inside the thoracic cavity below that of the outside air. The resulting pressure differential between the airways within the lungs and the outside air drives air from the outside through the respiratory airways and into the alveolar air sacs.

Inspiration

The lung tissue expands during the inspiratory phase of the breathing cycle. The lung tissue is elastic and the expansion that occurs during inspiration dynamically stretches lung tissue. This process requires energy in the form of muscular work that is done by the diaphragm to increase the volume of the thoracic cavity and to decrease the pressure in the thoracic cavity.

Expiration

When the diaphragm relaxes, the elastic tissue in the lungs relaxes to its normal level of relaxation. Air pressure in the lung then increases and exceeds that of the outside air. Air within the airways is then driven out of the lungs by the differences in pressure inside and outside of the lungs. This portion of the breathing cycle is called expiration. Expiration—in contrast to inspiration—is normally a passive process that does not require the body to utilize energy.

Gas Exchange—Diffusion

At the microscopic level, gas exchange between the bloodstream and the alveolar air is driven by diffusion. Diffusion is movement of particles from one region to another region that is driven by difference in the concentration of particles between the regions. The blood arriving at the capillaries surrounding the alveoli is pulmonary arterial blood—which is deoxygenated. The oxygen concentrations in this blood are much lower and the carbon dioxide concentrations are much higher than the air contained in nearby alveolar air sacs. The walls of the alveoli are extremely thin, which allows a fast rate of diffusion to reoxygenate the blood.

Microscopic Physiology

The microscopic physiology of the capillary/alveolar region provides the optimum possible conditions for diffusion to occur—very short diffusion distances with a minimum of physical barriers to the diffusion process. Oxygen molecules must diffuse through a one-cell thick alveolar wall then through a one-cell thick capillary wall and then through a cell membrane of a red blood cell. The reverse is true for carbon dioxide molecules, which are diffusing in the opposite direction—from the blood and into the alveolar air sacs. In the red blood cell, oxygen molecules bind to hemoglobin molecules.

This process reoxygenates the capillary blood and rids the blood of carbon dioxide. This blood is then delivered back to the heart for recirculation throughout the body.

Digestive System

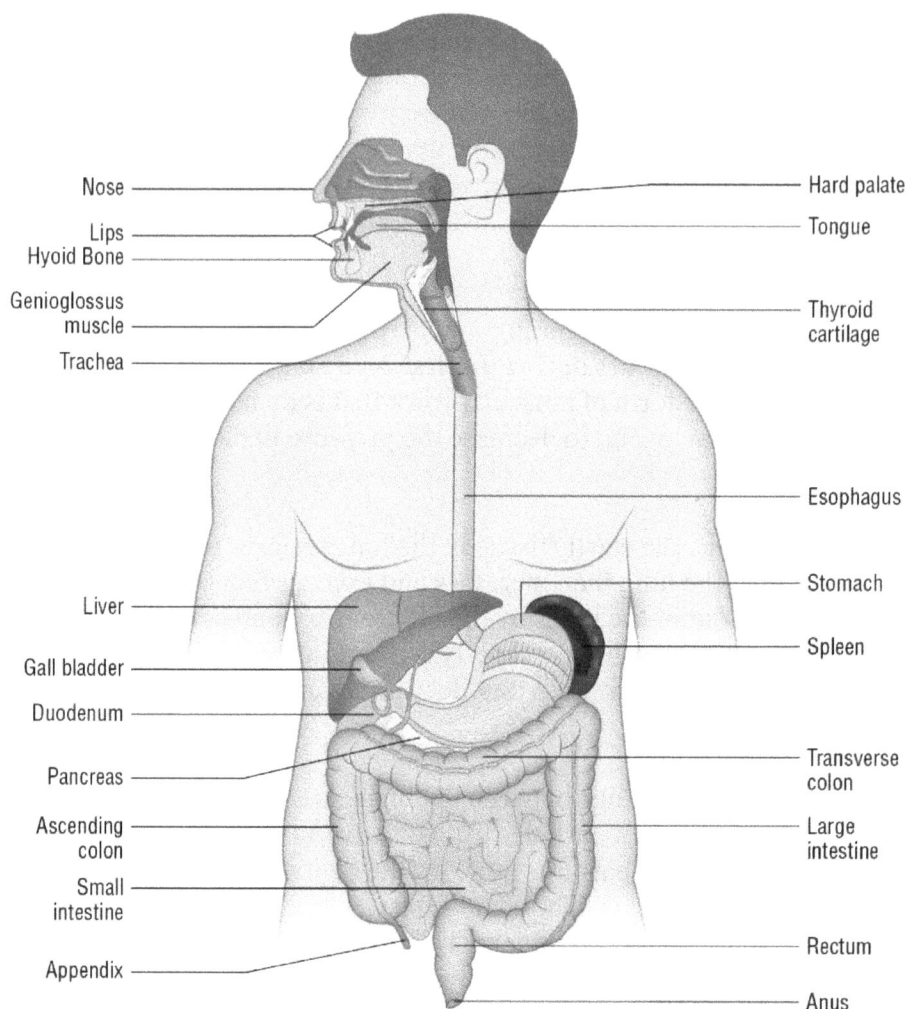

Nose — Hard palate

Lips — Tongue

Hyoid Bone

Genioglossus muscle — Thyroid cartilage

Trachea

Esophagus

Stomach

Liver — Spleen

Gall bladder

Duodenum

Transverse colon

Pancreas

Ascending colon — Large intestine

Small intestine

Rectum

Appendix — Anus

The Digestive Tract

The digestive tract, starting at the esophagus, follows the same path as the trachea, immediately posterior or dorsal to the trachea. At the bifurcation of the trachea, the esophagus continues inferiorly to the base of the thoracic cavity, where it passes through an opening in the muscular diaphragm and enters the abdomen. Just after entering the abdomen, the esophagus connects to the stomach. A muscular sphincter—the gastroesophageal (GE) sphincter—seals the passage of the digestive tract at the junction of the esophagus and the stomach. The GE sphincter opens only during the passage of ingested material from the esophagus into the stomach.

At the distal end of the stomach, the digestive tract continues as the small intestine. The duodenum region of the small intestine then accepts the stomach's contents. Another muscular sphincter (pyloric sphincter) seals the passageway between the stomach and duodenum. The sphincter opens at appropriate intervals to allow stomach contents to pass into the duodenum. In addition, substances produced by the liver and pancreas to aid the digestive process are secreted into the duodenum via the common bile duct. The digestive process continues as nutrients and water keep moving through the small intestine, starting at the duodenum and then passing through two subsequent segments of the small intestines, first the jejunum and then the ileum. The ileum connects to the first segment of the large intestine (the cecum).

At this point, all the nutrients and most of the water passing through the digestive tract have been absorbed. Indigestible bulk material continues to pass through the sequential segments of the large intestine, beginning with the cecum, and next the ascending, the transverse, and the descending colon. Most of the remaining water in the material within the large intestine is absorbed, and feces are formed during this stage through the digestive tract. The feces pass into the terminal segments of the large intestine (the sigmoid colon and the rectum) and then pass outside the body via defection through the anal sphincter.

The Digestive System

Along with the digestive tract anatomy already described, the digestive system also consists of salivary glands, the liver, the gallbladder, the pancreas, and a specialized regional venous circulatory system called the hepatic portal circulatory system. That system carries blood from capillary beds in the intestines to capillary beds in the liver. The salivary glands are in the oral cavity. The liver is on the right upper quadrant of the abdominal cavity, directly below the inferior surface of the diaphragm. The gallbladder is connected to the liver and nestled between liver lobes at the inferior surface of the liver. The pancreas is in the left upper quadrant of the abdomen, partially retroperitoneal (buried) in the dorsal abdominal wall.

The pancreatic duct and the gallbladder duct merge to form the common bile duct, which connects with the duodenum. An additional important anatomical relationship is that the stomach is anterior to the pancreas and inferior and to the left of the liver.

Digestive System Physiology

The function of the digestive system is to bring macronutrients, micronutrients, electrolytes, and water into the body. The macronutrients are carbohydrates, fats, and proteins. When dissolved in body fluids, electrolytes are the elemental ions Na+, K+, Ca++, Mg++, and Cl-. The micronutrients are vitamins and trace minerals. The digestive system also functions best when the diet includes indigestible plant fiber, which is composed primarily of cellulose.
An often-unappreciated fact regarding the digestive system is that, although the lumen (or canal) of the digestive tract is surrounded by the tissues and organs of the thorax and abdomen, the contents within the lumen of the digestive tract are literally outside the body. Nothing consumed orally and subsequently within the digestive lumen has been either absorbed by a cell of the body or passed through a surface epithelial cell layer into internal body regions.

The nutritional requirements of the body are the solid and liquid substances that must be consumed and then absorbed into the body. These substances include water, macronutrients, and micronutrients.

Peristaltic Motion

During swallowing, in the pharynx, the pulped food mass is compressed into a doughy consistency food-ball called a bolus. The bolus then passes into the esophagus. Beginning at the esophagus—and for the remaining journey through the digestive tract—the solid material in the food bolus will be propelled by rhythmic contractions of the digestive tract called peristalsis. This peristaltic motion is produced by smooth muscle cells in the walls of the digestive tract (esophagus, stomach, small intestines, and large intestines).

Intraluminal Barriers: The GE and Pyloric Sphincters

At the terminal (distal) portion of the esophagus, the food bolus must pass through a muscular sphincter. In biology, sphincters are rings of muscle tissue that can contract, just like the iris of the eye contracts, and thereby seal off a lumen (passageway), such as the lumen of the digestive tract. This process is called constriction; the relaxation of the sphincter reverses this action and opens the pathway, a process called dilation.

Normally, except when a food bolus is passing from the esophagus into the stomach, this sphincter—the gastroesophageal (GE) sphincter—is tightly constricted. This constriction occurs because the contents of the stomach are strongly acidic, roughly equivalent to the pH of battery acid. This stomach fluid will cause severe damage to any unprotected body tissues. When contents leak through the GE sphincter, heartburn occurs. A second muscular sphincter (the pyloric sphincter) is at the distal end of the stomach cavity, where the sphincter seals off the entryway to the initial segment of the small intestinal tract (the duodenum).

The Stomach

The stomach protects its inner wall lining from acidic injury by secreting large amounts of mucous onto the inner surface of the gastric lumen. To create this acidic environment, the stomach synthesizes and secretes hydrochloric acid. This highly acidic fluid by itself causes a widespread chemical breakdown of proteins and carbohydrates, but the stomach also synthesizes and secretes a powerful proteolytic (protein cutting) enzyme called pepsin. Pepsin is the first enzyme that engages in the enzymatic breakdown of all proteins.

Chyme

The stomach also engages is a considerable amount of mechanical digestion. The stomach walls are thick and constructed of several heavy muscle layers. This allows the stomach to generate powerful contractions that reduce food boluses into a slurry of water and partially digested lipids, proteins, and carbohydrates, collectively referred to as chyme.

The Small Intestine

At a time determined by the demands of the body, the stomach will release its contents into the adjacent distal segment of the digestive tract, the duodenum of the small intestine. The duodenum is the first of three continuous segments of the small intestine. The second segment is the jejunum, and the third and final segment is the ileum.

The Duodenum

The duodenum contains cells that synthesize and secrete the hormones secretin and cholecystokinin (CCK). Prior to stomach's releasing of its contents into the duodenum, these hormones are secreted into the bloodstream. The absorption of dietary iron occurs exclusively in the duodenum.

Bile

When arriving at the gallbladder, CCK stimulates the release of bile stored in the gallbladder into the gallbladder duct, which connects to the common bile duct. Bile then travels from the gallbladder duct into the common bile duct and then empties into the lumen of the duodenum. Bile that enters the duodenum is used to emulsify fats present in the digestive contents of the stomach once these contents are delivered into the duodenum.

Reproductive System

The male and female human reproductive systems are responsible for the generation of human offspring. The first stage of this process begins with the production of male and female gametes. Gametes, as a reminder, are the haploid (N) cells that result from meiotic cell division. In males, the gamete is a sperm cell; in females, the gamete is a mature ovum.

The second stage of this process is fertilization. During fertilization, male gametes are transported to the female reproductive system, and a sperm cell fuses with an ovum to produce a diploid (2N) cell, a zygote. The zygote is a hybrid cell that contains the following from the sperm cell and the ovum:

- **From the sperm cell:** one set of chromosomes 1 through 22 (the human autosomal chromosomes); one sex chromosome, which is either an X or Y chromosome.
- **From the ovum:** one set of chromosomes 1 through 22 and one X sex chromosome.

The resultant zygote has a full set of 22 pairs of autosomes and one pair of sex chromosomes (XX or XY). Zygotes with an X and a Y chromosome develop into male human offspring, and those with two X chromosomes develop into female offspring. The zygote then begins the process of cell division and cell differentiation, which eventually produces a mature human fetus capable of independent survival outside the female reproductive system. At this stage, the fetus is born from the mother to the outside world via the labor and delivery process.

The synthesis and secretion of the sex hormones—testosterone in the male and estrogen in the female—also occur in the gonads of the reproductive system.

Female Reproductive System

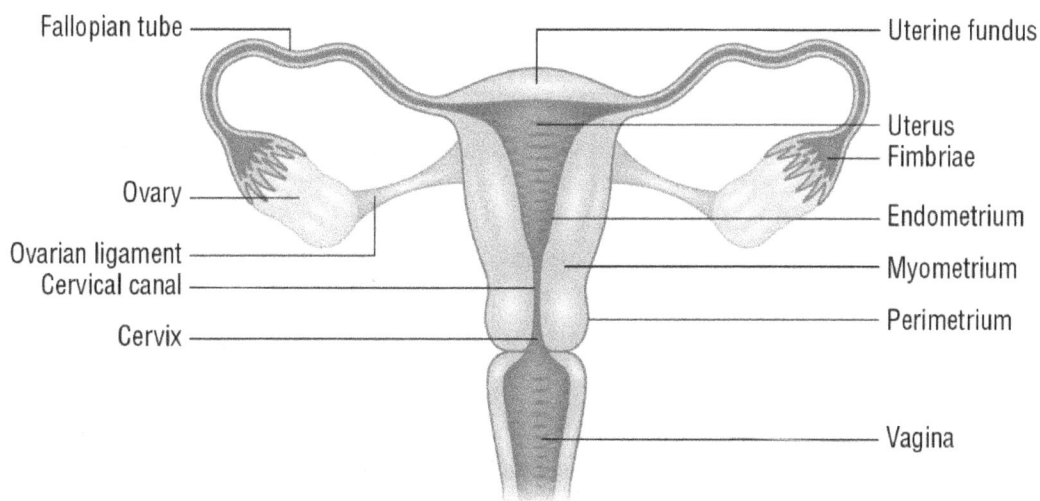

The female reproductive system consists of the external and internal female genitalia. The functions of the female reproductive system are the production of female gametes; the support of the fertilization of the fusion of female and male gametes to create a human zygote; and the physical support, protection, and nourishment of the development of the zygote to a mature human fetus and its subsequent delivery to the outside world. The gonads of the female reproductive system are also synthesize and release the female sex hormone estrogen.

The External Female Genitalia

The external female genitalia, as a group, are called the vulva. The vulva consists of the mons pubis—a mound of fatty tissue overlies the pubic bone and forms the vulva's anterior segment. The mons pubis comprises the labia majora, which are outer folds or lips divided into right and left labia by the pudendal cleft. The two folds of the labia majora are lateral to the underlying labia minora, clitoris, vaginal introitus (external opening), urethral meatus, the greater and lesser vestibular glands (Bartholin's glands and Skene's glands), and the vulvar vestibule.

The labia minora are structurally similar to the labia majora, laterally located adjacent and inferomedial to the labia majora, and adjacent and lateral to the central regions of the vulva. The central vulvar regions include the midline superiorly located clitoris and the centrally located vulvar vestibule. The urethral meatus and the vaginal introitus or orifice is in the midline of the vulvar vestibule. The urethral meatus is located immediately superior to the vaginal orifice.

The greater vestibular glands (Bartholin's glands) and the lesser vestibular glands (Skene's glands) are located lateral to the vaginal orifice. Bartholin's glands secrete mucous that provides lubrication of the vagina and the surrounding vestibular regions.

The Female Internal Reproductive System

The female internal reproductive system consists of four major components: the vagina, the uterus, the fallopian tubes, and the ovaries. In contrast to the male reproductive system, the female urethra does not communicate with any female reproductive structures and has no role in the female reproductive system.

The Vagina

The vagina is an anatomical tube consisting of muscular and fibrous tissue. The lumen of the vagina begins at the vaginal orifice and extends internally to the pelvic cavity, where it terminates at the cervix of the uterus. The cervix is the inferior portion of the uterus and protrudes into the lumen of the vagina. The walls of the vagina encircle the cervix, and the interior lining of the vaginal lumen is continuous with the external surfaces of the cervix.

The Uterus

The functions of the uterus are (1) to serve as a site for the implantation of a developing embryo and (2) to provide a continuous supportive, nurturing, and protective environment for the continued development of the embryo into a viable human fetus. When the fetus is sufficiently developed to survive outside the uterus, the uterus undergoes a series of muscular contractions that expel the fetus from the internal uterine cavity through the cervical canal and into the lumen of the vagina.

The uterus is a pear-shaped muscular organ in the pelvic cavity in a position immediately adjacent and dorsal to the urinary bladder and immediately adjacent and ventral to the rectum.

The uterus has four major anatomical regions: the cervix (neck of uterus), the internal os, the corpus (body of uterus), and the fundus (superior region of uterus). The conically shaped inferior segment of the uterus, the cervix, extends into the vagina and forms the cap to the internal end of the vagina. In the central cervix region, a passageway continuous with the lumen of the vagina extends into the central cavity of the uterus.

The walls of the uterus consist of three layers. The innermost layer, which includes the internal surface of the central uterine cavity, is the endometrium. The endometrium includes an innermost epithelial layer, which in turn consists of a basal layer and an overlying functional layer. The functional layer includes the surface layer cells exposed as the lining of the central uterine cavity. The functional layer consists of epithelial cells, mucous glands, and blood vessels that are responsive to various hormones.

The functional layer undergoes an approximately once-per-month cycle of growth, degeneration, and regeneration (menstrual cycle) that occurs in response to the variations in the levels of hormones that regulate the menstrual cycle. The middle layer of the uterus is called the myometrium. The myometrium is composed of several thick layers of smooth muscle tissue. The outermost encapsulating layer of the uterus (the parametrium) consists of a continuation of the peritoneum, which is the epithelial surface layer of the abdominal cavity. Structurally, the uterus is supported in its position within the pelvic cavity by three pairs of suspensory ligaments: the uterosacral, cardinal, and round ligaments.

The Fallopian Tubes

The fallopian tubes are a pair of structures that extend from superior-lateral positions on the uterus, one on the left and one on the right, medial to a position directly opposite of the respective left or right ovary. The fallopian tubes contain a central lumen lined with ciliated epithelium. One end of the lumen is continuous with the central cavity of the uterus, and the other end is open to the pelvic cavity and faces the respective ovary. A short gap exists between the ovary and the lateral opening of the lumen of the fallopian tube.

During ovulation, when a mature follicle within the ovary ruptures and releases a mature ovum (female gamete), the ovum is drawn into the fallopian tube by local peritoneal fluid currents generated by the motion of cilia within the fallopian tube. Once inside the tube, the ovum is carried by the same ciliary motions into the central cavity of the uterus. Fertilization of the ovum by a sperm cell (which sometimes occurs within the fallopian tubes) triggers a set of reactions that allow the developing embryo to implant within the wall of the endometrium of the uterus.

The Ovaries

The ovaries are the female gonads. Ovaries are 3 to 4 cm in size and ovoid shaped. Two ovaries are present in females, one each in the pelvic cavity on either the left or right side just medial to distal end of the respective left or right fallopian tube. The ovaries are connected to the uterus by the ovarian ligament and to the peritoneal wall of the pelvis by another ligament called the suspensory ligament.

In addition to being the primary estrogen-producing glands, the ovaries are organs that contain all a female's germ cells that will eventually mature and be released by the ovaries during ovulatory cycles. All these progenitor germ cells are present at birth in a human female's ovaries.

The general structure of an ovary includes an outer region called the cortex and an inner region called the medulla. The medulla of the ovary contains loose connective tissue that surrounds the blood vessels that provide the blood supply to the ovary.

The Ovarian Cortex

The ovarian cortex is composed of dense connective tissue, including fibroblast cells that can change functionally in response to various hormone levels. The cortex also has an outer layer of cuboidal epithelial cells called the germinal layer. While maturing into functional gametes (eggs), female germ cells acquire an organized collection of cells called granulosa cells. The granulosa cell mass and the embedded germ cell together are called an ovarian follicle. At all stages of development, the ovarian follicles are in the ovarian cortex.

Male Reproductive System

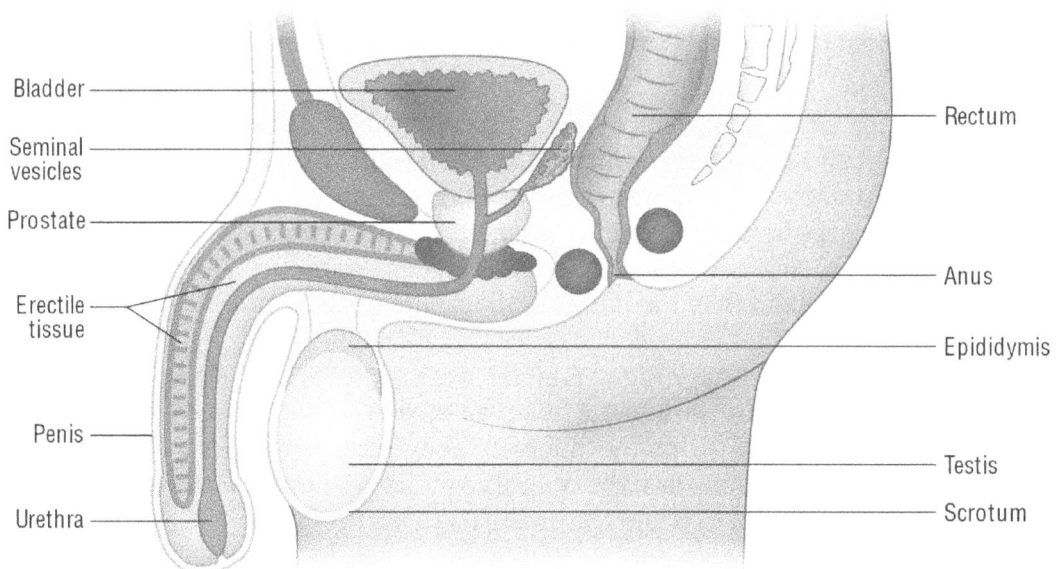

The male reproductive system consists of the external male genitalia (the penis, the scrotum, and the testis) and the internal male genitalia (the distal segment of the urethra, the seminal vesicles, and the prostate gland, bulbourethral glands, and Cowper's gland). The penis consists of a central canal (the urethra) that also serves as the passageway for the delivery of urine from the bladder to the exterior of the body, and the distensible surrounding erectile tissue (the corpus cavernosum). The distal end of the penis forms the head or glans of the penis, which contain the external opening of the urethra (the meatus and surrounding tissue called the foreskin).

The scrotum, an external anatomical pouch or sack consisting of skin and smooth muscle, is divided into two chambers. Each chamber contains a single testis along with the associated structures of the testis (the epididymis and the ductus deferens). The scrotum allows the testis to experience a slightly lower temperature environment than the internal body temperature. This lower temperature environment is necessary to allow the proper functioning of the spermatogenesis (sperm production) that occurs within the testis.

The testes are ovoid-shaped organs responsible for the first stages of the production of sperm cells. The testes are enclosed by a tough outer membrane (the tunica albuginea). The interior of the testis consists of a collection of thin coiled tubules called the seminiferous tubules. The cells lining the interior of the seminiferous tubules include specialized epithelial cells called Sertoli cells and germ cells capable of undergoing cell division and differentiation to produce sperm cells (spermatozoa).

The seminiferous tubules connect proximally to the rete testis, which is a short stalk of common connecting tubules where developing sperm cells are concentrated before proceeding to efferent ducts and into the epididymis. The epididymis is a highly convoluted tubule that forms a mass at the superior surface of the testis. Developing sperm cells are retained within the epididymis for 2–3 months. During this time, the developing sperm cells reach maturity.

The distal end of the epididymis is continuous with the vas deferens, which are short-length segments of tubules that connect the epididymis to the ejaculatory ducts in the interior of the pelvic cavity. The ejaculatory ducts connect to the urethra and have connections with ducts of the prostate gland, the bulbourethral glands, and Cowper's glands. These glands provide contributions to the seminal fluid that serves as the fluid medium that nourishes and supports the transportation of sperm cells during ejaculation.

Urinary System

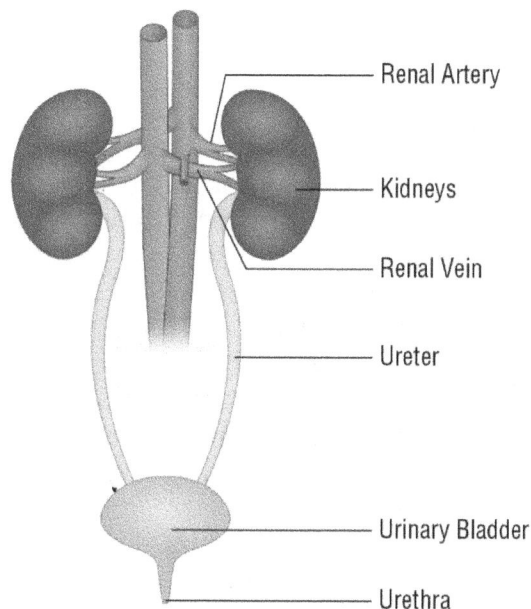

Renal Artery

Kidneys

Renal Vein

Ureter

Urinary Bladder

Urethra

The urinary system consists of the kidneys, renal arteries and veins ("renal" is an adjective meaning related to the kidney or of the kidney), ureters, urinary bladder, and urethra. The kidneys are bean-shaped and located, as previously mentioned, within the walls of the abdomen in a dorsolateral position on either side of the lumbar spine. This "buried in abdominal wall tissue" location is referred to as a retroperitoneal position (the pancreas is also in a partial retroperitoneal position).

The renal arteries carry blood to the kidneys that eventually arrives at capillaries surrounding microscopic filtering units called nephrons. Blood filtration occurs at these sites. Filtered blood from nephrons moves through venous networks and emerges from the kidneys within the renal vein. Filtered products from the nephrons pass through tubules that empty into a central collecting cavity in the kidney known as the renal pelvis.

The ureters (one per kidney) are thin tubes connecting the renal pelvis to the urinary bladder. The ureters transport the kidney's filtered liquid wastes (i.e., urine) from the renal pelvis to the urinary bladder. The urinary bladder is a distensible (inflatable) bag-like structure in the central anterior pelvic region of the abdominal/pelvic cavity. The bladder stores urine until it is released through another tube, the urethra.

The urethra carries the urine outside the body, exiting at the meatus (outer opening) of the glans penis in males and immediately anterior the entrance of the vagina in females. An additional important anatomical relationship of the urinary system is that the adrenal glands, which secrete many essential hormones as part of the endocrine system, are located directly adjacent to the superior surfaces of the kidneys, one adrenal gland per kidney.

The Kidneys

The kidneys have several critical functions in the human body. While kidneys produce urine, that is only the final stage of kidney function. The production of urine and its transport to the urinary bladder is the excretory function of the kidneys. This excretory function reflects the other functions of the kidney, which include maintaining an optimum volume of total body water and optimum concentrations of electrolytes within the fluid compartments of the body.

Additionally, the kidneys play a crucial role in maintaining an optimal pH of body fluids and an optimum blood pressure. The kidney removes soluble waste products from the body—most notably urea, bilirubin, and organic acids (e.g., uric acid and ammonia). The kidneys also have direct endocrine functions via producing the hormones renin, erythropoietin, and calcitriol.

Gross Anatomy

The two kidneys are each located anteriorly and laterally (either left or right) of the spine in a retroperitoneal (buried in abdominal wall) position in the posterior wall of the abdominal cavity. Both kidneys are immediately inferior to the diaphragm. While the left kidney is adjacent and posterior to the spleen, the right kidney is adjacent and posterior to the liver. The adult human kidneys are bean-shaped organs with an average size of about 10–13 cm in length, 5–7.5 cm in width, and 2–2.5 cm in thickness. The long axis of a kidney parallels the long axis of the body.

The lateral surfaces of the kidneys have a convex curvature, and the medial surfaces have a concave curvature. The upper region of the kidney is the superior pole, and the lower region is the inferior pole. In each kidney, an adrenal gland is located adherent to the superior pole.

Each kidney's outer surface is enclosed by a tough fibrous layer of tissue called the renal capsule. A layer of fat called the perinephric fat surrounds the renal capsule. The perinephric fat is surrounded by a connective tissue membrane called the renal fascia, which is surrounded by a second layer of fat (the paranephric fat layer). The renal hilum is a recessed region in the center of the medial surface of the kidney. The hilum contains the major blood vessels that supply the kidney (the renal artery and two renal veins) and the proximal end of the ureter.

The solid tissue of the kidneys is divided into two anatomical regions. The outer region is the renal cortex; the inner region is the renal medulla. The kidney is also subdivided into 10–15 renal lobes. The lobes are arranged sequentially like the wedges of an orange to produce the overall kidney structure. Each lobe consists of an upper or outer layer of renal cortex and a medial or deep cone-shaped region of renal medulla called a renal pyramid. The apex of each renal pyramid is called a papilla. Several adjacent renal papillae project into a cavity called a minor calyx. Several adjacent minor calyces fuse medially into a larger cavity called a major calyx. The major calyces empty into a central cavity called the renal pelvis, which narrows into a tube that becomes the ureter. The ureter exits the kidney through the renal hilum and continues inferiorly to merge with the urinary bladder. Collectively, the renal pelvis and the major and minor calyces form a continuous cavity called the renal sinus.

Integumentary System

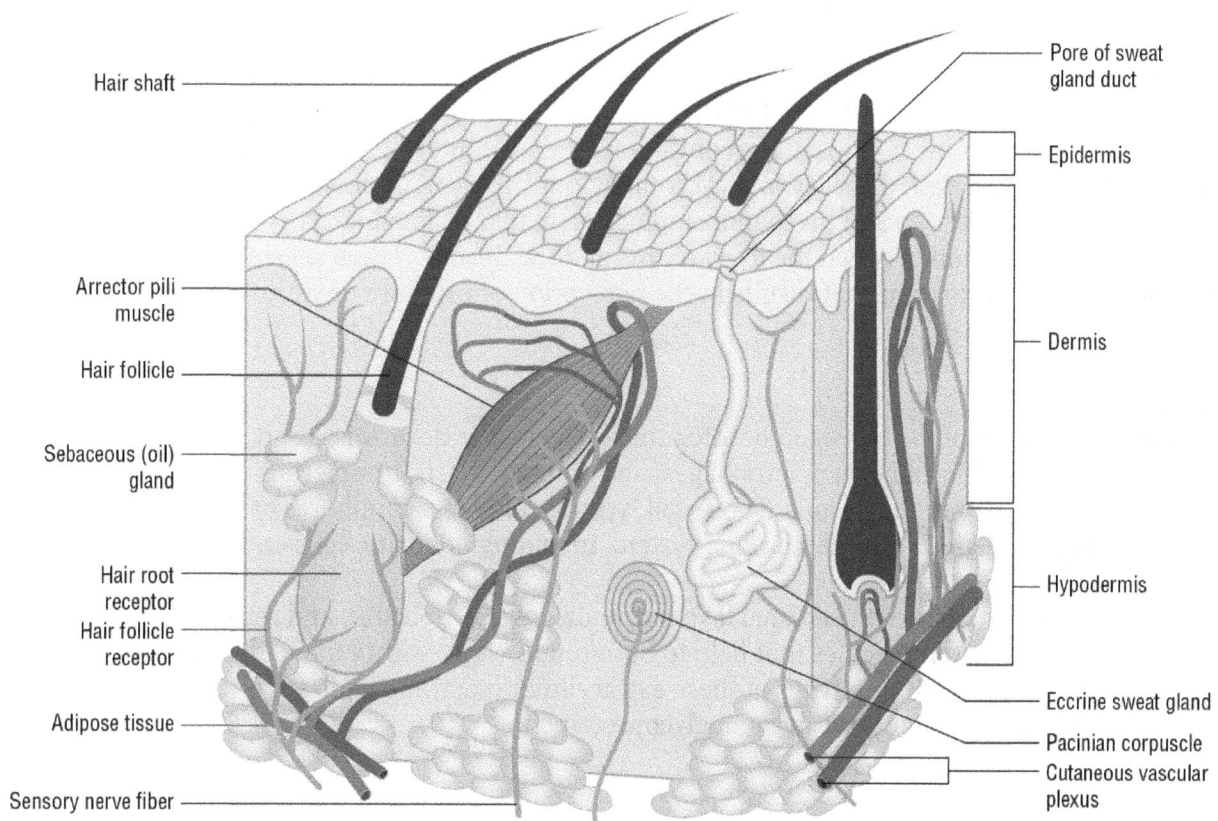

The integumentary system of the human body, or simply "the integument," is a multilayered sheath of tissues and associated cells and extracellular structural and functional components that completely encloses the interior of the body. The most superficial layer of the integumentary system is exposed to the external environment and forms the external surface of the body. Two of the most general primary functions of the integumentary system are (1) to provide a physical containment of the internal body contents and (2) to provide a physical and biochemical barrier to elements of the external environment. Several secondary functions of the integumentary system exist as well. Most of these functions, as a group, can be categorized as homeostatic functions because they all provide mechanisms to maintain a controlled and stable, yet adaptable internal environment distinctly separate from the external environment.

Layers of the Integument

The integument consists of a dermal or cutaneous layer and a subcutaneous or hypodermal layer. The dermal layer consists of two sub-layers, the dermis and the epidermis.

The Hypodermis (Subcutaneous Layer)

As the lowermost or deepest layer of the integument, the hypodermis (subcutaneous layer of the integument) consists primarily of loose adipose connective tissue, blood vessels, lymphatic vessels, and nerves. The hypodermis provides a transitional connective zone between the overlying dermal layer and the adjacent underlying body contents, usually outer skeletal muscle layers, but in some areas, bony structures. Such structures particularly include those over the knee and elbow joints and the anterior surfaces of the lower leg (the shins).

The adipocytes of the hypodermis are organized into small collections called lobules that are enmeshed in collagen fibers. Fibroblasts are sparsely distributed throughout the hypodermis. The hypodermis-dermis boundary is a continuous series of interdigitating invaginations of both layers into the other with direct structural connections provided by collagen and elastic fibers. One of the four major types of mechanoreceptors—lamellar or Pacinian corpuscles—are located at the boundary region between the hypodermis and the dermis. These sensory receptor cells provide tactile information that results in the perception of pressure or vibration.

The Dermis

As the middle layer of the three major integument layers, the dermis is composed of three primary cell types (fibroblasts, macrophages, and adipocytes), but numerous other types of cells are interspersed within the dermis. Those cell types include chromophores or melanocytes and various cells associated with the immune system, including dendritic cells and T-cells.

The extracellular matrix of the dermal layers contain collagen, elastin, and reticulin fibers and several types of macromolecules that help to both retain water within the matrix and serve other functions. The most common types of these extracellular macromolecules are glycosaminoglycans, proteoglycans, and glycoproteins.

The Dermal Reticular Layer

The dermis consists of two sub-layers: the papillary layer (superficial area adjacent to the epidermis) and the reticular dermis (deep thicker area beneath the papillary layer). The reticular layer is composed of dense connective tissue that contains dense amounts of collagen fibers, elastic fibers, and reticular fibers. These fibers provide the mechanical properties of tensile strength and elasticity to the integument. The roots of hair follicles, sweat glands, sebaceous glands, and sensory receptor cells are also implanted within the reticular layer of the dermis.

The Dermal Papillary Layer

The papillary layer is immediately superficial to the reticular layer. The primary type of tissue contained in the papillary layer is areolar connective tissue. Areolar connective tissue is a very loose arrangement of adipocytes, and collagen and elastin fiber with an abundance of gel-like extracellular matrix. These features allow substances to readily diffuse through the tissue.

The Dermal-Epidermal Interface

At the interface between the papillary layer of the dermis and the overlying superficial layer of the integument (i.e., the epidermis), the papillary layer projects numerous knob-like extensions of tissue called papillae between interdigitating ridges of the epidermis, called rete ridges. The result is a tight enjoining of the two integumentary layers. The papillae of the papillary layer contain tufts of capillaries or Meissner's corpuscles, which are sensory receptor cells adapted to provide information interpreted in the central nervous system as the sensation of light touch. Mid portions of hair follicles, sweat and sebaceous glands nerves, and lymphatic vessels also travel through the papillary dermis toward the epidermis.

The Epidermis

The most superficial layer of the integument is the epidermis. The epidermis has no direct blood supply and depends on diffusion for the supply of oxygen and nutrients and for transport of CO_2 and other waste products. The epidermis begins immediately adjacent at the superficial surface of the papillary layer of the dermis. The two layers are separated by a basement membrane (a common feature of almost all epithelial tissues), serves as an attachment surface for the lowermost layers of epithelial cells, and creates anchoring connections with loose connective tissue located beneath the basement membrane. The basement membrane provides the biomolecular features that allow the epidermis to adhere to the dermis. The basement membrane has several additional functions, such as immune system functions and cellular repair functions. The basement membrane has a complex structure consisting of multiple layers of fibrous proteins, including anchoring collagen fibers, substrate adhesion molecules (SAMS) integrins, and several other types of macromolecules. The basement membrane is also the last line of defense against the spread of cancerous cells that originate in the epithelium.

Regions of the Epidermis

The epidermis is composed of either four or five stratified regions depending on the local anatomical areas where the epidermis is located. Most areas consist of four regions: the stratum basale, stratum spinosum, stratum granulare, and stratum corneum. The epidermis of the palms of the hands and the soles of the feet is known as "thick skin" because it has five epidermal regions. The additional region of thick skin is the stratum lucidum, which is interposed between the stratum spinosum and the stratum granulare.

The Malpighian Layer

The deepest layer of the epidermis is the Malpighian layer, which is subdivided into the stratum basale or inner basal layer and the overlying stratum spinosum layer.

The basal layer (stratum basale): The basal layer is composed of columnar epithelial cells attached to the superficial surface of the underlying basement membrane by connective structures called hemidesmosomes. These cells are germinal epithelium that undergoes mitotic division to produce a continuous supply of cells that migrate toward the outer surface of the epithelium. While migrating, these cells undergo progressive stages of differentiation with varying characteristics that define the overlying regions of the epidermis. The basal layer also consists of melanocytes, Merkel cells, and associated cutaneous nerves and cells that participate in the inflammation reactions of the immune system. Melanocytes connect to keratinocytes and provide the pigment melanin to keratinocytes. Melanin provides a barrier to ultraviolet radiation and is the pigment that determines the degree of darkness for skin tone, a component of human racial characterizations. Merkel's cells and associated cutaneous nerves provide sensory information associated with the perception of light touch.

The stratum spinosum (spinous or prickle cell region): The stratum spinosum is the second of the two sub-layers of the Malpighian layer of the epidermis. The stratum spinosum region is located directly superficial to the inner basal layer. This region consists of polyhedral-shaped cells that are daughter cells of the basal epithelial progenitor cells. The stratum spinosum cells also undergo mitotic division contributing to the approximately five layers of epidermal cells within the region. The cells have a spiny or prickly appearance due to microfilament shortening within desmosomes that interconnect among the cells. The stratum spinosum cells synthesize large amounts of fibrillar proteins called cytokeratin, which aggregates within the cells to form tonofilaments.

Tonofilaments are assembled into desmosomes, which form tight junctions between the epidermal cells while continuing to differentiate and migrate toward the epidermal surface. As keratinocytes within the stratum spinosum continue to migrate upward and differentiate, the Golgi within the keratinocytes begin to produce lamellar bodies that contain a complex assortment of phosphor, glycosphingolipids, free fatty acids and enzymes that have antibiotic activity. These products will eventually participate in the formation of the complex extracellular matrix of the outer epidermal layers.

The Stratum Granulosum

The region of the epidermis adjacent and superficial to the stratum spinosum is the stratum granulosum. The region is three to four cells in thickness. The cells of the granular region have a high content of keratin granules that produce a granular microscopic appearance, hence the name "granulosum" for this layer. The cells of the layer are classified as keratinocytes, which do not divide in contrast to the cells of the stratum basale and the stratum spinosum. While continuing to be displaced toward the outer surface of the epidermis, keratinocytes become progressively flatter and more tightly compacted. In the palms and soles of humans, the stratum lucidum is a two-to-three cell-thickness region of the epidermis, adjacent and superficial to the stratum granulosum.

The Stratum Corneum

The most superficial region of the epidermis is the 10–30 cell-layer stratum corneum. Keratinocytes proceed through the final stages of cell differentiation to become corneocytes while moving from the stratum spinosum or stratum lucidum region to the stratum corneum. Corneocytes have ejected their cell nuclei (mature red blood cells also eject their cell nuclei) and are enveloped in a keratin protein matrix that, in turn, is surrounded by stacked layers of lipid molecules. The keratin proteins are connected to the cytoskeleton of corneocytes by structures called corneodesmosomes. This interconnection of corneocytes via keratin-corneodesmosomes-cytoskeleton networks creates the exceptional mechanical durability of the epidermis.

Glands of the Integument

The integument contains a variety of glands, most notably apocrine and eccrine sweat glands and sebaceous or oil glands. All these glands are exocrine glands. Exocrine glands secrete substances through a glandular duct (tube) onto the surface of epithelial tissue, either on the surface of the skin or on the luminal surface of an epithelial-lined hollow organ (e.g., the small intestine). In contrast, endocrine glands secrete substances directly into the bloodstream or lymphatic system.

Holocrine, Apocrine, and Merocrine Glands

Glands are also categorized based on the way they secrete substances. Three general types of secretory processes exist: holocrine, merocrine, and apocrine. Holocrine secretion occurs through the disintegration of the secretory cells when the disintegration of holocrine glandular cells releases the secretory substances present in the cytoplasm of the cells. Sebaceous glands of the integument are holocrine glands. The fragments of disintegrated glandular cells are also constituents of the secretions of holocrine glands. Apocrine secretion occurs through a budding of a cell membrane segment that forms vesicles that contain the secretory substances of the gland. Apocrine sweat glands are one of the two types of sweat glands in the integument. The cell membrane segments that bud off apocrine glandular cells are constituents of apocrine secretions. Human mammary glands are also apocrine glands.

The cellular fragment components of both holocrine and apocrine glands can obstruct the ducts of the glands. Obstructed glandular ducts can result in the formation of abscesses of the gland. The contents of these abscesses may become infected by bacteria and cause acne and other types of localized infections within the integument.

Merocrine glands utilize exocytosis to secrete their glandular products. No disintegration or budding of cell membranes occurs in the secretory cells of merocrine glands. The exocrine glands of the pancreas and virtually all endocrine glands are merocrine glands. The second type of sweat glands found in the integument (the eccrine sweat glands) is merocrine glands.

Sebaceous (Oil) Glands

Sebaceous or oil glands are widely distributed within the integument except for the soles of the feet and the palms of the hands. Sebaceous glands have ducts that most commonly communicate with the spaces adjacent to hair shafts within hair follicles, but a small percentage open directly onto the external epidermal surface. The glandular cells are in the dermis, usually adjacent to a hair follicle. Sebaceous glands are holocrine glands that synthesize and secrete a substance called sebum, which is an oily or waxy substance consisting of triglycerides, lipid esters, and free fatty acids.

Sebum provides an oily medium that contributes to the composition of the sweat layer on the surface of the skin. The oily component of sweat extends the cooling effects of evaporative sweating and prevents dehydration by increasing the adherence of the sweat layer to the surface of the skin. The free fatty acids contained in sebum lower the pH of the skin surface to a range of 4.5–5.0, a level that strongly inhibits the growth of potentially harmful microorganisms. In addition to the indirect antimicrobial effect provided by the lowering of skin pH, free fatty acids in sebum also provide strong, direct antimicrobial activity. The production of sebum can be influenced by various hormone levels; for example, testosterone stimulates sebum production, and estrogen inhibits sebum production.

Eccrine Sweat Glands

Eccrine glands are merocrine glands and are by far the most numerous and widely distributed sweat glands. These glands secrete a watery solution containing sodium and chloride ions. In addition, eccrine sweat contains bicarbonate ions, cytokines, immunoglobulins, and short-sequence polypeptides that have antimicrobial activity. The secretory cells of the glands are coiled deep in the dermis. Myoepithelial cells surround the secretory cells, and the contraction of these cells propels sweat solution through the eccrine duct and onto the skin surface. Eccrine sweat glands are innervated by autonomic nerve fibers that modulate sweat secretion in response to core body temperature levels and emotional stress (e.g., excitement or fear).

Apocrine Sweat Glands

The secretory cells and surrounding myoepithelial cells of apocrine sweat glands are in the dermis near the dermis-hypodermis interface. The duct of apocrine sweat glands—like those of most sebaceous glands—is usually located adjacent to hair shafts within hair follicles. But the distribution of apocrine sweat glands is limited to only a few regions on the surface of the body, primarily the axillae (armpits). The composition of apocrine sweat gland secretions differs significantly from eccrine sweat compositions.

Apocrine secretions have a high protein and carbohydrate content. Apocrine sweat combines with sebaceous gland secretions in hair shafts in the axillae, resulting in a cloudy viscous solution that clings to axillary hair and supports colonization by bacteria. Colonizing bacteria break down components of axillary sweat, and these breakdown products are responsible for the characteristic odor associated with the axillary regions.

Abnormalities of the Integument

Notable abnormalities (pathologies) of the integument include impetigo (a superficial staphylococcal bacterial infection) and cellulitis (a deep bacterial infection that extends into the hypodermis). Superficial viral infections are typically caused by papilloma virus (warts), but many generalized viral infections produce surface viral-containing vesicles, such as those associated with the herpes virus. Superficial tinea-species fungal infections cause the condition known as athlete's foot. Generalized viral and other infections often produce immune-related skin rashes, and many drug hypersensitivities also produce skin rashes and mild temporary blistering in the form of hives. In more serious cases, deep blistering and skin loss can occur with poison ivy reactions, severe drug sensitivity, and infectious and autoimmune reactions. Eczema is a common hereditary hypersensitivity reaction of the skin. Psoriasis is an often severe and debilitating condition resulting from excessive rates of cell division in the epidermis. Malignant melanoma is a particularly deadly and common cancer of melanocytes, usually related to excessive sun exposure. The resistance of the integument to infection is generally impaired by high levels of cortisol, which are often associated with prolonged periods of psychological stress.

Endocrine System

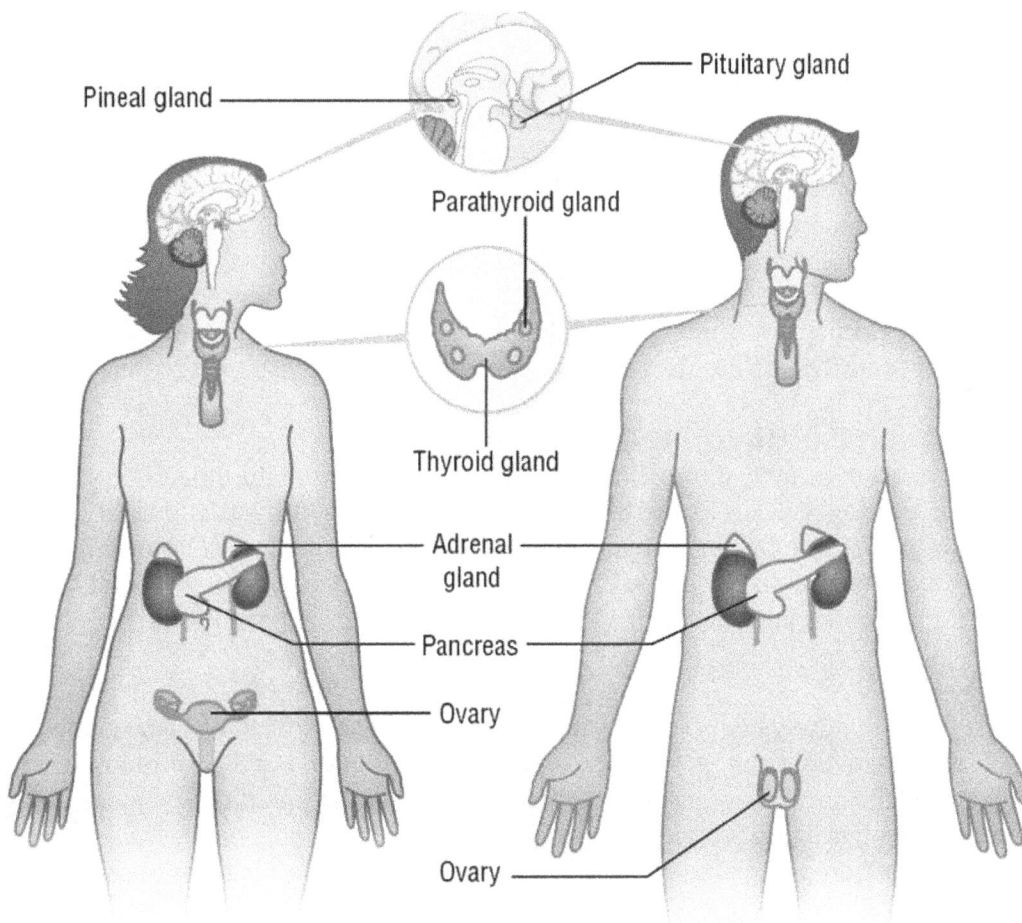

The endocrine system synthesizes and secretes hormones, which then exert a vast array of effects on the body. The endocrine system includes purely endocrine glands (whose sole function is the synthesis and secretion of hormones) and other tissues and organs that, in addition to their primary or co-functions, also synthesize and secrete hormones.

An important anatomical distinction exists between the two general types of glands, endocrine glands and exocrine glands. Exocrine glands do not necessarily secrete hormones and can secrete many other substances. The anatomical distinction for exocrine glands is that all exocrine glands secrete substances through a duct, which is a tube that leads to an anatomical surface (e.g., surface of the skin or intestinal tract). The common bile duct is one example.

All endocrine glands secrete hormones, and by anatomical definition, all endocrine glands secrete hormones directly into the bloodstream or the lymphatic system. In addition, by anatomical definition, no purely endocrine gland contains secretory ducts. For that reason, the endocrine glands are sometimes referred to as "ductless" glands.

The Hypothalamus and the Pituitary Gland

The hypothalamus and the pituitary gland are closely related anatomically. Together, these two structures serve as master controllers of the endocrine system through the secretion of hormones that regulate the levels of other hormones. The hypothalamus, a region of the brain that also synthesizes and secretes many critically important hormones, is in the inferior midbrain directly above the central region of the base of the cranial cavity. The pituitary gland is attached to the inferior portion of the hypothalamus by a connective stalk. The pituitary gland, which occupies a small depression or crater in the base of the skull called the sella turcica, secretes a wide variety of hormones. An important anatomical feature of the pituitary gland is that the posterior pituitary synthesizes only two hormones—oxytocin and vasopressin—and all other pituitary hormones are synthesized by the anterior pituitary.

The Pineal Gland

The pineal gland is located within the midbrain and is essentially at the anatomical center of the brain. The gland produces melatonin, which regulates sleep patterns and circadian rhythms.

The Thyroid and Parathyroid Glands

The thyroid glands are located superficially and to either side of the midline of the tracheal cartilage. Many anatomists classify the thyroid as a single gland with left and right lobes. The parathyroid glands are notable for being, in a sense, glands within glands. Four parathyroid glands are typically buried deeply in the thyroid gland, usually two per lobe. The thyroid glands secrete thyroid hormones and calcitonin. The parathyroids secrete parathyroid hormone (PTH).

The Pancreas

The pancreas is not a purely endocrine gland. Despite serving a critical exocrine gland function as a part of the digestive system, the pancreas' endocrine function is even more important. The pancreas secretes the hormones glucagon and, most importantly, insulin. The pancreas, as previously described, is in the upper-right quadrant of the abdomen, in a partially retroperitoneal position, immediately below the diaphragm and posterior to the stomach.

The Adrenal Glands

As previously discussed, the adrenal glands rest upon the superior surface of the kidneys, one gland per kidney. The glands' anatomical structure is significant in that the adrenal cortex (the surrounding outer layer) synthesizes the corticosteroid hormones, including cortisol and aldosterone, while the adrenal medulla (the central region) synthesizes epinephrine, norepinephrine, and dopamine.

The Gonads

The gonads have two important co-functions: the production of male or female gametes and the synthesis of sex hormones. In males, the gonads are the testicles and are located externally within the testicular pouches. The gonads synthesize the male sex hormone testosterone. In females, the gonads are the ovaries, which are located lateral to and at the level of the superior region of the uterus, one ovary on the left and one on the right. The distal entry into either the left or right fallopian tube is closely adjacent to the left or right ovary. The fallopian tubes provide a passageway into the uterine cavity. The uterus is a midline pelvic organ posterior to the urinary bladder and anterior to the rectum. The ovaries synthesize the female sex hormone estrogen.

Endocrine Physiology

While a large majority of the central nervous systems' responses are rapid in the form of electrical signals and muscular responses, the nervous system also exerts profound control over all aspects of the body by influencing the endocrine system. In contrast to direct nervous-signal-mediated control, which generally produces rapid but short-lived effects, hormonal effects are usually much slower in their actions and are often cumulative over longer periods of time, in some cases years or even decades. Many hormonal systems also function relatively independently of the central nervous system. In addition, many other hormones or hormone-like molecules are produced and secreted by virtually all tissues and organs of the body. For instance, the duodenum synthesizes and secretes the locally active hormones CCK and secretin.

The Hypothalamic Hormones

The hypothalamus is a critical brain region for the maintenance of homeostasis within the body. A primary mode of this regulation of homeostasis by the hypothalamus is through the release of hypothalamic hormones. The following primary hormones are secreted by the hypothalamus:

- **Thyrotropin releasing hormone (TRH):** This hormone acts on the anterior segment of the pituitary gland and stimulates the release of thyroid-stimulating hormone (TSH).
- **Corticotropin-releasing hormone:** This hormone also acts on the anterior segment of the pituitary gland and stimulates the release of adrenocorticotropin hormone (ACTH)
- **Growth hormone releasing hormone (GHRH):** This hormone stimulates the release of growth hormone (GH) from the anterior segment of the pituitary gland.
- **Gonadotropin-releasing hormone (GnRH):** This hormone stimulates the release of follicle-stimulating hormone (FSH) from the anterior segment of the pituitary gland.
- **Somatostatin (also known as growth-hormone-inhibiting hormone—GHIH):** This hormone inhibits the release of growth hormone and follicle-stimulating hormone from the anterior segment of the pituitary gland.

The Pituitary Gland Hormones

The pituitary gland is directly connected to the hypothalamus. Together, they regulate nearly all body functions via hormonal control. The two major functional/anatomical regions of the pituitary gland are the posterior pituitary and the anterior pituitary.

The Posterior Pituitary Gland Hormones

Many authorities consider the posterior pituitary to be part of the hypothalamus. The posterior pituitary secretes two hormones: oxytocin and vasopressin (AKA antidiuretic hormone—ADH).

Oxytocin

Oxytocin, often dubbed the "love hormone," plays a crucial role in social bonding, trust, and emotional connections. Produced in the hypothalamus and released by the pituitary gland, it influences childbirth, lactation, maternal behavior, and even impacts social interactions and stress regulation. Oxytocin triggers the milk letdown reflex in nursing mothers.

Vasopressin (or ADH)

Vasopressin is vital hormone that regulates blood pressure and the fluid balance of the body. The blood pressure effects are partially accomplished by ADH's effects on smooth muscle in the walls of blood vessels. ADH causes smooth muscle contraction in blood vessel walls, which in turn constricts blood vessel passageways. This results in an increase in blood pressure.

ADH also affects the kidney's microscopic filtering units—nephrons. There are an estimated one million nephrons per human kidney. ADH decreases the loss of water from the body by causing the nephrons to reabsorb water from fluids that have been filtered out of the bloodstream and are in the process of passing out of the kidney's filtering system and into the bladder.

Anterior Pituitary Gland Hormones
The hormones secreted by the anterior pituitary are described below.
- **Adrenocorticotropic hormone (ACTH):** ACTH is secreted continuously but at increased levels when the body is under physical or psychological stress and when blood glucose is too low. ACTH stimulates the cortex of the adrenal gland to release the corticosteroid hormone cortisol.
- **Thyroid-stimulating hormone (TSH):** TSH stimulates the thyroid gland to release thyroid hormones. Thyroid hormones are the primary hormones that establish the overall metabolic rates of the body.
- **Luteinizing hormone (LH) and Follicle-stimulating hormone (FSH):** LH and FSH are critical in the differentiation of cells to produce both male and female gametes and are the primary regulators of the female menstrual cycle.
- **Prolactin (PRL):** Prolactin stimulates glandular growth of mammary glands and subsequent production of milk in breastfeeding females.
- **Growth hormone (GH):** The levels of GH during childhood determines the maximum lean body mass and height that individuals can attain. This completion of growth is the physiological definition of adulthood.
- **Melanocyte-stimulating hormone (MSH):** The levels of MSH, particularly during prenatal (before birth) development, determines the darkness of skin color and is the basis for racial differences in skin color.

The Thyroid Hormones
The thyroid gland produces and releases two types of thyroid hormone, thyroxine (T4) and triiodothyronine (T3), and the hormone calcitonin. Notable effects of thyroid hormones include increases in the rates of protein synthesis, regulation of fat, protein and carbohydrate metabolism, promotion of cell differentiation, and enhancement of bone growth and regeneration. Excessively high or low levels of thyroid hormones can be fatal.

T3 and T4

Iodine atoms are included in the structure of the thyroid hormone and iodine deficiency leads to hypothyroidism and enlargement of the thyroid gland (this is called a goiter). The release of thyroid hormone is triggered by the pituitary hormone TSH. T3 is more potent than T4, but both hormones have the same effects. Thyroid hormones directly affect nearly every cell in the body and the overall effect is to increase the basal (baseline) metabolic activity of the body.

Calcitonin and Parathyroid Hormone (PTH)

PTH is synthesized and secreted by the parathyroid glands. PTH, along with the hormone calcitonin, plays a vital role in regulating the blood levels of calcium ion (Ca++). The activity of calcitonin and PTH occurs on cells involved in breaking down and regenerating the calcium-rich mineral hydroxyapatite—the major mineral that forms the extracellular matrix of bone.

The Pancreatic Hormones: Glucagon and Insulin

In addition to its exocrine function in the synthesis and release of digestive hormones and bicarbonate ions, the pancreas synthesizes and releases two hormones: glucagon and insulin. Both hormones are vital to maintaining proper levels of blood glucose. Insulin is also essential to most cells for the uptake of glucose into the cell. Insulin is produced by pancreatic islet cells. In type 1 diabetes, islet cells are attacked and destroyed by the body's own immune system. A lack of insulin can be fatal.

The Adrenal Cortical (Steroid) Hormones—Cortisol and Aldosterone

The adrenal cortical hormones are steroid hormones, which are modified versions of the cholesterol molecule. Other hormones are either small water-soluble molecules or polypeptides, which are amino acid chains.

Due to being based on a lipid type molecule, cholesterol, steroid hormones are fat-soluble rather than water-soluble. Steroid hormones are secreted into lymphatic vessels rather than blood vessels. The principal cortical hormones are the glucocorticoid steroid hormone cortisol and the mineral corticosteroid hormone aldosterone. The adrenal cortex also produces the precursor molecules transformed by the gonads into the male and female sex hormones, i.e., testosterone and estrogen, respectively.

Cortisol

Cortisol release is stimulated by the pituitary hormone ACTH. Cortisol has a wide range of actions, including to regulate the metabolism of fats, proteins, and carbohydrates. Cortisol also plays an important role in the immune system by suppressing the immune response. In addition, cortisol helps regulate glucose levels. Cortisol stimulates the liver to synthesize new glucose molecules through gluconeogenesis. Baseline levels of cortisol are essential to life.

Aldosterone

Aldosterone is a critical hormone in the regulation of blood pressure and electrolyte concentrations in the body. This regulation mechanism is highly complex and involves several other hormones in what is termed the renin-aldosterone-angiotensin hormone axis.

The Gonadal Hormones—Testosterone and Estrogen

The gonadal hormones—testosterone and estrogen—are synthesized in the testes in males and the ovaries in females, respectively. The sex hormones are synthesized from cholesterol-based precursors that are produced in the adrenal cortex. During the prenatal stage, testosterone is responsible for the development of male external genitalia. During adolescence, the sex hormones are responsible for the development of secondary sexual characteristics—pubic hair, testicular maturation, and breast development. Estrogen also appears to provide protection from coronary artery disease and osteoporosis in premenopausal females.

Immune and Lymphatic Systems

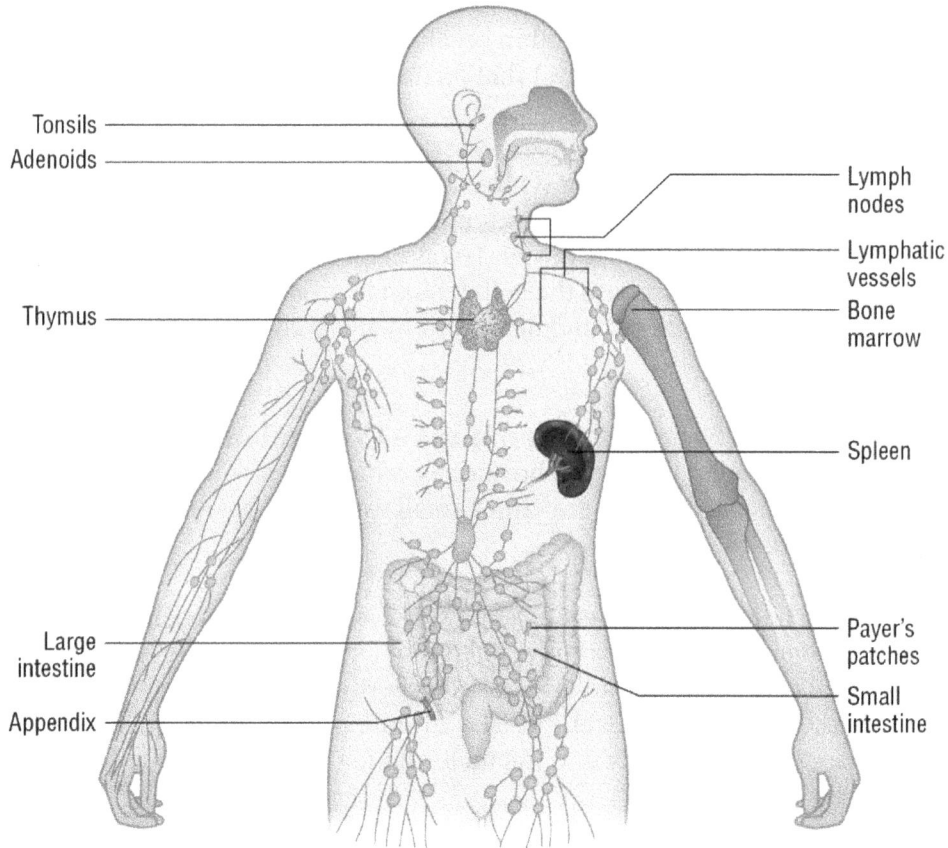

The immune system is a complex and widely distributed network of cells, organs, and other structures, while the lymphatic system is a body-wide circulatory system that includes lymphatic vessels, lymph nodes, and lymphoid organs. The lymphatic vascular system is closely associated with both the structure and distribution to the blood vessels of the cardiovascular system. The lymphatic system functions include the removal of excess fluids and debris from the extracellular or interstitial compartments of the body (area surrounding cells, not including spaces inside blood vessels). The lymphatic system also plays a key role in the immune system.

Capillary-size lymphatic vessels are found throughout the body. These vessels are terminal branches of the lymphatic vascular system. Lymphatic fluid moves from interstitial spaces into the lymphatic capillaries, then to progressively larger vessels, and finally to lymph nodes. Lymph nodes are nodular structures widely distributed throughout the body. Lymphatic fluid is filtered at lymph nodes and continues in vessels, leaving the lymph nodes to reach one of the two major lymphatic vessels—either the right lymphatic duct or the thoracic duct. The right lymphatic duct delivers lymph fluid into the right subclavian vein, and the thoracic duct delivers lymphatic fluid into the left subclavian vein.

The lymphatic circulation is also responsible for the absorption of fats and fat-soluble vitamins (vitamins A, C, D, and E) in the small intestines and subsequently for transport to the bloodstream.

Lymph Nodes
The anatomy of lymph nodes is significant for two key reasons: (1) the cortex of the lymph node is a site where T-cells accumulate and interact with B-cells, and (2) the medulla of lymph nodes is one of the anatomical regions where the maturation of B-cells occurs.

The Spleen
The spleen, the largest lymphoid organ in the body and one of the larger organs of the body in general, is in the left-upper quadrant of the abdomen just superior to the stomach and just inferior to the diaphragm. The spleen has structures that resemble lymph nodes containing B- and T-cells. It filters blood that arrives via the splenic artery arteries. The spleen contains macrophages that consume damaged and elderly red blood cells and recycles iron to the liver; and it also contains a large volume of white blood cells that serve as a readily accessible reserve for immune activities that may be required by the body.

The Thymus
The thymus is an organ in the midline of the thoracic cavity immediately posterior to the sternum and anterior to the trachea, directly between the lungs. The thymus is the organ where T-cells maturate.

The Appendix and the Tonsils
The appendix and the tonsils are also lymphoid organs that contain B- and T-cell functional regions. The appendix is an appendage of the cecum of the large intestine. The tonsils are in the lateral walls of the pharynx.

Bone Marrow
The medulla (central region) of most skeletal bones—and particularly the long bones of the arms and legs and the pelvic bones—contain bone marrow. Both red blood cells and white blood cells (including immature T- and B-cells) are produced in bone marrow.

Immune System Physiology
Most authorities would agree that the nervous system is probably the most complex system of the human body. At the same time, however, the human immune system is also extraordinarily complex, and decades of research remains to answer large gaps in the existing knowledge about this system. The immune system functions to protect the human body from foreign disease-causing biological and chemical agents. These agents include viruses, bacteria, and other single- and multi-cellular organisms. The immune system also protects the body from chemical products produced by disease-causing organisms (e.g., toxins). Finally, the immune system attempts to identify and contain or destroy dysfunctional or cancerous cells of the body.

There are various ways to categorize the immune system; one way is to define functions as either innate or adaptive immune system responses.

Innate Immune System
The innate immune system is a non-specific or generic immune system. It responds to pathogens and any other events that cause bodily injuries. In contrast to active immunity, innate immunity does not provide long-lasting resistance to repeated infection by the same organism.

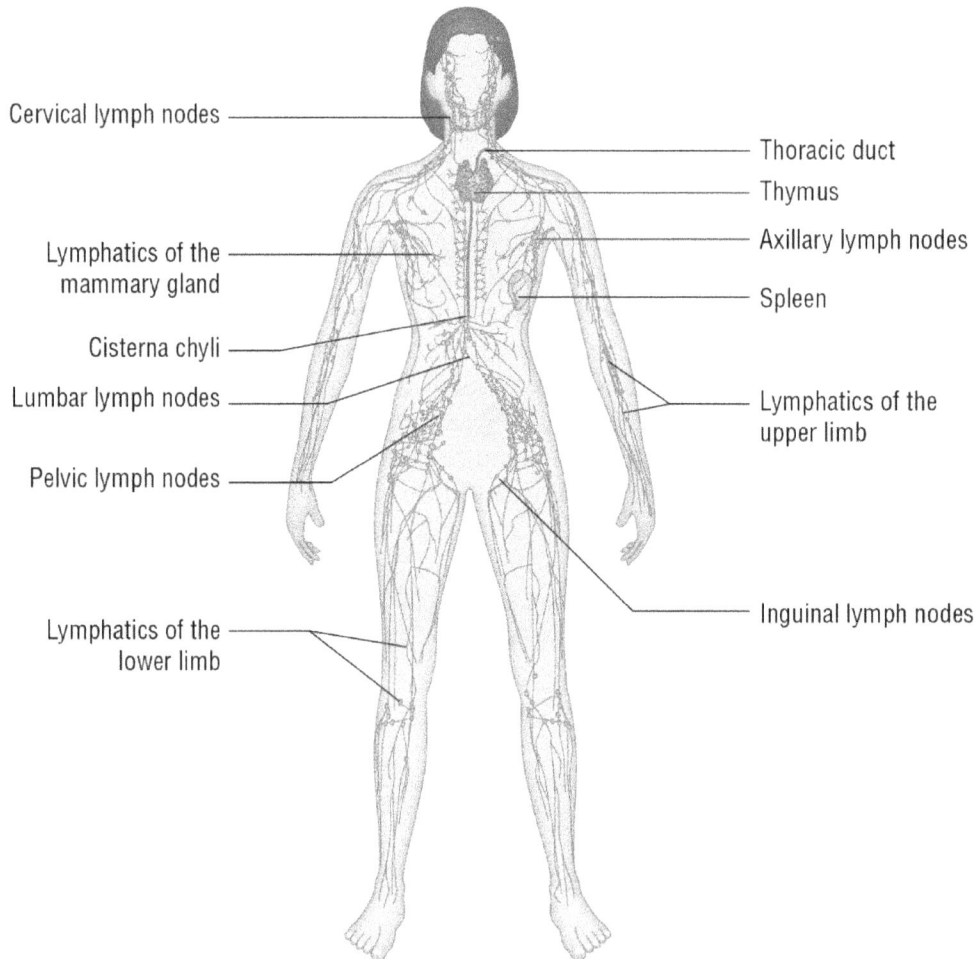

Cervical lymph nodes
Thoracic duct
Thymus
Axillary lymph nodes
Lymphatics of the mammary gland
Spleen
Cisterna chyli
Lumbar lymph nodes
Lymphatics of the upper limb
Pelvic lymph nodes
Inguinal lymph nodes
Lymphatics of the lower limb

Anatomical Barriers

The innate immune system consists of anatomical barriers and a variety of chemicals and cell types. The skin provides a physical barrier to pathogens and rids the skin surface of pathogens by desquamation (skin flaking), by sweating, and by the production of organic acids that create an unfavorable skin pH for pathogens. The continuous transport of mucus out of the respiratory tract by the motion of cilia provides physiological barriers to pathogens in the respiratory tract. The peristaltic motion of the intestines transports pathogens out of the digestive tract and gastric, and bile acids and digestive enzymes create a very hostile environment to most living organisms. Those organisms that do thrive in the digestive tract create a bio community that resists intrusion of other organisms. Saliva, mucous, and other bodily secretions contain a potent antibacterial compound called lysozyme.

Natural Killer Cells

If the barriers to a pathogen are breached, several innate defenses triggered. If the pathogen infects a cell of the body—usually in the form of a virus—the infected cell will alter its surface membrane molecules to alert natural killer (NK) cells that the cell is injured or infected. The NK cells attack the unhealthy cell by releasing perforins—small molecules that assemble on the target cell membrane and create holes or pores in the cell membrane. This process can be sufficient to kill the cell, but the NK cells also use the perorations created in the cell membrane to pass a potent toxin into the cell. The toxin has rapidly fatal effects on the unhealthy cell.

Sentinel Cells and Cytokines

Pathogens unconfined to the interior of cell are identified by monitoring cells of the innate immune system, AKA sentinel cells or surveillance cells. They recognize a limited number of molecular features common to most biological pathogens. As these enter the body, sentinel cells (usually macrophages) identify the pathogens and release molecules called cytokines.

Inflammation and the Complement Cascade

Cytokines are a class of intercellular signaling molecules that have a wide range of actions. One such action is the inflammatory reaction, which generates fever, causes vasodilation, and activates the complement cascade—a series of chemical reactions that produce a large amount of protein products that can directly kill pathogens or bind to pathogens and make them highly susceptible to destruction by macrophages.

Interferons

Interferons are a class of specific molecules released by many cells that progressively restrict the ability of viruses to continue infectious cycles within the body.

Macrophages

Macrophages are cells of the immune system that literally consume other cells—pathogens and injured or dead cells of the body—via a process called phagocytosis. Fever raises body temperature to levels unfavorable for viral infection processes. Swelling and increased blood flow begins the process of drawing a variety of types of immune cells to infection sites where an increasingly complex battle is waged to wall off the pathogens from further entry into the body and ultimately first kill the pathogens and then remove the cellular debris that results from this immunological warfare.

Histamine

Another class of effects that greatly enhances the local inflammatory reactions is the triggering of the release of histamine—this molecule causes local pain, increases fluid leakage from blood vessels at the infection site, resulting in swelling and causing vasodilation that results in an increased blood flow to the infected region.

Neutrophils

Another class of cytokine effects is the attraction of large numbers of neutrophils, which are a type of leukocyte, to the site of the pathogenic infection. This process involves the production of intercellular adhesion molecules (ICAMs) that neutrophils recognize and follow to the infection site. Upon encountering pathogens, neutrophils release granules of highly toxic compounds that destroy the cellular invaders.

As the innate immune response proceeds, a large number of additional inflammatory chemicals are produced. Several other cell types arrive and begin to create an inflammatory exudate of proteins, cells, and cytotoxic chemicals at the site of infection. When successful, the infection is walled off, pathogens are destroyed, and the damages are repaired.

Adaptive Immune System

The adaptive immune system consists of two major types of white blood cells called lymphocytes. The two types of lymphocytes are T-cells and B-Cells. B-cells produce antibodies, which are incredibly specific molecules designed to bind to a small molecule or a small region of a larger molecule. These small molecular regions are called antigens. Antigens are chemically foreign to the body and are considered "non-self" elements that the adaptive immune system recognizes and subsequently attempts to remove or deactivate by producing the specific antibody to the antigen or triggering immune cell actions that directly kill a pathogenic cell.

Humoral Active Immune Responses

In the humoral adaptive immune response, B-cells produce circulating antibodies that bind to antigens anywhere in the body. Interactions between circulating antigens, B-cell, and T-helper cell (a subtype of T-cell) trigger B cells to proliferate and produce large amounts of antibodies. When circulating antibodies bind these antigens, an antigen-antibody complex is formed, and this complex can be removed from the body by various mechanisms.

Cell-Mediated Active Immune Responses

The cell-mediated adaptive immune response involves the interaction of T-cells, B-cells, and antigen presenting cells or pathogen-capturing cells in the form of macrophages. In one type of cell-mediated response, a macrophage binds to a foreign cell, and then a T-helper cell binds to the macrophage. This binding action causes the T-helper cell to release cytokines that attract the cytotoxic T-cell to the T-helper/macrophage/pathogen cell complex. The cytotoxic T-cell, upon arrival, then kills the pathogenic cell.

Protective (Long-Term) Immunity

The innate immune system responds to pathogens and other substances that can injure cells (chemical, thermal, and physically inflicted injuries) in the same way every time. The adaptive immune system provides protective immunity. Once a particular antigen or pathogen has been identified by the adaptive immune system, the system is then primed to respond very quickly and very rapidly to clear the body of that particular antigen or pathogen if it attempts to infect the body in the future. This type of protective immunity can be artificially produced by the administration of vaccines. Typically, a vaccine is an injection of antigens in the form of killed or weakened pathogenic bacteria or viruses, which will result in long-term protective immunity to the dangerous native form of the bacterial or virus.

Passive Immunity

Passive immunity is a short-term immunity to pathogens that is acquired, rather than produced. For example, nursing infants acquire passive immunity to various pathogens by consuming antibodies formed by the mother and passed to the infant via breast milk. Once the supply of these antibodies stops, the immunity to the antibody-specific pathogens disappears in a few weeks or months.

VOCABULARY

You completed a crossword puzzle for the Vocabulary chapter in Module 3. Let's try another puzzle in this chapter. Below is a crossword puzzle to help you learn some additional words and expand your vocabulary.

Just like the earlier puzzle, the word list below contains all the words to solve the list of clues. As you solve each clue, enter the relevant word into the crossword puzzle and cross it off your word list.

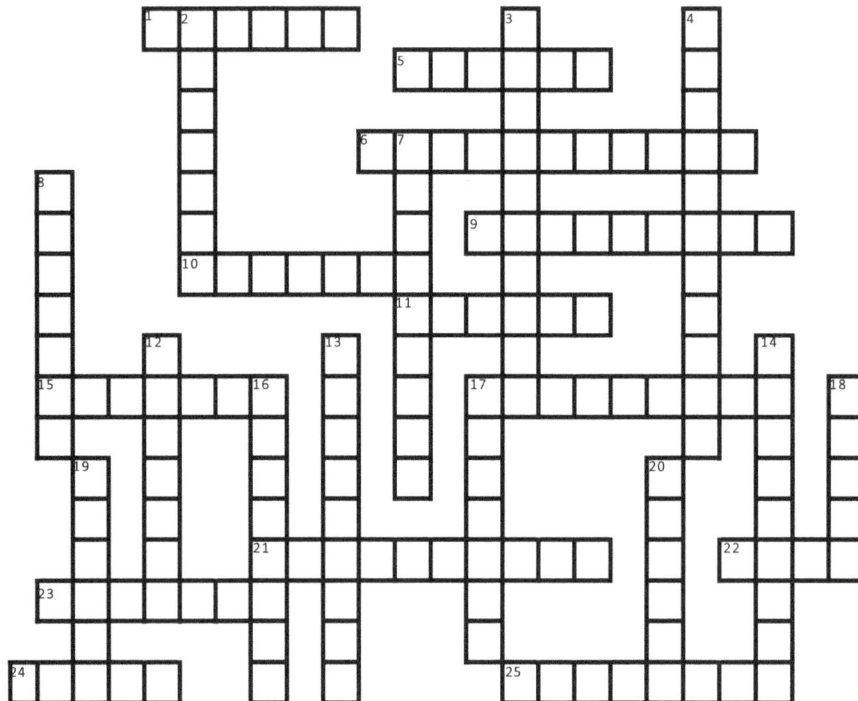

Word List

abdicate	fidget	profane
accost	hypocrite	reluctant
belligerent	inertia	spontaneous
boggy	jetty	sublime
canvass	limber	thrift
corrugated	menagerie	turmoil
defy	notary	vagrant
dilemma	obliterate	vestibule
eccentric	prestige	

Clues

Across

1. aggressively approach and speak to someone
5. flexible or supple
6. hostile and aggressive
9. unwilling or hesitant
10. moral or spiritual
11. a person authorized to perform legal formalities, usually relating to contracts or other documents
15. the mechanics principle where an object will remain in motion or at rest unless acted on by another force
17. a space adjacent to a main room or area
21. when a material is molded into a network of ridges
and grooves
22. resist or refuse to obey
23. a difficult choice
24. a small pier at which boats can dock
25. deep respect and admiration

Down

2. to survey someone about his/her opinion
3. completely destroy
4. suddenly or instantly
7. somewhat strange or unconventional
8. a great disturbance or uncertainty
12. irreverent or disrespectful
13. someone who claims to have certain principles or
beliefs, but docs not act in the same manner
14. a strange collection of items
16. to renounce or fail to carry out
17. a person without a settled home
18. very wet and muddy
19. a characteristic of being wise with money
20. wiggle or squirm about

Hopefully, solving this puzzle was a little easier for you than the first time around! Ready to see how you did? Head to the following page to check your answers against the solution.

Solution

Across

1. aggressively approach and speak to someone [ACCOST]

5. flexible or supple [LIMBER]

6. hostile and aggressive [BELLIGERENT]

9. unwilling or hesitant [RELUCTANT]

10. moral or spiritual [SUBLIME]

11. a person authorized to perform legal formalities, usually relating to contracts or other documents [NOTARY]

15. the mechanics principle where an object will remain in motion or at rest unless acted on by another force [INERTIA]

17. a space adjacent to a main room or area [VESTIBULE]

21. when a material is molded into a network of ridges and grooves [CORRUGATED]

22. resist or refuse to obey [DEFY]

23. a difficult choice [DILEMMA]

24. a small pier at which boats can dock [JETTY]

25. deep respect and admiration [PRESTIGE]

Down

2. to survey someone about his/her opinion [CANVASS]

3. completely destroy [OBLITERATE]

4. suddenly or instantly [SPONTANEOUS]

7. somewhat strange or unconventional [ECCENTRIC]

8. a great disturbance or uncertainty [TURMOIL]

12. irreverent or disrespectful [PROFANE]

13. someone who claims to have certain principles or beliefs, but docs not act in the same manner [HYPOCRITE]

14. a strange collection of items [MENAGERIE]

16. to renounce or fail to carry out [ABDICATE]

17. a person without a settled home [VAGRANT]

18. very wet and muddy [BOGGY]

19. a characteristic of being wise with money [THRIFT]

20. wiggle or squirm about [FIDGET]

Vocabulary-in-Context

Vocabulary-in-context questions ask you for the definition of a word as it is used within the context of the passage. The format of these questions resembles that of word knowledge questions. For vocabulary-in-context questions, you'll be given a word and asked to select the closest meaning from a list of four choices. Here's the difference between the two types of questions: While word knowledge questions test straightforward vocabulary, vocabulary-in-context questions often focus on words that can have more than one meaning. You will therefore need to use context clues from the passage to figure out which meaning is correct.

Notably, many questions on the TEAS 7 exam won't ask you to simply determine the meaning of a vocabulary word. Rather, instead of asking you for a synonym or definition of a vocabulary word, many questions will ask you what the vocabulary word "most closely means." For such questions, you'll need to use context clues and your existing vocabulary knowledge to determine which answer choice has the closest meaning to that of the vocabulary word.

To answer such questions, reread the sentence in the passage from which the word is taken. Come up with a prediction—your own definition or synonym of what the word means as used in that sentence. Then, look at the answer choices, and choose the one that best matches your prediction. Don't see your prediction among the answer choices? Then read each of the answer choices as part of the sentence, replacing the original word, and choose the one that makes the most sense.

Let's look at some examples.

Some of the questions you'll encounter will ask you to fill in the blank in a sentence. For the following questions, select the word that best completes the sentence.

1. The bolt was _____ , so it took a lot of effort to loosen the fastener.
   A. Rusted
   B. Shiny
   C. Loose
   D. Strong

Answer: A
Rationale: Using the context clues in the sentence, you can assume that the missing word is somehow related to the phrase "loosen the fastener." Something about the bolt made it difficult to remove. You can thus immediately eliminate "shiny" since it is not related to the action of removing a fastener. Likewise, "loose" is not correct because if the bolt were loose, it wouldn't be difficult to remove. "Strong" could possibly fit if there wasn't a better answer choice, but the word isn't typically used to describe how difficult a fastener is to remove. The word that best fits the sentence is therefore "rusted" because rust directly increases the difficulty of removing a fastener.

2. As the commanding officer's eyes widened and his face turned red, he proceeded to _____ the lance corporal.
   A. Tease
   B. Scold

      C. Compliment
      D. Correct

Answer: B
Rationale: Using the context clues in the sentence, you can assume that the missing word is somehow linked to widened eyes and a red face, which are associated with anger. You can immediately eliminate "tease" and "compliment" since those words connote lightheartedness and sincerity, not exactly aligning with the demeanor described in the sentence. "Correct" could fit if there wasn't a better answer choice, but the word isn't necessarily associated with widened eyes and a red face. The word that best fits the sentence is therefore "scold" because scolding connotes anger or irritation, both of which correlate with widened eyes and a red face.

Sure, these questions are easy overall, but they represent just one type of Vocabulary-in-Context questions you'll probably encounter on the exam. Here's another type: For the following questions, select the word that MOST CLOSELY means the same as the underlined word.

   3. The chairman of the board <u>abandoned</u> his position after a damaging scandal.
      A. Squandered
      B. Resigned
      C. Ignored
      D. Neglected

Answer: B
Rationale: All the answer choices connote negative characteristics of the position of chairman of the board, but only "resigned" most closely matches the underlined word. "Squandered" suggests a wasted opportunity. "Ignored" means deliberately taking no notice of. "Neglected" signifies a failure to pay attention to. "Resigned" indicates voluntarily leaving a job, which MOST closely means the same as "abandoned," leaving permanently.

   4. Sarah considered herself a <u>parsimonious</u> shopper. She loved finding great shopping deals.
      A. Cheap
      B. Frugal
      C. Economical
      D. Thrifty

Answer: A
Rationale: "Parsimonious" means being frugal to the point of stinginess. All the answer choices reflect the general meaning of "parsimonious," i.e., being careful with money, but only one choice has a negative association. "Frugal," "economical," and "thrifty" are all adjectives with a positive connotation, but "cheap" is usually used as a negative description. Thus, that term MOST closely means the same as "parsimonious," which has a negative connotation.

The following questions are a bit more difficult, but let's try a few more. For each question, select the word that LEAST LIKELY means the same as the underlined word.

   5. The evidence of the murder was <u>destroyed</u> before the trial.
      A. Devastated

      B. Obliterated
      C. Ruined
      D. Incinerated

Answer: D
Rationale: While all the answer choices can be used in place of "destroyed," "incinerated" suggests a specific type of damage: destruction by fire. Technically, "incinerated" is a logical answer, but the question isn't asking you which choice is not logical. The question is asking which choice LEAST likely means the underlined word. This question is a tough one, but on the exam, you should expect to see some questions like the prior one.

    6. While trying to negotiate a peace treaty, one side was being entirely <u>hostile</u> to the other.
      A. Belligerent
      B. Threatening
      C. Averse
      D. Combative

Answer: C
Rationale: While all the choices are mostly synonyms of "hostile," only one choice excludes a violent implication in its definition. "Averse" means strongly opposed to, but "belligerent," "threatening," and "combative" all suggest harm or death, as does "hostile."

For another type of question, you'll sometimes need to read a passage before answering the questions. Let's look at an example passage and some examples of related questions.

Passage
American elections consist of citizens voting for their government representatives. Today, this representation includes members of the U.S. Senate, but their inclusion was not always the norm. When the U.S. Constitution was first written, the people did not get to directly elect their senators. Instead, the senators were appointed by state legislators (who are elected directly by the people in their respective states). This process changed in 1913, however, with the 17th Amendment to the Constitution. This amendment allows for the direct election of U.S. Senators by the citizenry. While this election process can make senators more accountable to their constituents, since citizens will decide whether a senator will keep his/her job in the next election, the process diminishes the voice that state legislatures have in the federal government.

    1. The word <u>constituents</u> in the passage most closely means _____.
      A. Elements
      B. Employees
      C. Senators
      D. Voters

Answer: D
Rationale: By reading the choices back into the sentence, you can see that the best synonym for "constituents" is "voters." After all, voters decide whether to re-elect the senators. The word "constituents" on its own can have several meanings, including *voters, elements, members, components,* and *parts.* In the context of this passage, however, "voters" is the best answer.

2. The word <u>amendment</u> in the passage most closely means _____.
   A. Rule
   B. Principle
   C. Alteration
   D. Truth

Answer: C

Rationale: By reading the choices back into the sentence, you can see that the best synonym for "amendment" is "alteration." The passage states how the Constitution originally provided for senator selection. However, the passage also explains how the process changed after the 17th Amendment. Because "alteration" means "change," answer C is the best choice.

CRITICAL READING

When reading critically to answer questions based on provided passages on the TEAS 7, you'll want to know how to tackle inference questions and what signals can help you spot this type of question.

Inference Questions

Inference questions ask about ideas not directly stated, but rather implied by the passage. Such questions ask you to draw conclusions based on the information in the passage. Accordingly, inference questions usually include words such as *imply*, *infer*, or *conclude*, or may ask you what the author "would probably" think or do in each situation based on what was stated in the passage.

With inference questions, not going too far beyond the scope of the passage is important. You are not expected to make any guesses. Only one single correct answer—one that's a logical, next-step conclusion from what's presented in the passage—is relevant.

Let's look at some sample inference questions. Read the following passages, and use your inference skills to answer the questions that follow the passages. Remember that the inferences you make are not always obvious or directly stated in the passage.

Passage 1
Despite the practice being illegal in many states, some people set off their own fireworks at home each summer, especially on Independence Day. Most cities have public firework displays run by experienced professionals in a controlled environment, but many people still enjoy the thrill of setting off their own fireworks. However, this practice can be dangerous, and many people are injured each year from firework-related accidents. Having Independence Day fireworks in your own backyard is not worth the safety risk, especially when public firework displays are available in most areas.

    1.   The author of this passage would most likely support _____.
          A. The complete legalization of fireworks nationwide
          B. The reduction of public firework displays
          C. More rigorous enforcement of restrictions on home fireworks
          D. Promoting home fireworks use

Answer: D
Rationale: In the passage, the author takes a negative tone toward home fireworks use, citing the fact that the practice is dangerous, illegal in some areas, and unnecessary since many areas have safe public firework displays on holidays. Someone who is critical of home fireworks use would support strong enforcement of restrictions on their use.

Passage 2
A man took his car to the mechanic because the engine was overheating. The mechanic opened the hood to inspect the situation. He removed the radiator cap and could see that there was enough coolant in the radiator. Upon taking the car for a drive, he noticed that the engine would overheat at a stoplight but not on the highway.

1. According to the passage, what can you infer about the engine?
   A. The engine needs to be replaced
   B. The radiator is leaking
   C. The engine is operating normally
   D. The radiator fan is broken

Answer: D

Rationale: Although an overheating engine does indicate an abnormal condition, it does not necessarily indicate a catastrophic failure. Thus, the engine can hypothetically be repaired instead of replaced. The radiator was full of coolant, so that eliminates the possibility of a leak. When a vehicle is moving, the airflow across the radiator cools the coolant. However, when a vehicle is stationary, the fan is responsible for cooling the coolant. The fan not working correctly would explain why the car overheats at a stoplight but not on the highway.

Passage 3

One man in St. Paul Minnesota is making a difference for people in the community, and his impact was felt stronger than ever this Thanksgiving holiday. Jeff Ansorge once was in charge of almost 20 staff members and earned $80,000 a year as the head executive chef at a classy downtown Minneapolis restaurant. Only for the very well-off, the restaurant featured items such as a 24-ounce dry-aged porterhouse steak that went for almost $50. However, Jeff gave it all up to and has taken on the job as the head cook of a Salvation Army soup kitchen. While meals Jeff cooked at the restaurant would cost $40–$60, his meals are now free.

As head cook, he is making salmon, ribs, and stews for those who come to the Salvation Army Eastside Corps Community Center in St. Paul. For the Thanksgiving meal, Jeff made the traditional meal of turkey with stuffing, mashed potatoes and gravy, and extras such as cranberry sauce and rolls. Even the ambiance was completed with dinner being served on tables covered with white tablecloths and simple decorations. Jeff Ansorge, who is 40, says that it was a spiritual awakening that prompted him to make the move to the soup kitchen in October 2012, where he now makes just one-third of his previous salary.

While Jeff brought his culinary skills to his new role, his eye for bargain shopping and his ability to make food stretch has allowed the Salvation Army to serve great food and save money in the process as well. The Salvation Army works alongside the Second Harvest Heartland food bank, and with Jeff's help, they can now get 40-pound cases of mixed poultry for as little as five bucks. Jeff Ansorge also does his best to bring nutritional value to every meal that he serves. He knows that, for many who come to the soup kitchen, the food may be their only meal for the day. He's eliminated desserts and is working to cut back on the fat and sugars in meals, leaving more room for fresh fruits, fresh vegetables, and healthy meats.

1. Jeff is a caring and compassionate individual who has a deep sense of right and wrong and is likely governed by deeply held beliefs and ideas of mortality and civil duty.
   A. True
   B. False

Answer: A

Rationale: Several things mentioned in this passage can lead you to infer the statement about Jeff is true—he was raised in the Catholic faith, he works in a soup kitchen, volunteers, gave up a good job to help others, and genuinely seems to care about those less fortunate than himself.

2. All people who are well off and making good money dislike people like Jeff, who make those who are well off look bad.
    A. True
    B. False

Answer: A

Rationale: Nowhere in the passage is the detail in the question at all hinted at or implied.

Remember that inferences can be tricky things to master. But practice makes perfect, so keep at it!

ARITHMETIC REASONING

Scientific Notation

Scientific notation was originally developed as a simplified way for scientists to express extremely large or small numbers. In mathematics, scientific notation is used to easily compare large and small numbers. Let's look at how to translate a real number to its scientific notation equivalent.

Converting standard numbers to scientific notation is performed without calculation, although counting place values is still essential. Consider the following example:

> **Example:** The number 2,345,000 is equal to 2.345 * 1,000,000. By writing the value of 1,000,000 as 10^6 (10 multiplied by itself 6 times), the formulation of the scientific notation equivalent of the original number is completed: $2.345 * 10^6$.

Similarly, small decimal numbers can be written using scientific notation as well, as the following example shows:

> **Example:** The number 0.00736 is equal to 7.36 * 0.001. By writing the value of 0.001 as 10^{-3} (1 divided by 10, three times), the formulation of the scientific notation equivalent of the original number is completed: $7.36 * 10^{-3}$.

Instead of dividing (or multiplying) by 10, the translation to scientific notation can also be simplified by counting the number of places that the decimal point is transferred in the conversion process. In the first example, when the scientific notation was written, it began with writing 2.345. This number was formulated by moving the decimal point six places to the left in the original number. Therefore, the exponent of 10 was 6 (10^6).

Similarly, in the second example, the decimal part of the scientific notation number, 7.36, was written by moving the decimal point three places to the right. Therefore, the exponent of 10 was −3 (10^{-3}).

Using this method, no calculation is required. The included benefit is that the *significance* of numbers is easily determined. Answering the question about the number of significant figures for the two examples is a simple matter when using scientific notation. The number of digits in the decimal part of the scientific notation is always the number of significant figures. 2,345,000 has four significant figures, while 0.00736 has three. The zeros in these numbers are often referred to as *placeholders* when converting to scientific notation.

Notice that the exponent is NOT determined by counting zeros, but by counting the number of decimal places that are moved when formulating the scientific notation. The decimal part in scientific notation always has only one digit to the left of the decimal point.

MATHEMATICS KNOWLEDGE

Geometry

To tackle geometry questions on a mathematical reasoning test, you need to know a few formulas and rules. This section takes you through those basic rules. It covers intersecting lines, triangles, squares and rectangles, and circles.

Basic Vocabulary

Important vocabulary knowledge for geometry questions includes the following terms:

Line. A line is a set of all points between two endpoints. Lines have no area or width, only length.

Angle. An angle is the corner formed by two intersecting line segments; angles are measured in degrees. Degree measurements show the magnitude of the *sweep* of the angle. In the following figure, angle x is shown as the measure between the two-line segments.

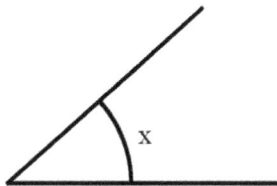

$360°$ describes the angle measurement all the way around a full circle. Half of that, $180°$, is the angle measurement across a straight line. Two lines at right angles to each other, called *perpendicular lines*, have an angle measurement of $90°$.

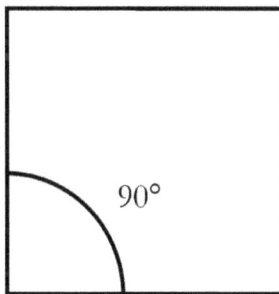

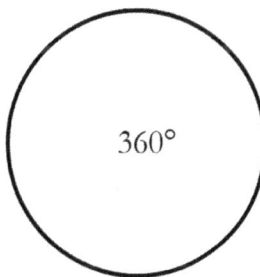

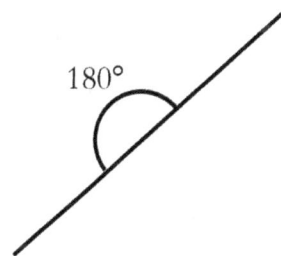

Area. The area is the measure of space inside a two-dimensional figure. Area has units of *length $*$ length*, or *length^2*. For example, room areas are described as square meters. Counties are described as being so many square kilometers. Each basic shape has a special formula for determining area.

Perimeter. The perimeter is the measure of the length around the outside of a figure.

Volume. For three-dimensional figures, the volume is the measure of space inside the figure. Volume has three dimensions: *length $*$ width $*$ height*. Accordingly, volume has units of *length³* (cubic length). For example, you may have heard *cubic meters* used to describe the volume of something like a storage unit. This formula applies only to square and rectangular three-dimensional shapes. Other figures have their own formulas for determining volume.

Intersecting Lines

Two important properties are crucial to know about pairs of intersecting lines:

1. They form angles that add up to 180° along the sides of each line.
2. They create two pairs of equal angles.

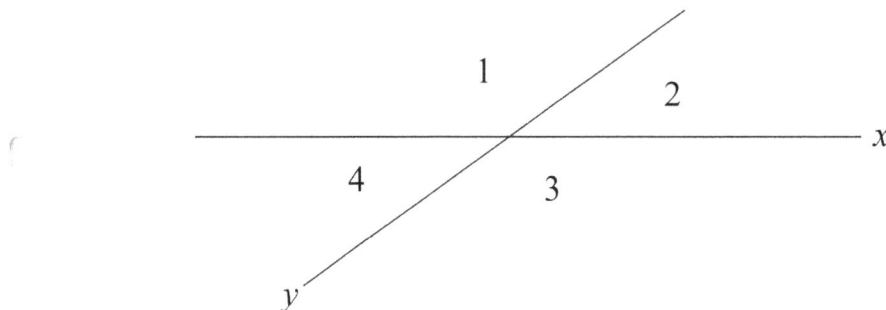

For example, in the diagram, line *x* intersects line *y*, forming the four angles 1, 2, 3, and 4. Any two angles along one side of a line will add up to 180°:

$$Angle\ 1 + Angle\ 2 = 180°$$
$$Angle\ 2 + Angle\ 3 = 180°$$
$$Angle\ 3 + Angle\ 4 = 180°$$
$$Angle\ 4 + Angle\ 1 = 180°$$

All four of the angles added together would equal 360°:

$$Angle\ 1 + Angle\ 2 + Angle\ 3 + Angle\ 4 = 360°$$

The two angles DIAGONAL from each other must be equal. For the preceding figure, the following is known:

$$Angle\ 1 = Angle\ 3$$
$$Angle\ 2 = Angle\ 4$$

This property is especially useful: If you are given any one of the angles, you can immediately solve for the other three. If you are told that *Angle 1* = 120°, for example, then you know that *Angle 2* = 180° − 120° = 60°. Since *Angle 3* = *Angle 1* and *Angle 4* = *Angle 2*, you now know all four angles.

Parallel/Perpendicular Lines

Parallel lines lie on the same 2-D plane (i.e., the page) and never intersect each other. The thing to remember about parallel lines is that, if a line intersects two parallel lines, the line will form a bunch of corresponding angles (like the ones discussed in the previous section). In addition, you can never assume that two lines are parallel just from a diagram. You need to be told or given enough information that you can deduce that two lines are parallel. The following diagram depicts an example of parallel lines, which always have the same slope.

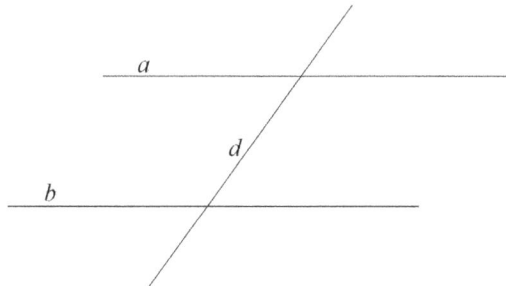

Lines *a* and *b* are parallel and are intersected by line *d*.

In the diagram, all four of the acute angles (the ones smaller than 90°) are equal. All four of the obtuse angles (the ones greater than 90°) are also equal. Why? Because a line intersecting parallel lines forms equivalent angles. This example is simply an expanded case of the intersecting lines concept discussed earlier.

Squares and Rectangles
By definition, a square has four sides of equal length and four 90° angles. A rectangle has two pairs of sides of equal length and four 90° angles. These angles mean that the sum of all four angles in a square or rectangle is 360°.

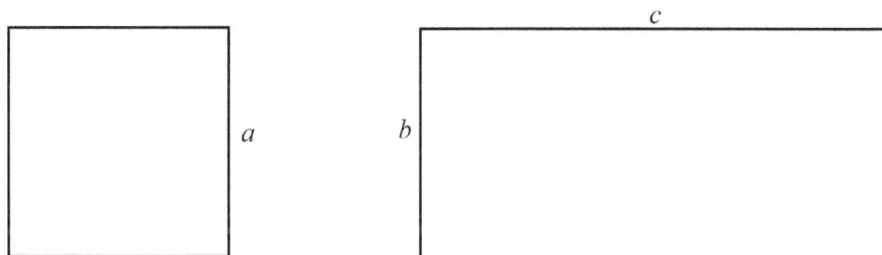

In that diagram, the shape on the left is a square. If you are given the length of side *a*, you automatically know the length of every side. You already know the measure of every angle as well because they are all 90°—the measure of right (perpendicular) angles.

The shape on the right is a rectangle. If given the length of side *b*, you know the length of the opposite side. But you do not know the length of the longer two sides unless lengths are given.

The **perimeter** of a square is the sum of all four of the line segments. Since the line segments are equal, the equation is as follows:

$$Perimeter\ of\ a\ square = 4 * (side\ length)$$

The perimeter of the given square is 4*a*.

The perimeter of the rectangle is also the sum of its sides. However, since there are two pairs of equal length sides in a rectangle, the equation is as follows:

$$Perimeter\ of\ a\ rectangle = 2 * (long\ side\ length) + 2 * (short\ side\ length)$$

The perimeter of the rectangle is $2b + 2c$.

The **area** of a square is its length times its width. Since length and width are the same for a square, the area is the length of one of its sides squared (that's where the term "squared" originated), and the equation to find the area is as follows:

$$Area = a2$$

For a rectangle, length times width is not equal to one side squared (the rectangle isn't a square, so the sides are not all the same length). The equation for the area of a rectangle is as follows:

$$Area = b * c$$

Triangles

A triangle is a polygon (closed shape) made of three separate line segments. While the four angles in a square and rectangle always add up to 360°, the three angles in a triangle always add up to 180°.

However, these angles are not always the same measure as they are for squares and rectangles.

See the following three distinct types of triangles:

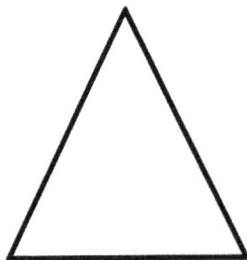

Equilateral
sides of same length
angles of 60°

Isosceles
two sides of same length
two angles of same measure

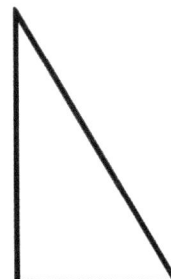

Right
one angle of 90°

The area of a triangle will always equal one half of the product of its base and its height. You can choose any side to be the base (the one at the bottom of the triangle is best), and the height of a triangle is the perpendicular line from the base to the opposite angle. The height is NOT the length of a side unless the triangle is a right triangle.

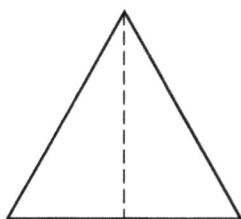

For example, in this triangle, the bottom leg is the base, and the dotted line is the height. The area can be calculated with the following formula:

$$A = \frac{1}{2}\,(base * height)$$

Another important formula to know when working with triangles is the Pythagorean theorem. This theorem tells you how to relate the lengths of the sides of right triangles—the ones that include 90° angles.

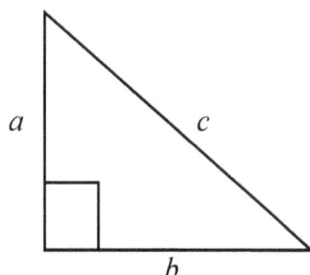

In the diagram, you have right triangle ABC. You know it's a right triangle because it has a 90° angle—not because it *looks* like a right triangle. Never assume the measure of an angle without being given that information. Side c is called the *hypotenuse*, which is the longest side of a right triangle. Sides a, b and c are related to each other according to the Pythagorean theorem:

$$c^2 = a^2 + b^2$$

Regardless of how the sides of the right triangle are labeled, however, the length of the longest side squared is equal to the sum of the lengths of the two shorter sides, each squared. You can expect to see a few problems on the test that will require you to use this relationship to solve the problems.

Here are some key details to remember about triangles:

- A triangle has three sides and three angles.
- The angles of a triangle will always add up to 180°.
- A triangle is a "right triangle" if one of the angles is 90°.
- If a triangle is equilateral, all angles are 60°, and all sides are the same length.
- The area of a triangle is one half times the base times the height.
- For right triangles, you can relate the lengths of the sides using the Pythagorean theorem.

Circles

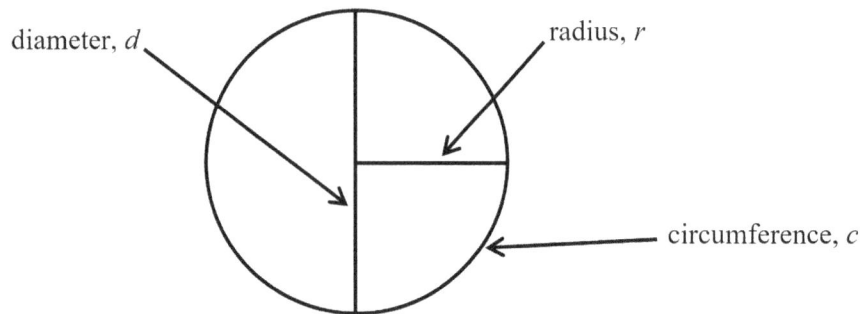

A circle is a figure without sides. Instead, a circle has a circumference with a set of points equidistant from the center of the circle.

Here are key details to remember about circles:

- The measurement around the outside of a circle is the **circumference**.
- The line segment from the center of the circle to the circumference is the **radius**.
- The line segment crossing the entire circle, passing through its center, is the **diameter**.
- The number of degrees in the central angle of a circle is 360°.

The circumference of a circle can be found using the following formula:

$$C = 2\pi r$$

In this formula, r is the radius (or the distance from the center of the circle to an outside point on the circle). If given the diameter, you can find the circumference using the following formula:

$$C = \pi d$$

The radius is twice the length of the diameter:

$$D = 2r$$

The area of a circle can be found using this formula:

$$A = \pi r^2$$

Therefore, the area is equal to the radius squared times the constant π (pronounced pi). Sometimes, answer choices are given with π as a part of the value, 2π, for example.

When you see such an answer, work out the problem without substituting the value of π (approximately 3.14). You can, in fact, estimate that π is 3.14 or $^{22}/_7$ in your calculations, but you'll end up with a decimal or fraction for your answer.

PRACTICE TEST 1

PRACTICE TEST 1.1: MATH

For each question, select the best answer.

1. Change the following mixed number to an improper fraction: $2\frac{1}{3}$.
    A. $5/3$
    B. $3/7$
    C. $7/3$
    D. $8/3$

2. Which of the following options is equivalent to 60% of 90?
    A. $0.6 * 90$
    B. $90 \div 0$
    C. $3/5$
    D. $2/3$

3. Convert the improper fraction $17/6$ to a mixed number.
    A. $1\frac{7}{6}$
    B. $2\frac{5}{6}$
    C. $\frac{6}{17}$
    D. $2\frac{7}{6}$

4. The decimal value of $7/11$ is _____?
    A. 1.57
    B. 0.70
    C. 0.6363...
    D. 0.77

5. The decimal value of $5/8$ is _____?
    A. 0.625
    B. 0.650
    C. 0.635
    D. 0.580

6. The fractional value of 0.5625 is _____?
    A. $7/15$
    B. $11/23$
    C. $5/8$
    D. $9/16$

7. The fractional value of 0.3125 is _____?
    A. $^5/_{16}$
    B. $^4/_{24}$
    C. $^6/_{19}$
    D. $^9/_{25}$

8. What is the value of the following expression if $a = 10$ and $b = -4$: $\sqrt{b^2 + 2 * a}$.
    A. 6
    B. 7
    C. 8
    D. 9

9. What is the greatest common factor of 48 and 64?
    A. 4
    B. 8
    C. 16
    D. 32

10. Solve for x in the following equation: $x = \frac{3}{4} * \frac{7}{8}$.
    A. $^7/_8$
    B. $^9/_8$
    C. $^{10}/_{12}$
    D. $^{21}/_{32}$

11. Find the value of $a^2 + 6b$ when $a = 3$ and $b = 0.5$.
    A. 12
    B. 6
    C. 9
    D. 15

12. What is the least common multiple of 8 and 10?
    A. 80
    B. 40
    C. 18
    D. 72

13. What is the sum of $^1/_3$ and $^3/_8$?
    A. $^3/_{24}$
    B. $^4/_{11}$
    C. $^{17}/_{24}$
    D. $^{15}/_{16}$

14. Solve the following equation: $x = (-9) * (-9)$.
    A. $x = 18$

    B. $x = 0$

    C. $x = 81$

    D. $x = -81$

15. Which fraction below falls between $^2/_3$ and $^3/_4$?

    A. $^3/_5$

    B. $^4/_5$

    C. $^7/_{10}$

    D. $^5/_8$

16. Which digit is in the thousandths place in the number: 1,234.567?

    A. 1

    B. 2

    C. 6

    D. 7

17. Which option below is the largest number?

    A. $^5/_8$

    B. $^3/_5$

    C. $^2/_3$

    D. 0.72

18. Which option below is the largest number?

    A. -345

    B. 42

    C. -17

    D. 3^4

19. Select the sequence below where all numbers fall between 4.857 and 4.858.

    A. 4.8573, 4.85735, 4.85787, 4.8598

    B. 4.857, 4.8573, 4.8578, 4.8579,

    C. 4.8571, 4.8573, 4.8578, 4.8579

    D. 4.8572, 4.8537, 4.8578, 4.8579

20. Which fraction below falls between 4 and 5?

    A. $^{11}/_3$

    B. $^{21}/_4$

    C. $^{31}/_6$

    D. $^{23}/_5$

21. Which number below does <u>not</u> fall between 7 and 9?

    A. $^{34}/_5$

    B. $^{29}/_4$

    C. $^{49}/_6$

D. $^{25}/_3$

22. If $\frac{4}{9}x - 3 = 1$, what is the value of x?
    A. $x = 9$
    B. $x = 8$
    C. $x = 7$
    D. $x = -4\frac{1}{2}$

23. What value is the solution for q in the following equation: $130 = q(-13)$?
    A. 10
    B. −10
    C. 1
    D. 10^2

24. Solve the following equation: $x = (-12) \div (-3)$.
    A. $x = -4$
    B. $x = -15$
    C. $x = 9$
    D. $x = 4$

25. Solve for r in the following equation: $p = 2r + 3$.
    A. $r = 2p - 3$
    B. $r = p + 6$
    C. $r = (p - 3) \div 2$
    D. $r = p - 3 \div 2$

26. Solve for x in the following equation: $x = 8 - (-3)$.
    A. $x = 5$
    B. $x = -5$
    C. $x = 11$
    D. $x = -11$

27. Evaluate the expression $7x^2 + 9x - 18$ for $x = 7$.
    A. 516
    B. 424
    C. 388
    D. 255

28. Evaluate the expression $x^2 + 7x - 18$ for $x = 5$.
    A. 56
    B. 42
    C. 38
    D. 25

29. Evaluate the expression $7x^2 + 63x$ for $x = 27$.
    A. 5,603

    B. 4,278

    C. 6,804

    D. 6,525

30. Sam worked 40 hours at d dollars per hour and received a bonus of $50. His total earnings were $530. What was his hourly wage?

    A. $18

    B. $16

    C. $14

    D. $12

31. The variable x is a positive integer. Dividing x by a positive number less than 1 will yield a(an) _____.

    A. Number greater than x

    B. Number less than x

    C. Negative number

    D. Irrational number

32. Amanda makes $14 an hour as a bank teller, and Oscar makes $24 an hour as an auto mechanic. Both work 8 hours a day, 5 days a week. Which equation below can be used to calculate how much money Amanda and Oscar make collectively in a 5-day week?

    A. $(14 + 24) * 8 * 5$

    B. $14 * 24 * 8 * 5$

    C. $(14 + 24)(8 + 5)$

    D. $14 + 24 * 8 * 5$

33. Seven added to four-fifths of a number equals 15. What is the number?

    A. 10

    B. 15

    C. 20

    D. 25

34. If the sum of two numbers is 360 and their ratio is 7:3, what is the smaller number?

    A. 72

    B. 105

    C. 98

    D. 108

35. Jean buys a textbook, a flash drive, a printer cartridge, and a ream of paper. The flash drive costs three times as much as the ream of paper. The textbook costs three times as much as the flash drive. The printer cartridge costs twice as much as the textbook. The ream of paper costs $10. How much does Jean spend in total for all supplies?

    A. $250

    B. $480

    C. $310

    D. $180

36. The area of a triangle equals one-half the base times the height. Which equation below is the correct way to calculate the area of a triangle with a base of 6 and a height of 9?

   A. $(6 + 9)/2$

   B. $\frac{1}{2}(6 + 9)$

   C. $2(6 * 9)$

   D. $\frac{(6 * 9)}{2}$

37. Calculate the value of the following expression: $2 + 6 * 3 * (3 * 4)^2 + 1$.

   A. 2,595

   B. 5,185

   C. 3,456

   D. 6,464

38. A rectangle with a length of $3x$ and a width of x has an area of $3x^2$. Write the area polynomial when the length is increased by 5 units and the width is decreased by 3 units: $(3x + 5)(x - 3)$.

   A. $3x^2 + 14x - 15$

   B. $3x^2 - 4x - 15$

   C. $3x^2 - 5x + 15$

   D. $3x^2 + 4x - 15$

39. A triangle with a base of $4x$ and a height of $7x$ has an area of $14x^2$, which is equal to $1/2$ times the base times the height. Write the area polynomial when the base is increased by 2 units and the height is increased by 3 units: $\frac{1}{2}(4x + 2)(7x + 3)$.

   A. $14x^2 + 14x + 6$

   B. $14x^2 + 14x + 3$

   C. $14x^2 + 13x + 3$

   D. $14x^2 + 28x + 3$

40. Momentum is defined as the product of mass times velocity. If your 1,250 kg car is traveling at 55 km/hr, what is the value of the momentum?

   A. 68,750 kg m/s

   B. 19,098 kg m/s

   C. 9,549 kg m/s

   D. 145,882 kg m/s

41. In her retirement accounts, Janet has invested $40,000 in stocks and $65,000 in bonds. If she wants to rebalance her accounts so that 70% of her investments are in stocks, how much money will she have to move from bonds?

   A. $33,500

   B. $35,000

   C. $37,500

   D. $40,000

42. Brian pays 15% of his gross salary in taxes. If he pays $7,800 in taxes, what is his gross salary?
    A. $52,000
    B. $48,000
    C. $49,000
    D. $56,000

43. In a high school French class, 45% of the students are sophomores, and 9 sophomores are in the class. How many total students are in the class?
    A. 16 students
    B. 18 students
    C. 20 students
    D. 22 students

44. Marisol's score on a standardized test was ranked in the 78th percentile. If 660 students took the test, approximately how many students scored lower than Marisol?
    A. 582 students
    B. 515 students
    C. 612 students
    D. 486 students

45. The population of Mariposa County in 2015 was 90% of its population in 2010. The population in 2010 was 145,000. What was the population in 2015?
    A. 160,000 people
    B. 142,000 people
    C. 120,500 people
    D. 130,500 people

46. Alicia must earn a score of 75% to pass an 80-question test. How many total questions can she miss and still pass the test?
    A. 20 questions
    B. 25 questions
    C. 60 questions
    D. 15 questions

47. A cell phone on sale at 30% off costs $210 after the discount. What was the original price of the phone?
    A. $240
    B. $273
    C. $300
    D. $320

48. In the graduating class at Emerson High School, 52% of the students are girls and 48% are boys. The class has 350 students. Among the girls, 98 plan to attend college. How many girls do not plan to attend college?
    A. 84 girls
    B. 48 girls
    C. 66 girls

D. 72 girls

49. The number of students enrolled at Two Rivers Community College increased from 3,450 in 2010 to 3,864 in 2015. What was the percent increase?
    A. 9%
    B. 17%
    C. 12%
    D. 6%

50. Produce is usually priced to the nearest pound. A produce scale has numerical values for pounds and ounces. Which weight below would you expect to be priced at 15 pounds?
    A. 15 pounds, 14 ounces
    B. 15 pounds, 10 ounces
    C. 14 pounds, 4 ounces
    D. 14 pounds, 14 ounces

51. Which number below is rounded to the nearest ten-thousandth?
    A. 7,510,000
    B. 7,515,000
    C. 7,514,635.8239
    D. 7,514,635.824

52. Measuring devices determine the precision of scientific measurements. If a graduated cylinder has a maximum of 10 cc's and has 10 increments between each whole number of cc's, which answer below is a correct representation of a volume measurement with this cylinder?
    A. 7 cc's
    B. 7.1 cc's
    C. 7.15 cc's
    D. 7.514 cc's

53. If a person can unload about 50 pounds in 15 minutes, estimate the time and labor force needed to unload 2.5 tons of 50-pound blocks from a truck based on 8-hour workdays.
    A. 1 person for 10 days
    B. 2 people for 1 day
    C. 4 people for 1 day
    D. 5 people for 5 days

54. In rush hour, you can usually commute 18 miles to work in 45 minutes. If you can travel an average of 5 miles per hour faster in the early morning (i.e., before rush hour), how much time would you estimate for the early commute to work?
    A. 50 minutes
    B. 40 minutes
    C. 30 minutes
    D. 20 minutes

55. During a 45-minute class period, you are taking a 50-question test with 20 multiple-choice questions and 30 true/false questions. If all questions have equal value, how

much time would you need to complete each question type if you are twice as fast at multiple-choice questions?

    A. 90 seconds per multiple-choice question; 45 seconds per true/false question

    B. 60 seconds per multiple-choice question; 30 seconds per true/false question

    C. 70 seconds per multiple-choice question; 35 seconds per true/false question

    D. 80 seconds per multiple-choice question; 40 seconds per true/false question

56. Your interview is scheduled for 8:00 in the morning, and you need to allow 20 minutes for your trip to the interview. You oversleep and leave 10 minutes late. How fast must you travel to get to your interview on time?

    A. Half as fast

    B. Twice as fast

    C. Three times as fast

    D. Four times as fast

57. A square meter is a square with 1-meter sides. If a meter is 1,000 millimeters, how many square millimeters are in a square meter?

    A. 100 square millimeters

    B. 1,000 square millimeters

    C. 10,000 square millimeters

    D. 1,000,000 square millimeters

58. In 4 years, Tom will be twice as old as Serena was 3 years ago. Tom is 3 years younger than Serena. How old are Tom and Serena?

    A. Serena is 28, Tom is 25

    B. Serena is 7, Tom is 4

    C. Serena is 18, Tom is 15

    D. Serena is 21, Tom is 18

59. Amy drives her car until the gas gauge is down to $1/8$ full. Then she fills the tank by adding 14 gallons. What is the total capacity of the gas tank?

    A. 16 gallons

    B. 18 gallons

    C. 20 gallons

    D. 22 gallons

60. Two rectangles are proportional. In other words, the ratio of length to width is the same for both rectangles. The smaller rectangle has a length of 8 inches and a width of 3 inches. The large rectangle has a length of 12 inches. What is the width of the larger rectangle?

    A. 4 inches

    B. 4.5 inches

    C. 6 inches

    D. 8.5 inches

PRACTICE TEST 1.2: SCIENCE

For each question, select the best answer.

1. Which of the following is present on bronchial epithelial cell membranes?
   A. Microvilli
   B. Cilia
   C. Flagella
   D. Dendrites

2. Emulsification of fats requires _____ and occurs in the _____.
   A. amylase; stomach
   B. bile; stomach
   C. amylase; small intestine
   D. bile; small intestine

3. Which of the following is a direct function of T-helper cells?
   A. Phagocytosis
   B. Cell lysis
   C. Circulating antibody production
   D. Cytokine secretion

4. Which of the following statements is true for blood pumped out of the heart?
   A. Passes through the pulmonary capillaries before returning to the left side of the heart
   B. Fully oxygenated
   C. Pumped out of the right ventricle via the aorta
   D. Reaches the lungs via the pulmonary veins before returning to the heart

5. Oxygen enters the circulatory system during _____.
   A. inspiration only
   B. inspiration and the interval between inspiration and expiration
   C. expiration and the interval between inspiration and expiration
   D. continuously throughout the entire respiratory cycle

6. Where do the integrative functions of the nervous system occur?
   A. Peripheral neurons
   B. Limbic system
   C. Cerebellum
   D. Autonomic nervous system

7. Which of the following opens periodically to allow the passage of stomach contents into the duodenum?
   A. Gastroesophageal sphincter
   B. Pyloric sphincter

  C. Sphincter of Oddi

  D. Anal sphincter

8. Which of the following is NOT part of the innate immune system in humans?

  A. Phagocytosis of foreign cells

  B. Stimulation of fever

  C. Production of antibodies

  D. The release and response to cytokines

9. Which of the following anatomical relations is correct for a normal adult human?

  A. Heart is ventral to the esophagus

  B. Wrist is proximal to the elbows

  C. Kidneys are medial to the abdominal aorta

  D. Urinary bladder is superior to the pancreas

10. Where is urea produced in humans?

  A. Liver

  B. Kidney

  C. Pancreas

  D. Red blood cells

11. Which of the following human organs does NOT receive both oxygenated and deoxygenated blood?

  A. Lungs

  B. Heart

  C. Liver

  D. Large intestine

12. Which of the following human skeletal muscle mostly contracts involuntarily?

  A. Masseters

  B. Diaphragm

  C. Biceps

  D. Tongue

13. In which of the following human organs does most ingested water get absorbed?

  A. Oral mucosa and the esophagus

  B. Esophagus and the stomach

  C. Small intestine

  D. Large intestine

14. Which of the following cell types binds to pathogen-associated molecular patterns (PAMPs)?

  A. Plasma cells

  B. Dendritic cells

  C. Natural killer (NK) cells

  D. T-helper cells

15. Which of the following statements is true regarding dietary protein intake in humans?
    A. Strict vegetarians have no protein intake
    B. It must include all 20 amino acids required for protein synthesis in the body
    C. Severe protein deficiency caused by inadequate protein intake during early childhood can result in a condition known as kwashiorkor
    D. The breakdown of proteins begins when they reach the ileum of the small intestine

16. Which of the following hormones inhibits the release of thyroid-stimulating hormone (TSH) and growth hormone?
    A. Somatostatin
    B. Luteinizing hormone (LH)
    C. Oxytocin
    D. Dopamine

17. What is the atomic weight?
    A. Measure of atomic activity
    B. Weight of protons and electrons of an atom
    C. Approximately equal to the weight of the protons and neutrons
    D. Approximately equal to the weight of neutrons and electrons

18. Which of the following three components are a nucleotide composed of?
    A. A carboxylic acid, a nitrogenous base, and a pentose sugar
    B. An amino acid, a hexose sugar, and a nitrogenous base
    C. A phosphate group, a pentose sugar, and a nitrogenous base
    D. A phosphate group, a hexose sugar, and an amino acid

19. Where does the diffusion of oxygen from inhaled air to the bloodstream occur?
    A. Bronchi
    B. Lungs
    C. Trachea
    D. Alveoli

20. Which of the following cellular organelles does not possess an outer encapsulating membrane?
    A. Mitochondria
    B. Ribosomes
    C. Chloroplasts
    D. Nuclei

21. Which of the following statements is true regarding a complete segment of mRNA and the DNA gene from which it was transcribed?
    A. The mRNA segment base sequence is identical to that of the DNA gene base sequence
    B. The mRNA segment base sequence is identical to that of the complementary DNA strand segment sequence

C. The mRNA segment base sequence is identical to that of the complementary DNA strand segment sequence except that adenine substitutes thymine in the mRNA base sequence

D. The mRNA segment base sequence is identical to that of the complementary DNA strand segment sequence except that uracil substitutes thymine in the mRNA base sequence

22. Which of the following is NOT a correct pair of physical quantities for SI units compared to British/English units?
    A. Watts: Horsepower
    B. Liters: Gallons
    C. Newtons: Joules
    D. All the above are appropriate pairs

23. In a covalent bond, two atoms share electrons in order to fill their _____.
    A. valence shells
    B. electromagnetic fields
    C. hydrocarbon molecules
    D. isotope

24. Which of the following is responsible for transmitting genetic information to a cell's ribosomes?
    A. Nucleosome proteins
    B. mRNA
    C. Sense strand of DNA
    D. tRNA

25. Which of the following terms represents the testicles and ovaries of the male and female reproductive systems?
    A. Gametes
    B. Gonads
    C. Sex chromosomes
    D. Zygote

26. Which of the following statements is correct for the processing of genetic information in human cells?
    A. A single unique sequence of genes codes a single unique protein
    B. A single unique three-base codon codes a single unique amino acid
    C. A single unique protein can only be coded by a single unique sequence of codons
    D. A single unique protein can only be coded by a single unique sequence of DNA bases

27. Where are neurotransmitters released in the peripheral nervous system?
    A. Myelin sheath
    B. Synapse
    C. Sarcomere

      D. Ganglia

28. Approximately how many miles are there in an 8K race?
      A. 4 miles
      B. 4.5 miles
      C. 5 miles
      D. 6.5 miles

29. What is the electric charge of an atom with equal numbers of electrons, neutrons, and protons?
      A. +2
      B. +1
      C. Zero
      D. -1

30. What are cells that mediate the immune response by phagocytosis or endocytosis called?
      A. Antigen-presenting cells (APCs)
      B. Red blood cells
      C. Antibody-producing cells
      D. Platelets

31. Adipose tissue is a type of _____.
      A. epithelial tissue
      B. connective tissue
      C. elastic tissue
      D. osseous tissue

32. In chemical reactions, a catalyst _____ of a reaction by _____.
      A. increases the efficiency; increasing the activation energy
      B. increases the efficiency; decreasing the activation energy
      C. increases the rate; increasing the activation energy
      D. increases the rate; decreasing the activation energy

33. Which of the following is the ground-state electronic configuration of a neutral atom of neon?
      A. $1s^2 2s^2 2p^6$
      B. $1s^2 2s^2 3s^2 3p^4$
      C. $2s^2 2p^2 3s^2 3p^2 3p^2$
      D. $6s^2 2p^2$

34. In biological chemical reactions, what does an increase in enzymatic activity indicate?
      A. Enzyme has increased its functional pH range
      B. Enzyme has increased its functional temperature range
      C. Enzyme has increased its effect on the rate of a chemical reaction
      D. Enzyme has increased the total number of reactions it is capable of catalyzing

35. Which of the following substances releases hydrogen ions by dissociation when in solution and has pH values lower than pure water?
    A. Bases
    B. Acidic substances
    C. Neutral substances
    D. None of the above

36. Which of the following proteins can stretch and relax?
    A. Keratin
    B. Elastin
    C. Ligaments
    D. Collagen

37. Which of the following is a site for steroid hormone production?
    A. Pancreas
    B. Adrenal gland
    C. Thyroid gland
    D. Thymus

38. Which of the following is a balanced chemical equation?
    A. $O_2 \rightarrow 2O^- + 2e^-$
    B. $2O_2 + 8H^+ + 8e^- \rightarrow 4H_2O$
    C. $4H^+ + 2O \rightarrow 2H_2O^+$
    D. $CH_4 + O_2 \rightarrow \frac{1}{2}CO_2 + \frac{1}{2}H_2O$

39. Which of the following intermolecular bonds cannot be broken down by human digestive enzymes?
    A. Peptide bonds
    B. B-glycosidic bonds
    C. Ester bonds
    D. Glycosidic bonds

40. Water molecules in the liquid state have _____ intermolecular bonding compared to water molecules in the solid state.
    A. the same type of
    B. stronger
    C. a different type of
    D. no

41. What is the electric charge of an atom when the number of electrons exceeds the number of protons?
    A. Neutral
    B. Positive
    C. Negative
    D. The electric charge is unknown

42. In a single chromosome, _____.
    A. every DNA strand contains genes
    B. there are always two copies for every gene
    C. every functional gene can be transcribed into an mRNA molecule
    D. there are at least 2 alleles for every gene

43. Which of the sequences shows the correct mRNA transcription of the following DNA sequence?

    DNA: AGC TAC CCG

    A. TCG ATG GGC
    B. UCG AUG GGC
    C. TCG UTG GGC
    D. CTA GCA AAT

44. In which of the following are ribosomes produced?
    A. Rough endoplasmic reticulum
    B. Peroxisomes
    C. Lysosomes
    D. Nucleoli

45. Ribosomes are to proteins as _____ is/are to DNA.
    A. amino acids
    B. codons
    C. RNA polymerase
    D. DNA polymerase

46. For double-stranded DNA, one strand is called the sense strand and the other is called the antisense strand. Which of the following occurs during the replication of double-stranded DNA?
    A. The sense strand is completely replicated before replication of the antisense strand begins
    B. The antisense strand is completely replicated before replication of the sense strand begins
    C. Either the sense or the antisense is replicated before replication of the complementary strand begins
    D. Replication of both strands occurs simultaneously

47. Which of the following is produced by the hypothalamus to improve mood?
    A. Glucagon
    B. Dopamine
    C. Prolactin
    D. Follicle-stimulating hormone

48. Which type of immunity do lymph nodes trigger?
    A. Innate immunity

    B. Adaptive immunity
    C. Incompatibility
    D. Myeloid lineage immunity

49. Which of the following are the structural categories of nitrogenous bases in nucleic acids?
    A. Purines and pyrimidines
    B. Thymine and uracil
    C. Nucleotides and nucleosides
    D. Pyrimidines and hydroxyurea

50. Which of the following is an R group of the amino acid lysine?
    A. $-COH$
    B. $-OH$
    C. CH_3
    D. NH_2

PRACTICE TEST 1.3: ENGLISH LANGUAGE

For each question, select the best answer.

1. Which of the answer choices show the set of words that best completes the following sentence?

   When asked if the sleeping pill had _____ him at all, the man replied that it did not have any _____; nonetheless, he realized that he _____ not attempt to drive his car that evening.

   A. affected; effect; ought
   B. affected; effect; aught
   C. effected; affect; ought
   D. effected; affect; aught

2. Which sentence makes the best use of grammatical conventions to ensure good clarity and concision?
   A. Hiking along the trail, the birds chirped loudly and interrupted our attempt at a peaceful nature walk.
   B. The birds chirped loudly, attempting to hike along the nature trail we were interrupted.
   C. Hiking along the trail, we were assailed by the chirping of birds, which hardly made our nature walk the peaceful exercise we had wanted.
   D. Along the nature trail, our walk was interrupted by loudly chirping birds in our attempt at a nature trail.

3. Which word from the following sentence is an adjective?

   A really serious modern-day challenge is finding a way to consume real food in a world of overly processed food products.

   A. really
   B. challenge
   C. processed
   D. consume

4. To improve sentence fluency, how could the following information best be conveyed in a single sentence?

   My daughter was in a dance recital. I attended it with my husband. She received an award. We were very proud.

   A. My daughter, who was in a dance recital, received an award, which made my husband and I, who were in attendance, very proud.
   B. My husband and I attended my daughter's dance recital and were very proud when she received an award.
   C. Attending our daughter's dance recital, my husband and I were very proud to see her receive an award.

    D. Dancing in a recital, my daughter received an award, and my husband and I, who were there, were very proud.

5. Which of the following sentences is punctuated correctly?
    A. Since the concert ended very late I fell asleep in the backseat during the car ride home.
    B. Since the concert ended very late: I fell asleep in the backseat during the car ride home.
    C. Since the concert ended very late; I fell asleep in the backseat during the car ride home.
    D. Since the concert ended very late, I fell asleep in the backseat during the car ride home.

6. Which of the answer choices below best completes the following sentence?

Negotiations with the enemy are never fun, but during times of war, _____ an unavoidable evil.

    A. its
    B. it's
    C. their
    D. they're

7. Which of the answer choices best completes the following sentence?

The a cappella group _____ looking forward to performing for the entire student body at the graduation ceremony.

    A. is
    B. are
    C. was
    D. be

8. What kind of sentence is the following statement?

I can't believe her luck!

    A. Declarative
    B. Imperative
    C. Exclamatory
    D. Interrogative

9. Identify the word causing an error in the following sentence:

Irregardless of the expense, it is imperative that all drivers have liability insurance to cover any personal injury that may be suffered during a motor vehicle accident.

    A. irregardless
    B. imperative
    C. liability
    D. suffered

10. Which of the following sentence is grammatically correct?
    A. Between you and me, I brang back less books from my dorm room than I needed to study for my exams.
    B. Between you and I, I brought back less books from my dorm room then I needed to study for my exams.
    C. Between you and me, I brought back fewer books from my dorm room than I needed to study for my exam.
    D. Between you and me, I brought back fewer books from my dorm room then I needed to study for my exams.

11. Which answer choice bests completes the following sentence with the proper antecedent agreement and the proper verb:

    Neither of _____ able to finish our supper.

    A. we; were
    B. we; was
    C. us; were
    D. us; was

12. Which word in the following sentence is used as a noun?

    The library books are overdue.

    A. The
    B. library
    C. books
    D. overdue

13. Which answer choice is a simple sentence?
    A. Mary and Samantha ran, skipped, and hopped their way home from school every day.
    B. Mary liked to hop, but Samantha preferred to skip.
    C. Mary loved coloring but disliked when coloring was assigned for math homework.
    D. Samantha thought Mary was her best friend, but she was mistaken.

14. Which answer choice is NOT a simple sentence?
    A. Matthew and Thomas had been best friends since grade school.
    B. Matthew was tall and shy, and Thomas was short and talkative.
    C. Matthew liked to get Thomas to pass notes to the little red-haired girl in the back row of math class.
    D. Matthew and Thomas would tease Mary and Samantha on the way home from school every day.

15. Which of the following sentences is punctuated correctly?
    A. "Theres a bus coming so hurry up and cross the street!" yelled Bob to the old woman.

B. "There's a bus coming, so hurry up and cross the street", yelled Bob, to the old woman.

C. "Theres a bus coming, so hurry up and cross the street,"! yelled Bob to the old woman.

D. "There's a bus coming, so hurry up and cross the street!" yelled Bob to the old woman.

16. Which of the following sentences is punctuated correctly?
    A. It's a long to-do list she left for us today: make beds, wash breakfast dishes, go grocery shopping, do laundry, cook dinner, and read the twins a bedtime story.
    B. Its a long to-do list she left for us today; make beds; wash breakfast dishes; go grocery shopping; do laundry; cook dinner; and read the twins a bedtime story.
    C. It's a long to-do list she left for us today: make beds; wash breakfast dishes; go grocery shopping; do laundry; cook dinner; and read the twins a bedtime story.
    D. Its a long to-do list she left for us today: make beds, wash breakfast dishes, go grocery shopping, do laundry, cook dinner, and read the twins a bedtime story.

17. Which of the following sentences is written in the first person?
    A. My room was a mess, so my mom made me clean it before I was allowed to leave the house.
    B. Her room was a mess, so she had to clean it before she left for the concert.
    C. You had better clean up your room before your mom comes home!
    D. Sandy is a slob and never cleans up her own room until her mom makes her.

18. Which of the following sentences adheres to the rules for capitalization?
    A. My second grade Teacher's name was Mrs. Carmicheal.
    B. The Pope gave a very emotional address to the crowd after Easter Sunday mass.
    C. The president of France is meeting with President Obama later this week.
    D. My family spent our summer vacations at grandpa Joe's cabin in the Finger Lakes region.

19. Which answer choice best completes the following sentence?

    The girl returning home after her curfew found the _____ up the stairs to her bedroom maddening as it seemed every step she took on the old staircase yielded a loud _____.

    A. clime; creak
    B. clime; creek
    C. climb; creek
    D. climb; creak

20. Which answer choice correctly completes the following sentence?

    By this time next summer, _____ my college coursework.

    A. I did complete
    B. I completed

    C. I will complete

    D. I will have completed

21. Which answer choice best completes the following sentence?

    The teacher nodded her _____ to the classroom _____, who was teaching a portion of the daily lesson for the first time.

    A. assent; aide
    B. assent; aid
    C. ascent; aide
    D. ascent; aid

22. Which of the following sentences is grammatically correct?
    A. No one has offered to let us use there home for the office's end-of-year picnic.
    B. No one have offered to let we use their home for the office's end-of-year picnic.
    C. No one has offered to let ourselves use their home for the office's end-of-year picnic.
    D. No one has offered to let us use their home for the office's end-of-year picnic.

23. Which answer choice best combines the following information into a single sentence?

    The tornado struck. It struck without warning. It caused damage. The damage was extensive.

    A. Without warning, the extensively damaging tornado struck.
    B. Having struck without warning, the damage was extensive with the tornado.
    C. The tornado struck without warning and caused extensive damage.
    D. Extensively damaging, and without warning, struck the tornado.

24. Which word in the following sentence is a verb?

    Carrying heavy boxes to the attic caused her to throw out her back.

    A. Carrying
    B. to
    C. caused
    D. out

25. Which answer choice best combines the following information into a single sentence?

    His lecture was boring. I thought it would never end. My eyelids were drooping. My feet were going numb.

    A. His never-ending lecture made my eyelids droop, and my feet were going numb.
    B. My eyelids drooping and my feet going numb, I thought his boring lecture would never end.
    C. His lecture was boring and would not end; it made my eyelids droop and my feet go numb.
    D. Never-ending, his boring lecture caused me to have droopy eyelids and for my feet to go numb.

26. Which answer choice correctly fills in the blanks in the following sentence?

Comets _____ balls of dust and ice, _____ leftover materials that_____ planets during the formation of _____ solar system.

    A. Comets is balls of dust and ice, comprised of leftover materials that were not becoming planets during the formation of its solar system.

    B. Comets are balls of dust and ice, comprising leftover materials that are not becoming planets during the formation of our solar system.

    C. Comets are balls of dust and ice, comprised of leftover materials that became planets during the formation of their solar system.

    D. Comets are balls of dust and ice, comprising leftover materials that did not become planets during the formation of our solar system.

For Questions 27–33, read the following paragraph and then answer each question based on the corresponding number following each word in bold, underlined text.

*John has **decide** (#27) to travel to visit his family for a week during the summer. He and his family **wants** (#28) to visit a new location and all meet up together. They have narrowed down the choices to either going to the beach, hiking in the mountains, or visiting a large metropolitan city like New York City. There are **alot** (#29) of factors to consider. While John **prefered** (#30) the great outdoors, his sister has aways dreamed of seeing the ballet or a show on Broadway. **John's** (#31) dad is eager to hike up a mountain and camp for a few days, but John would choose the beach for a more relaxing vacation if he had to **chose** (#32). John will be **most happiest** (#33) just to spend time with his family.*

27. What correction is needed for the underlined word preceding (#27)?
    A. decides
    B. will decide
    C. decided
    D. no change required

28. What correction is needed for the underlined word preceding (#28)?
    A. want
    B. wanted
    C. have want
    D. no change required

29. What correction is needed for the underlined word preceding (#29)?
    A. alott
    B. a lot
    C. lots
    D. no change required

30. What correction is needed for the underlined word preceding (#30)?
    A. prefers
    B. preferred

    C. prefer

    D. no change required

31. What correction is needed for the underlined word preceding (#31)?

    A. John

    B. Johns

    C. Johns'

    D. no change required

32. What correction is needed for the underlined word preceding (#32)?

    A. choose

    B. chooses

    C. choice

    D. no change required

33. What correction is needed for the underlined phrase preceding (#33)?

    A. most happier

    B. more happier

    C. happiest

    D. no change required

PRACTICE TEST 1.4: READING

For each question, select the best answer.

Questions 1–10 are based on the following passage about Penny Dreadfuls, a collection of serial novels with terror-based stories.

In the Victorian Era, Britain experienced social changes that resulted in increased literacy rates. With the rise of capitalism and industrialization during that period, people began to spend more money on entertainment, contributing to the popularization of the Penny Dreadfuls *serials. Improvements in printing brought two significant results: the production of newspapers, and Englands' fuller recognition of the singular concept of reading as a form of leisure; it was, in and of itself, a new industry. An increased capacity for travel via the invention of tracks, engines, and the coresponding railway distribution created both a market for cheap popular literature and the ability for it to be circulated on a large scale.*

The first penny serials were published in the 1830s to meet the above demand. Priced to be affordable to working-class readers, the serials were considerably cheaper than the serialized novels of authors such as Charles Dickens, which cost a shilling (twelve pennies) per part. Those who could not afford a penny a week, such as working class boys, often formed clubs sharing the cost and passed the flimsy booklets from reader to reader. Other enterprising youngsters would collect consecutive parts and then rent the volume out to friends.

The stories themselves were a mix of reprints, or sometimes rewrites, of gothic thrillers, and new stories about famous criminals. Other serials were thinly disguised plagiarized versions of popular contemporary literature. The Penny Dreadfuls *were influential since they were in the words of one commentator "the most alluring and low-priced form of escapist reading available to ordinary youth."*

In reality, the serial novels were overdramatic and sensational, but generally harmless. If anything, the Penny Dreadfuls, *although obviously not the most enlightening or inspiring of literary selections, resulted in increasingly literate youth in the industrial period. The wide circulation of this sensationalist literature, however, contributed to an ever-greater fear of crime in mid-Victorian Britain.*

1. Which answer choice has the correct punctuation for the third sentence in Paragraph 1?
   A. The existing punctuation is already correct.
   B. Improvements in printing brought two significant results: the production of newspapers and England's fuller recognition of the singular concept of reading as a form of leisure; it was, in and of itself, a new industry.
   C. Improvements in printing brought two significant results; the production of newspapers and Englands' fuller recognition of the singular concept of reading as a form of leisure; it was, in and of itself, a new industry.
   D. Improvements in printing brought two significant results: the production of newspapers, and England's fuller recognition of the singular concept of reading as a form of leisure; it was, in and of itself, a new industry.

2. In the first sentence of Paragraph 1, which of the following words should not be capitalized?
   A. Era
   B. Victorian
   C. Britian
   D. All should be capitalized

3. In the last sentence of Paragraph 1, which of the following words is misspelled?
   A. capacity
   B. via
   C. coresponding
   D. cheap

4. In the first sentence of the Paragraph 2, "the above demand" refers to the demand for which of the following antecedents in Paragraph 1?
   A. travel
   B. leisure
   C. industry
   D. market

5. Which of the following sentences is the clearest way to express the ideas in the third sentence of Paragraph 2?
   A. A penny a week, working class boys could not afford these books; they often formed sharing clubs that involved passing the flimsy booklets around from one reader to another reader.
   B. Clubs were formed to buy the flimsy booklets by working class boys who could not afford a penny a week that would share the cost, passing from reader to reader the flimsy booklets.
   C. Working class boys who could not afford a penny a week often formed clubs that would share the cost, passing the flimsy booklets from reader to reader.
   D. Sharing the cost were working class boys who could not afford a penny a week; they often formed clubs and passed, from reader to reader, the flimsy booklets around.

6. Which word in the first sentence of Paragraph 3 should be capitalized?
   A. stories
   B. gothic
   C. thrillers
   D. criminals

7. Which of the following versions of the final sentence of Paragraph 3 is correctly punctuated?
   A. The *Penny Dreadfuls* were influential since they were in the words of one commentator; the most alluring and low-priced form of escapist reading available to ordinary youth.

    B. The *Penny Dreadfuls* were influential since they were, in the words of one commentator, "the most alluring and low-priced form of escapist reading available to ordinary youth".

    C. The *Penny Dreadfuls* were influential since they were, in the words of one commentator, the most alluring and low-priced form of escapist reading available to ordinary youth.

    D. The *Penny Dreadfuls* were influential since they were, in the words of one commentator, "the most alluring and low-priced form of escapist reading available to ordinary youth."

8. In the first sentence of Paragraph 4, which of the following words is a noun?
   - A. serial
   - B. novels
   - C. sensational
   - D. generally

9. In the last sentence of Paragraph 4, which of the following words is an adjective?
   - A. circulation
   - B. literature
   - C. however
   - D. greater

10. The author wants to add a sentence to the passage that would list some of the books that were plagiarized into *Penny Dreadfuls*. Which paragraph would be the best place to add this information?
    - A. Paragraph 1
    - B. Paragraph 2
    - C. Paragraph 3
    - D. Paragraph 4

Questions 11–17 are based on the following passage about Martin Luther King Jr.

Martin Luther King Jr. was an American baptist minister and activist who was a leader in the African American Civil Rights Movement. He is best known for his role in the advancement of civil rights using nonviolent civil disobedience based on his Christian beliefs. In the United States, his racial equality efforts and his staunchly advocating civil rights are among, undoubtedly, culturally the most important contributions made by King to last century's society.

King became a civil rights activist early in his career. In 1955, he led the Montgomery bus boycott, and in 1957, he helped found the Southern Christian Leadership Conference (SCLC), serving as its first president. With the SCLC, King led an unsuccessful 1962 struggle against segregation in Albany, Georgia, and helped organize the 1963 nonviolent protests in Birmingham, Alabama. King also helped to organize the 1963 March on Washington, at which he delivered his famous I Have a Dream speech. There, he established his reputation as the greatest orator in American history.

On October 14, 1964, King justly received the Nobel Piece Prize for combating racial inequality through nonviolent resistance. In 1965, he helped to organize the famous Selma to Montgomery marches, and the following year he and SCLC took the movement north to Chicago to work on eliminating the unjust and much-despised segregated housing there. In the final years of his life, King expanded his focus to include opposition toward poverty and the Vietnam War, and in 1967, he gave a famous speech entitled "Beyond Vietnam." This speech alienated many of his liberal allies in government who supported the war, but to his credit, King never allowed politics to dictate the path of his noble works.

In 1968, King was planning a national occupation of Washington, D.C., to be called the Poor People's Campaign, when he was assassinated on April 4 in Memphis, Tennessee. His violent death was, not surprisingly, followed by riots in many U.S. cities.

King was posthumously awarded the Presidential Medal of Freedom and the Congressional Gold Metal. Martin Luther King, Jr. Day was established as a holiday in numerous cities and states beginning in 1971, and eventually became a U.S. federal holiday in 1986. Since his tragic death, numerous streets in the U.S. have been renamed in his honor, and a county in Washington State was also renamed for him. The Martin Luther King, Jr. Memorial on the National Mall in Washington, D.C., was dedicated in 2011.

11. In the first sentence of Paragraph 1, which of the following words should be capitalized?
    A. baptist
    B. minister
    C. activist
    D. leader

12. Which answer choice shows the best rewording of the final sentence from Paragraph 1 to improve clarity and concision?
    A. His efforts to achieve racial equality in the United States and his staunch public advocacy of civil rights are undoubtedly among the most important cultural contributions made to society in the last century.
    B. His efforts achieving equality in the United States and to staunchly advocate civil rights are undoubtedly among the most important contributions culturally and societally made in the last century.
    C. Racial equality and civil rights, staunchly advocated by King in the United States, are, without a doubt, last century's greatest contributions, in a cultural way, to society.
    D. Last century, King made cultural contributions to racial equality and civil rights, which are undoubtedly the greatest made in the previous century.

13. Which of the following phrases from Paragraph 2 should be placed inside quotation marks?
    A. Montgomery bus boycott
    B. Southern Christian Leadership Conference
    C. March on Washington
    D. I Have a Dream

14. In the first sentence of Paragraph 3, which of the following words is misspelled?
    A. nonviolent
    B. Piece
    C. combating
    D. racial

15. In the first sentence of Paragraph 5, which of the following words is misspelled?
    A. posthumously
    B. Presidential
    C. Medal
    D. Metal

16. Which of the following sentences from the passage provides context clues that convey the author's feelings about King?
    A. He is best known for his role in the advancement of civil rights using nonviolent civil disobedience based on his Christian beliefs. (Paragraph 1)
    B. King also helped to organize the 1963 March on Washington, at which he delivered his famous I Have Dream speech. (Paragraph 2)
    C. This speech alienated many of his liberal allies in government who supported the war, but to his credit, King never allowed politics to dictate the path of his noble works. (Paragraph 3)
    D. King was posthumously awarded the Presidential Medal of Freedom and the Congressional Gold Metal. (Paragraph 5)

17. The author is considering adding a paragraph about King's family to the passage. Should the author include the additional paragraph?
    A. Yes, because the information would add much-needed personal details.
    B. Yes, because the information would elaborate on information already provided.
    C. No, because the passage is about King's public life and works, and information about his family would be irrelevant.
    D. No, because information about his family has already been included, so an additional paragraph on that topic would be redundant.

For each remaining question, select the best answer.

18. Which of the following sentences uses correct punctuation for dialogue?
    A. "Hey, can you come here a second"? asked Marie.
    B. She briefly thought about his offer and then responded. "I think I will have to pass".
    C. "I am making pancakes for breakfast. Does anybody want some?" asked mom.
    D. The conductor yelled "All aboard"! and then waited for last minute travelers to board the train.

19. Which of the following is a compound sentence?
    A. She and I drove to the play together.
    B. I woke up early, so I could start my long-neglected household chores.
    C. The long-separated cousins ran, jumped, sang, and played all afternoon.
    D. I trembled when I saw him because his face was white as a ghost.

20. Which answer choice shows the best sequential order for the sentences below to form a logical paragraph?

    S1. *Walt Disney was a shy, self-deprecating, and insecure man in private but adopted a warm and outgoing public persona.*

    S2. *His film work continues to be shown and adapted; his studio maintains high standards in its production of popular entertainment, and the Disney amusement parks have grown in both size and number to attract visitors in several countries.*

    S3. *However, he had high standards and high expectations of those with whom he worked.*

    S4. *He nevertheless remains an important figure in the history of animation and in the cultural history of the United States, where he is considered a national cultural icon.*

    S5. *His reputation changed in the years after his death, from a purveyor of homely patriotic values to a representative of American imperialism.*

    A. S1, S2, S3, S4, S5
    B. S1, S3, S5, S2, S4
    C. S1, S4, S2, S3, S5
    D. S1, S3, S5, S4, S2

21. Which of the answer choices below is the meaning of the word <u>adopted</u> in the following sentence?

    Walt Disney was a shy, self-deprecating, and insecure man in private but adopted a warm and outgoing public persona.

    A. took
    B. began to use
    C. began to have
    D. legally cared for as one's own child

22. Which of the following sentences is written in the second person?
    A. You had better call and RSVP to the party right away before you forget.
    B. She had every intention of calling with a prompt reply to the invitation, but the week got hectic, causing her to forget.
    C. I am utterly hopeless at remembering things, so I will set up a calendar reminder for myself to call Jan about the party.
    D. "Did you forget to RSVP to the party?!" asked her exasperated roommate.

23. Which of the following sentences shows a proper pronoun-antecedent agreement?
    A. The author published several best-selling novels; some of it was made into films that were not as popular.
    B. Everyone should bring their parents to the town-wide carnival.
    C. Smart companies will do whatever necessary to hold onto its best employees.
    D. Parents are reminded to pick up their children from school promptly at 2:30 pm.

24. Which of the following sentences shows a proper subject-verb agreement?
    A. Danny is one of the only students who have lived up to his responsibilities as a newspaper staff member.
    B. One of my friends are going to be on a TV series starting this fall.
    C. Rice and beans, my favorite meal, reminds me of my native country, Puerto Rico.
    D. Most of the milk we bought for the senior citizens' luncheons have gone bad.

PRACTICE TEST 1 ANSWERS

PRACTICE TEST 1.1 ANSWERS: MATH

1. **Answer:** C. $^7/_3$

    Rationale: An improper fraction is a fraction whose numerator is greater than its denominator. To convert a mixed number, such as $2\frac{1}{3}$, to an improper fraction, multiply the whole number (2) times the denominator (3), and then add the result to the numerator (1). The numerator of the improper fraction then becomes that value (7). The result becomes the numerator of the improper fraction, which keeps the original denominator from the mixed number, as shown below:

    $$\frac{(2 * 3) + 1}{3} = \frac{7}{3}$$

2. **Answer:** A. $0.6 * 90$

    Rationale: To find 60% of 90, first convert 60% to a decimal by moving the decimal point two places to the left. Then multiply this decimal, 0.6, times 90.

3. **Answer:** B. $2\frac{5}{6}$

    Rationale: To convert an improper fraction to a mixed number, divide the numerator (in this case 17) by the denominator (in this case 6). With this conversion, you get 2 with a remainder of 5. Thus, 2 becomes the whole number portion of the mixed number, and the remainder is the numerator of the new fraction.

4. **Answer:** C. 0.6363...

    Rationale: The ratio $^7/_{11}$ implies division, so the decimal value can be determined by the long division problem of 7 divided by 11. The long division results in the repeating decimal 0.6363....

    A simpler method to find this decimal is as follows: The ratio $^7/_{11}$ is the product of 7 times $^1/_{11}$. The ratio $^1/_{11}$ is the repeating decimal 0.0909... Multiplying that decimal by 7 results in 0.6363..., which provides the same answer.

    If both options seem like the same amount of effort, remember that every fraction with 11 in the denominator can be determined in the same way.

5. **Answer:** A. .625

    Rationale: The ratio implies division, so $^5/_8$ can be determined by the long division problem of 5 divided by 8. The long division results in the decimal 0.625.

    A simpler method to find this decimal is as follows: The ratio $^5/_8$ is the product of 5 times $^1/_8$. The ratio $^1/_8$ is the decimal 0.125, so multiplying that decimal by 5 results in 0.625, which is the same answer.

If both options seem like the same amount of effort, remember that every fraction with 8 in the denominator can be determined in the same way.

6. **Answer:** D. $^9/_{16}$
Rationale: The numerator in the correct ratio will be equal to the given decimal times the correct denominator. The answer is simply a result of cross multiplying. But before doing that calculation, these problems can be simplified by eliminating the incorrect answers.

For example, answers A and B can both be eliminated due to being less than 0.5, or $^1/_2$. If you can't see that, then multiply .5 times 15 and .5 times 23. In answer A, .5 times 15 is 7.5 so $^7/_{15}$ is less than the fractional value of 0.5625. In answer B, .5 times 23 is 11.5 so $^{11}/_{23}$ is less than the fractional value of 0.5625.

Now, when evaluating fractional answers this way, you might look at answer C and realize that 0.6 times 8 equals 4.8. Since 4.8 is less than the numerator and 0.6 is larger than the given decimal value, answer C can also be eliminated.

7. **Answer:** A. $^5/_{16}$
Rationale: The numerator in the correct ratio will be equal to the given decimal times the correct denominator. The answer is simply a result of cross multiplying. But before doing that calculation, the problem can be simplified by eliminating impossible answers.

For example, answer B can be eliminated because it simplifies to $^1/_6$, which is much less than 0.3125. You can also see that by dividing 1 by 6, which becomes 0.167.

For answer D, the ratio $^9/_{25}$ is a simplified form of $^{36}/_{100}$, or 0.36, which is greater than 0.3125.

Now, evaluating fractional answers this way, you can eliminate answer C for a simple reason: 19 times 0.3125 will always leave a value of 5 in the ten-thousandths place because 19 times 5 equals 95. That means the product can never be the whole number 6, so answer C can be eliminated.

8. **Answer:** A. 6
Rationale: If $a = 10$, then $2x = 20$. The value of b^2 can be calculated as follows:

$$b^2 = (b) * (b)$$
$$b^2 = (-4) * (-4)$$
$$b^2 = 16$$

So now you have the following: $\sqrt{16 + 20}$ or $\sqrt{36}$

The square root of 36 is 6.

9. **Answer:** C. 16

Rationale: The greatest common factor of two numbers is the largest number that can be divided evenly into both numbers. The simplest way to answer this question is to start with the largest answer (32) and determine whether it can be divided evenly into 48 and 64. It cannot.

Now try the next largest answer (16). That number can be divided evenly into 48 and 64. Thus, 16 is the correct answer. The other answers are also factors, but the largest of them is 16.

10. **Answer:** D. $21/32$

   Rationale: To multiply fractions, multiply the numerators and the denominators. In this case, multiply 3 times 7 and 4 times 8. The correct answer is therefore $21/32$.

11. **Answer:** A. 12

   Rationale: Replace the letters with the numbers they represent, and then perform the necessary operations.

$$3^2 + 6(0.5)$$
$$9 + 3 = 12$$

12. **Answer:** B. 40

   Rationale: The least common multiple is used when finding the lowest common denominator. The least common multiple is the lowest number that can be divided evenly by both numbers.

   Here is a simple method to find the least common multiple of 8 and 10: (1) write 8 on the left side of your paper, (2) then add 8 and write the result, (3) then add another 8 to that number, and (4) write the result. Keep going until you have a list that looks something like below:

$$8 \quad 16 \quad 24 \quad 32 \quad 40...$$

   This partial list shows some multiples of 8. (If you remember your multiplication tables, these numbers are the column or row that go with 8.) Now do the same thing with 10.

$$10 \quad 20 \quad 30 \quad 40...$$

   This partial list shows multiples of 10. Eventually, similar numbers will appear in both rows. The smallest of these numbers is the least common multiple. There will always be more multiples that are found in both rows (if you were to continue listing multiples), but the smallest number is the least common multiple.

13. **Answer:** C. $17/24$

   Rationale: To add $1/3$ and $3/8$, you must find a common denominator. The simplest way to do so is to multiply the denominators: $3 * 8 = 24$. Therefore, 24 a common denominator. (This method will not always give you the lowest common denominator, but does in this case.)

Once you have found a common denominator, convert both fractions in the problem to equivalent fractions that have that same denominator. To do this conversion, multiply each fraction by an equivalent of 1, as shown in the following:

$$\frac{1}{3} * \frac{8}{8} = \frac{8}{24}$$

$$\frac{3}{8} * \frac{3}{3} = \frac{9}{24}$$

Now you can add $^8/_{24}$ and $^9/_{24}$ to solve the problem.

14. **Answer:** C. $x = 81$

    Rationale: When two numbers with the same sign (both positive or both negative) are multiplied, the answer is a positive number. Thus, the answer is C.

    Conversely, when two numbers with different signs (one positive and the other negative) are multiplied, the answer is negative.

15. **Answer:** C. $^7/_{10}$

    Rationale: The simplest way to solve this problem is to convert the fractions to decimals by dividing the numerators by the denominators: $\frac{2}{3} = 0.67$ and $\frac{3}{4} = 0.75$.

    Thus, the correct answer is a decimal that falls between those two decimal numbers.

    $$\frac{3}{5} = 0.6 \text{ (too small)}$$
    $$\frac{4}{5} = 0.8 \text{ (too large)}$$
    $$\frac{7}{10} = 0.7 \text{ (falls between 0.67 and 0.75)}$$
    $$\frac{5}{8} = 0.625 \text{ (too small)}$$

16. **Answer:** D. 7

    Rationale: In this number, the places are as follows:

    - 1 is in the thousands place.
    - 2 is in the hundreds place.
    - 3 is in the tens place.
    - 4 is in the ones place
    - 5 is in the tenths place.
    - 6 is in the hundredths place.
    - 7 is in the thousandths place.

17. **Answer:** D. 0.72

    Rationale: The simplest way to answer this question is to convert the fractions to decimals. To convert a fraction to a decimal, divide the numerator (the top number) by the denominator (the bottom number). The questions below show the conversions for answers A, B, and C:

$$5/8 = 0.625$$
$$3/5 = 0.6$$
$$2/3 = 0.67$$

The largest number is therefore 0.72, answer D.

18. **Answer:** D. 3^4
    Rationale: All positive numbers are larger than the negative numbers, so the only possible answers are 42 or 3^4. Since 3^4 equals 81 ($3 * 3 * 3 * 3$), answer D is correct.

19. **Answer:** C. 4.8571, 4.8573, 4.8578, 4.8579
    Rationale: The numbers 4.857 and 4.858 have an unlimited set of numbers between them, and the simplest method starts by adding another decimal place after the last digit of 4.857. When doing so, 4.8571 and 4.8572 are both greater than 4.857 but less than 4.858. Answer choices A, B, and D thus include numbers that are equal to or greater than the larger of the two, or less than both numbers. Only C has all numbers that fall within the 4.857 and 4.858. Answer C is therefore the correct choice.

20. **Answer:** D. $23/5$
    Rationale: The numbers 4 and 5 can be multiplied by the denominators (bottom numbers) in the answer set to first determine the improper fractions equating to 4 and 5, and then to determine which answers are correct. Only answer D is correct because $20/5$ and $25/5$ are the numbers that are less than and greater than the answer $23/5$, which falls between 4 (i.e., $20/5$) and 5 (i.e., $25/5$).

21. **Answer:** A. $34/5$
    Rationale: The numbers 7 and 9 can be multiplied by the denominators (bottom numbers) in the answer set to first determine the improper fractions equating to 7 and 9, and then to determine which answers are correct. Only answer A is correct because $34/5$ is less than $35/5$ (improper fraction denoting 7) and $45/5$ (improper fraction denoting 9), answer A does not fall between 7 and 9.

22. **Answer:** A. 9
    Rationale: Begin by subtracting the −3 from both sides of the equation (which is the same as adding +3). That step produces the following equation:

$$\frac{4}{9}x = 4$$

Now, to isolate x on one side of the equation, divide both sides by $4/9$. To divide by a fraction, invert the fraction and multiply, as shown below:

$$\frac{9}{4} * \frac{4}{9}x = \frac{4}{1} * \frac{9}{4}$$

You are left with the following: $x = \frac{36}{4} = 9$.

23. **Answer:** B. −10

    Rationale: To find the value of q, divide both sides of the equation by −13. When a positive number is divided by a negative number, the answer is negative. Answer B is therefore the correct choice.

24. **Answer:** D. $x = 4$

    Rationale: When you multiply or divide numbers that have the same sign (both positive or both negative), the answer will be positive. When you multiply or divide numbers that have different signs (one positive and the other negative), the answer will be negative. In this case, both numbers have the same sign, so the answer is a positive number, 4 (answer D).

25. **Answer:** C. $r = (p − 3) ÷ 2$

    Rationale: Begin by subtracting 3 from both sides of the equation:

    $$p − 3 = 2r$$

    Now, to isolate r on one side of the equation, divide both sides of the equation by 2:

    $$r = \frac{p − 3}{2}$$

26. **Answer:** C. $x = 11$

    Rationale: Subtracting a negative number is the same as adding a positive number. Therefore, $8 − (−3)$ is the same as $8 + 3$, both of which equal 11.

27. **Answer:** C. 388

    Rationale: The value can be expanded as 7 ∗ 49 added to 9 ∗ 7 with 18 subtracted from the total:

    $$(7 * 49) + (9 * 7) − 18$$

    The expression then becomes $343 + 63 − 18$, which equals 388.

28. **Answer:** B. 42

    Rationale: The value can be expanded as 25 (i.e., $5^2 = 25$) added to 7 ∗ 5 with 18 subtracted from the total:

    $$5^5 + (7 * 5) − 18$$

    The expression then becomes $25 + 35 − 18$, which equals 42.

There is another simple way to evaluate this expression. The expression can also be rewritten as the product of two expressions:

$$(x + 9)(x - 2)$$

If $x = 5$, then this product becomes $14 * 3$, which is also 42 (answer B).

29. **Answer:** C. 6,804

    Rationale: The simplest way to evaluate this expression is to rewrite it as the product of two expressions. Factoring common factors from the given expression becomes $7x(x + 9)$ since 7 and 9 are factors. Thus, $7x$ becomes 189 and $x + 9$ becomes 36. The product of 189 and 36 becomes 6,804. In the interest of eliminating incorrect answers, the product of the values in the "ones" column (i.e., the 9 in the 189 and the 6 in 35) is $6 * 9$, which is 54. The correct answer must end in 4, so the correct answer must be 6,804.

30. **Answer:** D. $12

    Rationale: Use the information given to write an equation:

    $$530 = 40d + 50$$

    When you subtract 50 from both sides of the equation, you get the following:

    $$480 = 40d$$

    Divide both sides of the equation by 40 to complete the equation:

    $$12 = d, \text{ Sam's hourly wage}$$

31. **Answer:** A. A number greater than x

    Rationale: When a positive number is divided by a positive number less than 1, the quotient will always be larger than the number being divided. For example, $5 \div 0.5 = 10$. If we solve this as a fraction, $5 \div (1/2)$ is the same as $5 * (2/1)$, which equals 10, since dividing by a fraction is the same as multiplying by the reciprocal.

32. **Answer:** A. $(14 + 24) * 8 * 5$

    Rationale: In the correct answer, $(14 + 24) * 8 * 5$, the hourly wages of Amanda and Oscar are first combined, and then this amount is multiplied by 8 hours in a day and 5 days in a week. One of the other choices, $14 + 24 * 8 * 5$, looks like the correct choice, but it is incorrect because the hourly wages must be combined before they can be multiplied by 8 and 5.

33. **Answer:** A. 10

    Rationale: The facts provided can be used to write the following equation:

    $$7 + \frac{4}{5n} = 15$$

First, subtract 7 from both sides of the equation to get the following equation:

$$\frac{4}{5n} = 8$$

Then, divide both sides of the equation by $\frac{4}{5}$. To divide by a fraction, invert the fraction so that $\frac{4}{5}$ becomes $\frac{5}{4}$, then multiply:

$$n = \frac{8}{1} * \frac{5}{4}$$
$$n = \frac{40}{4}$$
$$n = 10$$

34. **Answer:** D. 108

Rationale: The ratio of the two numbers is 7:3. Therefore, the larger number is $\frac{7}{10}$ of 360 and the smaller number is $\frac{3}{10}$ of 360. To find the smaller number, multiply the smaller fraction by the total of the two numbers:

$$\frac{3}{10} * \frac{360}{1} = \frac{1,080}{10} = 108$$

35. **Answer:** C. $310

Rationale: The individual costs of all these items can be expressed in terms of the cost of the ream of paper. Use x to represent the cost of a ream of paper. The flash drive costs three times as much as the ream of paper, so the drive costs $3x$. The textbook costs three times as much as the flash drive, so the book costs $9x$. The printer cartridge costs twice as much as the textbook, so the cartridge costs $18x$. Those values can then be plugged into the following equation:

$$x + 3x + 9x + 18x = 31x$$

The ream of paper costs $10, so $31x$ (the total cost) is $310.

36. **Answer:** D. $\frac{(6)(9)}{2}$

Rationale: The area of a triangle is one-half the product of the base and the height. Choices A and B are incorrect because they add the base and the height instead of multiplying them. Choice C is incorrect because it multiplies the product of the base and the height by 2 instead of dividing it by 2. Answer D is therefore the correct choice.

37. **Answer:** A. 2,595

Rationale: The steps in evaluating a mathematical expression must be carried out in a certain order, which is called "the order of operations." The following list shows the steps in order:

- **Step 1:** Parentheses: First do any operations in parentheses.

- **Step 2:** Exponents: Then do any steps that involve exponents.
- **Step 3:** Multiply and Divide: Multiply and divide from left to right.
- **Step 4:** Add and Subtract: Add and subtract from left to right.

One way to remember this order is to use the following mnemonic sentence: **P**lease **E**xcuse **M**y **D**ear **A**unt Sally.

To evaluate the expression in this question, follow the below steps:

- **Step 1:** Multiply the numbers in parentheses: $3 * 4 = 12$
- **Step 2:** Apply the exponent 2 to the number in parentheses: $12^2 = 144$
- **Step 3:** Multiply: $6 * 3 * 144 = 2{,}592$
- **Step 4:** Add: $1 + 2{,}592 + 1 = 2{,}595$

38. **Answer:** B. $3x^2 - 4x - 15$
    Rationale: The words in the problem convey that the new expression for the length is $3x + 5$, and the new width is represented by the expression $x - 3$. The area is represented by the product of $(3x + 5)(x - 3)$. Multiplying the two binomials together with the FOIL method means that the first term is the product of x and $3x$, or $3x^2$. All the multiple choice answers have the correct first term. However, the last term is the product of 5 and -3, or -15, which means that answer C is incorrect since the last term is $+15$.

    Since the middle term should show the difference of $5x$ and $-9x$, which is $-4x$, answer B is therefore the only correct answer. If you choose to use the box method to solve these products, you will see the same results and the same factors.

39. **Answer:** C. $14x^2 + 13x + 3$
    Rationale: The words in the problem convey that the new expression for the base is $4x + 2$, and the new height is represented by the expression $7x + 3$. The area is represented by the product of $\frac{1}{2}(4x + 2)(7x + 3)$. Multiplying the two binomials together with the FOIL method means that the first term is the product of $4x$ and $7x$ and $\frac{1}{2}$ or $14x^2$.

    However, the last term is the product of 2 and 3 and $\frac{1}{2}$, or 3, making answer A is incorrect.

    The middle term is $\frac{1}{2}$ the sum of $14x$ and $12x$, which is $\frac{26}{2}x$ or $13x$.

40. **Answer:** B. 19,098 kg m/s
    Rationale: Momentum is defined as the product of mass times velocity. The conversion of 55 km/hr to meters per second means multiplying by 1,000 and dividing by 3,600 (seconds per hour). That value, 15.28, must be multiplied by the 1,250 kg mass. The value of the momentum is therefore 19,098 kg m/s.

41. **Answer:** A. $33,500

Rationale: Janet has a total of $105,000 in her accounts ($40,000 in stocks, $65,000 in bonds). 70% of that amount (her goal for her stock investments) is $73,500. To reach that goal, she would have to move $33,500 from bonds to stocks.

42. **Answer:** A. $52,000

    Rationale: Convert 15% to a decimal by moving the decimal point two places to the left: 15% = 0.15. Using x to represent Brian's gross salary, the equation can be written as follows:

$$0.15x = \$7,800$$

To solve for x, divide both sides of the equation by 0.15. $7,800 divided by 0.15 is $52,000.

43. **Answer:** C. 20 students

    Rationale: First convert 45% to a decimal by moving the decimal point two places to the left: 45% = .45. Use x to represent the total number of students in the class, and then set up the following equation:

$$.45x = 9$$

Solve for x by dividing both sides of the equation by .45. Since 9 divided by .45 is 20, the correct answer is C.

44. **Answer:** B. 515 students

    Rationale: Marisol scored higher than 78% of the students who took the test. First, convert 78% to a decimal by moving the decimal point two places to the left: 78% = .78. Now multiply .78 times the number of students who took the test:

$$.78 * 660 = 514.8 \text{ or } 515 \text{ students (must be whole numbers)}$$

45. **Answer:** D. 130,500 people

    Rationale: The population of Mariposa County in 2015 was 90% of its population in 2010. Convert 90% to a decimal by moving the decimal point two places to the left: 90% = .90. Now multiply .90 times 145,000 (the population in 2010), as shown in the following equation:

$$.90 * 145,000 = 130,500$$

46. **Answer:** A. 20 questions

    Rationale: Alicia must have a score of 75% on a test with 80 questions. To find how many questions she must answer correctly, first convert 75% to a decimal by moving the decimal point two places to the left: 75% = .75. Now multiply .75 times 80:

$$.75 * 80 = 60$$

Alicia must answer 60 questions correctly to pass the test, but the question asks how many questions she can miss. If she must answer 60 correctly, then she can miss 20 questions and still pass the test.

47. **Answer:** C. $300
    Rationale: If the phone was on sale at 30% off, the sale price was 70% of the original price. Therefore, the answer can be obtained by solving the following equation for x:

$$\$210 = 70\% \text{ of } x$$

where x is the original price of the phone. When you convert 70% to a decimal, you get the following equation:

$$\$210 = .70 * x$$

To isolate x on one side of the equation, divide both sides of the equation by .70 to find the following:

$$x = \$300$$

48. **Answer:** A. 84 girls
    Rationale: First find the number of girls in the class by converting 52% to a decimal by moving the decimal point two places to the left:

$$52\% = .52$$

Now, multiply .52 times the number of students in the class:

$$.52 * 350 = 182$$

Of the 182 girls, 98 plan to attend college, so 84 do not plan to attend college.

$$182 - 98 = 84$$

49. **Answer:** C. 12%
    Rationale: To find the percent increase, you first need to know the amount of the increase. Enrollment went from 3,450 in 2010 to 3,864 in 2015. This change shows an increase of 414 students. Now, to find the percent of the increase, divide the amount of the increase by the original amount:

$$414 \div 3,450 = 0.12$$

To convert a decimal to a percent, move the decimal point two places to the right: 0.12 = 12%.

When a question instead asks for the percent of a decrease, you also divide the amount of the decrease by the original amount.

50. **Answer:** D. 14 pounds, 14 ounces
    Rationale: When rounding measurements to the whole number value, the measurement is usually rounded up to the next larger whole number if the measurement is halfway or closer to the next higher value. In this case, since a pound has 16 ounces, answer D is therefore the correct choice.

51. **Answer:** C. 7,514,635.8239
    Rationale: When rounding a number to a given place value, the next lower place value is used to determine whether the number is rounded up or down. The rounded value has its last significant digit in that place. Answer C has the number 9 in the ten-thousandths place. Notice the difference between ten-thousands and ten-thousandths; answer A is rounded to the ten-thousands place! Answer C is therefore the correct choice.

52. **Answer:** C. 7.15 cc's
    Rationale: When rounding a measurement, the value includes a precision of plus or minus half of the smallest increment measured. The lines on the cylinder would have the values of 7.00, 7.10, 7.20, each values a tenth of a cc. The actual value of the meniscus (i.e., the curved surface of a liquid as it sits in a graduated cylinder) that reads between tenths would be 7.15 cc's. Answer C therefore has a number with the correct precision.

53. **Answer:** C. 4 men for 1 day
    Rationale: When estimating, rounding before estimating is helpful. The summary of the solution to this problem includes a rate of 200 pounds per hour (15 minute per every 50 pounds). Two and one-half tons is 5,000 pounds. 5,000 pounds divided by 200 pounds per hour means 25 hours of labor are required. For 25 hours of labor, answer C (4 people for the day, or 32 labor hours) is the closest estimate. Answer A is 80 hours, B is 16 hours, and D is 200 hours.

54. **Answer:** B. 40 minutes
    Rationale: Here, the basic formula of distance equal to rate multiplied by time applies. Thus, the time required for the trip is the distance divided by the rate. 18 miles divided by $3/4$ (45 minutes is $3/4$ of an hour) is 24 miles per hour. The new rate would be 29 miles per hour (increase of 5 miles per hour). 18 divided by 29 is about 60% of an hour, or close to 40 minutes. The closest answer is 30 minutes, but that timing is only possible if the rate is 36 miles per hour! Estimating may require eliminating answers close to the correct answer.

55. **Answer:** C. 70 seconds per multiple-choice question; 35 seconds per true/false question
    Rationale: An estimate often implies the need to check potential answers for correctness. In this example, the basic assumption is that the time for multiple-choice problems will be twice the value as that of the true/false problems. Trying 1 minute for each multiple-choice question and a $\frac{1}{2}$ minute each for true/false question comes out to 35 minutes. Thus, answer B is not correct. The next closest answer is C, which comes out to 1,400 seconds (multiple choice) and 1,050 seconds (true/false) for the total of 2,450 seconds, which is close to the allowable 2,700 seconds (45 minutes). For answer D, the total comes out to 1,600 plus 1,200 seconds, or a total of 2,800 seconds, which is more than the allowable total of 2,700 second (i.e., 45 minutes).

56. **Answer:** B. Twice as fast
    Rationale: When estimating this answer, the formula of distance equal to rate multiplied by time applies. Thus, the speed required for the trip is the distance divided by the time. In this example, being 10 minutes late means half the amount of time needed to make the trip. Dividing by one-half means that the rate must be doubled, requiring you to drive twice as fast.

57. **Answer:** D. 1,000,000
    Rationale: The number of square units in this square meter is determined by 1,000 rows of 1,000 squares, each 1 millimeter square; 1,000 multiplied by 1,000 is 1,000,000 units.

58. **Answer:** B. Serena is 7, Tom is 4
    Rationale: Use S to represent Serena's age. Tom is 3 years younger than Serena, so his age is S − 3. In 4 years, Tom will be twice as old as Serena was 3 years ago. Thus, you can write the following equation:

    $$Tom + 4 = 2(Serena - 3)$$

    Now substitute S for Serena and S − 3 for Tom:

    $$(S - 3) + 4 = 2(S - 3)$$

    Simplify the equation, as shown in the following equation:

    $$S + 1 = 2S - 6$$

    Subtract S from both sides of the equation:

    $$1 = S - 6$$

    Add 6 to both sides of the equation to solve for the answer:

    $$7 = S, \text{ Serena's age}$$
    $$4 = S - 3, \text{ Tom's age}$$

59. **Answer:** A. 16 gallons
    Rationale: Amy drives her car until the gas tank is $^1/_8$ full. This means that it is $^7/_8$ empty. She fills it by adding 14 gallons. In other words, 14 gallons is $^7/_8$ of the tank's capacity. Draw a simple diagram to represent the gas tank.

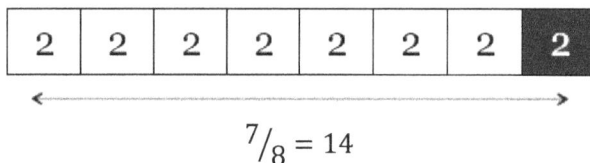

$$^7/_8 = 14$$

Each eighth of the tank is 2 gallons. Thus, the capacity of the tank is 2 * 8, or 16 gallons.

60. **Answer:** B. 4.5 inches

Rationale: The length of the larger rectangle is 12 inches, and the length of the smaller rectangle is 8 inches. Therefore, the length of the larger rectangle is 1.5 times the length of the smaller rectangle. Since the rectangles are proportional, the width of the larger rectangle must be 1.5 times the width of the smaller rectangle. The width can thus be calculated as follows:

$$1.5 * 3 \ inches = 4.5 \ inches$$

PRACTICE TEST 1.2 ANSWERS: SCIENCE

1. **Answer:** B. Cilia
   Rationale: Cilia are located on the outer membrane of bronchial epithelial cells. They are motile, hair-like extensions that help expel substances from the airways toward the pharynx. Microvilli are located on the villi of intestinal epithelial cells. They absorb water and nutrients. Flagella are located only on sperm cells in the human body. They promote the locomotion of the sperm. Dendrites are thin branching cellular extensions from neuron cell membranes. They receive and process signals from other neurons and transfer them to the neuron's cell body (soma).

2. **Answer:** D. bile; small intestine
   Rationale: Fat molecules are primarily hydrocarbons and are, therefore, water-insoluble. To absorb fats, the liver produces bile which is stored in the gall bladder and secreted into the duodenum. Bile breaks down large fat globules into smaller droplets that can be easily absorbed. The process of fat globule dissolution is called emulsification. Amylase is a digestive enzyme that breaks down certain carbohydrates. Amylase is produced by the salivary glands and the pancreas, which secrete it into the mouth and the small intestine, respectively.

3. **Answer:** D. Cytokine secretion
   Rationale: T-helper cells play a vital role in immune responses. They secrete cytokines through which the T-helper cells activate other cells of the immune system. These cytokines stimulate B cells to produce antibodies, activate killer T-cells, and stimulate macrophages to destroy ingested material.

4. **Answer:** A. It passes through the pulmonary capillaries before returning to the left side of the heart.
   Rationale: All blood pumped out of the heart passes through capillaries before returning to other heart chambers. It passes through the pulmonary capillaries before returning to the left side and through the systemic capillaries before returning to the right side of the heart. Blood pumped out of the right ventricle is deoxygenated. The blood then travels via the pulmonary artery to reach the lungs. Once blood is oxygenated in the lungs, it returns to the left atrium via the pulmonary veins. It then travels through the left ventricle and eventually reaches the aorta to be distributed to different parts of the body.

5. **Answer:** D. continuously throughout the entire respiratory cycle
   Rationale: Deoxygenated blood is pumped through alveolar capillaries continuously throughout the respiratory cycle. If oxygen did not diffuse into the capillaries throughout the entire respiratory cycle, then blood passing through the alveolar capillaries would not be oxygenated. This deoxygenated blood would then return to the left ventricle and mix with oxygenated blood, thus lowering the oxygen saturation level of blood being pumped out of the left ventricle. In normal individuals, blood pumped out of the left ventricle is nearly 100% oxygen saturated. There is no respiratory phase where oxygen does not diffuse into the circulatory system from the alveoli into the alveolar capillaries.

6. **Answer:** B. Limbic system
Rationale: The integrative functions of the nervous system occur in the brain (mainly in the limbic system and the neocortex). They refer to functions that are not directly involved in the processing of sensory inputs or in the activity of the motor and Autonomic centers. The main mechanisms in this category are those underlying the sleeping/waking cycle, consciousness, language, thinking (understanding, reason), memory (including learning), motivation (drives), and emotion (feelings).

7. **Answer:** B. Pyloric sphincter
Rationale: The pyloric sphincter opens at appropriate intervals to allow stomach contents to pass into the duodenum. The gastroesophageal sphincter opens during the passage of ingested material from the esophagus into the stomach. The sphincter of Oddi opens to release secretions of the liver and pancreas into the duodenum. The anal sphincter opens to let feces pass out of the body.

8. **Answer:** C. production of antibodies
Rationale: The innate immune system generates non-specific immune responses such as phagocytosis of foreign cells by macrophages, stimulation of fever by the release of interleukins, and the release and response to cytokines. Cytokines are generated by tissue injury triggered by a wide variety of infectious agents or chemicals. Innate immune responses occur through biochemical pathways and cell activities that do not involve antibodies or the recognition of specific antigens. Antibodies are produced by B-cells that are part of the human body's adaptive immune system.

9. **Answer:** A. Heart is ventral to the esophagus
Rationale: The term *ventral* is synonymous with anterior, while the term *dorsal* is synonymous with "posterior." The heart is anterior to the esophagus. "Proximal" means toward or closer to the trunk, while "distal" means away or farther from the trunk. The wrist is distal to the elbow. Medial means toward the center (sagittal plane) of the body, while lateral means away from the center of the body. The kidneys are lateral to the abdominal aorta. *Superior* means above a landmark, while *inferior* means below a landmark. The urinary bladder is inferior to the pancreas.

10. **Answer:** A. Liver
Rationale: Urea is a water-soluble, non-toxic molecule only synthesized in the liver's periportal hepatocytes by a group of enzymes. Its formation helps rid the body of the waste product ammonia generated by the catabolism of nitrogen-containing compounds such as nucleic acids and proteins. The kidneys excrete urea from the body. The pancreas produces digestive enzymes such as amylase, lipase, trypsinogen, and carboxypeptidase.

11. **Answer:** D. Large intestine
Rationale: All body organs receive an arterial supply of oxygenated blood. On the other hand, the lungs receive deoxygenated blood from the pulmonary artery, the heart receives deoxygenated blood from the superior and inferior vena cava, and the liver receives deoxygenated blood from the hepatic portal vein. The large intestine, like all other organs, only receives oxygenated blood.

12. **Answer:** B. Diaphragm

Rationale: The diaphragm is one of the muscles of respiration. It mostly contracts involuntarily, although in some instances a person could temporarily suppress respiration. The masseters are voluntary muscles that cause the lower jaw to close. The biceps are voluntary muscles involved in the movement of the forearm. The tongue is a voluntary muscle used in swallowing and articulation.

13. **Answer:** C. Small intestine
    Rationale: Although one of the primary roles of the large intestine is to absorb water, 80% of ingested water is absorbed through the small intestine. The oral mucosa, esophagus, and stomach don't absorb water.

14. **Answer:** B. Dendritic cells
    Rationale: Dendritic cells possess toll-like receptors on their cell membranes capable of binding to pathogen-associated molecular patterns (PAMPs) that are present on, or in, a wide variety of foreign substances. After recognizing and phagocytizing foreign substances, dendritic cells digest them and then present them as antigens on their outer cell membrane. Natural killer (NK) cells attack virally infected cells and cancer cells without interacting with other cells or substances of the adaptive immune system. Plasma cells synthesize and secrete antibodies. T-helper cells bind with and activate complementary T-cells to initiate the production of large amounts of antibodies.

15. **Answer:** C. Severe protein deficiency caused by inadequate protein intake during early childhood can result in a condition known as kwashiorkor
    Rationale: Kwashiorkor is a severe form of malnutrition that is usually fatal. It is the result of inadequate protein intake in children, usually after the age of 18 months. Strict vegetarians obtain their required dietary protein intake from non-animal sources, such as rice and legumes. Nine of the essential amino acids must be obtained through dietary intake, the remaining amino acids can be synthesized by the body. The breakdown of proteins begins within the stomach.

16. **Answer:** A. Somatostatin
    Rationale: Somatostatin, also known as growth hormone-inhibiting hormone (GHIH), inhibits the release of both growth hormone and thyroid-stimulating hormone from the anterior segment of the pituitary gland. Dopamine inhibits the pituitary release of prolactin. Luteinizing hormone (LH) and oxytocin are not inhibitory hormones.

17. **Answer:** C. Approximately equal to the weight of the protons and neutrons.
    Rationale: The atomic weight is the total weight of an atom. Therefore, the atomic weight is approximately equal to the number of protons and neutrons, with a little extra added by the electrons.

18. **Answer:** C. A phosphate group, a pentose sugar, and a nitrogenous base
    Rationale: The backbone of a continuous single DNA or RNA molecular chain is an alternating sequence of nucleotides. A nucleotide is a molecular subunit consisting of one of five possible nitrogenous bases bonded to a cyclic 5-carbon sugar (pentose sugar) that is bonded to a phosphate group. DNA and RNA segments are built from combinations of these nucleotides.

19. **Answer:** D. Alveoli
    Rationale: Alveoli are the terminal, sac-like, thin-walled structures of the bronchial tree. They have many capillaries surrounding their walls. This allows oxygen to diffuse easily from the air within the alveoli into the bloodstream. Once oxygen enters the bloodstream, it diffuses into the red blood cells and binds to their hemoglobin molecule. The red blood cells then carry oxygen to all body tissues through the circulatory system. The lungs are the respiratory organs where oxygen is inhaled and carbon dioxide is exhaled. The trachea and the bronchi serve as passages for air to the lungs.

20. **Answer:** B. Ribosomes
    Rationale: Ribosomes are protein complexes that float freely within a cell's cytoplasm or are attached to their endoplasmic reticulum. Ribosomes have no outer membranes. Mitochondria, chloroplasts, and the nuclei of eukaryotic cells are organelles that possess encapsulating membranes.

21. **Answer:** D. The mRNA segment base sequence is identical to that of the complementary DNA strand segment sequence except that uracil substitutes thymine in the mRNA base sequence
    Rationale: Just as DNA uses four bases (adenine, guanine, cytosine, and thymine), RNA uses four bases except that uracil is used instead of thymine in the RNA sequence.

22. **Answer:** C. Newtons: Joule
    Rationale: A watt is an SI unit of power, while horsepower is an English one that equals 745.69 watts. A liter is an SI unit of volume, while a gallon is an English one that equals 3.75 liters. A Newton is an SI unit of force, and a joule is an SI unit of energy.

23. **Answer:** A. valence shells
    Rationale: An electron shell, also called a principal energy level, represents the orbit followed by electrons around an atom's nucleus. Covalent bonds are chemical bonds that involve the sharing of electron pairs between atoms from their outermost electron shells called valence shells. Molecules formed through their atoms sharing electrons have the equivalent of full valence shells and thus have stable electronic configurations.

24. **Answer:** B. mRNA
    Rationale: Messenger RNA (mRNA) molecules are transcribed with genetic information from DNA. After transcription, mRNA leaves the nucleus and travels to the ribosomes in the cell's cytoplasm. Ribosomes read the genetic code of the mRNA and then assemble the protein that corresponds to the genetic information contained in the mRNA molecule.

25. **Answer:** B. Gonads
    Rationale: The gonads are the sexual organs of a species' males and females. The organs are responsible for producing male and female sex cells that create offspring by sexual reproduction. These sex cells are called gametes; female gametes are called eggs, while male gametes are called sperms. A sex chromosome is a chromosome involved in the determination of the sex of an individual. A zygote is a fertilized egg formed by the union of an egg and a sperm.

26. **Answer:** B. A single unique three-base codon codes a single unique amino acid
    Rationale: DNA is composed of a linear sequence of any of four different nitrogenous base subunits. These bases transmit genetic information in the form of three-base unit sequences called codons; 64 possible three-base sequences can be constructed from the combination of these four different DNA bases. Since there are only 20 amino acids, there can be more than one codon that codes for a given amino acid.

27. **Answer:** B. Synapse
    Rationale: Synapses are structures within the nervous system that permit a neuron (nerve cell) to pass an electrical or chemical signal to another neuron. They are considered junctions between two neurons. The narrow space between two neurons at a synapse is called the synaptic gap. One neuron releases neurotransmitters into the synaptic gap which diffuses across the gap and attaches to receptor sites on the other neuron. This results in the transmission of neural information.

28. **Answer:** C. 5 miles
    Rationale: A kilometer is approximately 0.621 miles. An 8K race refers to a race that spans across 8 kilometers. This distance converts to about 4.97 miles.

29. **Answer:** C. Zero
    Rationale: Electrons have an electric charge of -1, protons have an electric charge of +1, and neutrons have zero charges. Particles with opposite electric charges are attracted to one another by electromagnetic forces, while particles with the same electric charge repel each other. When an atom contains the same number of electrons and protons, the positive charges and negative charges neutralize each other, resulting in a net electric charge of zero.

30. **Answer:** A. Antigen-presenting cells (APCs)
    Rationale: APCs are a class of immune cells that mediate the cellular immune response by processing and presenting foreign antigens that they have acquired by phagocytosis or endocytosis from the extracellular environment for T-cells to recognize. Red blood cells are responsible for carrying oxygen throughout the body. Antibody-producing cells (B cells and plasma cells) are the primary components of the adaptive immune system. Platelets are small fragments of cells involved in the coagulation process.

31. **Answer:** B. connective tissue
    Rationale: Adipose cells of adipose tissue (fat cells) are classified as a type of connective cell. Epithelial tissues cover all surfaces of the body, line body cavities and hollow organs, and have other functions such as protection, secretion, absorption, and sensation. Elastic tissue is another type of connective tissue different than adipose tissue. Osseous tissue is present in bones.

32. **Answer:** D. increases the rate; decreasing the activation energy
    Rationale: The efficiency of a chemical reaction is the actual yield compared to the theoretical yield of the products of the reaction. This depends on the conditions under which the reaction occurs and is not affected by the presence of a catalyst. A catalyst increases the rate of a reaction by lowering its activation energy. Lowering the activation

energy increases the probability that the reactants will have sufficient energy to achieve the transition state so that the reaction can proceed to the final product state.

33. **Answer:** A. $1s^2 2s^2 2p^6$
    Rationale: The electron subshells of an atom, beginning from the lowest energy subshells, are 1s, 2s, 2p, 3s, 3d, and 3p. The s subshells are filled when they contain two electrons. The p subshells are filled when they contain six electrons. Neon has an atomic number of 10 and thus has 10 electrons. In the lowest energy state, the lowest available energy levels will be filled corresponding to an electron configuration of $1s^2 2s^2 2p^6$.

34. **Answer:** C. An enzyme has increased its effect on the rate of a chemical reaction
    Rationale: Enzyme activity is quantified for biochemical reactions as the amount of product generated per unit of time. It thus indicates how fast a reaction is occurring. The major factors that affect an enzyme's activity are temperature, pH, and the concentrations of the reactants and products of the reaction.

35. **Answer:** B. Acidic substances
    Rationale: The pH of pure water is 7, which is the neutral pH. Acids are substances that release hydrogen ions by dissociation when in solution. They have pH values lower than 7. Bases are substances that accept hydrogen ions when in solution and have pH values higher than 7.

36. **Answer:** D. Collagen
    Rationale: Collagen is an extracellular elastic structural protein found in tendons, cartilages, ligaments, and in the integumentary system. It can stretch and relax, in addition to, providing mechanical, protective, and structural properties. Keratin is an extracellular structural protein that provides protective and mechanical support to the outer layers of the skin, hair, and nails. Elastin is an extracellular structural protein that has extensibility and elastic recoil properties. A ligament is a structure that connects bones at joints.

37. **Answer:** B. Adrenal gland
    Rationale: Steroid hormones are produced in the adrenal gland, testes, and ovaries. The pancreas produces insulin and glucagon. The thyroid gland produces thyroid hormones. The thymus is the site for T-cell maturation and does not produce any hormones.

38. **Answer:** B. $2O_2 + 8H^+ + 8e^- \rightarrow 4H_2O$
    Rationale: A balanced chemical reaction is one where the number of atoms of distinct elements on both sides of the equation (i.e., reactants and products) are equal. Answer B is the only choice that meets these criteria.

39. **Answer:** B. B-glycosidic
    Rationale: Cellulose is found in dietary carbohydrates present in grains and vegetables. It is a glucose polymer formed of B-glycosidic bonds that cannot be broken by digestive enzymes. Peptide bonds are present between protein molecules and are broken down by the enzyme peptidase. Ester bonds are present between fats and lipids and are broken

down by the enzyme lipase. Amylase breaks down A-glycosidic bonds present in carbohydrates.

40. **Answer:** A. Same type of

   Rationale: Water molecules have the same types of intermolecular bonding whether they are in the liquid or solid state. What differs is that the kinetic energy of water molecules in the solid state is insufficient to overcome the intermolecular bonds that hold water molecules in a fixed position, while in the liquid state, water molecules have sufficient kinetic energy to change position within the liquid but insufficient to completely break free of intermolecular bonds and transform into the gaseous state.

41. **Answer:** C. Negative

   Rationale: When the number of electrons exceeds the number of protons, the atom has a net negative electric charge. This charge occurs because electrons have an electric charge of -1, while protons have an electric charge of +1; neutrons have zero charges.

42. **Answer:** C. every functional gene can be transcribed into an mRNA molecule

   Rationale: A gene is a sequence of DNA bases that can be translated into a protein. For that to happen, every gene is first transcribed into an mRNA molecule. A single chromosome contains a full set of genes. There may be more than one copy and more than one version of a given gene (called an allele) located on the chromosome. There are always at least two copies of every gene, but not two alleles for every gene such as the gene responsible for blood types which has 3 alleles. Only one strand of a double-stranded DNA molecule contains genes; the other one contains its complementary sequence, which cannot be transcribed into RNA.

43. **Answer:** B. UCG AUG GGC

   Rationale: For DNA, complementary base pairing occurs between adenine (A) and thymine (T), and between guanine (G) and cytosine (C). For RNA, the same complementary base relationship is true except that the complementary base of adenine is uracil (U). Choice B is the correct complementary base sequence for mRNA.

44. **Answer:** D. Nucleoli

   Rationale: Nucleoli are located within the nucleus of cells and are responsible for the production of ribosomes. Peroxisomes and lysosomes are intracellular vesicles that contain specific substances. Ribosomes are attached to the membrane of the rough endoplasmic reticulum but are not produced by them.

45. **Answer:** D. DNA polymerase

   Rationale: Ribosomes are intracellular organelles that synthesize proteins by reading RNA base sequences and connecting amino acids to form a protein. DNA polymerase synthesizes DNA through the process of replication. It replicates two strands of DNA simultaneously. RNA polymerase synthesizes mRNA molecules by reading DNA base sequences and connecting nucleotides to form mRNA. Codons are three-base sequences that code for specific amino acids.

46. **Answer:** D. Replication of both strands occurs simultaneously

Rationale: Replication of double-stranded DNA begins with the breaking of hydrogen bonds between a small sequence of complementary base pairs at a single site on the DNA molecule. This creates a gap in the DNA molecule that allows the DNA polymerase enzyme to enter and begin adding nucleotides with complementary bases to both the sense and antisense strands of the original DNA. Replication proceeds simultaneously on both strands.

47. **Answer:** B. Dopamine
    Rationale: Dopamine is a neurotransmitter, a chemical released by nerve cells to send signals to other nerve cells. It plays a major role in "reward-motivated behavior." Most types of reward increase the level of dopamine in the brain, and a variety of prescription and addictive drugs increase dopamine activity. Glucagon is produced by the pancreas to convert glycogen back into sugar. Follicle-stimulating hormone is produced by the pituitary gland and plays a role in sexual development and reproduction. Prolactin is produced in the pituitary gland and is responsible for milk production during lactation and the development of breast tissues.

48. **Answer:** B. Adaptive immunity
    Rationale: Lymph nodes are nodular structures that contain numerous antigen-presenting cells capable of triggering the adaptive immune system. The innate immunity includes leucocytes, phagocytes, the skin, and mucous membranes, which are our first line of defense against invading microorganisms. Examples of incompatibility are ABO and Rh blood incompatibility. The myeloid lineage includes monocytes, granulocytes, erythrocytes, and platelets, which are components of innate immunity.

49. **Answer:** A. Purines and pyrimidines
    Rationale: Purines and pyrimidines are the two structural categories of nitrogenous bases found in DNA and RNA. Purines are guanine and adenine, while pyrimidines are thymine, cytosine, and uracil. The major structural difference between the two is that purines have a two-ring structure and pyrimidines have a one-ring structure.

50. **Answer:** A. NH2
    Rationale: NH_2 is one of the functional R groups for the amino acid lysine.

PRACTICE TEST 1.3 ANSWERS: ENGLISH LANGUAGE

1. **Answer:** A. affected; effect; ought
   Rationale: Since a verb is needed in the first blank, "affected" not "effected" (a noun) will work, but the noun "effect" is correct in the second blank. "Ought," meaning "should" correctly completes the sentence, indicating he should not drive. "Aught" means zero, nothing, or none, so the term does not make sense in the context of the sentence.

2. **Answer:** C. Hiking along the trail, we were assailed by the chirping of birds, which hardly made our nature walk the peaceful exercise we had wanted.
   Rationale: Who was hiking along the trail? "We" were, so only option C works. The other options are dangling participles: In option B, the birds were not attempting to hike, so that doesn't make sense; in option A, again, the birds were hiking along the trail, so that makes no sense; and option D is just poorly constructed and makes the overall meaning unclear.

3. **Answer:** C. processed
   Rationale: "Processed" modifies "food products," so the term is an adjective. "Really" is an adverb modifying the adjective "serious." "Challenge" is a noun, which is a person, place, or thing. "Consume" is a verb, a word that shows action.

4. **Answer:** B. My husband and I attended my daughter's dance recital and were very proud when she received an award.
   Rationale: The clearest and most concise sentence is option B; all the information is included, is presented logically, flows smoothly off the tongue, and avoids wordiness.

5. **Answer:** D. Since the concert ended very late, I fell asleep in the backseat during the car ride home.
   Rationale: Option D is correct. "Since the concert ended very late" is a dependent clause (also sometimes called a subordinate clause) that explains why "I fell asleep...." Since the clause is dependent and appears at the beginning of the sentence, the only proper way to link the two clauses (one dependent, one independent) is with a comma.

6. **Answer:** D. they're
   Rationale: This question asks you to make a pronoun and antecedent agree by selecting the correct word choice. In the provided sentence, the antecedent is "negotiations"; since this term is a plural noun, the pronoun must also be plural. However, the blank is also missing a verb. The only option with a plural pronoun and a plural verb is the contraction "they're," option D.

7. **Answer:** A. is
   Rationale: "Group," a singular noun, is the subject of the sentence, so a singular verb is needed. Also needed is a present tense helping verb for "looking forward." The only option that satisfies both is choice A.

8. **Answer:** C. Exclamatory

Rationale: An exclamatory sentence is a type of sentence that expresses strong feelings by making an exclamation. Therefore, the option C is an exclamatory sentence.

9. **Answer:** A. irregardless
   Rationale: "Irregardless" is incorrect as it is a double-negative. The suffix "less" already indicates a lack of regard, so the addition of the negative prefix "ir" before the correct word, regardless, is unnecessary.

10. **Answer:** C. Between you and me, I brought back fewer books from my dorm room than I needed to study for my exam.
    Rationale: "Brought" is the correct past tense form of "bring." "Fewer" is the correct word to describe an exact number of items, whereas "less" is used to refer to an amount of something that cannot be exactly counted (e.g., sand, air, water). "Than" is the correct spelling of the word that shows a comparison between two things.

11. **Answer:** D. us; was
    Rationale: Words that follow prepositions are considered objective case; therefore "us" is the correct word. "Neither," a single pronoun, is the subject of the sentence, so a singular verb ("was") is needed to properly complete the sentence.

12. **Answer:** C. books
    Rationale: A noun is a person, place, or thing. While a "library" is usually used as a noun to denote a place where people can go to borrow books or look up information, this sentence uses the term as an adjective to modify "books," which is the only true noun in the sentence. "The" is an article, and "overdue" is an adjective.

13. **Answer:** A. Mary and Samantha ran, skipped, and hopped their way home from school every day.
    Rationale: A simple sentence is one that has one subject and one verb, though both the subject and verb can be compound. In this case, option A is a simple sentence; the one subject ("Mary and Samantha") is a compound; the one verb ("ran, skipped, and hopped") is also a compound one. The other answer options either have more than one subject or more than one verb.

14. **Answer:** B. Matthew was tall and shy, and Thomas was short and talkative.
    Rationale: A simple sentence is one that has one subject and one verb, though both the subject and verb can be compound. With two independent clause linked by the conjunction "and," the sentence in option B is the only compound sentence because it links the first independent clause/sentence ("Matthew was tall and shy") with the second independent clause/sentence ("Thomas was short and talkative").

15. **Answer:** D. "There's a bus coming, so hurry up and cross the street!" yelled Bob to the old woman.
    Rationale: "There's" is the subject and verb of the sentence written as a contraction, so the apostrophe is needed. A comma is needed before "so" because what follows the word is an imperative independent clause, meaning the clause has the implied subject of "you" because the quotation is a direct address toward the "the old woman." Without a comma before "so," the sentence in quotation marks would be a run-on sentence. When writing

dialogue, the punctuation is included inside the quotation marks; in this case, an exclamation is appropriate because Bob is warning the old woman to get out of the way of the oncoming bus. The use of the verb "yelled" is a clue that Bob's statement is exclamatory.

16. **Answer:** A. It's a long to-do list she left for us today: make beds, wash breakfast dishes, go grocery shopping, do laundry, cook dinner, and read the twins a bedtime story.
Rationale: "It's" is the subject and verb joined together in a contraction, so an apostrophe is needed. The sentence introduces a list, which requires preceding the list with a colon. Note that option C is unnecessarily uses semicolons, which are not grammatically needed. Semicolons are best used with complex lists where one or more of the list elements themselves either require commas or uses a conjunction. For example, "...wash breakfast dishes; go grocery shopping for apples, bananas, and pears; do laundry...") shows one list element that does both those things.

17. **Answer:** A. My room was a mess, so my mom made me clean it before I was allowed to leave the house.
Rationale: The use of the possessive pronoun "my" and the singular pronoun "I" indicates that the sentence is written from the first-person perspective. "You" and "your" are second-person pronouns; "her" and "him" are third-person pronouns.

18. **Answer:** C. The president of France is meeting with President Obama later this week.
Rationale: When referring to the "president of France," "president" is just a noun denoting the position, so the term is not capitalized. In the case of "President Obama," "President" is the title by which he is addressed and precedes his name, so the term is a proper noun and requires capitalization. The other options are incorrectly capitalized.

19. **Answer:** D. climb; creak
Rationale: "Climb" is the proper spelling to denote ascending the stairs; "clime" refers to climate. "Creak" denotes a squeaky sound, while "creek" denotes a stream or small moving waterway.

20. **Answer:** D. I will have completed
Rationale: The future perfect tense indicates that an action will have been finished at some point in the future. This tense is formed with "will" plus "have" plus the past participle of the verb (which can be either regular or irregular in form). "By this time next summer" is the clue that lets you know the coursework will be done some time in the future.

21. **Answer:** A. assent; aide
Rationale: The word "assent" means approval, which is what the teacher wants to do to show encouragement to a novice teacher who is currently the teacher's "aide" or assistant in the classroom. "Ascent" denotes a climb; "aid" is a verb denoting the action of helping.

22. **Answer:** D. No one has offered to let us use their home for the office's end-of-year picnic.
Rationale: "No one," a singular pronoun, requires a singular verb ("has"). "Us" is an objective case pronoun, which is needed to follow the verb "to let." "Ourselves" is a

reflexive case pronoun, which is not needed in this sentence. "We" is subjective. "Their" shows possession of "home," and when spelled as "there," the term denotes location (e.g. here or there).

23. **Answer:** C. The tornado struck without warning and caused extensive damage.
Rationale: Incorporating all the information from the four sentences logically and concisely, option C is the best choice.

24. **Answer:** C. caused
Rationale: "Caused" is the verb in this sentence; "Carrying" is the subject. Though the latter term may look like a verb, "carrying" is a gerund (a verb acting as a noun) that is the subject. Deleting extraneous words would help clarify this aspect. Here's the sentence rewritten in its most basic form: "Carrying caused her to throw out her back." This basic form makes it clear that "carrying" is the subject and not a verb.

25. **Answer:** B. My eyelids drooping and my feet going numb, I thought his boring lecture would never end.
Rationale: This sentence most clearly and concisely conveys all the information in the four provided sentences. The structure is parallel, and no awkward or extraneous words are included.

26. **Answer:** D. Comets are balls of dust and ice, comprising leftover materials that did not become planets during the formation of our solar system.
Rationale: "Comets" is a plural subject requiring a plural verb ("are"), and "comprising" (meaning "made up of") explains that comets are made of leftover materials that "did not" (in the past) become planets during the formation of "our" solar system. "For the first blank, "is" (option A) would not work because it's a singular verb. For the second blank, "comprised of" is redundant due to "of" (options A and C). For the third blank, past tense is needed, and only option D uses a past tense verb in that part of the sentence. For the fourth blank, the only pronoun that works logically is "out," which only options B and D use. Thus, only option D meets the requirements for all four blanks.

27. **Answer:** C. decided
Rationale: The use of "has" implies the need for present perfect tense, which is used to refer to past actions (making the decision) related to or continuing into the present. "will decide" implies the future, and "decided" implies the action is not related to the present or something that continues into the present.

28. **Answer:** A. want
Rationale: The subject is a plural compound subject because of the "and" in "he and his family," so a verb in plural form ("want") is needed. "Wants" is the singular form of the verb, so using it creates a subject-verb disagreement.

29. **Answer:** B. a lot
Rationale: The correct spelling of the term is "a lot" (two words). Spelling it as a single word is a misspelling.

30. **Answer:** A. prefers
    Rationale: A present tense verb is needed because the statement is one that remains true/exists in the present. "Preferred" is past tense, and "prefer" would create a subject-verb agreement since "John" needs to be singular and "prefer" is plural.

31. **Answer:** D. no change required
    Rationale: "John's" is the correct possessive form as John is a singular person. "Johns" has no possessive element and implies there are two Johns. "Johns'" forms a plural possessive, also implying there are two Johns.

32. **Answer:** A. choose
    Rationale: The only verb that fits the context is "choose," option. "Chooses" creates a subject-verb disagreement since "he" is singular. "Choice" is a noun rather than a verb."

33. **Answer:** C. happiest
    Rationale: "Most happier" is grammatically incorrect" because "most" is a superlative, and the superlative form of "happy" is "happiest" (option C). "More happier" is redundant because "happier" is the comparative form of "happy" and thus inherently conveys the "more" element.

PRACTICE TEST 1.4 ANSWERS: READING

1. **Answer:** B. Improvements in printing brought two significant results: the production of newspapers and England's fuller recognition of the singular concept of reading as a form of leisure; it was, in and of itself, a new industry.
   Rationale: Changes were needed to avoid an inaccurate comma and an inaccurate possessive. The two results listed after the colon in the sentence are both dependent clauses rather than independent ones, so no comma is needed before "and." In addition, the possession of recognition for the singular concept of reading by England needs to be shown with an apostrophe plus "s." Putting the after the "s" implies there are two Englands by first making the term plural and then adding the possessive. Option C incorrectly uses a semicolon, which requires a complete independent clause on each side of the punctuation. Option D uses the correct possessive for "England's," but does not omit the unnecessary comma before "and."

2. **Answer:** A. era
   Rationale: In the term "Victorian era," only "Victorian" is a proper noun (named after Queen Victoria, who ruled for over 60 years) that should be capitalized. "Era" is a noun referring to a specific period in history, so "era" should not be capitalized. The other words in options B and C should both remain capitalized as they are proper nouns.

3. **Answer:** C. coresponding
   Rationale: The correct spelling is corresponding.

4. **Answer:** D. market
   Rationale: In the relevant sentence, "the above demand" refers to the "market" (for cheaper literature) mentioned in the last sentence of Paragraph 2.

5. **Answer:** C. Working class boys who could not afford a penny a week often formed clubs that would share the cost, passing the flimsy booklets from reader to reader.
   Rationale: This sentence most clearly and concisely expresses the idea of book sharing among working boys who could not afford to spend a penny every week to buy the *Penny Dreadfuls*.

6. **Answer:** B. gothic
   Rationale: The word Gothic is a proper adjective referring to a specific genre of literature. None of the other words in the sentence should be capitalized.

7. **Answer:** D. The *Penny Dreadfuls* were influential since they were, in the words of one commentator, "the most alluring and low-priced form of escapist reading available to ordinary youth."
   Rationale: Since the sentence includes a direct quote, the last part of the sentence needs to be in quotation marks. Offsetting commas also need to be used around "in the words of one commentator" due to the length of the prepositional phrase. The period at the end of the sentence needs to be inside the quotation marks.

8. **Answer:** B. novels

Rationale: A noun is a person, place, or thing. "Novels" is a plural noun that denotes a thing that can be read. "Serial" and "sensational" are adjectives; "generally" is an adverb.

9. **Answer:** D. greater
   Rationale: An adjective is a word that describes a noun. In this sentence, "greater" is an adjective describing the noun "fear." "Circulation" and "literature" are nouns; "however" is an adverb.

10. **Answer:** C. Paragraph 3
    Rationale: Paragraph 3 mentions that *Penny Dreadfuls* were often plagiarized versions of other popular literature at the time, so that paragraph would be the best place to add a sentence of the supporting detail about the books that were plagiarized.

11. **Answer:** A. baptist
    Rationale: As the word identifies King's religion, "Baptist" should be capitalized. The other options are not proper nouns and are thus not capitalized.

12. **Answer:** A. His efforts to achieve racial equality in the United States, and his staunch public advocacy of civil rights are undoubtedly among the most important cultural contributions made to society in the last century.
    Rationale: Using parallel structure and avoiding wordiness, option A is the clearest and most concise of the versions. The other versions of the sentence have both wordiness, excessive comma use (causing choppy, awkward flow).

13. **Answer:** D. I Have a Dream
    Rationale: "I Have a Dream" is the title of a speech and should therefore be inside quotation marks. The other list options are not titles that require quotation marks.

14. **Answer:** B. Piece
    Rationale: "Piece" should be spelled Peace, as in harmony or an absence of fighting.

15. **Answer:** D. Metal
    Rationale: "Metal" should be spelled "Medal," as in an award or honor, not "metal," which refers to a naturally occurring element or raw material.

16. **Answer:** C. This speech alienated many of his liberal allies in government who supported the war, but to his credit, King never allowed politics to dictate the path of his noble works. (Paragraph 3)
    Rationale: The phrase "to his credit" and the description of his works as "noble" provide clues that the author has a positive perspective about Martin Luther King and the role his activism played in American history.

17. **Answer:** C. No, because the passage is about King's public life and works, and information about his family would be irrelevant.
    Rationale: The focus of the passage is about King's work as a minister and activist, so details about his family are unrelated to this focus and therefore should be left out.

18. **Answer:** C. "I am making pancakes for breakfast. Does anybody want some?" asked mom.
Rationale: Only option C correctly includes sentence punctuation for quoted statements: punctuation for dialogue should be inside quotation marks, which is illustrated with mom asking if anyone wants pancakes; the question mark is within the quotation marks.

19. **Answer:** B. I woke up early, so I could start my long-neglected household chores.
Rationale: Option B contains two simple sentences that, when combined, form a compound sentence. A compound sentence consists of at least two independent clauses either connected by a comma and coordinating conjunction, or connected with a semicolon (and no coordinating conjunction).

20. **Answer:** D. S1, S3, S5, S4, S2
Rationale: The most logical progression of ideas is in option D. The topic of Disney's public persona is introduced and then contrasted with his treatment of people at work. Details about the transformation of his persona from that of an American patriot to an imperialist should come next. Finally, the paragraph is wrapped up with statements about the importance of his work and his current legacy in popular culture.

21. **Answer:** C. began to have
Rationale: The sentence is discussing the contrast between Disney's private and public personas, stating that he began to have a public persona that differed significantly from the way he acted in private.

22. **Answer:** A. You had better call and RSVP to the party right away before you forget.
Rationale: Statements that show a direct address and use the pronoun "you" take the second-person perspective. Though the exclamation in option D uses the pronoun "you," the term appears in a quoted statement; the sentence itself is really in the third person. Only option A is an example of second-person writing.

23. **Answer:** D. Parents are reminded to pick up their children from school promptly at 2:30 pm.
Rationale: Only option D makes proper use of pronouns and their antecedents: in option A, "novels" and "it" do not agree. In B, "everyone" and "theirs" don't' agree. In C, "companies" and "it" do not agree.

24. **Answer:** C. Rice and beans, my favorite meal, reminds me of my native country Puerto Rico.
Rationale: Option C is the only sentence in which the subject ("rice and beans"/"meal") and verb ("reminds") agree. In A, "one" and "have lived" do not agree. In B, "one" and "are going" do not agree. In D, "most" (of the milk) or "it" does not agree with "have gone."

PRACTICE TEST 2

PRACTICE TEST 2.1: MATH

For each question, select the best answer.

1. The population of a town increased from 12,500 to 15,000 over the past decade. What is the percentage increase in the town's population?

    A. 17%
    B. 18%
    C. 19%
    D. 20%

2. Find the median in the following series of numbers: 80, 78, 73, 69, 100.
    A. 69
    B. 73
    C. 78
    D. 80

3. Solve the following equation: $x = \sqrt{11 * 44}$.
    A. $x = 36$
    B. $x = 24$
    C. $x = 18$
    D. $x = 22$

4. A barrel is currently $3/5$ full of syrup. If 150 liters more syrup is added to the barrel, it becomes completely full. What is the total capacity of the syrup barrel?

    A. 325 liters
    B. 350 liters
    C. 375 liters
    D. 400 liters

5. Which number below is the largest?
    A. −345
    B. 42
    C. −17
    D. 3^4

6. Which number below is a prime number?
    A. 81
    B. 49
    C. 59
    D. 77

7. The area of a trapezoid equals one-half the sum of the lengths of the parallel sides times the perpendicular height (h) between the two. Which equation below shows the correct way to calculate the area of the depicted trapezoid?

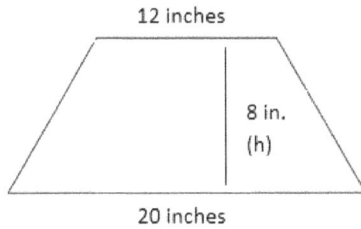

   12 inches

   8 in. (h)

   20 inches

   A. $\frac{1}{2} + (12 + 20) \div 8$

   B. $(20 + 8) * 12 \div \frac{1}{2}$

   C. $\frac{1}{2} * \frac{(20*8)}{12}$

   D. $\frac{1}{2} (12 + 20) * 8$

8. Evaluate (i.e., calculate the value of) the following expression: $2 + 6 * 3 * (3 * 4)^2 + 1$.
   A. 2,595
   B. 5,185
   C. 3,456
   D. 6,464

9. If $x \geq 9$, what is a possible value of x?
   A. 2^3
   B. 9
   C. -34
   D. 8.5

10. Solve the following equation: $x = (-22) * (-22)$.
   A. $x = 44$
   B. $x = 0$
   C. $x = 484$
   D. $x = -484$

11. Solve the following equation: $x = a^2 * a^3$.
   A. $x = a$
   B. $x = a^5$
   C. $x = 1$
   D. $x = 0$

12. A baker is preparing a recipe that requires 5 ingredients that must still be purchased: all-purpose flour, coconut sugar, free-range eggs, generic butter, and real vanilla extract. The coconut sugar costs twice the cost of the flour. The cost of the free-range eggs is twice as much as double the cost of the flour. The cost of the generic butter is three times

the cost of the flour. The cost of the real vanilla extract is four times the cost of the flour. The all-purpose flour costs $2. What will be the total cost of all 5 ingredients?

 A. $26

 B. $27

 C. $28

 D. $29

13. What is the smallest possible integer value of x in the following equation: $x > 2^2 - 4$?

 A. 3

 B. 5

 C. 6

 D. 7

14. In a local hospital, 65% of the nursing staff are registered nurses (RNs), while the remaining 35% are licensed practical nurses (LPNs). The hospital employs a total of 200 nurses. Among the RNs, 45 nurses have more than 5 years of experience. How many registered nurses have less than 5 years of experience?

 A. 139 registered nurses

 B. 45 registered nurses

 C. 87 registered nurses

 D. 21 registered nurses

15. A cell phone on sale for 30% off costs $210 after the discount. What was the original price of the phone?

 A. $240

 B. $273

 C. $300

 D. $320

16. Four subtracted from three-eighths of a number equals 48. What is the number?

 A. 116

 B. 120

 C. 124

 D. 128

17. The sum of two numbers is 360, and their ratio is 7:3. What is the smaller number of the two?

 A. 72

 B. 105

 C. 98

 D. 108

18. Michael must consume a total of 104 ounces of fluids to meet his daily hydration goal. If he has already consumed 25% of that goal, how many more ounces of fluids does he need to drink to reach his goal?

 A. 64 ounces

 B. 72 ounces

    C. 78 ounces
    D. 80 ounces

19. Carmen has a box that is 18 inches long, 12 inches wide, and 14 inches high. What is the volume of the box?
    A. 44 cubic inches
    B. 3,024 cubic inches
    C. 216 cubic inches
    D. 168 cubic inches

20. The lines in the diagram below are _____.

    A. Parallel
    B. Perpendicular
    C. Acute
    D. Obtuse

21. Find the area of the shape below.

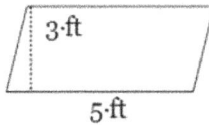

    A. 16 square feet
    B. 7.5 square feet
    C. 15 square feet
    D. 30 square feet

22. Which number below is the largest?
    A. $5/8$
    B. $3/5$
    C. $2/3$
    D. 0.72

23. It took Charles four days to write a history paper. He wrote 5 pages on the first day, 4 pages on the second day, and 8 pages on the third day. If Charles ended up writing an average of 7 pages per day, how many pages did he write on the fourth day?
    A. 11 pages
    B. 8 pages
    C. 12 pages
    D. 9 pages

24. Which option below is equivalent to the following equation: $\frac{5}{mp} \div \frac{p}{4}$?

    A. $\frac{5p}{4mp}$

    B. $\frac{20}{mp^2}$

    C. $\frac{20mp}{4mp}$

    D. $\frac{4mp}{5p}$

25. What is the approximate area of the portion of the square below that is <u>not</u> covered by the circle?

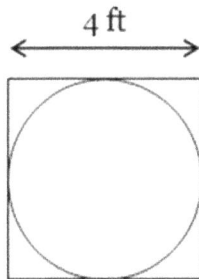

    A. 4.14 square feet
    B. 3.44 square feet
    C. 6.25 square feet
    D. 5.12 square feet

26. Danvers is 8 miles due south of Carson and 6 miles due west of Baines. If a driver could drive in a straight line from Carson to Baines, how many miles would the trip be?

    A. 8 miles
    B. 10 miles
    C. 12 miles
    D. 14 miles

27. Lourdes rolls a pair of 6-sided dice. What is the probability that the result (the sum of the numbers on the top of both dice) will equal 10?

    A. $^1/_{36}$
    B. $^2/_{36}$
    C. $^3/_{36}$
    D. $^4/_{36}$

28. Four friends plan to share equally the cost of a retirement gift. If one person drops out of the arrangement, the cost per person for the remaining three would increase by $12. How much does the gift cost?

    A. $144
    B. $136
    C. $180
    D. $152

29. What option below shows the factorial of 5?
    A. 25
    B. 5 and 1
    C. 120
    D. 125

30. Which digit is in the thousandths place in the following number: 1,234.567?
    A. 1
    B. 2
    C. 6
    D. 7

31. What is the mode in the following set of numbers: 4, 5, 4, 8, 10, 4, 6, 7?
    A. 6
    B. 4
    C. 8
    D. 7

32. Which number below is a perfect square?
    A. 5
    B. 15
    C. 49
    D. 50

33. Sarah sells handmade jewelry and earns $8 for each piece she sells, while Mike runs a small bakery and earns $50 for each batch of bread he bakes. Each day, Sarah sells 40 pieces of jewelry, and Mike bakes 15 batches of bread. Which equation below can be used to calculate how much money Sarah and Mike make collectively in a 7-day week?
    A. $[(8 * 40) + (50 * 15)] * 7$
    B. $\frac{(8*40)+(50*15)}{7}$
    C. $[(8 * 40) + 7)] + [(50 * 15) + 7)]$
    D. $(8 + 40 + 50 + 15) * 7$

34. The number of spectators at the 2024 NFL Super Bowl game was 59% of the number of spectators at the 1980 NFL Super Bowl. Rounding to the nearest whole number, how many people attended the 2024 Super Bowl if the 1980 game had 103,985 spectators?
    A. 60, 229 people
    B. 61, 351 people
    C. 62, 420 people
    D. 63,500 people

35. What is the sum of $^5/_8$ and $^3/_{16}$?
    A. $^7/_8$
    B. $^{10}/_{16}$
    C. $^{10}/_{24}$
    D. $^{13}/_{16}$

36. Maryanne is 6 years younger than Rich. Twenty-two years ago, Rich was 10 years older than half of Maryanne's age. How old are Maryanne and Rich today?
    A. Rich is 32, Maryanne is 26
    B. Rich is 34, Maryanne is 28
    C. Rich is 36, Maryanne is 30
    D. Rich is 38, Maryanne is 32

37. A rectangle's length is three times its width. The area of the rectangle is 48 square feet. How long are the sides?
    A. Length = 12, width = 4
    B. Length = 15, width = 5
    C. Length = 18, width = 6
    D. Length = 24, width = 8

38. Which option below shows the prime factorization of 24?
    A. $24 = 8 * 3$
    B. $24 = 2 * 2 * 2 * 3$
    C. $24 = 6 * 4$
    D. $24 = 12 * 2$

39. x is a positive integer. Dividing x by a positive number less than 1 will yield _____.
    A. A number greater than x
    B. A number less than x
    C. A negative number
    D. An irrational number

40. Solve the following equation: $x = 8 - (-3)$.
    A. $x = 5$
    B. $x = -5$
    C. $x = 11$
    D. $x = -11$

41. Which statement below is true?
    A. The square of a number is always less than the number.
    B. The square of a number may be either positive or negative.
    C. The square of a number is always a positive number.
    D. The square of a number is always greater than the number.

42. Jerry's height at age 10 was in the 65% percentile. If there are 110 students in Jerry's fourth-grade class, approximately how many fourth-graders are shorter than Jerry?
    A. 63 fourth-graders
    B. 67 fourth-graders
    C. 71 fourth-graders
    D. 76 fourth-graders

43. Rebecca saved d dollars every week for 5 years and received $1,000 total in birthday money during the same period. How much money did Rebecca save each week if she saved a total of $16,600 over the 5-year period?
    A. $30
    B. $40
    C. $50
    D. $60

44. Solve for r in the following equation: $p = 2r + 3$.
    A. $r = 2p - 3$
    B. $r = p + 6$
    C. $r = \frac{p+3}{2}$
    D. $r = \frac{p-3}{2}$

45. What is the least common multiple of 4 and 6?
    A. 24
    B. 36
    C. 12
    D. 10

46. Solve the following equation: $x = -42 \div -7$.
    A. $x = -35$
    B. $x = -49$
    C. $x = 6$
    D. $x = -6$

47. Convert the improper fraction $\frac{23}{8}$ to a mixed number.
    A. $3\frac{6}{8}$
    B. $\frac{8}{23}$
    C. $2\frac{3}{8}$
    D. $2\frac{7}{8}$

48. What value of q is a solution to the following equation: $130 = q(-13)$?
    A. 10
    B. −10
    C. 1
    D. 10^2

49. Find the value of $x^2 + 4y$ when $x = 10$ and $y = 3.75$.
    A. 150
    B. 125
    C. 115
    D. 105

50. Which of the following is equal to half a billion?
    A. 50,000,000
    B. 500,000,000
    C. 500,000
    D. 50,000,000,000

51. If the radius of the circle in the diagram below is 4 inches, what is the perimeter of the square?

    A. 24 inches
    B. 32 inches
    C. 64 inches
    D. 96 inches

52. Solve for x in the following equation: $x = \frac{5}{6} * \frac{2}{3}$
    A. $x = \frac{3}{5}$
    B. $x = \frac{5}{9}$
    C. $x = \frac{4}{7}$
    D. $x = \frac{7}{8}$

53. Which answer represents the relationship between x and y in the below table?

x	y
0	7
3	13
5	17
7	21
8	23

    A. $y = x + 7$
    B. $y = 4x + 1$
    C. $y = 2x + 10$
    D. $y = 2x + 7$

54. When you add two numbers, the sum is 480. If the ratio of the two numbers is 5:1, what is the smaller number?
    A. 60
    B. 70
    C. 72

    D. 80

55. In a local bakery, 30% of the pastries sold are croissants. If the bakery sold 24 croissants yesterday, how many pastries were sold?
    A. 78 pastries
    B. 80 pastries
    C. 82 pastries
    D. 84 pastries

56. What is the perimeter of the below figure?

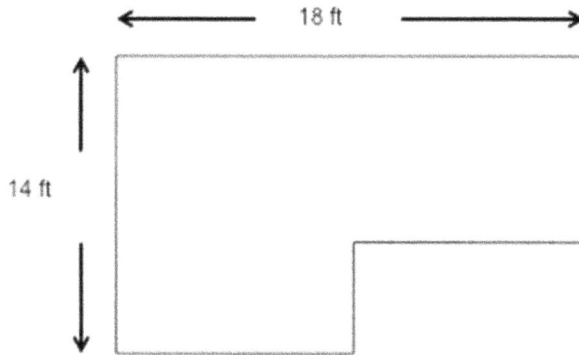

    A. 64 feet
    B. 72 feet
    C. 84 feet
    D. 96 feet

57. What exponent should replace the question mark in the following equation: $15{,}200 = 1.52 * 10^?$?
    A. 2
    B. 3
    C. 4
    D. 5

58. Which option below is equal to 0.0065?
    A. $6.5 * 10^{-2}$
    B. $6.5 * 10^{-3}$
    C. $6.5 * 10^{-4}$
    D. $6.5 * 10^{-5}$

59. At a lunch cart, there are 2 orders of diet soda for every 5 orders of regular soda. If the owner of the lunch cart sells 112 sodas a day, how many are diet and how many are regular?
    A. 28 diet, 84 regular
    B. 32 diet, 80 regular
    C. 34 diet, 82 regular
    D. 36 diet, 84 regular

60. What is the greatest common factor of 72 and 96?
    A. 8
    B. 16
    C. 24
    D. 48

PRACTICE TEST 2.2: SCIENCE

For each question, select the best answer.

1. What is the primary functional difference between smooth endoplasmic reticulum and rough endoplasmic reticulum?
   A. The smooth endoplasmic reticulum does not participate in the synthesis of products destined for external secretion
   B. The smooth endoplasmic reticulum does not participate in the synthesis of proteins
   C. The rough endoplasmic reticulum does not participate in the synthesis of products destined for external secretion
   D. The rough endoplasmic reticulum does not participate in the synthesis of proteins

2. Which of the following is a universal feature of all living cells?
   A. External cell membrane
   B. External cell wall
   C. Nucleus
   D. Mitochondria

3. Which of the following terms would NOT be used to define the relative position of one body structure to the other?
   A. Caudal
   B. Coronal
   C. Ventral
   D. Inferior

4. Which of the following intracellular structures is responsible for the whip-like motion of the flagellum of a human sperm cell?
   A. Thick filaments
   B. Actin filaments
   C. Microtubules
   D. Intermediate filaments

5. What are the linear backbones of DNA formed of?
   A. Alternating nitrogenous bases of thymine and uracil
   B. Alternating deoxyribose sugars and phosphate groups
   C. Alternating nucleotides of ribose and deoxyribose
   D. Alternating nitrogenous bases and glucose groups

6. Which of the following is a possible nitrogenous base sequence for both a codon and an anticodon?
   A. ACG
   B. GCT
   C. UTC
   D. AGU

7. Which of the following organelles works with the smooth endoplasmic reticulum to process, package, and transport a variety of synthesized products throughout the cell?
   A. Ribosomes
   B. Golgi apparatus
   C. Cili
   D. Mitochondria

8. Which of the following is the major extracellular structure that provides protective and mechanical support to the outer layers of skin, hair, and nails?
   A. Fibrillin
   B. Collagen
   C. Keratin
   D. Melatonin

9. Choose the correct pair of terms that correctly completes the following statement:

   In the human male reproductive system, _____ cells produce _____.

   A. tunica albuginea; primary spermatids
   B. Sertoli; follicle-stimulating hormone (FSH)
   C. spermatogonia; luteinizing hormone (LH)
   D. Leydig; testosterone

10. Choose the pair of terms that correctly completes the following statement:

    In humans, the _____ joint has a greater range of motion than the _____ joint.

    A. elbow; knee
    B. sacroiliac; atlantoaxial
    C. elbow; shoulder
    D. knee; hip

11. Which of the following is a component of cell membranes and a precursor for the synthesis of steroid hormones, cortisol, aldosterone, progesterone, and the sex hormones testosterone and estrogen?
    A. Lipoproteins
    B. Triglycerides
    C. Amino acids
    D. Cholesterol

12. Which of the following is the primary function of the pulmonary surfactant?
    A. Prevention of the rupture of alveoli during maximal inspiration
    B. Prevention of the collapse of alveoli during expiration
    C. Increased solubility of oxygen in the solution between the alveoli and capillary endothelium
    D. Decreased viscosity of bronchiolar mucous secretions

13. Which cavity is enclosed by the inner walls of the thorax, the abdominal wall muscles, and the inner surface bones of the pelvis and associated muscles?
    A. Abdominal/pelvic cavity

   B. Thoracic cavity
   C. Ventral cavity
   D. Dorsal cavity

14. Which layer of the integumentary system has poor thermal conduction and thus acts as an insulator to protect against excessive heat transfer between the inside of the body and the external environment?
   A. Epidermis
   B. Hypodermis
   C. Dermis
   D. Stratum corneum

15. What is the next structure that blood will pass through in the following sequence: Right atrium → tricuspid valve → right ventricle?
   A. Pulmonary valve
   B. Pulmonary artery
   C. Pulmonary vein
   D. Right lung

16. Which of the following is the most likely origin of a blood clot that lodges in the right pulmonary artery?
   A. Peripheral lower limb vein
   B. Aorta
   C. Left atrium
   D. Main pulmonary vein

17. Which of the following is a lymphocyte lineage cell?
   A. Eosinophils
   B. Plasma cells
   C. Monocytes
   D. Basophils

18. Which of the following molecules is present on the cell membrane of antigen-presenting cells?
   A. Human leukocyte antigens
   B. ABO glycoproteins
   C. Rh-factor proteins
   D. Cadherin-class cell-adhesion molecules

19. Which of the following is NOT a function of the sympathetic nervous system?
   A. Redirection of blood flow from the intestines to the skeletal muscles
   B. Inhibition of peristalsis
   C. Dilation of the bronchi
   D. Reduction of the strength and contractility of the heart

20. Which of the following leads to suppressing the secretion of the hormone glucagon?
   A. High protein content of the stomach chyme

B. Activation of the sympathetic nervous system

C. A meal with high simple carbohydrate content

D. The hormone cholecystokinin

21. Which of the following is a correct cause-and-effect sequence in the digestive process?

    A. Cholecystokinin secretion → increased somatostatin secretion → increased pancreatic amylase secretion

    B. Cholecystokinin secretion → increased bile secretion → increased fat emulsification

    C. Secretin secretion → increased gastric mucous secretion → increased pepsin secretion

    D. Secretin secretion → increased gastric HCL secretion → increased pepsin activation

22. The male and female sex hormones are regulated by the _____ through the release of _____, which regulates the synthesis and release of _____ and _____ by the _____ pituitary.

    A. pineal; GnRH; testosterone; estrogen; anterior

    B. pineal; GHIH; PRL; LH; posterior

    C. hypothalamus; GHRH; testosterone; estrogen; posterior

    D. hypothalamus; GnRH; LH; FSH; anterior

23. What type of muscle is located throughout the body, particularly in the muscular layers of the respiratory system, the digestive system, and the circulatory system, and is regulated by the autonomic nervous system?

    A. Smooth muscles

    B. Skeletal muscles

    C. Cardiac muscles

    D. Voluntary muscles

24. Which of the following structures consists of dense connective tissue?

    A. Collagen, keratin, and elastin

    B. Ligaments, tendons, cartilage, and the lower structural layers of the dermis of the skin

    C. Epidermal, subcutaneous, and dermal layers of the skin

    D. Bones, blood, plasma, and extracellular proteins

25. What is the electron configuration for boron (atomic number 5)?

    A. $1s^2 2s^3$

    B. $1s^2 2s^2 2p^1$

    C. $1s^2 2s^2 3s^1$

    D. $2s^2 2s^2 2p^1$

26. Which of the following would result in the accumulation of lactic acid in muscles?

    A. Activation of the sympathetic nervous system

    B. Depletion of glycogen stored in the liver

    C. Inadequate amount of oxygen delivered to the muscles

    D. Inadequate levels of pyruvate within the muscles

27. Which of the following is an effect of activation of the parasympathetic nervous system?
    A. Increased activity of the sinoatrial node
    B. Decreased smooth muscle contractions in the digestive tract
    C. Direct inhibition of deep tendon reflexes
    D. Contraction of smooth muscle in the walls of arterioles in skeletal muscles

28. Which of the following hormones has a direct effect on blood vessels, causing the contraction of smooth muscle cells located in the vessel walls?
    A. Angiotensin-converting enzyme
    B. Renin
    C. Angiotensin II
    D. Aldosterone

29. Which of the following elemental groups has the lowest electronegativity?
    A. Halogens
    B. Noble gases
    C. Alkali metals
    D. Transition metals

30. What is the most abundant blood cell type?
    A. Proteins
    B. Erythrocytes
    C. Leukocytes
    D. Thrombocytes

31. Which of the following chemical reactions generates a large amount of heat energy?
    A. Decomposition
    B. Dissociation
    C. Evaporation
    D. Combustion

32. _____ are either fatty acids or cholesterol.
    A. Lipids
    B. Monosaccharides
    C. Amino acids
    D. Glycogen

33. Which of the following is a type of tissue present in the hypodermis with the corresponding function of the tissue's main cellular component?
    A. Epithelial - mechanical barrier
    B. Epithelial - energy storage
    C. Connective - mechanical barrier
    D. Connective - energy storage

34. Which of the following hormones is NOT synthesized in the pituitary gland?
    a. Prolactin

b. Melatonin
c. Oxytocin
d. Adrenocorticotropic hormones

35. Which of the following hormones has rapid effects like those caused by the activation of the sympathetic nervous system?
    A. Insulin
    B. Thyroid hormones (T3 and T4)
    C. Testosterone
    D. Aldosterone

36. Which of the following is NOT a non-metal element?
    A. Platinum
    B. Carbon
    C. Nitrogen
    D. Oxygen

37. What is the name of the process where reactants bind to the active site of an enzyme followed by configuration changes of the enzyme molecule to orient the reactants in an optimum position for the chemical reaction to occur?
    A. Denaturation
    B. Active site orientation
    C. Induced fit
    D. Inhibition

38. Which ONE of the following joint types is different from the other three?
    A. Intervertebral discs
    B. Temporomandibular joint
    C. Manubriosternal joint
    D. Pubic symphysis

39. Where does the initial filtration of blood by the kidney occur?
    A. Renal pelvis
    B. Adrenal cortex
    C. Collecting ducts
    D. Glomeruli

40. What is the kidney's response to antidiuretic hormone?
    A. Increased secretion of urea
    B. Decreased osmolality of extracellular fluid in the renal medulla
    C. Increased permeability of the renal tubules to water
    D. Decreased secretion of glucose

41. What is the hormonal response of the central nervous system to an undesirably high plasma osmolarity?
    A. Increased secretion of corticotropin-releasing hormone
    B. Decreased secretion of corticotropin-releasing hormone
    C. Increased secretion of antidiuretic hormone

    D. Decreased secretion of antidiuretic hormone

42. Choose the pair that correctly completes the following statement: _____ causes the kidneys to release _____.
    A. an undesirably low plasma sodium concentration; renin
    B. an undesirably high plasma sodium concentration; renin
    C. an undesirably low plasma sodium concentration; aldosterone
    D. an undesirably high plasma sodium concentration; aldosterone

43. Which of the following is completely reabsorbed by the kidney under normal physiological circumstances?
    A. Glucose
    B. Sodium
    C. Bicarbonate ion
    D. Urea

44. What is the physiological purpose of sodium reabsorption in the kidneys?
    A. Sodium ion conservation
    B. Potassium ion excretion
    C. Concentration of urine
    D. Acidification of urine

45. What general shape do structural proteins have?
    A. Globular
    B. Fibrillar
    C. Biconcave
    D. Spherical

46. Which of the following is a DIRECT physiological effect of angiotensin II?
    A. Increased blood pressure
    B. Increased renal medullary osmolality
    C. Decreased permeability of renal tubules to water
    D. Redistribution of gastrointestinal blood flow

47. What is the name of the DNA strand transcribed by RNA polymerase?
    A. Homologous
    B. Complementary
    C. Sense
    D. Antisense

48. Which of the following does not participate in the immune response to viral infections?
    A. T-cells
    B. Interferons
    C. Chief cells
    D. Plasma cells

49. What is the mechanism of action of antivenom in snakebite victims?
    A. Blockade of the cell membrane molecular targets of snake venom

    B. Proteolytic destruction of the snake venom

    C. Non-enzymatic deamination of the snake venom

    D. Deactivation of the snake venom by antigen-specific antibody binding

50. The influenza vaccine provides _____ immunity to the influenza virus.
    A. active innate
    B. active humoral
    C. passive cellular
    D. passive innate

51. Which of the following pairs correctly completes the following sentence?

    T-cells originate from cells located in the _____ and reach maturity in the _____.

    A. bone marrow; cortex of the spleen
    B. bone marrow; thymus
    C. thymus; cortex of the spleen
    D. cortex of the spleen; thymus

52. Among the four cardinal signs of localized infection, which of the following is NOT the DIRECT result of increased vascular permeability?
    A. Redness and swelling only
    B. Redness and heat only
    C. Swelling and pain only
    D. Pain and heat only

53. Which of the following is an autoimmune disease?
    A. Type 1 diabetes mellitus
    B. Cystic fibrosis
    C. Sickle cell anemia
    D. Peptic ulcer

54. Where are dietary triglycerides hydrolyzed by the enzyme lipase?
    A. Endoplasmic reticulum
    B. Small intestine
    C. Liver
    D. Stomach

55. Which of the following chemical reactions correctly represents the formation of a peptide bond between two amino acids, AA_1, and AA_2?
    A. $AA_1 + AA_2 \rightarrow AA_1 - AA_2 + H_2O$
    B. $AA_1 + AA_2 \rightarrow AA_1 - AA_2 + CO_2 + NH_3$
    C. $AA_1 + AA_2 \rightarrow AA_1 - AA_2 + 2\ glucose$
    D. $AA_1 + AA_2 + NAD^+ \rightarrow AA_1 - AA_2 + CO_2 + NADH$

Practice Test 2.3: English Language

For each question, select the best answer.

1. Which of the answer choices show the set of words that best completes the following sentence?

   My early morning flight tomorrow _____ before 6:00 am, so I will be _____ to bed early tonight.

   A. depart; gone
   B. departs; going
   C. departed; going
   D. departing; going

2. Which of the answer choices show the set of words that best completes the following sentence?

   I want to paint my house, but I need to find the original paint color code to _____ that _____ a match.

   A. insure; it's
   B. ensure; its
   C. insure; its
   D. ensure; it's

3. Which of the answer choices show the set of words that best completes the following sentence?

   We are all going over _____ to pick up our gear, and _____ we will be ready for our camping trip.

   A. there; than
   B. their; than
   C. there; then
   D. they're; then

4. Which of the answer choices show the set of words that best completes the following sentence?

   I'm so excited to watch _____ performance tonight; I know _____ going to do great!

   A. your; your
   B. you're; you're
   C. you're; your
   D. your; you're

5. Which of the following sentences has the correct structure and grammar?
   A. My grandmother's house was built over 100 years ago if you can believe it.
   B. My grandmother's house, was built over 100 years ago, if you can believe it.
   C. My grandmothers house was built over 100 years ago, if you can believe it.
   D. My grandmothers house, was built, over 100 years ago if you can believe it.

6. Which of the following sentences has the correct structure and grammar?
    A. I listened to the instructor's lesson but interpreted a different meaning.
    B. I listened to the instructors lesson but interpreted a different meaning.
    C. I listened to the instructors lesson but inferred a different meaning.
    D. I listened to the instructors lesson but inferenced a different meaning.

For Questions 7–15, read the following paragraph and then answer each question based on the corresponding number following each word in bold, underlined text.

*We've decided to start a business and **will opening** (#7) a gourmet coffee shop. I've always loved coffee, and it is my favorite part of the morning when I begin the day. I did not set out with a goal of being **a business** (#8) owner of a coffee shop. It started because, after trying **dozen** (#9) of types of brands and types of beans, **I realize** (#10) I wanted to try roasting coffee beans myself to get the exact flavor profile I liked best. After a lot of learning through trial and error, I finally discovered what I think is the perfect cup of coffee. **Me and my friends and family** (#11) agree that they loved it, so I hope that the rest of my community will too. If it has the **affect** (#12) I think it will, we could **some day** (#13) open more shops. I **acknowlege** (#14) that this is a lofty goal, but I hope that my hard work will **payoff**. (#15)*

7. What correction is needed for the underlined word preceding (#7)?
    A. will have opened
    B. will be opening
    C. will be opens
    D. no change required

8. What correction is needed for the underlined word preceding (#8)?
    A. businesses
    B. business's
    C. business'
    D. no change required

9. What correction is needed for the underlined word preceding (#9)?
    A. a dozen
    B. dozens'
    C. dozens
    D. no change required

10. What correction is needed for the underlined word preceding (#10)?
    A. realizing
    B. will realize
    C. realized
    D. no change required

11. What correction is needed for the underlined word preceding (#11)?
    A. My friends and family agree
    B. My friends, and family, agree

C. I and my friends and family agree
D. no change required

12. What correction is needed for the underlined word preceding (#12)?
    A. affects
    B. effect
    C. effects
    D. no change required

13. What correction is needed for the underlined word preceding (#13)?
    A. some days
    B. some-day
    C. someday
    D. no change required

14. What correction is needed for the underlined word preceding (#14)?
    A. aknowledge
    B. acknowledge
    C. acknolege
    D. no change required

15. What correction is needed for the underlined word preceding (#15)?
    A. pay-off
    B. pays off
    C. pay off
    D. no change required

PRACTICE TEST 2.4: READING

For each set of questions, read the passage, and then answer the related questions by selecting the best answer.

Passage 1

The United States Treasury operates the Bureau of Engraving and Printing (BEP), a subsidiary where the nation's supply of paper money is designed and manufactured. But to call American currency "paper" money is a slight misnomer that understates its unperceived complexity and intrinsic technological sophistication. The treasury goes to extraordinary lengths to safeguard cash from counterfeiters. One of the most fundamental ways is by printing not on paper per se, but on a proprietary blend of linen and cotton. American money is more akin to fabric than paper, and each printed bill is a phenomenal work of art with masterful craftsmanship.

The most frequently counterfeited denominations are the $20 bill, preferred by domestic counterfeiters, and the $100 note, which is the currency of choice for foreign forgers. To make the copying of twenties more difficult, the BEP uses color-shifting ink that changes from copper to green in certain lights. Evidence of this ink can be seen in the numeral 20 located in the lower right corner on the front of $20 bills. A portrait watermark—which is a very faint, rather ethereal image of President Jackson—is also juxtaposed into the blank space to the right to his visible and prominent portrait. Additionally, a security ribbon, adorned with a flag and the words "USA Twenty," is printed on and embedded into the bill. When exposed to ultraviolet light, the thread glows with a greenish hue. Twenties also include an almost subliminal text that reads "USA20." This micro-printed text is well-camouflaged within the bill. With the use of a magnifying glass, the micro text can be found in the border beneath the treasurer's signature.

The $100 bill has similar security features, including color-shifting ink, portrait watermarks, security threads and ribbons, raised printing, and micro-printing. These units of currency, dubbed "Ben Franklins" in honor of the statesman whose face graces the $100 bill, also boast what the BEP describes as a 3-D security ribbon. The ribbon has bells and numbers printed on it. When tilted, the currency appears to have images of bells that transform into the numeral 100. When the bill is tilted side to side, the bells and 100s seem to move in a lateral direction.

Security threads woven into each different denomination have their own respective colors, and each one glows a different color when illuminated with ultraviolet light. Fine engraving or printing patterns appear in various locations on bills too, and many of these patterns are extremely fine. The artists who create them for engraving also incorporate non-linear designs as the waviness can make successfully counterfeiting the currency exponentially more difficult. The surface of American currency is also slightly raised, giving it a subtly, but distinct tactile characteristic.

1. Which of the following conclusions can logically be drawn from the first paragraph of the passage?
   A. Linen and cotton are more expensive printing materials than paper.
   B. The current process of printing money is reflective of decades of modifications.

      C. Counterfeiting of American money is an enormous problem.

      D. The artistry inherent in the making of American money makes it attractive to collectors.

2. Which of the sentences below, if added to the end of the passage, would provide the best conclusion to both the paragraph and the passage?

      A. It is clear from all these subtly nuanced features of the various bills that true artistry is at work in their making.

      B. Yet despite all these technological innovations, the race to stay ahead of savvy counterfeiters and their constantly changing techniques remains a never-ending endeavor.

      C. Due to the complexities involved in the printing of money, these artists are consequently well-paid for their skills.

      D. Thus, many other countries have begun to model their money-printing methods on these effective techniques.

3. The passage is reflective of which of the following types of writing?

      A. Descriptive

      B. Narrative

      C. Expository

      D. Persuasive

4. This passage likely comes from which of the following documents?

      A. Pamphlet for tourists visiting the United States Treasury

      B. Feature news article commemorating the bicentennial of the Bureau of Engraving and Printing

      C. Letter from the U.S. Treasury secretary to the president

      D. Public service message warning citizens about the increased circulation of counterfeit currency

5. Which of the following is an example of a primary source document?

      A. Pamphlet for tourists visiting the United States Treasury

      B. Feature news article commemorating the bicentennial of the Bureau of Engraving and Printing

      C. Letter from the U.S. Treasury secretary to the president

      D. Public service message warning citizens about the increased circulation of counterfeit currency

6. Which of the following describes the word <u>intrinsic</u> as it is used in the first paragraph of the passage?

      A. Amazing

      B. Expensive

      C. Unbelievable

      D. Inherent

Passage 2

In the Middle Ages, merchants and artisans formed groups called "guilds" to protect themselves and their trades. Guilds appeared in the year 1000, and by the 12th century, analogous traders—such as wool, spice, and silk dealers—had formed their own guilds. _____, towns like Florence, Italy, boasted as many as 50 merchants' guilds. With the advent of guilds, apprenticeship became a complex system. Apprentices were to be taught only certain things, and then the apprentices were to prove they possessed certain skills, as determined by the guild. Each guild decided the length of time required for an apprentice to work for a master tradesperson before being admitted to the trade.

7. The topic sentence of the above passage is _____.
    A. In the Middle Ages, merchants and artisans formed groups called "guilds" to protect themselves and their trades.
    B. Guilds appeared in the year 1000, and by the 12th century, analogous traders—such as wool, spice, and silk dealers—had formed their own guilds.
    C. With the advent of guilds, apprenticeship became a complex system.
    D. Apprentices were to be taught only certain things, and then the apprentices were to prove they possessed certain skills, as determined by the guild.

8. The main idea of the passage is that _____.
    A. wool, spice and silk dealers were all types of merchant trades during the Middle Ages
    B. Florence, Italy was a great center of commerce during the Middle Ages
    C. merchant guilds originated in the Middle Ages and became extremely popular, eventually leading to a sophisticated apprenticeship system
    D. apprenticeships were highly sought after; therefore, merchants had many skilled workers to choose from to assist the merchants in their trades

9. From the content of the passage, it can be reasonably be inferred that _____.
    A. prior to the inception of guilds, merchants were susceptible to competition from lesser skilled craftspeople peddling inferior products or services
    B. most merchants were unscrupulous businesspersons who often cheated their customers
    C. it was quite easy to become an apprentice to a highly skilled merchant
    D. guilds fell out of practice during the Industrial Revolution due to the mechanization of labor

10. As used in the second sentence, <u>analogous</u> most closely means _____.
    A. obsolete
    B. inferior
    C. similar
    D. less popular

11. Which of the following is the best signal word or phrase to complete the fill-in-the-blank space in the passage?
    A. Up until that time
    B. Before that time

    C. By that time
    D. After that time

Passage 3

Certainly we must face this fact: if the American press, as a mass medium, has formed the minds of America, the mass has also formed the medium. There is action, reaction, and interaction going on ceaselessly between the newspaper-buying public and the editors. What is wrong with the American press is what is in part wrong with American society. Is this, _____, to exonerate the American press for its failures to give the American people more tasteful and more illuminating reading matter? Can the American press seek to be excused from responsibility for public lack of information as TV and radio often do, on the grounds that, after all, "we have to give the people what they want or we will go out of business"? —Clare Boothe Luce

12. What is the primary purpose of this text?
    A. To reveal an innate problem in American society
    B. To criticize the American press for not taking responsibility for their actions
    C. To analyze the complex relationship that exists between the public and the media
    D. To challenge the masses to protest the lack of information disseminated by the media

13. From which of the following is the above paragraph most likely excerpted?
    A. Newspaper editorial letter
    B. Novel about yellow journalism
    C. Diary entry
    D. Speech given at a civil rights protest

14. Which of the following is an example of a primary source document?
    A. Newspaper editorial letter
    B. Novel about yellow journalism
    C. Diary entry
    D. Speech given at a civil rights protest

15. As used in the fourth sentence in the passage, <u>illuminating</u> most closely means _____.
    A. intelligent
    B. sophisticated
    C. interesting
    D. enlightening

16. Which of the following options is the best signal word or phrase to fill in the blank?
    A. so
    B. however
    C. therefore
    D. yet

17. What is the author's primary attitude toward the American press?

    A. Admiration
    B. Perplexity
    C. Disapproval
    D. Ambivalence

18. Which of the following identifies the mode of the passage?
    A. Expository
    B. Persuasive/argumentative
    C. Narrative
    D. Descriptive

19. Based on the passage, which of the following can most likely be concluded?
    A. The author has a degree in journalism
    B. The author has worked in the journalism industry
    C. The author is seeking employment at a newspaper
    D. The author is filing a lawsuit against a media outlet

Passage 4

The game today known as "football" in the United States can be traced directly back to the English game of rugby, although there have been many changes to the game. Football was played informally on university fields more than a hundred years ago. In 1840, a yearly series of informal "scrimmages" started at Yale University. It took more than 25 years, _____, for the game to become a part of college life. The first formal intercollegiate football game was held between Princeton and Rutgers teams on November 6, 1869, on Rutgers' home field in New Brunswick, New Jersey, and Rutgers won.

20. Which of the following sentences, if added to the end of the paragraph, would provide the best conclusion?
    A. Despite an invitation to join the Ivy League, Rutgers University declined, but later joined the Big Ten Conference instead.
    B. Football was played for decades on school campuses nationwide before the American Professional Football Association was formed in 1920 and then renamed the National Football League (NFL) two years later.
    C. Women were never allowed to play football, and that fact remains a controversial policy at many colleges and universities today.
    D. Football remains the national pastime, despite rising popularity for the game of soccer due to increased TV coverage of World Cup matches.

21. Which of the following options is the best signal word or phrase to fill in the blank ?
    A. however
    B. still
    C. in addition
    D. alternatively

Passage 5

Modernism is a philosophical movement that arose during the early 20th century. Among the factors that shaped modernism were the development of modern societies based on industry and the rapid growth of cities, followed later by the horror of World War I. Modernism rejected the science-based thinking of the earlier Era of Enlightenment, and many modernists also rejected religion. The poet Ezra Pound's 1934 imperative to "Make it new!" was the touchstone of the movement's approach toward what it saw as the now obsolete culture of the past. A notable characteristic of modernism is self-consciousness and irony concerning established literary and social traditions, which often led to experiments concerned with HOW things were made, not so much with the actual final product. Modernism had a profound impact on numerous aspects of life, and its values and perspectives still influence society in many positive ways today.

22. According to the passage, what is the overarching theme of the modernist movement?
    A. Rejection of the past and outmoded ideas
    B. Appreciation of urban settings over natural settings
    C. A concentration on method over form
    D. A focus on automated industry

23. As used in the passage, <u>touchstone</u> most closely means _____.
    A. challenge
    B. basis
    C. fashion
    D. metaphor

24. Which of the following statements from the passage can be described as an opinion?
    A. Among the factors that shaped modernism were the development of modern societies based on industry and the rapid growth of cities, followed later by the horror of World War I.
    B. The poet Ezra Pound's 1934 imperative to "Make it new!" was the touchstone of the movement's approach toward what it saw as the now obsolete culture of the past.
    C. A notable characteristic of modernism is self-consciousness and irony concerning established literary and social traditions, which often led to experiments focused on HOW things were made, not so much with the actual final product.
    D. Modernism had a profound impact on numerous aspects of life, and modernist values and perspectives still influence society in many positive ways today.

Passage 6

The modern Olympics are the leading international sporting event featuring summer and winter sports competitions in which thousands of athletes from around the world participate in a variety of competitions. Held every two years, with the Summer and Winter Games alternating, the Games are a modern way to bring nations together, _____ allow for national pride, and facilitate sportsmanship on a global scale. Having withstood the test of time over many centuries, the Olympics are the best example of the physical achievements of humankind.

The creation of the modern Games was inspired by the ancient Olympic Games, which were held in Olympia, Greece, from the 8th century BC to the 4th century AD. The Ancient Games events were fewer in number than modern games and were examples of very basic traditional forms of competitive athleticism. Many running events were featured; other events included a pentathlon (consisting of a jumping event, discus and javelin throws, a foot race, and wrestling), boxing, wrestling, pankration, and equestrian events. Fast forward to the modern state of this ancient athletic competition, and the Olympic movement during the 20th and 21st centuries has resulted in several changes to the Games, including the creation of the Winter Olympic Games for ice and winter sports, which for climate reasons, would not have been possible in ancient Greece. The Olympics have also shifted away from pure amateurism to allowing participation of professional athletes, a change met with criticism when first introduced, as many felt the change detracted from the original spirit and intention of the competition.

Today, over 13,000 athletes compete at the Summer and Winter Olympic Games in 33 different sports and nearly 400 events. The first, second, and third-place finishers in each event receive Olympic medals: gold, silver, and bronze, respectively. And every country hopes to be able to go home with many of these medals, as they are truly still a point of pride for each nation to be recognized for some outstanding achievement on the world stage, however briefly.

25. Which of the following options is the best signal word or phrase to fill in the blank in Paragraph 1?
    A. despite
    B. however
    C. instead of
    D. as well as

26. Which of the following words from the last sentence of Paragraph 2 has a negative connotation?
    A. shifted
    B. allowing
    C. change
    D. detracted

27. Which of the following statements based on the passage would be considered an opinion?
    A. The ancient Olympic games were held in Olympia, Greece.
    B. The Olympic games are the best example of humanity's physical prowess.
    C. When the Games were changed from pure amateurism to allowing professional athletes to participate, the change displeased many people.
    D. Today, 33 different sports are represented at the Olympic Games.

Passage 7

A day or two later, in the afternoon, I saw myself staring at my fire, in a room at an inn I had booked based on foreseeing that I would spend some weeks in London. I had just come in and, having decided on a spot for my luggage, sat down to consider my room. It was on the ground floor, and the fading daylight reached it in a sadly broken-down condition. It struck me that the room was stuffy and unsocial, with its moldy smell and its decoration of lithographs and waxy flowers—it seemed an impersonal black hole in the huge general blackness of the inn itself. The uproar of the neighborhood outside hummed away, and the rattle of a heartless hansom cab passed close to my ears. A sudden horror of the whole place came over me, like a tiger-pounce of homesickness that had been watching its moment. London seemed hideous, vicious, cruel and, above all, overwhelming. Soon, I would have to go out for my dinner, and it appeared to me that I would rather remain dinnerless, would rather even starve, than go forth into the hellish town where a stranger might get trampled to death, and have his carcass thrown into the Thames River.

28. Based on the passage above, the author's attitude toward his experience in London can best be described as _____.
    A. awe
    B. disappointment
    C. revulsion
    D. ambivalence

29. Which type of document is this passage likely excerpted from?
    A. Travel guide
    B. Diary entry
    C. News editorial
    D. Advertisement

30. Which of the following documents would likely NOT be considered a primary source document?
    A. Travel guide
    B. Diary entry
    C. News editorial
    D. Advertisement

31. Based on the content of the passage, which of the following statement is a reasonable conclusion?
    A. The author is quite wealthy.
    B. The author has been to London before.
    C. The author is traveling to London based on the recommendation of a friend.
    D. The author will not be traveling to London again.

For each remaining question, select the best answer.

32. Which of the sentences below illustrates the proper use of punctuation for dialogue?
    A. "I have a dream", began Martin Luther King, Jr.

B. "Can you believe I've been asked to audition for that part," asked Megan excitedly?

C. "You barely know him! How can you marry him?" was the worried mom's response to her teenager's announcement of marriage.

D. "Remain seated while the seatbelt signs are illuminated." Came the announcement over the airplane's loudspeaker system.

33. Which of the sentences below is NOT in the second person?
    A. Lincoln started his "Gettysburg Address" with "Four score and seven years ago."
    B. Did you know that anyone can audition for the school play?
    C. Make sure to close the window before leaving!
    D. "Remain seated while the seatbelt signs are illuminated," came the announcement over the airplane's loudspeaker system.

34. Which of the following sentences is an example of an imperative sentence?
    A. "I have a dream," began Martin Luther King, Jr.
    B. Megan excitedly asked, "Can you believe I've been asked to audition for that part?"
    C. "You barely know him! How can she marry him?" was the worried mom's response at her teenager's announcement of marriage.
    D. Please remain seated while the seatbelt signs are illuminated.

35. Which of the following words means "the act of cutting out"?
    A. Incision
    B. Concision
    C. Excision
    D. Decision

36. Which of the following words refers to an inflammation?
    A. Appendectomy
    B. Colitis
    C. Angioplasty
    D. Dermatology

37. Which of the following words refers to a cancer?
    A. Neuropathy
    B. Hysterectomy
    C. Oncology
    D. Melanoma

38. Which of the following conditions is associated with the nose?
    A. Hematoma
    B. Neuralgia
    C. Rhinitis
    D. Meningitis

39. Which of the following words refers to the study of something?
    A. Gastroenterology

B. Gastritis
C. Psychosis
D. Psychopath

PRACTICE TEST 2 ANSWERS

PRACTICE TEST 2.1 ANSWERS: MATH

1. **Answer:** D. 20%
   Rationale: To find the percentage increase, you first need to know the amount of the increase. The population increased from 12,500 to 15,000 over the past decade. This change shows an increase of 2,500 people. Now, to find the percent of the increase, divide the amount of the increase by the original amount:

   $$2,500 \div 12,500 = 0.20$$

   To convert a decimal to a percent, move the decimal point two places to the right:

   $$0.20 = 20\%$$

   When a question instead asks for the percent of a decrease, you also divide the amount of the decrease by the original amount.

2. **Answer:** C. 78
   Rationale: To find the median in a series of numbers, arrange the numbers in order from smallest to largest:

   $$69, 73, 78, 80, 100$$

   The number in the center is the median.

   If there are an even number of numbers in the series—for example, 34, 46, 52, 54, 67, 81—then the median will be the average of the two numbers in the center. In this example, the median will be 53 (the average of 52 and 54). Remember: The median is different from the average.

3. **Answer:** D. 22
   Rationale: This question asks you to find the square root of 11 times 44. First, do the multiplication:

   $$11 * 44 = 484$$

   Now multiply each of the possible answers by itself to see which one is the square root of 484. Since $22 * 22 = 484$, the answer is D.

4. **Answer:** C. 375 liters
   Rationale: If $^3/_5$ full of water, the barrel is $^2/_5$ empty. The 150 liters added to fill the barrel is therefore $^2/_5$ of the barrel's capacity. Draw a simple diagram to represent the barrel.

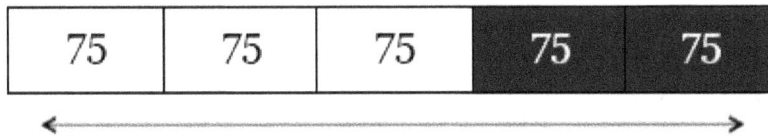

$$^2/_5 = 150 \text{ liters}$$

Each fifth of the barrel is 75 liters. Thus, the total capacity of the barrel is 5 * 75, or 375 liters.

5. **Answer:** D. 3^4
   Rationale: Positive numbers are larger than negative numbers, so this fact limits the possible answers to 42 and 3^4, the latter of which equals $81(3 * 3 * 3 * 3)$. Thus, the answer is D.

6. **Answer:** C. 59
   Rationale: A prime number is a whole number greater than 1 that can be divided evenly only by itself and 1. In this question, only 59 fits that definition.

   Conversely, 81 is not prime because it can be divided evenly by 9; 49 is not prime because it can be divided evenly by 7; and 77 is not prime because it can be divided evenly by 7 and 11.

7. **Answer:** D. $\frac{1}{2}(12 + 20) * 8$
   Rationale: The area of a trapezoid is one-half the product of the parallel sides (top and bottom) times the perpendicular height between the two. Choice A is incorrect because it uses the wrong mathematical operators in multiple areas. Choice B is incorrect because it adds the bottom base with the height rather than top base; the formula also divides rather than multiplies by $\frac{1}{2}$. Choice C is incorrect because it divides the sum of the bases rather than multiples by them. Thus, the answer is D.

8. **Answer:** A. 2,595
   Rationale: The steps in evaluating a mathematical expression must be carried out in a certain order, which is called the "order of operations." The following list shows the steps in order:

   - **Step 1:** Parentheses: First do any operations in parentheses.
   - **Step 2:** Exponents: Then do any steps that involve exponents.
   - **Step 3:** Multiply and Divide: Multiply and divide from left to right.
   - **Step 4:** Add and Subtract: Add and subtract from left to right.

   One way to remember this order is to use the mnemonic sentence below:
   Please **E**xcuse **M**y **D**ear **A**unt **S**ally.

   To evaluate the expression in this question, follow the below steps:

- **Step 1:** Multiply the numbers in Parentheses: $3 * 4 = 12$
- **Step 2:** Apply the Exponent 2 to the number in parentheses: $12^2 = 144$
- **Step 3:** Multiply: $6 * 3 * 144 = 2,592$
- **Step 4:** Add: $1 + 2,592 + 1 = 2,595$

9. **Answer:** B. 9
   Rationale: The symbol ≥ means "greater than or equal to." The only answer that is greater than or equal to 9 is answer B.

10. **Answer:** C. $x = 484$
    Rationale: When two numbers with the same sign (both positive or both negative) are multiplied, the answer is a positive number. Thus, the answer is C.

    Conversely, when two numbers with different signs (one positive and the other negative) are multiplied, the answer is negative (-484 in this case).

11. **Answer:** B. $x = a^5$
    Rationale: When multiplying numbers that have the same base and different exponents, keep the base the same and add the exponents. In this case, $a^2 * a^3$ becomes $a^{(2+3)}$ or a^5.

12. **Answer:** C. $28
    Rationale: The individual costs of all the items can be expressed in terms of the cost of the all-purpose flour ($2). Use x to represent the cost of the flour. The coconut sugar costs twice the cost of the flour, so the sugar costs $2x$. The cost of the free-range eggs is twice as much as double the cost of the flour, so the eggs cost $(2 * 2x)$. The cost of the generic butter is three times the cost of the flour, so the butter costs $3x$. The cost of the real vanilla extract is four times the cost of the flour, so the vanilla extract costs $4x$. Those values can then be plugged into the following equation:

$$x + 2x + (2 * 2x) + 3x + 4x = 14x$$

The all-purpose flour costs $10, so $14x$ (the total cost) is $28.

13. **Answer:** C. 6
    Rationale: Solve the equation below:

    i. $x > 3^2 - 4$
    ii. $x > 9 - 4$
    iii. $x > 5$

We know that x is greater than 5, so the answer could be either 6 or 7. However, the question asks for the smallest possible value of x, so the correct answer is 6.

14. **Answer:** B. 45 registered nurses
    Rationale: First, find the number of registered nurses (RNs) working at the hospital. Convert 65% to a decimal by moving the decimal point two places to the left:

$$65\% = .65$$

Now, multiply .65 times the number of RNs working at the hospital:

$$.65 * 200 = 130$$

Of the 130 RNs, 45 have more than 5 years of experience, so to college, so 85 have less than 5 years of experience.

$$130 - 45 = 85$$

15. **Answer:** C. $300
    Rationale: If the phone was on sale at 30% off, the sale price was 70% of the original price. Therefore, the answer can be obtained by solving the following equation for x:

$$\$210 = 70\% \text{ of } x$$

where x is the original price of the phone. When you convert 70% to a decimal, you get the following equation:

$$\$210 = .70 \times x$$

To isolate x on one side of the equation, divide both sides of the equation by .70:

$$x = \$300$$

16. **Answer:** D. 128
    Rationale: The facts provided can be used to write the following equation:

$$\frac{3}{8}n - 4 = 48$$

First, add 4 to both sides of the equation:

$$\frac{3}{8}n = 48$$

Then, divide both sides of the equation by $\frac{3}{8}$. To divide by a fraction, invert the fraction so that $\frac{3}{8}$ becomes $\frac{8}{3}$, then multiply:

$$n = \frac{48 * 8}{3}$$
$$n = \frac{384}{3}$$
$$n = 128$$

17. **Answer:** D. 108

Rationale: The ratio of the two numbers is 7:3. Therefore, the larger number is $\frac{7}{10}$ of 360 and the smaller number is $\frac{3}{10}$ of 360. To find the smaller number, multiply the smaller fraction by the total of the two numbers, as shown in the equation below:

$$\frac{3}{10} * \frac{360}{1} = \frac{1,080}{10} = 108$$

18. **Answer:** C. 78 ounces

    Rationale: Michael must consume 104 ounces to meet his daily hydration goal; he has already consumed 25%. To calculate how many more ounces he must drink to meet the goal, first convert 25% to a decimal by moving the decimal point two places to the left: 25% = .25. Now multiply .25 times 104:

$$.25 * 104 = 26$$

    Michael has thus drunk 26 ounces of his goal (i.e., 104 ounces), but the question asks how many ounces he has left to drink to meet his goal. Since he must drink 104 ounces of fluids a day, subject the number of ounces he has already drunk from the total goal:

$$104 - 26 = 78$$

    Thus, if he must drink 104 ounces, Michael still needs to drink 78 ounces to meet his goal.

19. **Answer:** B. 3,024 cubic inches

    Rationale: The formula for the volume of a rectangular solid is $length * width * height$. Therefore, the volume of this box is calculated using the following formula:

$$18 * 12 * 14 = 3,024 \; cubic \; inches$$

20. **Answer:** B. Perpendicular

    Rationale: Two lines that form a right angle are called perpendicular.

21. **Answer:** C. 15 square feet

    Rationale: This shape is called a parallelogram. The area of a parallelogram equals the base times the height, as calculated in the following equation:

$$5 \; feet * 3 \; feet = 15 \; square \; feet$$

22. **Answer:** D. 0.72

    Rationale: The simplest way to answer this question is to convert the fractions to decimals. To convert a fraction to a decimal, divide the numerator (the top number) by the denominator (the bottom number). The questions below show the conversions for answers A, B, and C:

$$^5/_8 = 0.625$$

$$^3/_5 = 0.6$$
$$^2/_3 = 0.67$$

The largest number is therefore 0.72, answer D.

23. **Answer:** A. 11 pages
    Rationale: If Charles wrote an average of 7 pages per day for four days, he wrote a total of 28 pages. He wrote a total of 17 pages on the first three days, so he must have written 11 pages on the fourth day.

24. **Answer:** B. $\frac{20}{mp^2}$
    Rationale: To divide by a fraction, invert the second fraction and multiply.

$$\text{so } \frac{5}{mp} \div \frac{p}{4} \text{ becomes } \frac{5}{mp} * \frac{4}{p}$$

$$\text{and } \frac{5}{mp} * \frac{4}{p} = \frac{20}{mp^2}$$

25. **Answer:** B. 3.44 square feet
    Rationale: First, find the area of the square by multiplying the length of a side by itself. The area of the square is 16 square feet. Then, find the area of the circle by using the following formula: $A = \pi r^2$.

    The symbol π equals approximately 3.14. The letter r is the radius of the circle. In this case, r is half the width of the square (or 2), so $r^2 = 4$. The area of the circle is calculated as follows:
    $$A = 3.14 * 4$$
    $$A = 12.56$$

    To find the area of the square not covered by the circle, subtract 12.56 square feet from 16 square feet, which equals 3.44 square feet.

26. **Answer:** B. 10 miles
    Rationale: If you made a simple map with the three cities, it would look like the following diagram:

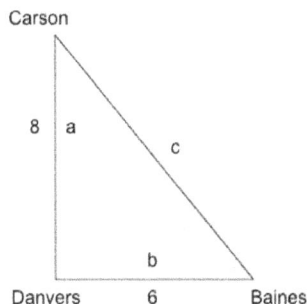

The preceding figure is a right triangle. The longest side of a right triangle is called the hypotenuse. The two legs of the triangle are labeled a and b. The hypotenuse is labeled c. You can find the length of the hypotenuse (the distance between Caron and Baines) with the following equation:

$$a^2 + b^2 = c^2$$

In this case, the equation would be calculated as follows:

$$8^2 + 6^2 = c^2$$
$$64 + 36 = c^2$$
$$100 = c^2$$

To find c, ask the following question: What number times itself equals 100? The answer is 10.

27. **Answer:** C. $^3/_{36}$
    Rationale: When you roll a pair of 6-sided dice, there are 36 possible combinations of numbers (or outcomes). There are six numbers on each of the dice, so there are $6 * 6$ possible combinations. Only three of those combinations will yield a total of 10: $4 + 6$, $5 + 5$, and $6 + 4$. Much of the time, probability answers will be given in the form of simplified fractions. In this case, the correct answer could also have been $^1/_{12}$.

28. **Answer:** A. $144
    Rationale: When one person dropped out of the arrangement, the cost for the remaining three went up by $12 per person for a total of $36. This means that each person's share was originally $36. There were four people in the original arrangement, so the cost of the gift was 4 * $36, or $144.

    Or alternatively, let $4x$ equal the original cost of the gift. If the number of shares decreases to 3, then the total cost is $3(x + 12)$. Those expressions must be equal:

    $$4 = 3(x + 12)$$
    $$4x = 3x + 36$$

    Subtracting $3x$ from both sides, obtains the following:

    $$x = 36$$

    Then the original price of the gift was 4 times 36, or $144.

29. **Answer:** C. 120
    Rationale: The factorial of a number is the product of all the integers less than or equal to the number. The factorial of 5 is $5 * 4 * 3 * 2 * 1 = 120$. The factorial is written this way: 5!

30. **Answer:** D. 7

Rationale: In this number, the places are as follows:

- 1 is in the thousands place
- 2 is in the hundreds place
- 3 is in the tens place
- 4 is in the ones place
- 5 is in the tenths place
- 6 is in the hundredths place
- 7 is in the thousandths place

31. **Answer:** B. 4
    Rationale: The mode is the number that appears most often in a set of numbers. Since 4 appears three times, it is the "mode."

32. **Answer:** C. 49
    Rationale: A perfect square is the product of an integer times itself. In this question, 49 is a perfect square because it is the product of $7 * 7$.

33. **Answer:** A. $[(8 * 40) + (50 * 15)] * 7$
    Rationale: In the correct answer, $[(8 * 40) + (50 * 15)] * 7$, the first set of parentheses inside the brackets calculates how many how much Sarah makes per day selling 40 pieces of jewelry at $8 each. The second set of parentheses inside the brackets calculates how much Mike makes per day selling 15 batches of bread for $50 each. The results of both operations are then added together to give the total combined daily earnings for Sarah and Mike. The resulting amount is then multiplied by 7 days.

34. **Answer:** B. 61,351 people
    Rationale: The number of spectators at the 2024 NFL Super Bowl was 59% of the number of spectators at the 1980 NFL Super Bowl (103, 985 people). To solve for the answer, first convert 59% to a decimal by moving the decimal point two places to the left: 59% = .59. Now multiply .59 times 103,985 (the number of spectators at the 1980 game in 1980), as shown in the following equation:

$$.59 * 103,985 = 61,351.15$$

Since the answer calls for the nearest whole number, B is the correct answer.

35. **Answer:** D. $^{13}/_{16}$
    Rationale: To add $^{5}/_{8}$ and $^{3}/_{16}$, you must find a common denominator. The simplest way to do this is to multiply the denominators: $8 * 16 = 128$. Therefore, 128 is a common denominator. However, this method will not always give you the lowest common denominator (LCD), which in this case would be 16.

Using the LCD, convert both fractions in the problem to equivalent fractions that have that same denominator. To do this conversion, rewrite each fraction with the common denominator of 16:

$$\frac{5}{8} = \frac{5*2}{8*2} = \frac{10}{16}$$

$$\frac{3}{16} * \frac{1}{1} = \frac{3}{16}$$

Now you can add $^{10}/_{16}$ and $^{3}/_{16}$ to solve the problem, so the correct answer is $^{13}/_{16}$.

36. **Answer:** C. Rich is 36, Maryanne is 30

Rationale: Use R to represent Rich's age, and M to represent Maryanne's age. Maryanne is 6 years younger than Rich, $M = R - 6$. Twenty-two years ago, Rich was 10 years older than ½ of Maranne's age:

$$Rich - 22 = 10 + \frac{1}{2}[(Maryanne - 6) - 22]$$

Now substitute R for Rich and R - 6 for Maryanne:

$$R - 22 = 10 + \frac{1}{2}[(R - 6) - 22]$$

Simplify the equation, as shown in the steps below:

$$R - 22 = 10 + \frac{1}{2}(R - 28)$$
$$R - 22 = 10 + \frac{R}{2} - 14$$
$$R - 22 = \frac{R}{2} - 4$$

Then take the following steps: multiply both sides of the equation by 2 to remove the fraction, subtract R from both sides of the equation, and add 44 to both sides of the equation to solve for R:

$$2R - 44 = R - 8$$
$$R - 44 = -8$$
$$R = 36 \, Rich's age$$

Finally, calculate Maryanne's age:

$$Maryanne's \, age = R - 6$$
$$Maryanne's \, age = 36 - 6$$
$$Maryanne's \, age = 30$$

Thus, Rich is 36, Maryanne is 30.

37. **Answer:** A. Length = 12, width = 4

Rationale: Use w to represent the width of the rectangle. The length is three times the width, so the length is $3w$. The area of the rectangle is the length times the width, so the area is $w * 3w$, or $3w^2$:

$$3w^2 = 48$$

Divide both sides of the equation by 3 to get the following:

$$w^2 = 16$$

Therefore, $w = 4$, the width of the rectangle, and $3w = 12$, the length of the rectangle

38. **Answer:** B. $24 = 2 * 2 * 2 * 3$
   Rationale: The prime factors of a number are the prime numbers that divide that number evenly. The prime factorization of a number is a list of the prime factors that must be multiplied to yield that number.

   The simplest method of finding the prime factorization is to start with a simple multiplication fact for that number. In this case, the following is a good choice:

   $$24 = 6 * 4$$

   The prime factorization of 24 includes the prime factorization of both 6 and 4. Therefore, since $6 = 2 * 3$ and $4 = 2 * 2$, the prime factorization of 24 must be the following:

   $$24 = 2 * 2 * 2 * 3$$

39. **Answer:** A. A number greater than x
   Rationale: When a positive number is divided by a positive number less than 1, the quotient will always be larger than the number being divided. For example, $5 ÷ 0.5 = 10$. If we solve this as a fraction, $5 ÷ (1/2)$ is the same as $5 * (2/1)$, which equals 10, since dividing by a fraction is the same as multiplying by the reciprocal.

40. **Answer:** C. $c = 11$
   Rationale: Subtracting a negative number is the same as adding a positive number. Therefore, $8 - (-3)$ is the same as $8 + 3$, both of which equal 11.

41. **Answer:** C. The square of a number is always a positive number.
   Rationale: When two numbers with the same sign (positive or negative) are multiplied, the product is always positive. When a number is squared, it is multiplied by itself, so the numbers being multiplied have the same sign. Therefore, the product is always positive.

   The square of a number greater than 1 is always greater than the original number. But the square of a positive number less than one (e.g., 0.5) is always less than the original number.

42. **Answer:** C. 71 fourth-graders

Rationale: Jerry is taller than 65% of students in his class. To find the number of students shorter than Jerry, first convert 65% to a decimal by moving the decimal point two places to the left: 65% = .65. Now multiply .65 times the number of students in Jerry's fourth-grade class:

$$.65 * 110 = 71.15 \text{ fourth-grade students, or } 71 \text{ (must be a whole number)}$$

43. **Answer:** D. $60

Rationale: Use the information given to write an equation. First, determine how many weeks are in 5 years (each year has 52 weeks):

$$5 * 52 = 260 \text{ weeks}$$

The total amount Rebecca saved from her weekly savings is thus $260d$. She also received $1,000 total in birthday money over the 5 years. Together, her total savings amounts to $20,600. Now write the equation to solve for the answer:

$$260d + 1,000 = 16,600$$

When you subtract 1,000 from both sides of the equation, you get the following:

$$260d = 15,600$$

Divide both sides of the equation by 260 to complete the equation:

$$d = \$60, \text{ the amount Rebecca saved each week for 5 years}$$

44. **Answer:** D. $r = \frac{p-3}{2}$

Explanation: Begin by subtracting 3 from both sides of the equation to get the following:

$$p - 3 = 2r$$

Now, to isolate r on one side of the equation, divide both sides of the equation by 2 to get the following:

$$r = \frac{p - 3}{2}$$

45. **Answer:** C. 12

Rationale: The least common multiple (LCM) is used when finding the lowest common denominator. The LCM is the lowest number that can be divided evenly by both numbers.

Here is a simple method to find the least common multiple of 4 and 6 (1) write 4 on the left side of your paper, (2) then add 4 and write the result, and (3) then add another 4 to that number and write the result. Keep going until you have a list that looks something like the following list:

$$4\ 8\ 16\ 20\ 24\ 28...$$

This partial list shows some multiples of 4. (If you remember your multiplication tables, these numbers are the column or row that go with 4.) Now do the same thing with 10.

$$6\ 12\ 18\ 24...$$

This partial list shows multiples of 6. Eventually, similar numbers will appear in both rows. The smallest of these numbers is the LCM. There will always be more multiples that are found in both rows (if you were to continue listing multiples), but the smallest number is LCM.

46. **Answer:** C. $x = 6$
Rationale: When you multiply or divide numbers that have the same sign (both positive or both negative), the answer will be positive. When you multiply or divide numbers that have different signs (one positive and the other negative), the answer will be negative. In this case, both numbers have the same sign, so the answer is a positive number, 6 (answer C).

47. **Answer:** D. $2\frac{7}{8}$
Rationale: To convert an improper fraction to a mixed number, divide the numerator (23) by the denominator (8). In this case, you get 2 with a remainder of 7. The 2 becomes the whole number portion of the mixed number, and 7 becomes the numerator of the new fraction.

48. **Answer:** B. −10
Rationale: To find the value of q, divide both sides of the equation by −13. When a positive number is divided by a negative number, the answer is negative.

49. **Answer:** C. 115
Rationale: Replace the letters with the numbers the letters represent in $x^2 + 4y$, and then perform the necessary operations, as shown below:

$$10^2 + 4(3.75)$$
$$100 + 15 = 115$$

50. **Answer:** B. 500,000,000
Rationale: A billion is 1,000 million (1,000,000,000). Half a billion is 500 million (500,000,000).

51. **Answer:** B. 32 inches
Rationale: The radius of a circle is one half of the diameter, so the diameter of this circle is 8 inches. The diameter is a line that passes through the center of a circle and joins two points on its circumference. If you study this figure, you can see that the diameter of the circle is the same as the length of each side of the square. The diameter is 8 inches, so the perimeter of the square is 32 inches (8 + 8 + 8 + 8).

52. **Answer:** B. $x = \frac{5}{9}$

    Rationale: To multiply fractions, multiply the numerators and the denominators of the fractions in the equation $x = \frac{5}{6} * \frac{2}{3}$. In this case, multiply 5 by 2, and 6 by 3. The correct answer is therefore $\frac{10}{18}$, which can be reduced to $\frac{5}{9}$.

53. **Answer:** D. $y = 2x + 7$

    Rationale: The simplest way to answer this question is to determine which of the equations would work for all the values of x and y in the table. Choices A and D would work when $x = 0$ and $y = 7$, but A would not work for any other values of x and y. Choice B would work when $x = 3$ and $y = 13$, but it would not work for any other values of x and y. Choice C would not work for any of the values of x and y. Only choice D would be correct for each ordered pair in the table.

54. **Answer:** D. 80

    Rationale: If we call the smaller number x, then the larger number is $5x$. The sum of the two numbers is 480, so the following equation can be used to solve for x:

$$x + 5x = 480$$
$$6x = 480$$
$$x = 80$$

55. **Answer:** B. 80 pastries

    Rationale: To solve this problem, first convert 30% to a decimal by moving the decimal point two places to the left: $30\% = .30$. Use x to represent the total number of pastries in the class, and then set up the following equation:

$$.30x = 24$$

    Solve for x by dividing both sides of the equation by .30. Since 24 divided by .30 is 80, the correct answer is B.

56. **Answer:** A. 64 feet

    Rationale: The dimensions of the left side and the top side of this figure are provided, but how do you find the dimensions of the other sides? Look at the two horizontal lines on the bottom of the figure. Together, the lines are as wide as the top side of the figure, so they must be 18 feet when measured together. Now look at the two vertical lines on the right side of the figure. Together, the vertical lines are as tall as the left side of the figure, so the lines must be 14 feet when measured together. Thus, the perimeter of the figure is $14 + 18 + 14 + 18$, or $32 + 32 = 64 \, feet$.

57. **Answer:** C. 4

    Rationale: Make a list of the powers of 10.

    - $10^2 = 100$
    - $10^3 = 1,000$

- $10^4 = 10,000$
- $10^5 = 100,000$

When you divide 15,200 by 1.52, you get 10,000. Therefore, the correct exponent is 4. That exponent is also the number of places the decimal must be moved in the number 1.52 to make the number 15,200.

58. **Answer:** B. $6.5 * 10^{-3}$
    Rationale: Make a list of the negative powers of 10:

    - $10^{-2} = 0.01$
    - $10^{-3} = 0.001$
    - $10^{-4} = 0.0001$
    - $10^{-5} = 0.00001$

    Now multiply each of these numbers by 6.5 to see which one gives you 0.0065. The decimal must be moved 3 places to the left in the number 6.5 to make the number 0.0065.

59. **Answer:** B. 32 diet, 80 regular
    Rationale: If the owner sells 2 diet sodas for every 5 regular sodas, then $2/_7$ of the sodas sold are diet and $5/_7$ are regular. Multiply these fractions by the total number of sodas sold, as follows:

    $$\frac{2}{7} * \frac{112}{1} = \frac{224}{7} = 32 \; diet \; sodas$$

    $$\frac{5}{7} * \frac{112}{1} = \frac{560}{7} = 80 \; regular \; sodas$$

    Remember: When multiplying a fraction by a whole number, dividing by the denominator first is usually simpler. Then multiply by the numerator.

60. **Answer:** C. 24
    Rationale: The greatest common factor of two numbers is the largest number that can be divided evenly into both numbers. The simplest way to answer this question is to start with the largest answer (48) and determine whether it can be divided evenly into 72 and 96. It cannot.

    Now try the next largest answer (24). That number can be divided evenly into 72 and 96. Thus, 24 is the correct answer. Answers A and C are also factors, but 24 is the largest number that can be divided evenly into both 72 and 96.

PRACTICE TEST 2.2 ANSWERS: SCIENCE

1. **Answer:** B. The smooth endoplasmic reticulum does not participate in the synthesis of proteins
   Rationale: The smooth endoplasmic reticulum does not contain ribosomes, which are present in the rough endoplasmic reticulum. Ribosomes are required for protein synthesis. Both rough and smooth endoplasmic reticulum are involved in the synthesis of products destined for transport and secretion out of the cell into the external environment.

2. **Answer:** A. External cell membrane
   Rationale: An external cell membrane (plasma membrane) is a feature of all living cells. Plants, fungi, and bacteria also possess at least one outer cell wall; however, human and other animal cells do not. Bacterial cells do not possess a nucleus or mitochondria.

3. **Answer:** B. Coronal
   Rationale: Caudal, ventral, and inferior are all anatomical positions. *Caudal* means nearer to the tail of the body. *Ventral* means at or nearer the frontal surface of the body. *Inferior* means near the feet. *Coronal*, along with sagittal and cross-sectional, refers to the axial planes of the body. *Coronal* is not used to express anatomical relations in the body.

4. **Answer:** C. Microtubules
   Rationale: The human sperm's flagellum is constructed from an internal bundle of microtubules that interact with a microtubule-organizing structure at the base of the flagellum. Individual microtubules slide sequentially back and forth within the flagellum, causing a whipping motion that causes the forward motion of the sperm cells. Thick (myosin) filaments are critical for muscle contraction, and actin microfilaments are involved in functions that require active, purposeful movement of cells; however, neither are present in the flagellum. Intermediate filaments are structural elements of the cytoskeleton of cells and do not contribute to the function of the flagellum.

5. **Answer:** B. Alternating deoxyribose sugars and phosphate groups
   Rationale: A DNA molecule is usually double-stranded. Each strand is composed of linear backbones of alternating deoxyribose sugars and phosphate groups.

6. **Answer:** A. ACG
   Rationale: The nitrogenous base thymine (T) occurs in DNA molecules but not in RNA molecules, while the nitrogenous base uracil (U) occurs in RNA molecules but not in DNA molecules. The remaining nitrogenous bases—adenine (A), cytosine (C), and guanine (G)—occur in both RNA and DNA. Codons are DNA 3-base sequences, and anticodons are RNA 3-base sequences. Answer A is the only possible choice that can occur in both an RNA and a DNA sequence.

7. **Answer:** B. Golgi apparatus
   Rationale: The Golgi apparatus is a highly folded series of membrane compartments. It works with the smooth endoplasmic reticulum to process, package, and transport a wide

variety of products synthesized in the cell. Frequently, these products are packaged into secretory vesicles that are subsequently secreted out through the cell membrane into the external environment. Ribosomes are small, spherical complexes of proteins and RNA that transcribe mRNA transcripts to assemble the coded protein. Cilia are hair-like extensions of the cell membrane involved in locomotion. The mitochondria contain enzymes that convert nutrients into energy.

8. **Answer:** C. Keratin
   Rationale: Keratin is a major extracellular structural protein. It provides protective and mechanical support to the outer layers of the skin and is the primary component of hair and nails. Collagen is an extracellular structural protein that has different mechanical properties. Fibrillin is a glycoprotein necessary for the formation of elastin in connective tissue. Melatonin is a hormone produced by the pineal gland and is responsible for the sleep-wake cycles.

9. **Answer:** D. Leydig; testosterone
   Rationale: Leydig cells are present in the testes and are responsible for producing testosterone in the male reproductive system. The tunica albuginea is the fibrous outer membrane of the testes and does not directly participate in the production of any type of cell. Sertoli cells produce substances that support the development of sperm precursor cells; however, Sertoli cells do not produce FSH. Spermatogonia are the progenitors of mature sperm cells and do not produce LH.

10. **Answer:** A. elbow; knee
    Rationale: The elbow and knee joints are synovial hinge joints that allow flexion and extension. However, the elbow joint additionally allows the head of the radius to pivot at its articulation with the distal end of the humerus, thus allowing for an additional range of motion known as supination and pronation. Therefore, the elbow's range of motion is greater than that of the knee joint. The sacroiliac joint connects the sacrum with the iliac bone of the pelvis on both sides of the lower spine. This joint is a non-synovial ligamentous joint that has a highly limited range of motion. The hip and shoulder joints are both synovial ball-and-socket joints that have a much greater range of motion than the hinge joints of the knee and elbow.

11. **Answer:** Cholesterol
    Rationale: Cholesterol is an important component of cell membranes and a precursor molecule for the synthesis of steroid hormones, cortisol, aldosterone, progesterone, and the sex hormones testosterone and estrogen. Most of the cholesterol used by the body is synthesized and not of dietary origin. Lipoproteins carry cholesterol through the bloodstream to reach the cells. Triglycerides are a type of fat used in energy production. Amino acids are the building blocks of proteins.

12. **Answer:** B. Prevention of the collapse of alveoli during expiration
    Rationale: The pulmonary surfactant decreases the surface tension of the fluid layer lining the internal surface of the alveoli. The surface tension of fluid layers on a concave surface, such as the internal surface of the spherical-shaped alveoli, increases as the radius of the alveoli decreases. Without the pulmonary surfactant, the surface tension of the fluid layer within the alveoli would increase during expiration to a point where the

alveoli could completely collapse. This collapse would prevent re-inflation of the alveoli on subsequent inspiration.

13. **Answer:** C. Ventral cavity
    Rationale: The ventral cavity is enclosed by the inner walls of the thorax (the thoracic muscles, ribs, sternum, and thoracic vertebrae); the inner surfaces of the ventral, lateral, and dorsal abdominal wall muscles; and the inner surfaces of the bones and associated muscles of the pelvis. The ventral cavity is divided into an upper cavity (the thoracic cavity) and a lower cavity (the abdominal/pelvic cavity) by the diaphragm. The major contents of the thoracic cavity are the heart and lungs, while the major contents of the abdominal and pelvic cavities are the intestines, the digestive organs, the urinary bladder, and the uterus and ovaries (in females).

14. **Answer:** B. Hypodermis
    Rationale: An important function of the integumentary system is thermoregulation, which allows the body to maintain a constant, optimum internal temperature range. The hypodermis contains adipose tissue that has poor thermal conduction and thus acts as an insulator to protect the body against excessive heat transfer to the external environment. The dermis provides protection and sensation to the skin and produces sweat and oil. The epidermis (also called the stratum corneum) is the outermost layer of the skin that protects against hazardous substances.

15. **Answer:** A. Pulmonary valve
    Rationale: Blood flows from the right atrium through the tricuspid valve to the right ventricle and then through the pulmonary valve to the main pulmonary artery.

16. **Answer:** A. A Peripheral lower limb vein
    Rationale: The pulmonary arteries are part of the right circulatory system. Blood clots in the pulmonary arteries (pulmonary embolism) originate from locations in the right heart circulation unless there is an abnormal connection between the left and right atria. Pulmonary embolisms most commonly originate from blood clots in large deep veins of the lower limbs. The other choices are all located on the left side of the heart circulation.

17. **Answer:** B. Plasma cells
    Rationale: The lymphocyte lineage gives rise to natural killer cells: T lymphocytes, B lymphocytes, and plasma cells. The myeloid lineage gives rise to basophils, neutrophils, eosinophils, macrophages, and platelets.

18. **Answer:** A. Human leukocyte antigens
    Rationale: The major histocompatibility complex (MHC) Class I human leukocyte antigens (HLA) are present on the cell membranes of dedicated or professional antigen-presenting cells of the immune system. ABO and Rh factor molecules are restricted to red blood cell membranes. Cadherin-class cell-adhesion molecules are primarily involved in structural functions related to binding with the extracellular matrix molecules.

19. **Answer:** D. Reduction of the strength and contractility of the heart

Rationale: The sympathetic nervous system releases neurotransmitters to the cardiac muscle and smooth muscle located in the bronchi, the intestinal tract, and the walls of blood vessels. These generate a response to environmental circumstances that require aggressive and highly energetic responses (fight or flight responses). The sympathetic nervous system increases the force of contraction of the heart, increases heart rate, increases blood pressure, redirects blood flow from the intestines to the skeletal muscles, inhibits peristalsis, and dilates bronchi.

20. **Answer:** C. A meal with high simple carbohydrate content
    Rationale: The most common stimulus for the release of the hormone glucagon is low levels of glucose in the bloodstream. Glucagon induces the liver to break down stored glycogen into glucose molecules. The glucose molecules are then secreted into the bloodstream to restore the blood glucose to normal levels. Conversely, high blood glucose levels suppress the release of glucagon. A meal high in simple carbohydrates will result in high levels of blood glucose since simple carbohydrates are easily hydrolyzed by digestive enzymes into glucose molecules that are rapidly absorbed into the circulation.

21. **Answer:** B. Cholecystokinin secretion → increased bile secretion → increased fat emulsification
    Rationale: Cholecystokinin released from the duodenum triggers the release of bile from the gallbladder into the duodenum. Bile emulsifies fat. Somatostatin is a hormone secreted by the duodenum, pancreas, and anterior pituitary gland that inhibits HCl and gastrin secretion from the stomach. Secretin is a hormone released by the duodenum that inhibits HCl secretion in the stomach and stimulates the release of bicarbonate by the pancreas.

22. **Answer:** D. hypothalamus; GnRH; LH; FSH; anterior
    Rationale: The male sex hormone, testosterone, is produced in the testes. The synthesis and secretion of testosterone are regulated by the hypothalamus through the release of gonadotrophin-releasing hormone (GnRH), which regulates the synthesis and release of luteinizing hormone (LH) and follicle-stimulating hormone (FSH) by the anterior pituitary. Both FSH and LH stimulate the testes to synthesize and release testosterone. The female sex hormone, estrogen, is produced in the ovaries. Once estrogen level reaches a critical level at about day 15 of the menstrual cycle, the estrogen level sends feedback to the hypothalamus and the pituitary gland, resulting in a spike in FSH and LH levels. The LH spike stimulates ovulation.

23. **Answer:** A. Smooth muscles
    Rationale: Smooth muscles are the type of muscle located throughout the body, particularly in the muscular layers of the respiratory system, the digestive system, and the circulatory system. Cardiac and smooth muscles are not under voluntary control and are regulated by the autonomic nervous system. Cardiac muscles are the muscles that form the heart. Skeletal muscles are voluntary muscles formed of individual cells that have endomysium and epimysium connections that allow for the free movement of cells.

24. **Answer:** B. Ligaments, tendons, cartilage, and the lower structural layers of the dermis of the skin

Rationale: Dense connective tissue has a high fibrous protein content within its ground substance. These fibers are composed primarily of collagen and variable amounts of elastic fibers with fibroblasts distributed among the extracellular fibers. Dense connective tissue forms ligaments, tendons, cartilage, and the lower structural layers of the dermis of the skin.

25. **Answer:** B. 1s22s22p1
    Rationale: For any given number of electron shell levels, the s orbitals are lower energy than the p orbitals and thus fill before electrons begin to occupy positions in the p orbitals. Therefore, the electron configuration for boron is $1s^2 2s^2 2p^1$.

26. **Answer:** C. Inadequate amounts of oxygen delivered to the muscles
    Rationale: Lactic acid (lactate) production in muscles results from the anaerobic conversion of pyruvate (a product of glycolysis) to lactic acid. This process generates energy; however, it is inefficient compared to the oxidative metabolism of glucose. Inadequate oxygen supply shifts energy production to this anaerobic pathway. Additionally, oxygen is required to convert lactate back to pyruvate. In an oxygen-deficient environment, muscles cannot convert lactate back to pyruvate, and consequently, lactate levels rise within the muscles. Activation of the sympathetic nervous system, depletion of glycogen stores in the liver, and inadequate levels of pyruvate within muscles do not result in the accumulation of lactic acid in the muscles.

27. **Answer:** D. Contraction of smooth muscle in the walls of arterioles in voluntary muscles
    Rationale: Activation of the parasympathetic nervous system produces physiological changes associated with the rest and digestive functions. The contraction of smooth muscle in the walls of arterioles in voluntary muscles redirects blood flow from voluntary muscles to the digestive system. Increased sinoatrial node activity increases heart rate; decreased activity of smooth muscle contractions in the digestive tract slows peristalsis and inhibits digestion. Both are opposite to the parasympathetic effects. There are no direct autonomic effects on deep tendon reflexes.

28. **Answer:** C. Angiotensin II
    Rationale: Angiotensin II has a direct effect on blood vessels, causing the contraction of smooth muscle cells located in their walls. This contraction results in an increase in blood pressure. Angiotensin II is a potent vasoconstrictor. It also stimulates the release of aldosterone from the adrenal gland. Aldosterone causes the kidneys to increase their reabsorption of sodium, helping to restore normal plasma ion concentrations. Renin is produced in the kidneys and controls the production of aldosterone. Angiotensin-converting enzyme causes the conversion of angiotensin I to angiotensin II.

29. **Answer:** B. Noble gases
    Rationale: The noble gases (Group 13) do not need additional electrons and therefore have no electronegativity. Halogens (Group 17) are one electron short of completing their valence octet and are thus the most electronegative. The alkali metals (Group 1) are 7 electrons short of completing their valence octet and hence have the lowest electronegativity.

30. **Answer:** B. Erythrocytes

Rationale: Blood cells are erythrocytes, leukocytes, and thrombocytes (platelets). Erythrocytes account for 99% of blood elements, while leukocytes and platelets account for 1%. Proteins are not blood cells. Proteins make up 6%–8% of the plasma.

31. **Answer:** D. Combustion
    Rationale: Exothermic reactions are those that generate or emit heat into the environment, whereas endothermic reactions are those that absorb heat from the environment. All combustion reactions are self-sustaining and highly exothermic. Decomposition, dissociation, and evaporation are all examples of endothermic reactions.

32. **Answer:** A. Lipids
    Rationale: Nearly all types of lipids are formed of either fatty acids or cholesterol. Monosaccharides are the simplest carbohydrates. Amino acids are the building blocks of proteins. Glycogen is the stored form of glucose.

33. **Answer:** D. Connective - energy storage
    Rationale: The hypodermis is the deepest of the three layers of the skin. The layer is primarily formed of loose connective tissue with a high content of adipocytes. The primary function of the adipocytes is fat storage, which serves as an energy reserve for the body. Adipocytes also provide some mechanical cushioning properties to the skin while allowing interstitial fluids and cells to freely pass through the hypodermis. These unique properties of the hypodermis differ from the epidermis's protective role.

34. **Answer:** B. Melatonin
    Rationale: Melatonin is produced by the pineal gland, while the other answer options are products of the pituitary gland.

35. **Answer:** B. Thyroid hormone (T3 and T4)
    Rationale: Activation of the sympathetic nervous system induces a level of overall alertness, priming the body for high-energy situations and an increased metabolic state. Thyroid hormones also induce increased metabolic activity. Individuals with excessive levels of thyroid hormone (hyperthyroidism) and those with extreme activation of the sympathetic nervous system experience similar symptoms. Insulin is responsible for the cellular uptake of glucose for energy use. Testosterone is the major male sex hormone responsible for male physical characteristics and reproduction. Aldosterone regulates sodium and potassium levels in the blood, thus regulating blood pressure.

36. **Answer:** A. Platinum
    Rationale: Platinum is a transition metal. Carbon, nitrogen, and oxygen are all non-metals.

37. **Answer:** C. Induced fit
    Rationale: Enzymes are biological catalysts that are extremely complex three-dimensional protein structures. Enzymes lower the activation energies of biological reactions by attracting reactants to a specific site on the enzyme known as the active site. As reactants bind to the active site, the configuration of the site changes in a manner that orients the reactants in the optimum manner for the chemical reaction to occur. This process is called the induced fit mechanism for enzymatic activity. The activity of an

enzyme is defined by the rate at which the reaction it catalyzes occurs. The higher the enzymatic activity, the greater the rate of the reaction.

38. **Answer:** B. Temporomandibular joint
    Rationale: The intervertebral discs, manubriosternal joint, and pubic symphysis are all united by cartilages and have no joint activity. The temporomandibular joint is a highly mobile synovial joint that allows for chewing by moving the lower jaw (mandible).

39. **Answer:** D. Glomeruli
    Rationale: Arterial blood arrives for filtration by the kidneys via the renal artery. The renal artery undergoes several branchings to form renal arterioles that extend throughout the renal cortex. Branches of these arterioles form tufts of capillaries that occupy the invagination of a Bowman's capsule. A Bowman's capsule is a balloon-like expansion of the proximal renal tubule. The combined region of capillary tufts and Bowman's capsule is called a glomerulus. There are over one million glomeruli in the renal cortex. The walls of the capillary tufts are permeable to water and dissolved solutes such as electrolytes, urea, and other substances. The pressure inside these capillaries exceeds that of the surrounding extracellular space and the fluid within Bowman's capsule. This pressure gradient drives water and dissolved solutes out of the capillary tufts and into the lumen of Bowman's capsule. The solution that enters the capsule's lumen is called a *filtrate*. The filtrate is then collected in the collecting ducts and flows to the renal pelvis and eventually to the ureters. The adrenal cortex is not part of the kidney and has no role in the formation of urine.

40. **Answer:** C. Increased permeability of the renal tubules to water
    Rationale: The antidiuretic hormone enhances the permeability of the renal tubules and collecting ducts to water. As a result, water diffuses out of the filtrate solution and into the renal medulla, where it can be reabsorbed into the circulation. This process concentrates urine and reduces the loss of additional water from the body through the urinary system. The antidiuretic hormone does not affect the secretion of urea, the osmolality of extracellular fluid in the renal medulla, or the secretion of glucose.

41. **Answer:** C. Increased secretion of antidiuretic hormone
    Rationale: Osmoreceptors in the hypothalamus and the pituitary gland directly detect plasma osmolality from adjacent capillaries. When plasma osmolality is undesirably high, the osmoreceptors relay this information to the pituitary gland. The pituitary gland then releases antidiuretic hormone that increases the permeability of the renal tubules and collecting ducts to water. The result is the diffusion of water out of the filtrate solution and into the renal medulla, where it can be reabsorbed into the circulation. This process concentrates urine and reduces the loss of additional water from the body through the urinary system.

42. **Answer:** A. an undesirably low plasma sodium concentration; renin
    Rationale: The kidneys can directly detect the sodium concentration of plasma within renal arterioles. In response to an undesirably low plasma sodium concentration (and to low blood pressure), the kidneys release the hormone renin. Renin leads to the production of angiotensin II, a potent vasoconstrictor that stimulates the release of aldosterone from the adrenal gland. Aldosterone causes the kidneys to increase the

reabsorption of sodium, thus helping to restore plasma ion concentrations to normal levels.

43. **Answer:** A. Glucose
Rationale: Under normal circumstances, glucose molecules that are filtered from the blood into the renal tubule are completely reabsorbed from the filtrate. Glucose in the urine is an abnormal finding and often indicates the presence of diabetes mellitus. Sodium, urea, and bicarbonate are normally present in urine and are not completely reabsorbed from renal tubule filtrate.

44. **Answer:** C. Concentration of urine
Rationale: The loop of Henle is a U-shaped segment of the renal tubules located between the proximal and distal convoluted tubules. The bottom part of the "U" of the loops of Henle is in the renal medulla. The ascending limb of the loop excretes sodium into the interstitium of the medulla, thus creating very high osmolality. The renal collecting tubules pass through the medulla on their way to the sinuses of the renal pelvis. The collecting tubules are impermeable to sodium and other solutes, while the tubules permeability to water can be adjusted by various hormonal influences. When the collecting tubules are maximally permeable to water, water diffuses out of the collecting tubules into the medulla. The maximal concentration of urine (or the maximum osmolality of the urine) produced is slightly lower than the osmolality of the medulla. When the osmolality of the collecting tubules and the medulla are nearly equal, the driving force for the diffusion of water disappears.

45. **Answer:** B. Fibrillar
Rationale: Structural proteins have a fibrillar (fiber-like) or elongated shape, as opposed to globular or spherical proteins, which typically have enzymatic or transport functions. The biconcave shape is seen in red blood cells but not in proteins.

46. **Answer:** A. Increased blood pressure
Rationale: Angiotensin II is the active form of angiotensin hormone. Activation of angiotensin begins with the release of the hormone renin from the kidneys. Angiotensin II has a direct effect on blood vessels by causing the contraction of smooth muscle cells located in their walls. This contraction results in an increase in blood pressure. Additionally, angiotensin II has a direct effect on the proximal renal tubules to increase sodium reabsorption. Angiotensin II stimulates the release of the hormone aldosterone, which has additional effects on the kidney.

47. **Answer:** D. Antisense
Rationale: The DNA strand transcribed by RNA polymerase is called the antisense strand. The other DNA strand is called the sense strand.

48. **Answer:** C. Chief cells
Rationale: Chief cells in the parathyroid gland secrete parathyroid hormone, which is responsible for maintaining normal calcium levels. The gastric chief cell releases pepsinogen and chymosin. T-cells circulate the body to find viral infections. Interferons are created by virally infected cells in the body; they are small proteins that help prevent

the virus from replicating. Plasma cells help fight viral infections by creating antibodies to the virus.

49. **Answer:** D. Deactivation of the snake venom by antigen-specific antibody binding
    Rationale: Antivenom is created by injecting snake venom into lab animals and collecting the animals' blood serum afterward. The immune system of animals produces antibodies against the antigens present on the venom molecules. In affected human subjects treated with antivenom, these antibodies bind to the venom molecules, neutralizing them and enhancing their clearance from the body.

50. **Answer:** B. active humoral
    Rationale: The influenza virus contains viral shell proteins recognized by T-helper cells. The T-helper cells activate B-cells. Activated B-cells are then differentiated into plasma cells, which actively release antigen-specific antibodies into the blood circulation. These antibodies are short-lived and protect against influenza infection after a few days. Additionally, some of the activated B-cells differentiate into long-lived memory cells that generate a much stronger and more rapid antibody response to subsequent encounters with the influenza virus. This antibody response is part of the active immune response and is categorized as a humoral response.

PRACTICE TEST 2.3 ANSWERS: ENGLISH LANGUAGE

1. **Answer:** B. departs; going
   Rationale: The flight departure time is accurate regardless of the time it's stated if the departure will not occur after 6:00 am on the day of the flight. Thus, a present tense verb ("departs") is needed. In the second blank, a future tense verb ("going") is needed because "will be" conveys that going to bed early has not yet happened. Only choice B fits both of those verb tense requirements.

2. **Answer:** D. ensure; it's
   Rationale: "Ensure" means "to make certain of something," whereas "insure" is protection against a possible future event, such as car insurance in case of an accident. "It's" is the contraction of "it is."

3. **Answer:** C. there; then
   Rationale: "There" is a place. "They're" is a contraction representing "they are," and "their" shows possession of something. "Then" indicates an order of something following another event. "Than" is used to compare things (e.g., "a horse is bigger than a dog").

4. **Answer:** D. your; you're
   Rationale: "Your" is a possessive pronoun showing that what follows the pronoun belongs to "you" (as the person being spoken to). "You're" is a contraction representing "you are."

5. **Answer:** A. My grandmother's house was built over 100 years ago if you can believe it.
   Rationale: "Grandmother's" is the proper grammatical usage since the term implies possession, as does the apostrophe. No commas are necessary in this sentence.

6. **Answer:** A. I listened to the instructor's lesson but interpreted a different meaning.
   Rationale: This question is partially a trick one because "infer" and "interpret" are extremely confusing and regularly misused in speech, but option A is the only possible correct answer because the apostrophe in "instructor's" implies possession regarding who is giving the lesson.

7. **Answer:** B. will be opening
   Rationale: The future tense is needed since the business is not yet opened. Thus, choice B is correct.

8. **Answer:** D. no change required
   Rationale: The underlined word preceding (#8) is grammatically correct.

9. **Answer:** C. dozens
   Rationale: The surrounding context and phrasing imply more than one dozen. Since option B is a possessive (which isn't needed in the relevant sentence), that leaves only option C as the correct answer.

10. **Answer:** C. realized

Rationale: A past-tense verb is needed because the sentence is explaining something that happened 100% in the past and is not ongoing.

11. **Answer:** A. My friends and family agree
    Rationale: Neither "me" nor "I" are needed in the phrasing because the sentence is about the friends and family, which omits option A. Since option B has grammatically unnecessary and awkward offsetting commas, only option A can be correct.

12. **Answer:** B. effect
    Rationale: "Effect" means to result in something, while "affect" means to "create or produce a change." To check whether "effect" is the right word, replace it with "result." In this case, if the shop does well, the result (or "effect") will be opening more shops.

13. **Answer:** C. someday
    Rationale: "Someday" is an adverb that describes some unknown or undefined point in the future. As two words, "some day" refers to a singular day even when the specific day is either unknown or unspecified (e.g., "I have a doctor's appointment some day next month"). In "some days," "some" is an adjective modifying the noun "days."

14. **Answer:** B. acknowledge
    Rationale: Option B shows the correct spelling of this commonly used but frequently misspelled word.

15. **Answer:** C. pay off
    Rationale: "Payoff" is incorrect because it's the noun form, and the word in question is being used as a future-tense verb. Thus, "pay off," option C, is correct because, when the term is a verb, the two-word spelling is used. "Payoff" means the climax, success, or profit from doing something, while "pay off" in this context means to yield good results or succeed, especially after putting in a lot of effort. "Pay-off" is a form of the word that is no longer (or very rarely) used as language has instead evolved to spell the term as one word.

PRACTICE TEST 2.4 ANSWERS: READING

1. **Answer:** C. Counterfeiting of American money is an enormous problem.
    Rationale: C is the best option given that the passage includes the following: "The Treasury goes to extraordinary lengths to safeguard cash from counterfeiters."

2. **Answer:** B. Yet, despite all these technological innovations, the race to stay ahead of savvy counterfeiters and their constantly changing techniques remains a never-ending endeavor.
    Rationale: The main point of the passage is to emphasize the extent of counterfeiting and detail the technology used to counteract such constantly changing fraudulent activity. The focus of option B best aligns with that point.

3. **Answer:** C. Expository
    Rationale: An expository essay is one in which an idea is investigated and expounded upon, and an argument is clearly and concisely laid out to present evidence concerning that idea. In this case, the idea being investigated and expounded upon is anti-counterfeiting techniques.

4. **Answer:** A. Pamphlet for tourists visiting the United States Treasury
    Rationale: The style and specific subject matter both indicate that the passage is most likely from an informational pamphlet written for visitors to the Bureau of Engraving and Printing.

5. **Answer:** C. Letter from the U.S. Treasury secretary to the president
    Rationale: A primary source document is one that was created and serves as a firsthand source of information or evidence about a particular period. Only the personal letter would meet the criteria of a primary source.

6. **Answer:** D. Inherent
    Rationale: Technological sophistication is inherent (or naturally found) in the making of American money, so much so that to call it "paper" does not fully reveal the high complexity involved in creating money.

7. **Answer:** A. In the Middle Ages, merchants and artisans formed groups called "guilds" to protect themselves and their trades.
    Rationale: The first sentence is the topic sentence because it introduces the main idea of the paragraph.

8. **Answer:** C. merchant guilds originated in the Middle Ages and became extremely popular, eventually leading to a sophisticated apprenticeship system.
    Rationale: The guild system's origins and development are the main idea of the paragraph. The other options are too narrow in focus to constitute a main idea.

9. **Answer:** A. prior to the inception of guilds, merchants were susceptible to competition from lesser skilled craftsmen peddling inferior products or services.

Rationale: It can be inferred that, if guilds were instituted, there must have been a need for merchants to safeguard themselves and their livelihoods from threats.

10. **Answer:** C. similar
    Rationale: The sentence conveys that the spice, silk, and wool dealers were tradespeople similar to other merchants who had set up guilds.

11. **Answer:** C. By that time
    Rationale: The passage introduces the inception of guilds and their development over time, chronologically. Based on the previous sentence in the passage (i.e., before the fill-in-the-blank sentence), guilds clearly grew in popularity over the centuries, until towns like Florence had 50 guilds by the 12th century. "By that time" most clearly states this increase and development over time.

12. **Answer:** B. To criticize the American press for not taking responsibility for their actions
    Rationale: Luce is clearly criticizing the press for not taking responsibility to disseminate enlightening information to the public and for instead blaming the public for not asking for "tasteful and more illuminating" reading matter.

13. **Answer:** A. Newspaper editorial letter
    Rationale: Given the paragraph's opinionated style and serious, critical tone, the excerpt is most likely from a longer letter printed in the op-ed section of a newspaper.

14. **Answer:** C. Diary entry
    Rationale: The diary entry (which would likely provide firsthand thoughts, feelings, and opinions about current life or world events, as witnessed by the author) would qualify as a primary source document of evidence or information concerning a particular period. While potentially primary sources, the other options are not guaranteed to be given the lack of specifics regarding the content; thus, option C is the best choice.

15. **Answer:** D. enlightening
    Rationale: <u>Illuminating</u> reading matter is that which would be enlightening and provide necessary information to the public.

16. **Answer:** C. therefore
    Rationale: Luce is using a cause-and-effect argument here, but she is questioning the excuse of the press to not do their job as a result of certain demands of the public, which would "therefore exonerate the American press for its failures to give the American people more tasteful and more illuminating reading matter."

17. **Answer:** C. disapproval
    Rationale: Luce clearly disapproves of the press and their practice of serving up a lack of news to the public "on the grounds that, after all, [they] have to give the people what they want or [the press] will go out of business."

18. **Answer:** B. Persuasive/argumentative

Rationale: Luce uses several modes of writing here, but overall, she is critical of the American press and arguing that they are at fault for not giving the American public useful information or "illuminating reading matter."

19. **Answer:** B. The author has worked in the journalism industry
    Rationale: The author clearly understands the business of the media, as well as its public responsibility to inform citizens. Thus, it can be concluded that she likely has worked in the journalism industry. None of the other statements can reasonably be concluded based on the content of the passage.

20. **Answer:** B. Football was played for decades on school campuses nationwide before the American Professional Football Association was formed in 1920, and then renamed the National Football League (or the NFL) two years later.
    Rationale: This statement adds additional information to the paragraph about the progression of the game of football in the U.S. and therefore appropriately concludes the paragraph. The other statements either discuss topics not related directly to football or add additional information that is slightly off topic.

21. **Answer:** A. however
    Rationale: The sentence is explaining that, despite the appearance of football as a sport on some college campuses and the annual scrimmages occurring at Yale, 25 years passed before football became a regular activity in college life. "However" best shows this contrast when compared to the other options.

22. **Answer:** A. Rejection of the past and outmoded ideas
    Rationale: From the paragraph, modernism is clearly mostly concerned with rejecting the ideas of the past—such as the science of the Enlightenment and old ideas about religion—and instead focuses on creating what is "new."

23. **Answer:** B. Basis
    Rationale: Pound's suggestion to "make it new" was the basis or touchstone of the modernist movement's outlook and approach to interpreting the world and society.

24. **Answer:** D. Modernism had a profound impact on numerous aspects of life, and modernist values and perspectives still influence society in many positive ways today.
    Rationale: The author's description of modernism's influence as being "positive" is clearly an opinion about the nature of the influence. The other statements are factually based, providing general information about the modernist movement.

25. **Answer:** D. as well as
    Rationale: This sentence discusses all the positive benefits that result from the continuation of the Olympic Games in the present day, but rather than the benefits being listed in a three-element list, the detail about national pride is building off the idea of bringing nations together, so "as well as" is the correct signal phrase to convey that relationship with the related ideas.

26. **Answer:** D. Detracted

Rationale: The idea that allowing professional athletes to participate in the games would cause people to believe it "detracted" from the intentions of the original Olympics is a negative notion. The idea suggests that this change would take away from the games, instead of adding something positive.

27. **Answer:** B. The Olympic games are the best example of humanity's physical prowess.
    Rationale: This statement is the opinion of the author as there is no indication that this idea has been tested or proven in any way. Rather, the statement is simply what the author believes or feels, as indicated by the subjective "best" and "prowess," which implies the author finds the physicality of athletes to be impressive.

28. **Answer:** C. revulsion
    Rationale: The author uses phrasing like "moldy smell" and "black hole" to describe his rented room in the inn, and "heartless" and "hideous" to describe the environment of London. He also added that he "would rather even starve" than go out to find himself a meal in the "hellish town where a stranger might get trampled to death." These expressions are strong negative sentiments that clearly indicate his revulsion to the city.

29. **Answer:** B. Diary entry
    Rationale: The personal and frank tone that the author uses to describe his hotel room and his private fears about going out into the city of London for dinner suggest that the passage would have been written in a journal or diary.

30. **Answer:** D. Advertisement
    Rationale: A primary source document is one that was created from firsthand experience under a period of study of a particular event, moment in time, situation, etc. A travel guide, diary entry, and news editorial could all potentially be primary sources that chronicle a firsthand experience. The only one that would likely NOT qualify as a primary source is the advertisement. Advertisements are usually meant to persuade others to engage in an experience, make a purchase, or take a certain action. Plus, advertisements are often not completely based in personal experience and may not even be factual.

31. **Answer:** D. The author will not be traveling to London again.
    Rationale: The author is clearly unhappy with his lodging and finds London to be a generally disagreeable place, so he would be very unlikely to visit London again. The other statements are not reasonable conclusions that can be made from the content of the passage.

32. **Answer:** C. "You barely know him! How can you marry him?" was the worried mother's response at her teenager's announcement of marriage.
    Rationale: Sentence punctuation is always inside quotation marks. Option B places the comma correctly, but the question mark at the end of the sentence is incorrect for dialogue. Therefore, only option C is punctuated correctly for dialogue.

33. **Answer:** A. Abraham Lincoln started his famous "Gettysburg Address" with the following words: "Four score and seven years ago."

Rationale: The second-person perspective uses the pronoun "you" or features a direct address. The first sentence is the only one not written in the second person; the use of "Abraham Lincoln" and "his" illustrates second person.

34. **Answer:** D. Please remain seated while the seatbelt signs are illuminated.
    Rationale: An imperative statement is one that gives a direct command and implies the subject of "you." Option D is imperative; the announcement is directly commanding the passengers to remain seated.

35. **Answer:** C. Excision
    Rationale: The prefix "Ex-" means "out," which serves as the relevant clue here. "Excision" refers to a surgical procedure done to cut out something unwanted or unnecessary.

36. **Answer:** B. Colitis
    Rationale: The suffix "-itis" refers to inflammation, so "colitis" is an inflammation of the colon.

37. **Answer:** D. Melanoma
    Rationale: The suffix "-oma" refers to a tumor or cancer, so "melanoma" refers to a cancer of the skin (coming from melanin, which gives human skin its color). "Oncology" is the study of cancer, but does not refer to cancer itself.

38. **Answer:** C. Rhinitis
    Rationale: The root "rhino" refers to the nose or nasal area, so "rhinitis" is an inflammation of the nasal passages.

39. **Answer:** A. Gastroenterology
    Rationale: The suffix "-logy" refers to the study of some discipline or area; therefore, gastroenterology is the study or examination of the gastrointestinal area of the body.